SENTENCING

The Decision as to Type,

Length, and Conditions of Sentence

SENTENCING

The Decision as to Type, Length, and Conditions of Sentence

BY
ROBERT O. DAWSON

The Report of the American Bar Foundation's Survey of the Administration of Criminal Justice in the United States

* *

FRANK J. REMINGTON
Editor

LITTLE, BROWN AND COMPANY
BOSTON 1969 TORONTO

LIBRARY OF CONGRESS CATALOG CARD NO. 77-79881

SECOND PRINTING
(FIRST PAPERBACK PRINTING, 1974)

Published simultaneously in Canada
by Little, Brown & Company (Canada) Limited

PRINTED IN THE UNITED STATES OF AMERICA

THE AMERICAN BAR FOUNDATION, CHICAGO

1968-1969

DEDICATION

Dedicated to the late Albert James Harno, member of the Project Advisory Committee on the study of the Administration of Criminal Justice — teacher, scholar, administrator, leader of his profession, public servant, and friend.

> Basic to legal research is the postulate that laws are established to regulate human conduct and to promote social solidarity. Many laws do not achieve these ends. They do not function well, or have outlived their original purpose, or are poorly administered. The way to determine whether a given law is accomplishing the end for which it was intended is to find out how it works. This involves getting the facts about its operation. . . . Only after the facts are known can we be prepared to project remedial measures.
>
> Albert J. Harno
> 1966 University of Illinois
> Law Forum x (Summer 1966)

PREFACE

Sentencing deals with the imposition of sentence and the granting and revocation of probation and parole. These are the final stages of the criminal justice process and in a sense the last words of the law on crime and its control. Yet analysis of the sentencing process brings to the surface the question of efficacy that is latent in all aspects of the administration of criminal justice: Does the whole business from arrest through punishment really have practical consequences?

On this question the verdict of the past, from biblical times at least, has been emphatically positive: Of course the identifying, accusing, trying, convicting, and punishing of society's offenders chastens them and deters others. The verdict of contemporary common consent is in accord; the only question these days seems to be how severe we must become in order that the criminal law will work. Upon this premise, the problems of criminal law enforcement can be reduced to two questions of efficiency: How to get as many offenders as possible through the procedural mill to the point of sentencing; and, at the point of sentencing, how to distribute the short supply of punishments so that maximum rectifying effects will be achieved.

It is inappropriate here to explore whether the premise is well founded. This is occasion only for noting that if the premise is wrong — if threats of punishment have only modest efficacy in crime control — then we have a lot of backtracking to do in criminal law policy. For present purposes, it may be assumed what common sense suggests — that threats of punishment are a significantly effective means toward control of crime. Even on that premise, however, there is an enormous gap between the idea of a system of punishments and a system of punishments that is operational. Professor Dawson's study can be considered an analysis of that gap.

The present volume considers the procedural aspects of sentencing and parole. There is an intimate connection between the question of punishment or rehabilitation measures and the question of sentencing and parole procedures. The connection may be said to be this: Where the dispositional alternatives open to the sentencing judge or paroling authority are few and unsatisfactory, then the scope and depth of the inquiry that goes into the sentence or parole decision tends to be correspondingly modest. The same is true with regard to revocation of probation or parole. This connection is not a rule of law but a rule — even if a loose one — of human behavior: Neither court nor probation officer nor attorney nor defendant is really very interested in pursuing an elaborate inquiry into the defendant's psycho-social background and his prospects for rehabilitation if the alternatives in fact presented are between a relatively empty period in jail or prison and a relatively unsupervised period out of jail or prison. The only real question is whether the defendant will soon do it again, and that is a proposition speculative in the extreme. Perhaps the only thing clear is that the defendant wants to stay out of jail whatever else.

Professor Dawson explores a range of possibilities in sentencing procedure, juxtaposing the statutory proposals of the American Law Institute's Model Penal Code and the National Council on Crime and Delinquency's Model Sentencing Act against the realities of criminal law administration. These statutory proposals differ from each other but both specify procedural standards — particularly regarding presentence investigation — that well exceed those observed in the field. The thrust of these reform proposals is thus toward more thorough investigation of the offender and his rehabilitation prospects. The means toward this end include both administrative investigation by caseworkers and judicial inquiry through the adversary process. With regard to parole and its revocation, the same reform impetus is felt. To the extent these reform movements bear fruit, the authorities who lay and lift sentence will hear much more about the offender than they did in the procedures disclosed in the present volume.

Most observers would agree that procedural refinement is overdue in sentencing and parole processes. And most would agree that more thorough investigation should be made of the offender and his prospects for rehabilitation. But neither of these procedural reforms can have much positive effect on correctional decisions unless those decisions really lead somewhere: when the facilities, personnel, and programs are available to carry out what diagnosis indicates. Penetrating diagnosis has little point in medicine if therapy is limited to tourniquets, and the same point holds in the penal system. This means that long-run improvement in sentencing is in the hands of the legislature, for it controls the purse strings that can make more resources available if it is so willed.

Within the limitations imposed by available treatment resources, however, formidable issues of policy remain with regard to sentence and parole procedures. A basic issue concerns the genuineness of the tribunal's interest in having "the facts" about the offender — his family history, vocational experience, psychological makeup, etc. Some skepticism about such "facts" is of course warranted because we know little about which of them auger well for rehabilitation and which do not. But something more than healthy skepticism seems to be at work in the day-to-day routine of sentence and parole decision-making. One has the sense that the judges and parole board members oscillate between really wanting to know about the defendant and "not wanting to be confused with the facts." Would information disturb settled though unspoken sentencing rules of thumb? This apparent ambivalence might warrant further exploration and analysis.

A related phenomenon, and perhaps an explanation of the ambivalence, is the tension for the involved officials — investigating officer, judge, parole board member — between carrying out their roles in a satisfactory way and getting a dirty job done tolerably well. The presentence investigating officer wants to deliver "professional" presentence reports about the offender. Pursuit of this professional interest requires reference to facts and background circumstances whose relevance is dictated by professional probation theory. Yet the officer's recommendations must also achieve a suitably high acceptance rate with the court, which translates itself into a "feedback" process in which the presentence investigator to greater or lesser degree writes what he expects the trial judge would like to read. The same phenomenon exists regarding prison officials' recommendations to the parole authority.

Similar tensions exist for counsel. The prosecutor has to appear "tough" enough to satisfy the police department and yet not so inflexibly tough that the sentencing judge may come to regard prosecutorial recommendations as merely party line. Defense counsel has a kindred dilemma, aggravated by the fact that most criminal defendants have an irradicable suspicion that their lawyers have sold out. Defense counsel's dilemma can be resolved in part by letting the defendant himself "tell his story" to the judge at the time of sentence. Doing so gives him some satisfaction that he has had his day in court — a most important consideration — and may even help the court do its job. On the other hand, criminal defendants are not conspicuous for their ability to deal successfully in interpersonal relations, including that of trying to persuade a judge to go easy on them. It is common report of defense counsel that they let their man talk, whether at trial or at the time of sentencing, only with severest reservations. The defendant may only confirm what the judge suspects, that he is a no-good.

The problem of the offender's direct participation reappears in more complicated form in the parole decision. Sense of fairness and a desire to show the man that his case is being considered militate for letting him have a say. On the other hand, giving him his say lengthens an already overlong parole hearing calendar and demonstrates to the offender how cursory the board review of his case really is. Moreover, in time the prison inmate becomes schooled in the rhetoric of clemency pleading; grade school dropouts start talking about life adjustment. At this point one would suppose a professional spokesman could do at least as well.

Another theme that emerges from Professor Dawson's study is the struggle for exercise of authority in sentencing policy. This is a complex conflict whose participants can be roughly grouped into three categories: the hard-liners, who want mandatory sentences of considerable stiffness; the soft-liners, who want low ceilings on penalties and strong pressure for probation; and those in the middle who want to give the trial court broad discretion in fixing sentence. The first two camps have similar strategy in that they want the legislature rather than the judiciary to establish sentencing policy. On what legislative policy ought to be, however, the hard-liners and soft-liners are of course at odds. In most jurisdictions the result is that the judiciary has very wide sentencing discretion, either explicitly or because there are equivalent means open — such as conviction of a lesser offense — which the judiciary can follow when inclined. In practice, therefore, sentencing decision is essentially an exercise of judicial discretion guided — one could say hampered — by legislative specifications that restrict without directing.

Against the backdrop of data developed by Professor Dawson in this volume, the debate over sentencing policy between hard line and soft line assumes a somewhat unreal character. The closer one gets to the situation, the more difficult it is to adhere with enthusiasm to any "line" — hard or soft. One simply cannot make categorical statements about corrigibility for any general class of offenders — whether arrayed by type of offense, age and social background, or some other factor. True enough, we can predict that an offender with a long record is an unpromising prospect for rehabilitation, and that one who has a record of stable family and employment relationships is otherwise, but a feeling of surprise does not spring out of this finding. Still, if we could get more people to accept even these humble propositions, perhaps the legislatures would abandon the attempt to straighten the crooked simply by making threats of greater punishment.

As in the previous volumes in this series, Professor Frank Remington of the Law School at the University of Wisconsin has played a key role in the author's development of his material. In writing the sentencing volume, Professor Dawson also was greatly helped by repeated consultation with Professor Frank Miller, his then colleague at Washington University in St. Louis. In addition, Professor Dawson has asked that acknowledgment be paid to the following institutions for their encouragement and financial support: the School of Law, University of Wisconsin; the Schools of Law and Social Work, Washington University; the School of Law, University of Texas; the Ford Foundation; and the American Bar Foundation.

The Committee on Administration of Criminal Justice of the American Bar Foundation, under the chairmanship of Walter P. Armstrong, Jr., has approved this study for publication. Neither the committee nor the Foundation, however, assumes responsibility for the positions taken by the author. Publication of this work by the American Bar Foundation signifies only that it is regarded as valuable and responsible. The analyses, conclusions, and opinions expressed herein are the author's and not those of the Foundation, its officers and directors, or others associated with its work.

Geoffrey C. Hazard, Jr.
Executive Director
American Bar Foundation

EDITOR'S FOREWORD

Sentencing is the last in a series of volumes dealing with the total criminal justice process, from detection of crime to the final release of an offender from parole. The other volumes are *Detection of Crime, Arrest, Prosecution,* and *Conviction.*

The scope of *Sentencing* is broader than its title may seem to indicate. Not only is the initial imposition of sentence by the trial judge explored, but also subsequent correctional decisions, such as the decisions to revoke probation, to grant parole, and to revoke parole. Some correctional issues of great importance, however, are not dealt with. Correctional decision-making processes that involve a potentially great effect upon the liberty of the offender are concentrated on: the choice between probation and prison, the parole decision, and probation and parole revocation. Treatment and control decisions made about the prison inmate not involving his release have been excluded, partly because of inadequacy of data and partly out of the need to limit the size of the book. Correctional treatment of the misdemeanant is also excluded, because the felony correctional system presents the correctional process in its most sophisticated and complicated version. With all its inadequacies, the felony system is undoubtedly the "model" toward which the misdemeanant system strives. However, there remains great need in the future to look carefully at the correctional treatment of the misdemeanant offender, if only to prevent an almost literal "corruption" of the criminal justice process. The common sentence for a so-called minor offender, such as the drunk or the streetwalking prostitute, is a small money fine, a short jail sentence, or probation without meaningful supervision. Whichever the choice is, no very significant objective is achieved either for the individual offender or for the community. This fact has had a seriously detrimental impact upon the operation of the criminal justice system. The system is designed on the apparent assumption that the conviction and correctional treatment of offenders are the important objectives. For example, the exclusionary rule of evidence assumes that police will desire to achieve a conviction and will therefore be influenced by the knowledge that evidence illegally obtained is not admissible. When conviction and correctional treatment do achieve some significant objective, the exclusionary rule of evidence may affect enforcement practice. When conviction is not followed by meaningful correctional treatment, it is likely that alternatives to the criminal justice system will be turned to. If formal alternatives such as civil commitment do not exist, as is often the case, law enforcement may resort to a "practical" alternative, such as locking up the drunk and the prostitute and releasing them the next morning. This kind of "helping" (for the down-and-out drunk) or "harassment" (for the streetwalking prostitute) is usually without lawful basis. The only real alternative to this kind of improvisation is the development of methods for dealing with these difficult social problems outside the criminal justice process or developing sensible correctional programs for the "minor offender." Perhaps no more important or difficult task confronts us today than developing appropriate methods for dealing with the minor offender. Experience in dealing with the serious offender is often helpful in devising better ways of dealing with the misdemeanant, but it is obvious that a great deal more needs to be done.

Because *Sentencing* is the final volume in the series, it is appropriate here to give brief attention to the major emphasis of the American Bar Foundation's Administration of Criminal Justice Series as a whole, as well as to the major emphasis within this volume. What that emphasis is and how it developed are important in assessing the contributions and limitations of the Foundation's research effort.

The objective at first was to study all things that might be of interest to anyone concerned about criminal justice administration. This was obviously a kind of naive empiricism and, in practical terms, was impossible of achievement, even if the objective had been desirable. The need was for focus, for a conceptual framework which would influence the gathering of data and structure the written reports. This focus was slow in developing and really took form only in the process of putting together the several volumes. The delay had the obvious disadvantages of inefficiency in the gathering of data and, to a degree, a lack of precision in the major objectives of the written series. However, the advantage was gained of letting the data, the study itself, exert a strong influence on the emphasis ultimately decided upon.

No doubt empirical research, well done, contributes by furnishing descriptive data that make possible a better understanding of the processes being studied. This series does constitute a significant contribution to understanding how the criminal justice system works. But equally important, empirical research contributes to forming a valid judgment about what is of greatest significance in the processes being described. Whether significance is determined more by the data or by the values and interests of the researcher is difficult to tell, but it is apparent that both are involved.

The series focuses on two basic aspects of criminal justice administration: (1) the study of the process of criminal justice as a system, one which must be studied as a whole if individual decisions and agencies are to be adequately understood; (2) a study of the exercise of discretionary power by criminal justice agents and agencies.

The Total System Approach

As in the other volumes in the series, an effort is made to view specific processes in the context of the over-all system. The American Bar Foundation's Administration of Criminal Justice Series demonstrates clearly that basic understanding and improvement of any aspect of criminal justice administration require understanding and improvement at other stages. A good police and court system, for example, is not likely to be effective without adequate correctional programs and resources.

It is also apparent that the practitioner cannot function effectively without knowledge of the total system. Gone, for example, is the day when the lawyer's contribution was made primarily in the courtroom. Increasingly, lawyers are being called upon to function in the police station and with respect to important correctional decisions such as probation and parole revocation. These new responsibilities can be adequately discharged only when the lawyer understands how the total criminal justice system works.

There are important research objectives achieved by looking at the system as a whole. Some of these can be briefly identified.

1. Understanding the over-all criminal justice system makes it apparent that an effort to eliminate discretion at one stage in the process is likely to be reflected by an administrative accommodation at another stage. Thus, legislative prescription of a high mandatory sentence for certain offenders is likely to result in a reduction in charges at the prosecution stage, or if this is not done, by a refusal of the judge to convict at the adjudication stage. The issue with respect to legislative requirements of high mandatory sentences thus is not solely whether certain offenders should be dealt with severely, but also how the criminal justice system will accommodate to the legislative change.

2. Discretionary decisions made at any stage of the process commonly have an important impact upon decisions made at other stages. For example, police decisions on enforcement priorities ob-

viously control the "intake" of the criminal justice system and affect the kinds of cases which find their way through prosecution and conviction to correctional treatment. In turn, the nature of correctional treatment has substantial impact upon enforcement priorities. Other things being equal, police are likely to give priority to making cases which will result in effective correctional treatment. For example, the institution of a special program for dealing with sex offenders helps police to feel that something significant can be done for convicted offenders. As a consequence, a case that once would have been handled by reducing the charge to disorderly conduct may now be pursued on a charge of incest or taking indecent liberties.

3. Because of the reciprocity of all stages of the criminal justice process, there is obvious need for effective communication between the agencies involved. A judicial decision in one case to suppress illegally obtained evidence may have been designed to affect police practices, whereas in another case a decision calling for an unusually long prison sentence may be aimed at correctional treatment of the particular offender. This study of the over-all criminal justice process has made clear that decisions by one agency are commonly not understood by other agencies. Often a decision designed to have a constructive impact is misunderstood, with the consequence that a process of nullification sets in. Obviously better communication and better coordination are needed. Because the judge is at the pivotal point in the system and because he often does try to exercise control over the practices of other agencies, the court is probably the agency in the best position to achieve administrative coordination. Yet, the trial judiciary has repeatedly failed to realize the important responsibility which it has for administration, not only of the court calendar but also of the over-all criminal justice process.

The Exercise of Discretionary Power

Kenneth Culp Davis recently said:

> A more significant concept than "informal procedures" is "administrative discretion," because the most significant action is taken not merely in choosing which course to follow in something so orderly as informal adjudication but also in answering such questions as whether, when, and whom to investigate; whether to initiate some kind of action and whether to continue or discontinue it; whether, when, and whom to prosecute; whether and when to make rules and what content to put into them; whether to make policy statements and what to say; whether

> and how to advise and supervise regulated parties. Discretionary power is vastly broader than informal adjudication. Perhaps the exercise of discretionary power is the lifeblood of the administrative process.[1]

Study of the criminal justice system makes very clear that the "exercise of discretionary power is the lifeblood" of the criminal justice process and thus is emphasized throughout the American Bar Foundation series.

The importance of the exercise of discretionary power is so obvious that it would not warrant emphasis were it not for the fact that it has commonly been ignored. At a time when the exercise of discretion by economic regulatory agencies was being given careful attention, little attention was given to decisions of comparable significance in the government's effort to control antisocial behavior through the criminal justice process. Too often it was assumed that the police task was ministerial, that the lawyer's function was controlled by elaborate rules governing pretrial and trial procedures, and that the correctional process involved only privileges rather than important rights of convicted offenders. In fact, as this and other volumes in the series clearly show, each criminal justice agency does exercise broad discretionary power which has an important impact upon individuals and the community as a whole. This is true of the exercise of police and prosecutor discretion and the largely informal decisions made in the plea-bargaining process. It is particularly true in the area of sentencing and correctional treatment. Throughout the criminal justice process the optimum situation would seem to be to achieve sufficient administrative flexibility to allow for the positive contribution of the expertise of the agency involved but at the same time to have methods which insure that administrative decision-making is responsive to the legitimate interests of the community and that there are sufficient safeguards to insure against administrative arbitrariness. Though easily stated, this objective is difficult to achieve, and one of the major — and as yet unresolved — issues in criminal justice administration is the proper balance between administrative flexibility and control through rules of law and formal procedures of decision-making. This is a major question for corrections, which has only recently been confronted with the need to respond to demands for increased attention to "due process," to proposals for increased legislative control over correctional decision-making, and to increasing willingness of the judiciary to review correctional practices and policies.

It is not clear why lawyers have not considered the criminal jus-

[1] Davis, Administrative Law, Cases — Text — Problems 70-71 (1965).

tice system as an important object of study and concern. Probably the reason lies in the economics of the legal profession: representation of clients before economic regulatory agencies was obviously important, while representation of clients before "social regulatory agencies" seemed neither necessary nor economically very feasible. Whatever the reason, the neglect has been detrimental to the criminal justice system. Police and correctional agencies are important — in many ways the most important — members of the administrative branch of government. They have important policy-making responsibility, but it has usually not been acknowledged and, as a consequence, has not been carried out openly or well.

In a sense the American Bar Foundation Series is only of historical interest, because most empirical research is outdated by the time it is completed. Institutions change, and data no longer accurately describe the institutions and processes dealt with. Certainly there have been great changes in this country during the past ten years, and these changes have had a profound impact upon government efforts to deal with antisocial behavior. Indeed, the decade has come to be known as a period of social revolution, so great have the changes been, particularly in the large urban areas. Though this is true, it does not follow that the Administration of Criminal Justice Series or the issues stressed are less significant than they were ten years ago. Indeed the changes have made it more important to understand the criminal justice system, its strengths and limitations, and to confront more directly than we have in the past the important administrative policy decisions which must be made. There is greater awareness than ever before that decisions by individual police officers and policies of police departments have a major impact upon urban communities. There is awareness also that the traditional conception of probation and parole as privileges will no longer withstand challenge. Thus understanding of the exercise of discretionary power in correctional administration is as important as it is in other aspects of the criminal justice process.

Though understanding the criminal justice process as a total system and understanding the exercise of discretionary power are of great importance, there are other questions of central importance, some of which are neglected in this research, for example, the question of the relationship of the criminal justice system to other systems for the prevention and control of antisocial behavior. The criminal justice process is only one way — and not necessarily the most effective way — of dealing with important social problems.

An understanding of the administration of criminal justice is not complete if there is a failure to take into account its impact upon the community, particularly the ghetto community. The widespread civil disorder of recent summers has created a situation which makes imperative the reassessment of the relationship of the police, the courts, and corrections with the ghetto. Current police investigative practices may alienate the ghetto community and thus contribute more to the risk of widespread disorder than they contribute to the solution of crime. As the police function is re-evaluated, so also will be the total function of the criminal justice system as a means of social control.

Basic changes are obviously necessary. But they are likely to be realistically conceived and effectively implemented only if they are grounded upon a thorough understanding of the criminal justice system today.

SUMMARY OF CONTENTS

PART IV

TABLE OF CONTENTS

CHAPTER 2

PART II

CHAPTER 3

CHAPTER 4

CHAPTER 7

CHAPTER 8

CHAPTER 9

CHAPTER 10

CHAPTER 11

PART IV

CHAPTER 15

CHAPTER 16

CONCLUSION

SENTENCING

The Decision as to Type,

Length, and Conditions of Sentence

INTRODUCTION

The Correctional Process in Current Criminal Justice Administration

This volume is about the stages of criminal justice administration that occur after conviction of crime. The corrections segment of the criminal justice system is a decision-making process for determining what to do with the convicted offender — whether to commit him to prison or permit him to live in the community under probation supervision; if he is permitted to live in the community, what kinds of controls to impose upon him, for how long, and how to determine whether community living should be terminated in favor of commitment to prison; if he is comitted to prison, to determine how long he should be incarcerated and whether he should be released unconditionally or under supervision; and, if he is released under supervision, for how long, under what conditions, and subject to recommitment for what conduct. This volume, then, is not about one decision made at a single time and place, but about a process that involves a number of interrelated decisions that may span several years in a given case and involve a number of different decision makers.

A major purpose of the criminal justice system is to identify in a legally acceptable manner those persons who should be subjected to control and treatment in the correctional process. If corrections does not properly perform its task, the entire criminal justice system suffers — an inefficient or unfair correctional process can nullify the efforts of courts, prosecutors, and police alike. Conversely, the manner in which these agencies perform their tasks has an important impact upon the correctional process: A person who has been unfairly dealt with prior to conviction is a poor subject for rehabilitation.

One of the major goals of the correctional process is the rehabilitation of the convicted offender. How well this goal is achieved and at how much sacrifice of other goals are currently matters of considerable controversy. Despite the importance of determining the effectiveness of the correctional process in achieving the rehabilitation goal, this volume deals with that only incidentally. Its major purpose is not to determine the recidivism rates produced by various methods of correctional treatment nor to suggest ways in which the effectiveness of the process can be enhanced. Those tasks have been undertaken in other books.[1] The principal focus of this volume is upon the exercise of discretionary power in the correctional process and upon the methods of control used to insure against abuse. Because the correctional process involves the use of governmental authority over the liberty of individuals, it must be fair as well as effective, that is, it must conform to notions of decision-making regularity and responsibility that normally accompany governmental action of a coercive nature. To focus upon the exercise of discretionary power is not to suggest that the correctional process as it presently operates is unfair. Nor is it to suggest that the same safeguards against unfairness that characterize the criminal trial and, increasingly, pretrial decision making, should be imposed upon the correctional process. Rather, the point is that the exercise of discretionary power in the correctional process is so important to offenders and the community alike that it should be the object of continued attention.

The volume is organized into four parts. Part I deals with presentence information. It examines methods of obtaining presentence information used in practice — the presentence investigation, the postplea of guilty hearing, the sentence hearing, and the psychiatric examination — and the methods used to assure accuracy of information obtained.

Part II deals with the probation system. Once the trial judge has obtained the available information about the offense and offender, he must begin to make a series of sentencing decisions. Although statutes sometimes preclude probation, the trial judge usually has authority to place the defendant on probation or to impose a prison sentence. In practice this choice, when it is available under applicable statutes, resolves itself into an inquiry as to whether the defendant is a suitable candidate for probation, a prison commitment resulting automatically from a determination of unsuitability. Therefore, the basic choice between probation and incarceration is examined in Part II. In addition, Part II examines decisions that must be made if probation is granted, that is, selection of probation conditions, probation supervision decisions, and the question of probation revocation.

Part III deals with determining the length of incarceration. If the trial judge decides the defendant is not suited for probation, or

[1] E.g., Glaser, The Effectiveness of a Prison and Parole System (1964).

a statute precludes probation, or the defendant had been placed on probation which was revoked, a prison commitment is imposed. When that occurs, a determination as to the length of incarceration must be made. Far from being a simple matter of judicial sentencing, that determination results from several interrelated decisions made at different times by trial judges, executive clemency authorities, parole boards, and parole officers. Part III examines the trial court selection of the minimum or maximum sentences, parole eligibility requirements and their manipulation by executive clemency authorities, the decision to grant or deny parole, parole conditions, supervision, and revocation.

Part IV deals with the relationship between the correctional process and the legal system. It is an examination of the importance of discretion in the correctional process and of legislative, judicial, and administrative efforts to guide and control its exercise. It also examines the function of counsel in controlling discretion.

Empirical study of the correctional process raises a number of interesting and important issues. Those that seem most important are briefly discussed here.

a. *Obtaining adequate and accurate presentence information.* There is general agreement that the trial judge should be provided with enough information to permit him intelligently to exercise the sentencing choices available to him and that such information should be accurate. It is normally assumed that adequate information can be obtained only through the presentence investigation and that the question of accuracy resolves itself into whether the presentence investigation report is disclosed to the defendant or his attorney. Empirical study indicates, however, that the problem of assuring adequate and accurate presentence information is more complex than commonly assumed. The use in Milwaukee of a judicial proceeding, called the postplea of guilty hearing, as the basic source of presentence information, supplemented in selected cases by a presentence investigation, raises the issue whether it is an acceptable alternative to the routine use of the presentence investigation. If it is, it may have advantages over the presentence investigation because it conserves limited probation staff resources. It also provides a high degree of accuracy, since all information is channeled through a hearing in the presence of the defendant and his attorney, who have an opportunity to cross-examine witnesses and to present defense evidence. The practice also indicates that inadequate attention has been given to ways of assuring accuracy of the presentence report other than disclosing it to the defendant or his attorney. Little attention has been given to whether administrative steps taken during the presentence investigation to assure accuracy can be relied upon or whether the trial judge can assure accuracy independently of disclosure of the report to the defense. These issues are discussed in Part I. To a more limited extent analogous issues exist in assuring adequate and accurate information for other correctional decisions, such as the decision to grant or deny parole or decisions to revoke probation or parole. These are discussed in Parts II and III in connection with discussions of the decisions themselves.

b. *Role of the trial judge in the probation system.* In legal conception, the trial judge has responsibility for operation of the probation system. He has exclusive legal authority to grant or deny probation, to select probation conditions, to determine the length of the probation period, and to revoke probation. While there is recognition that many of these responsibilities are executed through probation staff, empirical study indicates that the large, urban probation department has a much more substantial role in operating the probation system than commonly assumed. The probation staff determines important supervision policies with little or no judicial participation. The probation conditions routinely imposed by trial judges are often formulated by the probation department. Judicial decisions to revoke probation are made only with respect to those probation violators whom the staff has decided to return to court for a revocation hearing. Probation staff recommendations on the choice between incarceration and probation, while advisory in form, often assume great importance in determining whether probation is granted. What should be the role of the trial judge in the probation system? Should he attempt to exercise the kind of detailed control contemplated by law? Or should he attempt to make basic policy decisions, leaving the details of administration to the staff? Discussion in Part II attempts to identify the roles played in practice by the trial judge and the probation staff.

c. *The statutory sentencing structure.* While there is almost unanimous agreement that statutory restrictions upon judicial discretion to place offenders on probation are undesirable, there is considerable current controversy over the function of the trial judge in selecting the length of the sentence when a prison commitment is imposed. The Model Penal Code proposes that the trial judge have no discretion to select the maximum sentence, that it should be fixed by statute on the basis of the offense for which the defendant was convicted.[2] Other recent proposals favor retaining judicial discretion in selecting the maximum.[3] Denial of judicial

[2] Model Penal Code §6.06 (Proposed Official Draft, 1962).
[3] Model Sentencing Act §9 (1963).

discretion to select the maximum sentence is advocated as a means of reducing sentence disparity and as a way of postponing the individualization of the length of incarceration until the parole decision, when the offender's prison rehabilitative progress is known. Yet, practices in Kansas and Michigan, which deny judicial discretion to select the maximum, indicate that inadequate attention has been given to what happens when the legislatively fixed maximum is implemented in criminal justice administration. The practice indicates that the felt need to give sentence concessions to encourage guilty pleas may lead to a practice of charge reductions to provide these concessions when judicial discretion to do so is denied by statute. This, in turn, may severely limit the ability of the legislatively fixed maximum to achieve its stated goals. The importance of the legislative choice of sentencing structure for prison commitments and the administrative consequences of that choice are discussed in Part III.

d. *Criteria for correctional decision-making.* Legislatures, courts, and commentators commonly assume that the considerations that enter into correctional decision-making are related either to the rehabilitation of the offender or the protection of society. Other criteria are assumed not to be used frequently or to be of doubtful propriety. Yet in practice, correctional decisions are based on numerous criteria only some of which conform to these commonly held assumptions. Thus, the encouragement of guilty pleas very commonly influences the decision to grant or deny probation and judicial selection of the length of the prison sentence. Securing restitution to the victim of the offense or support for the offender's family are often important considerations influencing the decision to grant or deny probation. The use of the parole decision to support discipline within correctional institutions and the desire to insulate the parole system from public criticism are considerations that frequently influence parole decision-making. It seems clear that common assumptions about the criteria used in correctional decision-making are inaccurate, and careful attention should be given to the full range of criteria actually used. These matters are discussed in Parts II and III.

e. *Equality of treatment in correctional decision-making.* Sentence disparity — differences in probation decisions and prison sentences that cannot be attributed to legitimate differences in cases — has received considerable public attention and discussion. Proposals for appellate court review of sentencing decisions and for legislatively-fixed sentences are justified in part as means of reducing sentence disparity. Yet, it seems clear that inadequate attention has been given to the capability of means used in practice to reduce sentence disparity or to minimize its harmful effects. Consideration has not been given to the extent to which subsequent correctional decisions are capable of minimizing the effects of disparity in selecting the length of the sentence. Adequate consideration has also not been given to the use of devices such as the sentencing council employed by federal trial judges in Detroit as a means of reducing sentence disparity. In addition to the failure to take account of means used in practice to reduce disparity or minimize its effects, there has been a failure to consider disparity in other correctional decisions. Thus, in practice there is clear evidence of disparity in probation revocation, in granting and denying parole, and in parole revocation. Yet discussion of disparity continues to focus exclusively upon sentencing. These matters are discussed in Parts II and III.

f. *Controlling discretion in the correctional process.* Traditionally, the assumption has been made that, in order to be effective in rehabilitating offenders and protecting society, the correctional process must operate with a maximum of internal flexibility and a minimum of outside interference. Legislatures have traditionally been careful to avoid detailed regulation of the correctional process and appellate courts have refused to intervene, except under extraordinary circumstances. As a result, correctional decision makers possess broad discretion, that is, they are authorized by law to make decisions with little or no legal guidance or control. The basic assumption of the process — that broad discretion is necessary and desirable — is presently undergoing extensive reexamination. A growing body of opinion perceives a need for greater control over the exercise of discretion in the correctional process. Attention has focused almost exclusively upon the desirability of greater legislative control over the process and upon the need for more appellate court intervention in correctional decision-making. By contrast, little attention has been devoted to the availability of administrative controls over discretion. Adequate consideration has not been given to the capacity of correctional agency policy-making and systems of administrative review to provide sufficient controls. Yet, in practice administrative controls do exist, although they would have to be strengthened considerably if primary reliance is to be placed upon them. Also, administrative controls may have substantial advantages over simple reliance on legislative and judicial controls because they are capable of preserving flexibility where it is needed and of providing real control over the details of administration upon which much of the fairness of the process depends. There is a comparable failure to consider the function of counsel in controlling discretion, other than his obvious role in facilitating the use of judicial controls by challenging correctional decisions. How to guide and control discretion in the correctional process is probably the most important of the issues raised in this volume. It pervades the entire book, but it is discussed as a distinct issue in Part IV.

PART I

Presentence Information

The ideal course would be to require a pre-sentence investigation in every case that comes before the court. We recognize, however, that facilities and personnel do not now make this possible. The problem at the present time is rather to assure that our limited resources in this area are used where they are needed most; the problem of the future is to expand those resources to the point where they are reasonably adequate for the discharge of this important task.

American Law Institute,
Model Penal Code §7.07,
Comment (Tent. Draft
No. 2, 1954)

I could not operate without a postplea of guilty hearing. In addition to using it to assure myself that defendants who plead guilty actually are guilty, I use it as a source of presentence information. There are many offenders I can place on probation or sentence to prison on the basis of the information obtained from the postplea hearing and in those cases there is no reason to refer the defendant for a presentence investigation.

Statement by Wisconsin
trial judge

There is general agreement that the trial judge should be given enough information about the offense and offender to permit him to exercise intelligently the sentencing choices available, and that the information upon which he relies in sentencing should be accurate. It is also generally agreed that more presentence information is needed than that which is available in most misdemeanor cases, and even in felony cases in some jurisdictions.

It is often assumed that the only way of obtaining adequate presentence information is through the presentence investigation and report,[1] supplemented in selected cases by a psychiatric examina-

1 A presentence investigation is an inquiry by a probation officer into the circum-

tion. Certainly, this is the assumption that underlies the above quotation from the Model Penal Code as well as the provision that would require a presentence investigation and report in all serious cases.[2] Similarly, a Michigan statute requires a presentence investigation and report in all felony cases.[3] Yet, as the statement by the Wisconsin trial judge indicates, the postplea of guilty hearing[4] may be an acceptable alternative to the presentence investigation and report as the routine method of obtaining presentence information. In Milwaukee such a hearing is conducted in guilty plea cases and a presentence investigation is ordered only if the trial judge feels he has not obtained adequate information from the hearing. Sufficient consideration has not been given to whether this or other alternatives exist to routine reliance upon the presentence investigation and report. That such consideration is justified seems clear from a comparison of the postplea of guilty hearing used in Milwaukee with the routine use of presentence investigations and reports in Detroit.[5]

---

stances of a criminal offense and the background and personal characteristics of the offender. The information obtained is presented to the sentencing judge in a written report. A detailed discussion of presentence investigations and reports appears in Chapter 1.

[2] Model Penal Code §7.07 (Proposed Official Draft, 1962) would require a presentence investigation and report when the defendant has been convicted of a felony, is less than twenty-two years of age, or will receive an extended term for a misdemeanor.

[3] Mich. Stat. Ann. §28.1144 (1954).

[4] A postplea of guilty hearing is an informal trial court hearing in which testimony about the circumstances of the offense is presented by a police officer and testimony about the defendant's background is presented by the defendant and, occasionally, others as well. A detailed discussion of the postplea of guilty hearing, as it was observed in Milwaukee, appears in Chapter 1.

[5] A comparison might involve these considerations: (1) Because the defendant and his attorney are present at the postplea hearing, the risk of the trial judge relying on inaccurate information in sentencing seems less than when the presentence investigation is used. This imbalance is corrected somewhat when the presentence report is disclosed to the defendant or his attorney and is corrected even more when steps are taken to provide reasonable assurance that investigating probation officers make an effort to prevent inaccurate information from being included in the report, and that trial judges take reasonable steps to assure accuracy apart from disclosing the report to the defense. (2) The typical presentence report is more complete than the information yielded by the postplea hearing; specifically, it usually contains more information about the defendant's background than typically brought out in a postplea hearing. However, when presentence investigations are routinely used, there is a tendency to truncate the report and to eliminate much of this information. Furthermore, in many cases the defendant's background (other than his official criminal record) is viewed by the trial judiciary as being relatively unimportant because the nature of the offense or the defendant's criminal record makes either probation or imprisonment the clear choice. Finally, if the trial judge feels inadequately informed on this point by the postplea hearing, he can order a presentence investigation directed to the defendant's background. (3) The presentence report typically contains the investigating probation officer's analysis of the offender and a recommendation on disposition of the case, while in the postplea hearing the

Because it is assumed that adequate presentence information can be obtained only through the presentence investigation and report, the problem of assuring reliability of information obtained has also been considered only in relation to the presentence report. Furthermore, public discussion has focused upon only one aspect of the reliability of the presentence report, that is, whether it should be disclosed to the defendant or his attorney. However, data discussed in Part I make it clear that the problem of assuring reliability of presentence information should be considered in a much broader focus. It is clear, for example, that sufficient consideration has not been given to devices designed to assure that probation officers conducting presentence investigations include only reliable information in the resulting presentence reports. Furthermore, if a postplea of guilty hearing, or similar device, is regarded as an acceptable alternative to the routine use of presentence investigations, the problem of assuring reliability of information becomes one of determining whether the hearing was conducted in such a manner to provide reasonable assurance of reliability.

Data discussed in Part I are also relevant to the longstanding controversy about whether the presentence report should be disclosed to the defendant or his attorney. Proponents of disclosure have urged its necessity to assure accuracy of the presentence report. Opponents have urged the necessity of nondisclosure to avoid losing confidential sources of information, to avoid the harmful psychological effects disclosure may have on defendants, and to avoid the administrative burdens created by extensive and fre-

---

trial judge is denied the benefit of this advice. However, in many cases the nature of the offense or the criminal record determines the disposition, and finer points of analysis are not considered even when they are presented. Again, if in a particular case the trial judge wishes the benefit of this advice, he can order a presentence investigation to obtain it. (4) A presentence report presents information in a form that is convenient for use by officials making later correctional decisions, while the postplea hearing is limited to assisting the trial judge in sentencing. Furthermore, if a presentence investigation is not conducted, its equivalent may be conducted when the offender is placed on probation or committed to prison. However, a transcript of the postplea hearing can be made, as it is in Milwaukee, and, if made available to probation or prison officials, it provides most of the information they would obtain by independent investigation. (5) The postplea of guilty hearing has the advantage of conserving limited probation staff resources by avoiding the necessity of conducting a presentence investigation in every case. However, it could be argued that the presentence investigation conserves police and judicial resources. (6) The postplea of guilty hearing can provide assurance that the guilty plea comes from a defendant who actually is guilty, as well as providing basic presentence information. It could be argued that a postplea hearing or similar device is necessary for guilty plea verification and, therefore, would be readily available for presentence information purposes. On the other hand, it could be argued that the presentence report can also be used to verify guilty pleas. For a discussion of devices used to verify guilty pleas, see Newman, Conviction: The Determination of Guilt or Innocence Without Trial 7-21 (1966).

quent cross-examination of investigating probation officers by defense attorneys.[6] Yet, available data fail to support most of these assumptions. The risk of frequent and prolonged cross-examination of the investigating probation officers, or any of his sources of information, seems unlikely to materialize. No such instances were observed in Milwaukee where reports are regularly disclosed to defense counsel. Presentence reports, at least in busy urban courts, rarely contain information provided by so-called "confidential sources" — persons who would be unwilling to provide information if the report were disclosed to the defense. The great majority of the information in presentence reports comes from two sources — extensive interviews with the defendant and official police reports. The argument that disclosure is necessary to assure accuracy of presentence reports fails to take account of alternative ways of assuring accuracy. In short, data discussed in Part I suggest that many of the assumptions underlying the arguments advanced in the disclosure controversy are without foundation in fact. A basic rethinking about presentence information is needed. Chapter 1 discusses methods used in practice to obtain presentence information; Chapter 2 deals with the problem of assuring reliability of presentence information obtained.

[6] There is a great deal of literature on the question of disclosure of the presentence report. For one of the more interesting debates on the subject, see Higgins, Confidentiality of Presentence Reports, 28 Albany L. Rev. 12 (1964); Roche, The Position for Confidentiality of the Presentence Investigation Report, 29 Albany L. Rev. 206 (1965); Higgins, In Response to Roche, 29 Albany L. Rev. 225 (1965).

CHAPTER 1

Methods of Obtaining Presentence Information

There are substantial variations among jurisdictions in the availability of presentence information in serious cases. In some states, the trial judge must base his sentencing decision upon the defendant's prior criminal record and the brief statements made by the defendant, the defense counsel, and the prosecuting attorney in court immediately before sentencing. This was true in Kansas at the time of the field survey.[1] In other states, however, much more information is available. The presentence investigation is the most common method of obtaining information for sentencing. One is conducted in every felony case in Detroit, and in Milwaukee one is conducted when the trial judge decides that more information is needed than obtained through the postplea of guilty hearing. In addition, psychiatric examinations are available and used selectively in Detroit and Milwaukee.[2]

[1] This is all the information normally available in misdemeanor cases in many jurisdictions. See McIntyre, Law Enforcement in the Metropolis 158-159 (1967); The President's Commission on Law Enforcement and Administration of Justice, Task Force Report: The Courts 31 (1967). The movement to obtain adequate information for sentencing has largely been confined to serious cases; however, the suggestion has been made that it would be feasible to provide a brief version of the presentence report in many misdemeanor cases. See the President's Commission on Law Enforcement and Administration of Justice, Task Force Report: Corrections 19 (1967). As stated previously, this volume is concerned mainly with the correctional process in serious cases.

[2] Since very little presentence information was available in Kansas at the time of the field survey, this chapter and Chapter 2 concentrate upon Michigan and Wisconsin. Furthermore, within those two states emphasis is upon the presentence information available in Detroit and Milwaukee. This is because more data were gathered in those two cities; it is also consistent with the emphasis of this entire series on the administration of criminal justice in urban areas.

Michigan and Wisconsin, like many states, have dual systems of probation supervision and presentence investigation, some areas being served by a state department and others by a local department. In Wisconsin, presentence investigations and probation supervision outside of Milwaukee County are the responsibility of the State Department of Public Welfare; within Milwaukee County these functions are performed by a local probation department, the Milwaukee County Municipal and

It is important to understand the functions and limits of each method of obtaining presentence information; the various methods do not yield the same kind of information. For example, the postplea of guilty hearing yields information primarily on the circumstances of the offense and the defendant's criminal record, while the typical presentence report, although it is concerned with the offense, concentrates somewhat more completely on the defendant's background and present attitudes. It is also important to understand the differences among the various methods of obtaining presentence information in terms of the reliability of the information obtained. For example, the postplea hearing probably yields more reliable information than the presentence report, especially if the contents of the report are not disclosed to the defendant or his attorney. The problem of the reliability of presentence information is discussed in Chapter 2. In this chapter, concern is with the various methods of obtaining presentence information and the impact of these methods on the kind of information obtained.

A. The Postplea of Guilty Hearing

1. *The nature of the hearing.* The postplea of guilty hearing is important in the sentencing of serious offenders in Milwaukee, although the hearing is neither required nor recognized by Wisconsin law.[3] It was devised by a judge of the felony court to assure that defendants who plead guilty are guilty of the offense charged and to serve as a method of obtaining presentence information.[4] Al-

District Court Probation Department. In Michigan, outside of Wayne County, presentence investigations and probation supervision are the responsibility of the Michigan Department of Corrections; in Wayne County, outside of Detroit, they are the responsibility of the Wayne County Circuit Court Probation Department; and in Detroit, they are the responsibility of the Recorder's Court Probation Department.

3 Although the postplea of guilty hearing is neither required nor specifically authorized by Wisconsin law, if such a hearing is conducted Wisconsin law requires that a transcript of it, and all other proceedings before the court, accompany the defendant to the correctional institution if he is sentenced to a term of incarceration. Wis. Stat. Ann. §252.20 (1957). Kansas statutes required that the trial judge submit to the correctional institution to which he has sentenced a convicted felon any information he may possess concerning the nature of the offense and the characteristics of the offender. Presumably, this general requirement would include a transcript of a postplea of guilty hearing if one were conducted. See Kan. Laws 1903, Ch. 375, §3, repealed by Kan. Laws 1957, Ch. 331, §37. No postplea hearings were observed in Kansas. They were used only occasionally in Michigan.

4 The postplea hearing also assists the judge in determining whether the plea was entered voluntarily and with knowledge of the charge and the consequences of pleading guilty to it. The judge indicated that a further reason for the hearing is that it helps prevent successful attack on the validity of the conviction by putting facts on the record, including testimony of the defendant himself, that would not otherwise be recorded.

though concern here is with the latter function,[5] the fact that the postplea of guilty hearing is also a device for verifying the guilty plea affects the kind of presentence information obtained through its use.[6]

The postplea of guilty hearing usually takes place at the time of the arraignment on the information or indictment. Usually the sequence of events is (i) for the defendant to indicate a desire to plead guilty; (ii) for the judge to conduct a hearing to determine whether the plea of guilty should be accepted; (iii) if there is adequate basis for accepting the plea, for the judge to do so and enter a judgment of guilty; and (iv) for the judge to ask whether anything further needs to be said prior to sentencing. Occasionally, after a case is set for trial on a plea of not guilty, a defendant will change his plea to guilty.[7] Most of the postplea hearing is devoted to presentation of the state's evidence. Normally, the first person to testify is the investigating police officer. He describes the circumstances of the offense and the process of investigation that resulted in the defendant's apprehension and prosecution. There is occasionally questioning by the court, and there may be cross-examination by the defendant or his attorney. The police officer concludes his testimony by giving the judge a written statement of the defendant's prior criminal record. That usually completes the state's case.[8] The defendant is then requested to testify. The judge informs him he is free to refuse, but few elect not to testify. His attorney, or the judge if he is unrepresented, questions him concerning his background and the reasons he committed the offense. The defense attorney usually attempts to develop mitigating circumstances, such as the defendant's cooperation with the police in their investigation. The prosecuting attorney normally elicits a statement from the defendant that the testimony of the investigating police officer was accurate. The trial judge then questions the defendant about

[5] The guilty plea verification function of the hearing is discussed in Newman, Conviction: The Determination of Guilt or Innocence Without Trial 19-20 (1966).

[6] This helps to explain why the postplea hearing is focused more on the circumstances of the offense and less on the background of the defendant than is sometimes true of presentence investigations.

[7] There may be a number of reasons for this. In multi-judge courts the defense attorney may use a not guilty plea as a method of selecting a trial judge whom he has reason to believe will be sympathetic to his client. In jurisdictions in which plea bargaining with the prosecutor occurs, the initial not guilty plea may be entered to secure bargaining advantages. In Milwaukee, where neither of these considerations was operative at the time of the field survey, it is likely that many not guilty pleas were entered simply to provide more time for the defense attorney to investigate the case to determine whether the defendant should plead guilty.

[8] Occasionally, the state calls other witnesses, such as the victim of the offense. This occurs routinely only in nonsupport prosecutions. In those cases, the state uses two witnesses: the wife or former wife of the defendant and the investigating officer for the welfare department that provided aid to her and their children.

his prior criminal record by reading descriptions of arrests and convictions from the written statement and requesting verification of their accuracy. The defendant usually does not present other witnesses.[9] The trial judge then either pronounces the defendant guilty of the offense to which he pleaded guilty or refuses to accept the plea and dismisses the prosecution without prejudice to the opportunity of the prosecutor to file a more accurate charge.

If the judge pronounces the defendant guilty, he gives immediate consideration to the problem of sentencing by conducting a sentence hearing.[10] He solicits recommendations, information, and arguments as to the proper sentence and whether a presentence investigation should be ordered. The prosecuting attorney, the defendant, and the defense attorney all join in this discussion. In many cases the judge places the defendant on probation or sentences him to prison on the basis of the information thus obtained, without ordering a presentence investigation.[11] In such cases he immediately disposes of the case, briefly stating his reasons for the decision reached. When the judge orders a presentence investigation, the case is continued, usually for two weeks, to allow time to conduct the investigation. After the judge reads the presentence report, he discusses it with the prosecuting attorney, the investigating probation officer, and the defense attorney in his chambers immediately before sentencing. After this discussion, the defendant is asked in open court whether he wishes to make a statement and further discussion may occur. The judge then disposes of the case.

2. *The nature of the presentence information obtained.* The kind of presentence information the postplea hearing yields must be understood if intelligent comparisons are to be made between the hearing and the presentence investigation as alternative methods of obtaining information for sentencing decisions. The Milwaukee postplea of guilty hearing is helpful in this regard even though it may differ from postplea hearings in other jurisdictions due to the informal nature of the device. The Milwaukee hearing yields information in five general areas: the circumstances of the offense, uncharged offenses admitted by the defendant, his criminal record, his degree of cooperation with the police in their investigation, and his social history. In Milwaukee the circumstances of the offense and the criminal record receive emphasis, while the defendant's social history receives relatively little attention.[12]

[9] Occasionally character evidence may be offered by the defendant's wife, friends, or employer.

[10] See pages 51-55.

[11] For a discussion of the criteria used to decide whether to order a presentence investigation when there has been a postplea of guilty hearing, see pages 24-26.

[12] This may reflect the sentencing criteria used by the Milwaukee trial judge, who

a. *Circumstances of the offense.*

Illustration No. 1: The defendant had pleaded guilty to armed robbery. A detective from the police department was sworn in as the first witness. Questioning by the prosecuting attorney revealed that on the night of the offense the defendant entered a tavern that had no other customers at the time, ordered and drank one drink, and then ordered a second. When the bartender served the drink, the defendant pulled out his revolver and announced that this was a hold-up. He then went behind the bar, and the bartender opened the cash register and gave the defendant more than $60.

The investigating police officer describes the circumstances of the offense through questioning by the prosecuting attorney. His testimony concerns many events that he did not personally observe. It is based upon information gathered by the police department by interviewing the victim and other witnesses and, often, upon the defendant's confession, although the written confession is not itself introduced into evidence. The police officer then describes the process of investigation leading to arrest of the defendant.[13] The testimony about the offense and apprehension of the defendant is not substantially different from the written arrest report made by the police department.[14] In jurisdictions that routinely use the presentence investigation, the arrest report is usually incorporated into the presentence report or paraphrased in it.[15]

Occasionally, the court asks the police officer to clear up ambiguities in his testimony or to expand a point of particular interest to the judge. In cases involving personal injury to the victim, for example, the judge frequently questions the police officer concerning the extent of the victim's injuries and his progress in recovery.

---

seems to give greatest emphasis to the circumstances of the offense and the defendant's criminal record. It is equally possible, however, that the relative lack of social history reflects the fact that the postplea hearing may be a poor device for obtaining such information.

13 In the illustration case, for example, the police officer testified as follows: A few days later, while investigating another robbery, a police officer went to a particular tavern and noticed the defendant in a group of three men, one of whom resembled the person he was seeking. He followed the defendant and his two companions outside and observed them get into a car and drive off. The police officer followed. He finally caught up with the car, had it pull over to the curb, and with drawn gun ordered the defendant and his two companions out of the car. A search followed and on one of them a pistol was found. When asked about it, the person said that he was merely holding it for the defendant. When the defendant was asked about this by the police officer he readily admitted that the pistol was his. He was arrested and interrogated at police headquarters where he quickly confessed to the tavern robbery.

14 Indeed, in some cases the testifying police officer has written the arrest report and may be using it in court to refresh his memory.

15 See pages 27-30.

The defense attorney usually does not cross-examine the police officer extensively about the circumstances of the offense. The defendant in his testimony sometimes offers what he considers to be mitigating circumstances related to the offense, such as provocation by the victim or the defendant's intoxication at the the time of the offense.[16]

b. *Uncharged offenses.*

Illustration No. 2: The defendant had pleaded guilty to a charge of forging a payroll check that he had stolen from his employer. The defendant was represented by counsel. Prior to calling the first witness, the prosecuting attorney stated: "Your honor, by stipulation of the parties the state will offer testimony regarding three additional forgeries for which this defendant has not been formally prosecuted, with the request that the Court consider those additional matters in determining the sentence and with the understanding that the state will seek no warrants in connection with them." The Court accepted the stipulation. The investigating police officer then testified that the defendant stole fifty-five blank payroll checks from his employer and, using his employer's check protector, executed fourteen of them, of which he cashed only four.

Many persons arrested for one offense have in addition committed other offenses. Once the police obtain sufficient evidence to assure conviction of the offense for which the offender was arrested, they attempt to secure from him admissions as to other offenses that he committed. This technique, which frequently results in a defendant admitting a large number of other offenses, is successful partly because of police assurances that the defendant will not be prosecuted for the admitted offenses.[17] In jurisdictions that do not use the postplea of guilty hearing, the admitted, but uncharged, offenses are brought to the attention of the court in the presentence report. There is little doubt that the uncharged offenses influence the judge's sentencing decisions.[18]

In Milwaukee the uncharged offenses are brought to the attention of the court through the investigating police officer's testimony admitted into evidence by stipulation of the parties. For the defendant this has some advantages over simply describing the uncharged offenses in the presentence report. If the defendant receives what the police and prosecutor consider an inadequate

16 In the illustration case, for example, the defendant testified that he had visited a number of bars on the day of the robbery, was drunk when he committed the offense, and used the money to buy more liquor.

17 This system, called the "clean-up process," is described in detail in Miller, Prosecution: The Decision to Charge a Suspect with a Crime (forthcoming).

18 See Chapters 3 and 7.

sentence on the offense charged, there may be a temptation to prosecute him for one of the other offenses which he admitted. Although this occurs infrequently, the legality — at any rate the fairness — of such a subsequent prosecution may present difficult problems. Without a stipulation of the type used in Milwaukee, it is questionable whether the defendant can successfully prevent a subsequent prosecution on the theory that the police assured him he would not be prosecuted, because the court may take the view that the police have no authority to bind the state by that kind of promise. However, when the prosecuting attorney stipulates in court that the state will not prosecute for the other offenses, the defendant's chances of preventing a subsequent prosecution are greatly improved.[19] Furthermore, admitting testimony in a postplea hearing concerning the uncharged offenses provides the defendant with an opportunity to test the truthfulness of the information given to the judge,[20] an opportunity that is often lacking when the uncharged offenses are simply described in the presentence report.[21]

c. *Criminal record.*

> *Illustration No. 3:* The defendant had pleaded guilty to a charge of theft. At the conclusion of his testimony, the investigating police officer gave the judge a written statement of the defendant's criminal record. After the defendant had testified, the judge questioned him on the accuracy of the document by reading each item and asking whether he had in fact been arrested or convicted for that offense. In each instance the defendant indicated that the record was accurate.

As part of their investigation, the police obtain information about whether the defendant has ever previously been arrested or convicted. They search the local police department records and obtain the defendant's F.B.I. record. In those jurisictions that do not use the postplea of guilty hearing, the defendant's criminal record is included in the presentence report when a presentence investigation is conducted.[22] In Milwaukee the investigating police officer

[19] A Model Penal Code provision would bar subsequent prosecution in this situation: "When the defendant has asked that other crimes admitted in open court be taken into account when he is sentenced and the Court has not rejected such request, the sentence shall bar the prosecution or conviction of the defendant in this State for any such admitted crime." Model Penal Code §7.05(4) (Proposed Official Draft, 1962).

[20] Miller, Prosecution (forthcoming), indicates that some of the admitted offenses may not in fact have been committed by the person admitting them.

[21] Defendant's opportunity to challenge the truthfulness of uncharged offenses alleged to have been committed by him depends upon whether the contents of the presentence report are disclosed to him or his attorney and whether the timing and extent of disclosure are such as to permit challenge before sentence is imposed.

[22] See pages 27-30.

simply gives the judge the record at the end of his testimony, and the judge then questions the defendant concerning the accuracy of the record. Occasionally, the defendant denies a particular arrest or conviction or offers something by way of explanation of it. Sometimes the judge asks the defendant whether he has ever been convicted of an offense not shown on the record; occasionally, a defendant answers such a question affirmatively. Arrests not resulting in conviction are included in the defendant's criminal record, and frequently an arrest for a certain offense is shown with no indication of the disposition of the case. When that occurs, the judge may ask the defendant what happened in the case. The defendant's experiences in juvenile court are also included as part of his record. Verification of the defendant's prior criminal record by the judge may not occur when the record is simply included in the presentence report.[23]

d. *Defendant's cooperation with the police.*

Illustration No. 4: Defendant had pleaded guilty to a charge of theft from the person. In cross-examination of the investigating police officer, the defense attorney asked, "How was the defendant? Was he cooperative?" to which the police officer replied, "He was very cooperative." Later the defense attorney emphasized the defendant's cooperation with the police as argument for probation or a light sentence.

In deciding whether to place a defendant on probation[24] or in selecting the length of the sentence if he is committed to prison[25] the trial judge in Milwaukee takes into account the defendant's plea of guilty and whether he cooperated with the police in their investigation. It is routine in the postplea of guilty hearing for the defendant's attorney to ask the investigating police officer whether the defendant was cooperative in the investigation. Usually cooperation assumes the form of the defendant confessing to the offense for which he was arrested, but it may also involve admitting other offenses, locating stolen property, or implicating accomplices. In jurisdictions that do not use a postplea of guilty hearing that information typically is contained in the presentence report — when there is one.

e. *Defendant's social history.*

Illustration No. 5: The defendant had pleaded guilty to armed robbery. After the investigating police officer had testified, the defendant took the stand and testified as follows: He

[23] In Detroit, where the presentence report is not disclosed, there is often no verification of prior criminal record.

[24] See Chapter 3.

[25] See Chapter 6.

> recently had been separated from his wife, and divorce proceedings were under way because his wife was bearing a child by another man. In his despondency, some days prior to the offense he had purchased the gun in question for the purpose of going after the man who had fathered the child. The defendant had not gotten to this man, and he claimed that he was only thinking about doing something to him. On the day of the offense he had been drinking rather heavily and visited many bars. Gradually he was becoming broke and went into a bar for a drink. He admitted fully that he committed the offense and used the money to purchase liquor. Since the separation of the defendant from his wife, he had been living with his own parents and working, but not regularly. Defense counsel asked the defendant if he had used any threatening words during the robbery, such as would suggest an intent to kill or do violence if his demands were not met. The defendant denied that he had. The defendant then was questioned by the prosecuting attorney, who asked him whether the statements made by the police officer were substantially correct, and the defendant admitted they were.

The defendant in his testimony typically relates a certain amount of background information about himself and usually attempts to explain why he committed the offense. Typically, the defendant relates what he considers to be the major events in the recent years of his life, including marital difficulties, other violations of the law, employment history, mental health, etc. Very little attention is devoted to his early childhood, relationship to his parents, or early educational experiences. It is rare for anyone other than the defendant to testify to matters that would normally be called social history.[26] The social history content of the postplea hearing reflects the defendant's idea (and that of his counsel) of what the court will recognize as relevant social and psychological events in the defendant's immediate past. The completeness and sophistication of the presentations vary but are usually fairly straightforward and traditional in concepts of motivation and blameworthiness.

In some presentence reports more attention is given to the defendant's social history than in the Milwaukee postplea of guilty hearing. In other presentence reports, emphasis is placed upon the circumstances of the offense and comparatively little attention is given to social history. It seems clear that some judges would regard the social history content of the postplea hearing as inade-

[26] "Social history" is used here to include all information about the defendant other than the circumstances of the present offense and his official criminal record.

quate. In most cases, the Milwaukee trial judge considers it to be sufficient, but in those in which he does not he orders a presentence investigation with instructions to concentrate on social history.

B. The Presentence Investigation

1. *The decision to conduct a presentence investigation.* In most states that have facilities for presentence investigation the trial judge has discretion to order one or to sentence the defendant without one.[27] An issue of current debate is whether a presentence investigation should be required by law in all cases, or at least in all cases involving the possibility of long-term incarceration. Proponents of such a requirement assert that the presentence report is so important and useful a sentencing aid that trial judges should not have discretion to dispense with it. They contend further that, when the defendant is placed on probation or sentenced to a term of incarceration, the correctional authority will have to conduct a comparable investigation anyway in order to make sensible treatment and custodial decisions. Objections to such a requirement tend to be based on the assumption that, because of limitations on the manpower of most probation departments, making presentence investigations mandatory would greatly reduce the effectiveness of the supervisory functions of the departments to the detriment of probationers and the community. Current discussion of whether presentence investigations should be made mandatory has not taken into account the alternative methods of obtaining presentence information. Experiences in Michigan and Wisconsin are instructive.

In Michigan presentence investigations are required by law in felony cases.[28] In addition, judges of Detroit's Recorder's Court routinely order presentence investigations in all high misdemeanor[29] cases. Postplea of guilty hearings are rarely used. Yet this

[27] See Advisory Council of Judges of the National Council on Crime and Delinquency, Model Sentencing Act, Art. II, Comment (1963).

[28] Mich. Stat. Ann. §28.1144 (1954) provides in part: "Before sentencing any person charged with a felony, and, if directed by the court, in any other case where any person is charged with a misdemeanor within the jurisdiction of the court, the probation officer shall inquire into the antecedents, character and circumstances of such person or persons, and shall report therein in writing to such court or magistrate. If such person is committed to a state penal institution or the Detroit house of correction, a copy of such pre-sentence investigation report and, if a psychopathic or psychiatric examination of such person has been made for the court, a copy of the report thereon shall accompany the commitment papers. . . ."

[29] The term "high misdemeanor" is used by personnel of Recorder's Court to designate a misdemeanor that carries a penalty in excess of ninety days or $100 or both. Misdemeanors that carry lesser penalties ("low misdemeanors") are disposed of in a different division of Recorder's Court than high misdemeanors and felonies.

does not mean there is no attempt to verify the factual accuracy of pleas of guilty. That part of the presentence report which deals with the circumstances of the offense is sometimes used by judges for plea verification. Indeed, in one Michigan jurisdiction that is the primary purpose of the presentence investigation.[30] Thus, the presentence investigation, like the postplea of guilty hearing, may serve both as a source of sentencing information and as an aid in verifying pleas of guilty. The content of the presentence report varies depending upon which of these is emphasized.

In Wisconsin, on the other hand, the trial judge has discretion not to order a presentence investigation, except in certain sex offense cases.[31] In Milwaukee, the trial judge determines whether a presentence investigation is needed after the postplea of guilty hearing has been conducted. One judge said that in many cases he could determine from the postplea of guilty hearing that the offender was immediately worthy of probation. Conversely, he said that a similar situation could exist in which several types of individuals and their offenses were not worthy of probation, and there would seem to be little reason to refer them for a presentence investigation. In deciding whether to order a presentence investigation, the judge considers a number of factors, any one of which might result in an investigation: (1) whether there is any conflict in testimony as to the circumstances of the offense; (2) whether there is doubt as to the extent of personal injury or property loss to the victim of the offense; (3) whether there was any testimony in the hearing indicating that a more detailed inquiry into the defendant's social history might produce helpful information; and (4) whether the defendant or his counsel requests a presentence

---

Because high misdemeanors and felonies are treated the same for most purposes by the law, Recorder's Court judges feel they should be treated the same with respect to presentence investigations even though the law makes a distinction in that instance.

[30] The presentence report produced by the Wayne County Circuit Court Probation Department is devoted largely to a careful description of the circumstances of the offense drawn from the police, the defendant, and other witnesses. It contains relatively little information of the social history kind. In this respect it resembles the information obtained through the Milwaukee postplea of guilty hearing. One reason for this may be that both devices function as the principal plea verification method in each jurisdiction. Another factor may be that most of the personnel of the Wayne County Circuit Court Probation Department are former police officers, persons who would be expected to be oriented toward this type of investigation. The Wayne County Circuit Court has criminal jurisdiction for all areas within Wayne County outside the City of Detroit; Recorder's Court has criminal jurisdiction in Detroit.

[31] The Wisconsin Sex Offenders Act requires a commitment to the Department of Public Welfare for a psychiatric and presentence investigation prior to sentencing in certain sex cases. For further discussion, see Chapter 7.

investigation.[32] When a presentence investigation is ordered to clarify a specific area of the case, the judge instructs the probation department to give particular attention to that problem.[33]

Comparison thus can be made between a system in which a presentence investigation is a standard ingredient of sentencing, as in Detroit, and in which it is relied upon only selectively, as in Milwaukee. This, indeed, is a dimension of the problem of obtaining adequate presentence information that is usually ignored. Most proponents of mandatory presentence investigation view the only alternative as that of sentencing based on no presentence information at all or, at best, on only that information obtained in a hasty and routine sentence hearing.[34] But, as the Milwaukee experience indicates, that does not exhaust the alternatives; the postplea of guilty hearing can, and does, produce most of the information typically contained in a presentence report, and it can, and does, serve as a way of screening out those cases in which a presentence investigation would apparently serve no useful sentencing purpose.

The question whether presentence investigations should be made mandatory is not easily answered. In addition to the considerations usually advanced, a number of factors must be taken into account: whether making presentence investigations mandatory precludes, as a practical matter, the development of a postplea of guilty hearing proceeding; whether the presentence report can perform the plea verification function as well as the postplea hearing and, if it can, what effect this has on its suitability as a sentencing aid; and whether some combination of postplea hearing and presentence investigation might be required.[35]

2. *Sources of information for the presentence investigation.* It is important to understand the presentence investigation process, especially what sources of information are used by the investigating

[32] The reasons for ordering a presentence investigation are, of course, literally without limit. On one occasion, for example, police testimony indicated that the defendant might be connected with a professional car theft ring. The trial judge ordered a presentence investigation to determine whether this suspicion could be substantiated or refuted.

[33] The probation department receives a transcript of the postplea of guilty hearing almost immediately in all cases referred to it for presentence investigation. That transcript is used to determine why the judge ordered the investigation and to furnish leads to fruitful areas of investigation.

[34] See pages 51-55.

[35] Another consideration of great importance is the relative reliability of presentence information obtained through the postplea of guilty hearing and the presentence investigation. This is a very complex problem, having as its variables, among others, whether the defendant is represented by competent counsel with opportunity to cross-examine the investigating officer (and, perhaps, his sources of information) and opportunity to introduce evidence in rebuttal. The broader question of the relative reliability of methods of obtaining presentence information is discussed in Chapter 2.

probation officer. This is particularly important because the current debate over the confidentiality of the presentence report[36] is based in substantial measure upon assumptions concerning the relative importance of the various sources of information used in the investigation, particularly so-called confidential sources. After understanding what sources of information are used, an informed judgment can be made about whether the resulting report should be held in confidence from the defendant and his counsel.

a. *The police.* The police department is a principal source of information for the investigating probation officer. In Detroit, when an offender is referred to the probation department for a presentence investigation, the police department provides the investigating probation officer with its "arrest report," a written description of the arrest and investigation.[37] This statement is incorporated into the presentence report[38] and is the probation officer's primary source of information about the offense.[39] The police department also furnishes the probation officer with the defendant's "rap sheet," a written statement of his prior arrests and convictions.[40] The rap sheet, which is incorporated into the presentence

[36] The issue of confidentiality of the presentence report is discussed in Chapter 2 in the broader context of a discussion of methods of assuring reliability of all types of presentence information.

[37] The investigating police officer transmits the arrest report to the probation officer soon after referral of the case for presentence investigation. Nonsupport cases usually do not involve the police. Instead, they originate in the Adjustment Division of Recorder's Court Probation Department. See note 43 *infra* this chapter. If the offender is successfully prosecuted after informal efforts to compel performance of support obligations have failed, he is referred to the Domestic Relations Division for presentence investigation. The Adjustment Division routinely submits to the Domestic Relations Division a statement that contains the same information contained in the police department's arrest report. In fact, the same form is used for both reports.

[38] In one case, the following arrest report was submitted to the investigating probation officer:

"At 1:15 A.M., Patrolmen R and F investigated a 1949 automobile that had been stolen at Iroquois and Lafayette. They investigated the above subject, who was trying to start the car and found that he did not have a key or registration for the car. Officers found that tinfoil had been used to jump the ignition. Subject also had two screwdrivers and a key for a jukebox on his person.

"On being questioned subject stated that on the night in question he had been in a theater. Later he met some men in a hotel parking lot. He decided to take the above car and go for a ride. He further stated that he fashioned a jumper out of tinfoil, started the car, and had gone only five blocks when the car stalled. He was arrested by the officers as he was trying to get it started.

"The defendant later pleaded guilty before Judge S to unlawfully driving an automobile away. The defendant also cleared up a breaking and entering and safe job in St. Claire, Michigan."

[39] Further information about the offense is usually obtained from interviewing the defendant and only rarely from interviewing the victim or witnesses.

[40] In nonsupport cases the Adjustment Division obtains the defendant's criminal record from the police department's record bureau and tansmits it to the investigating probation officer.

report, lists all the defendant's arrests, whether they resulted in release, charge and dismissal, or conviction and usually indicates the disposition of each such arrest. Finally, if the defendant during in-custody interrogation admitted to offenses other than those for which he was arrested, a description of the offenses admitted is forwarded to the probation officer conducting the presentence investigation.[41] This document, termed a "clean-up sheet," is incorporated into the presentence report.

The rap sheet submitted to the investigating probation officer by the police department does not include arrests or court action experienced by the defendant while he was legally a juvenile.[42] Although some of this information is available to the probation department, no effort is made to obtain it unless the defendant is under the age of twenty-one at the time of referral for presentence investigation. In that event, the presentence investigation is conducted by the Youth Division of Recorder's Court Probation Department [43] and a check of the defendant's juvenile record is routinely made.

This information is available from two sources: the police department and the juvenile court. The investigating probation officer usually obtains the information from the police department, which maintains a separate record of all arrests of individuals un-

[41] The probation department may not know of some offenses the defendant has admitted. If the defendant admitted offenses at the time of a prior arrest, it is unlikely that the current presentence report will reflect them. Admitted offenses are not recorded in the police department's record bureau and thus do not appear on the rap sheet. If the defendant had previously been referred for a presentence investigation, the files of the probation department may reflect the prior admitted offenses, but if the previous presentence report was prepared by a different division of the probation department, its file probably will not be checked. It is possible, therefore, for an offender to have an extensive record of admitted offenses that are not known to the probation department and thus will not be known to the sentencing judge.

[42] The Michigan juvenile code places exclusive original jurisdiction in the juvenile court for minors under the age of seventeen. Mich. Stat. Ann. §27.3178(598.2) (a) (1962). The juvenile court has authority to permit a sixteen-year-old minor alleged to have committed a felony to be tried in criminal court. Mich. Stat. Ann. §27.3178-(598.4) (1962). It has concurrent jurisdiction with the criminal court over certain minors who are seventeen, eighteen, or nineteen years of age. Mich. Stat. Ann. §27.3178 (598.2)(d) (1962).

[43] The Probation Department of Recorder's Court has six divisions: Adjustment Division, Misdemeanant Division, Men's Felony Division, Women's Division, Domestic Relations Division, and Youth Division. The Adjustment Division does not conduct presentence investigations: its primary function is negotiating and collecting nonsupport payments prior to court action. The Misdemeanant Division conducts very few formal presentence investigations; a representative of that Division is present in Recorder's Court when low misdemeanors are adjudicated and provides the judge with the defendant's criminal record and, occasionally, oral information concerning his background and a recommendation as to disposition of the case. The other four divisions do conduct presentence investigations.

der the age of seventeen. This information is not contained in the criminal record bureau, the source of information for the rap sheet. The probation officer may obtain this information by taking notes from the police records, but he is not permitted to duplicate them or remove them from the files, because the police assume that would violate the confidentiality required by law for juvenile records.[44] When the police first make contact with a juvenile, they make out a "history sheet" regardless of whether court action is contemplated. This information, which evaluates the juvenile in his school and work, neighborhood relations, home conditions, and parental and family relations, is available to the investigating probation officer.

The police department's juvenile record is restricted to information about arrests. Unlike the adult records, no information relating to the disposition of the case subsequent to arrest is maintained in the juvenile records, possibly because the police may interpret the juvenile code's confidentiality provisions as precluding the recording of such information.[45] If information concerning the disposition of a juvenile case is desired, the juvenile court records must be consulted. In an informal opinion, the legal adviser to the judges of Recorder's Court expressed the view that the juvenile code does not preclude the disclosure of an individual's juvenile court record in a presentence report when he is later convicted of a criminal offense.[46] Nevertheless, probation officers rarely obtain juvenile court records. They explain their reluctance to seek these records on the grounds that they add little to the records available

[44] Mich. Stat. Ann. §27.3178(598.23) (1962) provides: "A disposition of any child under this chapter, or any evidence given in such case, shall not in any civil, criminal or any other cause or proceeding whatever in any court, be lawful or proper evidence against such child for any purpose whatever, except in subsequent cases against the same child under this chapter." It is not clear how, if at all, this provision affects police record-keeping procedures, but it is the only provision arguably related to them.

[45] See note 44 *supra*.

[46] Mich. Stat. Ann. §27.3178(598.28) (1962) provides in part: "The court shall maintain records of all cases brought before it. Such records shall be open only by order of the court to persons having a legitimate interest." See note 44 *supra*. The author of the legal opinion, after examining several statutory provisions, reached this conclusion: "For the best interest of the juvenile ward, or one who was so originally, as well as the interest of the public, the facts relating to a juvenile record should be at the disposal of the court which has to determine whether or not one accused of crime is to be given probation. . . . It isn't using his record against the child, but for him. As a ward of the state he should be protected. If he gets probation, he will still be a ward of the state in a sense, subject to probation protection by a different court.

"By statute the fact of a juvenile disposition is barred as evidence against such child. This logically does not in my opinion, preclude its use to help authorities to decide on protective probation instead of a criminal sentence."

through the police department[47] and that the juvenile court has, over the years, been inconsistent in permitting access to the records, periodically making them unavailable to probation officers conducting presentence investigations.[48]

In Milwaukee the investigating probation officer obtains essentially the same information from the police department as does his counterpart in Detroit. When a case is referred to the probation department for presentence investigation following the postplea of guilty hearing, a transcript of that hearing accompanies the referral. From the transcript, the investigating officer obtains the police department's description of the offense, the defendant's criminal and juvenile record, and a description of admitted but uncharged offenses.[49] This information is repeated in the presentence report.

b. *The defendant.* The defendant is an important source of information for the probation officer conducting a presentence investigation. The officer usually initiates the investigation by interviewing the defendant and often he will interview him several times during the course of the investigation.[50] Other sources of information, such as the victim, witnesses, defendant's family and friends, or the records of social agencies having previous contact with the defendant, are usually consulted, if at all, to verify information given by the defendant in the interviews.

[47] The following is an example of a juvenile court record incorporated into a presentence report:

10-17-49	Larceny — probation.
1-29-51	Violation of probation, larceny of bicycle — probation continued.
11-19-51	Violation of probation, breaking and entering, larceny and truancy, admitted to Boy's Republic.
3-11-52	Violation of probation, maladjustment, returned to Boy's Republic.
10-7-52	Violation of probation, maladjustment, released. Probation continued, placed in foster home.
6-23-53	In court for changing plan, probation continued in own home.
5-28-54	Probation terminated, case dismissed.

[48] One probation officer said he does not bother to check the records of the juvenile court. He complained that the records made available by the juvenile court were not of much assistance. "The juvenile court goes on a confidence kick occasionally although they are cooperative. . . . On the other hand, records of the Youth Bureau of the Detroit Police Department are not considered confidential and therefore can be safely included in a presentence report." He acknowledged that the records of the Youth Bureau are not always complete and do not always show the disposition made. However, all arrests made by the Youth Bureau are not ultimately referred to juvenile court. Also, the Youth Bureau has detailed facts concerning the offense for which the subject was picked up.

[49] See pages 19-22.

[50] In addition, the defendant may be interviewed by the investigating probation officer's supervisor. This procedure is followed in some divisions of the Recorder's Court Probation Department. Since its major purpose is to verify information obtained by the investigating probation officer and to check on the quality of the investigation, rather than to obtain new information from the defendant, this procedure is discussed in Chapter 2 in the context of assuring reliability of presentence information.

The defendant is usually requested to relate the circumstances of the offense. He almost always admits to committing the offense, but often his description of its circumstances is helpful in understanding the reasons for its commission. His statement is usually incorporated into the presentence report as "Defendant's version of the offense." For example, the following appeared in a report of a case in which the defendant had pleaded guilty to second degree murder of her husband:

> Defendant states that she and her husband had not been getting along for the last few years. He was running around and, as a result of her attempting to get him to stay home, they quarreled almost continuously. During these quarrels he threatened to do her bodily harm. She stated further that he had a baby by another woman and that even though he did not support the baby, as far as she knew, he always was short of money. She stated it was difficult for her to remember what was said prior to the present offense. She said she never wanted to do anyone any harm and was extremely regretful for having committed the present offense.

The defendant's statement and the police department arrest report are usually all the information the probation officer secures concerning the circumstances of the offense.

The defendant is always the principal source of information (often the only one) concerning his social history, i.e., his health, family history, present family situation, social activities, educational achievements, and economic circumstances. Often the probation officer questions the defendant on his present state of health and summarizes briefly the information obtained, such as "He is in good health" or "Defendant complains of excessive nervousness. Shortly before the present offense she had a miscarriage and was hospitalized." The probation officer obtains from the defendant a description of his family history and present family situation. The officer's concern with this information varies depending upon several circumstances. In Detroit, if the case involves an adult who has committed an offense unrelated to his family situation, the probation officer attempts to elicit information concerning the defendant's relationship with his parents, his siblings, and his wife and children, without trying to analyze the family situation in detail. If the defendant is a youth, additional attention is given to describing the current home situation. When the offense is nonsupport, there is an attempt to determine the exact nature of the relationship between the wife and husband.[51] Although the pri-

[51] Nonsupport cases are virtually the only ones in which it is routine procedure to interview the victim of the offense (the defendant's wife) as well as the defendant.

mary purpose is to determine need for support and ability to pay,[52] there is also an effort to ascertain the extent to which the wife is at fault and, particularly, whether the husband and wife are collaborating to defraud welfare authorities.[53]

The probation officer usually seeks to describe the defendant's mode of life, under such headings as religion, recreation, and interests. Virtually all of this information comes from the defendant. The Youth Division of the Recorder's Court Probation Department pays particular attention to the defendant's "Interests and Activities":

> Defendant's use of leisure time is relatively poor. The greater part of his time is spent with persons of questionable character, some of whom have served prison sentences or are presently on probation. He indicates no interest in furthering his education. States he is not addicted to narcotics, does not gamble, drinks beer when he can acquire some by means of an older person purchasing it for him. Smokes cigarettes; claims a heterosexual adjustment having had intimate physical relations with girls known to be promiscuous sexually. No serious accident, venereal disease, or tuberculosis.

The probation officer questions the defendant concerning his educational achievements. The discussion of this in the presentence report is often very brief: "Finished eighth grade in Kentucky at age sixteen, quit to work in coal mine." [54] Finally, the probation officer normally questions the defendant concerning his employment status. Usually this information is not verified by checking

[52] The defendant's willingness and ability to make support payments as a condition of probation are important criteria in determining whether he will be placed on probation or sentenced to prison. See Chapter 3.

[53] The problem usually involves the so-called "man in the house" disqualification from Aid to Families with Dependent Children. Under this rule, aid may not be paid to a family when the father is living with them, even if he is unemployed and the family needs assistance for that reason. Sometimes a probation officer investigating a nonsupport case suspects that the defendant is living with his family, which is receiving AFDC. In such cases, it is the usual practice to contact the welfare authorities to relate the causes of the suspicion and to intensify the investigation into the defendant's home situation. In Detroit, the public welfare authorities provide a liaison man to the probation department to facilitate such cooperation.

[54] The Youth Division of the Recorder's Court Probation Department gives more emphasis to the defendant's educational background than do the other divisions. In one case, the following information was obtained from the defendant and was related in the presentence report:

"Education: The defendant began school at the age of five and left school at the age of sixteen, after having completed tenth grade. Prior to attending high school, he mentioned he had attended Detroit Public Schools, but because of continual skipping, was sent to Boy's Republic and later to a foster home in Penobscot. Claims he acquired an average education. For the greater part of the time he received excellent marks and did not fail any subjects. However, this no doubt is questionable since defendant does not indicate a good basic education."

with the asserted employer.[55] When restitution is to be secured to the victim of the offense or when the defendant is to be compelled to make family support payments,[56] the probation officer's inquiry into the defendant's employment and financial status is conducted in considerably more detail: The defendant's ability to make required restitution or support payments is an important factor in determining whether he will be placed on probation.[57]

c. *Field observations and additional interviews.* Very little use is made of field observations in either Detroit or Milwaukee in conducting presentence investigations. Occasionally, the investigating probation officer may visit the defendant's home, sometimes to observe conditions there, more often to interview members of the defendant's family who are not able to appear at the probation office. The only cases in which interviews with persons other than the defendant are routinely made are nonsupport cases, in which the defendant's wife is interviewed to determine the extent of need for support and whether any payments have been made by the defendant.

d. *Probation department files.* In Detroit, the investigating probation officer usually checks the files of his division of the probation department to ascertain whether the defendant has previously been supervised by that division. If there was a prior period of supervision, information concerning that experience is included in the presentence report:

> *Former Probation Period:* Defendant was supervised by this department on two prior occasions. On November 17, 1954, she was given a four-month probation period by Your Honor on a charge of accosting and soliciting. Her case was closed with improvement. Again, on November 10, 1955, the defendant was placed on one year's probation by Judge A on a charge of uttering and publishing [a forged instrument]. This case, too, was closed with improvement and, at the time it was closed, the defendant was in Rest Haven. Our record indicates, however, prior to going to Rest Haven the defendant was placed in Memorial Hospital and refused to stay. The superintendent had requested this office to obtain a warrant for her in order to keep her there. She made her own hospital plan with Rest Haven and entered there.

[55] One reason given for this was that in many cases it is not particularly significant whether the defendant presently has employment, while checking with the asserted employer would in some cases result in dismissal if the defendant is in fact employed.

[56] Probation, if granted, will be conditioned upon the defendant's making restitution or support payments. See Chapter 4.

[57] See Chapter 3.

The files of other divisions of the probation department usually are not checked to determine whether the defendant has ever been under the supervision of another division. This is due, in part, to a lack of a central indexing system. When a presentence investigation is being conducted by the Women's Division, the files of other departments are checked if the defendant has been involved with a male. Any information obtained is included in the presentence report:

> *Men's Probation:* We find that Sylvester had been on probation for drunkenness, and his case is to close next month. His probation officer had no knowledge of the fact that the boy had been living with defendant.

e. *Public and private social agencies.* Information is obtained only infrequently from public and private social agencies. In Detroit the probation officer may occasionally check with the parole authorities if there is a record of defendant's having been on parole. The Women's Division checks with parole authorities if the spouse of a female offender has a prior or current parole status. The information obtained is included in the presentence report:

> *Parole Board:* Contacted Ike's parole officer and learned from him that Ike was returned on February 26, 1957. He stated that the case against him is weak, but from narcotics officers it was learned that Ike is still associated with dope. He claimed to be employed, but there were conflicting statements made by him and his alleged employers. In addition, he was unable to account for money which he claimed to have earned by working. Ike was extremely antagonistic and would not cooperate with a plan for him to be hospitalized at the United States Public Health Service Hospital at Lexington, Kentucky.

With the exception of the Women's Division, however, there is no systematic attempt to use information possessed by parole authorities.[58]

The Youth Division routinely contacts the psychological clinic of the board of education in conducting presentence investigation. Officers of the Division consider this an important source of information. One officer said that, if the boy lives in a rough and relatively high delinquency neighborhood, he may have a long behavioral history which usually starts in school. As a consequence, such boys are usually referred to the psychological clinic when in school.

[58] The Wisconsin State Department of Public Welfare makes its records available to the Milwaukee probation department if a defendant undergoing presentence investigation has been under probation or parole supervision by the state agency. The extent, if any, to which that resource is used is unknown.

The clinic, therefore, has a wealth of information, both psychological and social. In many instances in which individuals are having problems, the teachers will have visited the home and will have provided valuable social data. The other divisions of the probation department do not routinely make use of this resource.

In Detroit it is not usual practice for the investigating probation officer to check with the Social Service Exchange to ascertain prior contacts with social agencies, nor does the probation department systematically register its cases with the Exchange. Some probation officers claimed they were not allowed sufficient time to check with the Exchange; others thought the information obtained from that source not particularly helpful.

Clearly, inadequate indexing and retrieval systems and high caseloads result in much information loss. How valuable the information lost would be is another matter, but some relevant information is never retrieved, and other information gets retrieved anew each time a defendant is re-convicted.

3. *The presentence report.*

a. *Content of the presentence report.* The general outline of the presentence report is usually specified by departmental regulation. Normally, the investigating probation officer is expected to obtain information under each of the applicable headings of a report form and to present that information in the presentence report. In Milwaukee, for example, the presentence report form requests information under the following headings: identification of the defendant, the court in which the case is pending, the offense charged, the plea, the circumstances of the present offense, employment status, assets, prior criminal and juvenile record, complainant's background, defendant's marital history, education, religion, membership in social organizations, parole status if any, present status of defendant's children, social history, military record, health record, and summary and recommendation by the probation department. Substantially the same content is specified for presentence reports by the Detroit Recorder's Court Probation Department and many other probation departments.[59]

b. *Variations in the content of the presentence report.* Although the general outline of the presentence report remains stable within a particular probation department and does not vary significantly from department to department, it is nevertheless true that there are significant differences in presentence reports. One major variation is in the extent to which the defendant's background is em-

[59] See Model Penal Code §7.07(3) (Proposed Official Draft, 1962) for a similar indication of the scope of the presentence report. See also Administrative Office of the United States Courts, The Presentence Investigation Report (Pub. No. 103, 1965).

phasized in the report; another is the extent to which the probation officer interprets and evaluates the data obtained. Three factors appear to account for these and similar variations in presentence reports: the purpose of the investigation, the background and training of the investigating officer, and whether the contents of the report are disclosed to the defendant or his attorney.

(1) *The purpose of the investigation.* Presentence investigations are conducted in every felony case in Detroit and in Wayne County outside of Detroit. The investigations are conducted by different organizations: those in Detroit by the Recorder's Court Probation Department, and those in Wayne County outside of Detroit by the Wayne County Circuit Court Probation Department. Both use approximately the same general outline for the presentence report, yet the report in Wayne County contains much greater emphasis upon the circumstances of the offense than that in Detroit, while it contains less emphasis upon the defendant's background. One factor apparently contributing to this difference is that the presentence report in Detroit is used simply as an aid to sentencing, while in Wayne County it is used in addition as a device to verify the accuracy of the guilty plea.[60] The emphasis of the Wayne County report is better adapted to plea verification, because of the detailed examination into the circumstances of the offense, than is the report typically produced by the Recorder's Court Probation Department.

Because presentence investigations are conducted selectively in Milwaukee, the purpose of the investigation may have an even greater impact upon the content of the report than in Michigan. When a case is assigned for investigation, the probation department receives a transcript of the postplea of guilty hearing. From that transcript, the reason the judge ordered the investigation can often be determined. In those cases in which the judge has a specific reason and it appears on the transcript, the probation department tends to concentrate on that aspect of the case and the presentence report emphasizes it. If, for example, the judge indicates on the record that he is ordering the investigation to obtain more information concerning the defendant's residence plans, the probation department will concentrate its investigation in that area. On other occasions the judge may indicate that he is interested in the extent of restitution that should be required if the defendant is given probation; in such cases, the probation department attempts to determine the exact extent of the loss of the victim of the offense. And in one case, the probation department believed that a defendant had been referred for investigation only to please the

[60] See Newman, Conviction 14-18 (1966).

defense attorney who had requested it. It spent very little time investigating and the presentence report was quite short.

(2) *The background and training of the investigating officer.* The educational background of the investigating probation officer also affects the contents of the presentence report. That the Wayne County presentence report concentrates on the circumstances of the offense has already been noted. This doubtless is explained in part by the fact that many Wayne County probation officers, unlike those in Detroit and Milwaukee, are former police officers. They are accustomed to investigating the circumstances of offenses but not the background of the offender; their presentence investigation produces a document which in scope is like an expanded arrest report.

The effect of educational background and training upon the presentence report was noted by the Chief Probation Officer in Detroit in discussing a new in-service training program instituted in his department. He said that, as a result of the training program, he has already received much improved presentence reports, even from older employees who had no formal training. They have become aware of the type of social data desired by institutions in their classification programs and in planning for parole. Much of the detailed social information usually excluded from presentence reports in the past is now being included and verified, the latter being of special importance. Names and addresses of relatives, employers, etc., are being detailed in the reports, and residences of relatives verified along with respective employers. In the past, probation officers frequently did not verify such information and upon further check by the Department of Corrections personnel it would be discovered that the relatives' residences or employers given by the subjects to the probation department and unverified were frequently false.

(3) *Disclosure of the presentence report.* In Milwaukee the presentence report is regularly disclosed to the defendant's attorney. A number of probation officers noted that this practice had the effect of excluding from the presentence report matters that might be controversial and likely to be questioned by the defendant's attorney. The investigating officer is more likely to exclude information that he cannot verify if the report is disclosed; also, he may not include information, such as psychiatric reports obtained from other persons, that he considers confidential.[61]

c. *Evaluations and recommendations by the probation department.* In addition to factual information, most presentence reports

[61] The effects of disclosure on the contents of the report are discussed in more detail in Chapter 2.

contain the probation department's evaluation of the defendant and a recommendation for or against probation. The Detroit probation department made the following evaluation of one case:

> *Summary and Evaluation:* Defendant is a twenty-four-year-old woman of average intelligence who is emotionally unstable, poorly adjusted, and a sex delinquent. She has lived in Detroit for about six years, is employed, and admits that she has been a prostitute for that length of time. She also admits that she has been using marijuana for the past three years. We feel that her antisocial behavior has become too well established to be changed by supervision.

The department's recommendation is usually limited to a statement favoring probation or incarceration. It normally does not express an opinion concerning the conditions or length of the probationary period or the length of incarceration. In those cases in which statutes prohibit probation,[62] the department makes no recommendation. The practice in Milwaukee is identical.

(1) *The process of arriving at a departmental recommendation.* In Detroit the investigating probation officer may or may not include his own recommendation in the presentence report. The supervisor of his division reads the report and, in some instances, personally conducts a further interview with the defendant. The supervisor then drafts a covering letter in which he briefly states the facts and expresses the recommendation of the department. If the supervisor personally interviews the defendant, he may conclude that the facts differ from those stated by the investigating probation officer. Consequently, the supervisor may make a recommendation contrary to that made by the investigating officer. Faced with such conflicting information and advice, the judge may return the case to the probation department for clarification or may appeal to another agency, such as the police department. One judge stated that he had, on occasion, contacted the police department to verify facts when there was conflict in the report of the probation department. In one case the investigating officer recommended confinement. The supervisor recommended probation based on a factual assumption which differed from that of the investigating officer. The latter had reported that the offender had been operating a gambling racket. The supervisor, on the other hand, stated that the offender was working in the real estate business. When the judge contacted the police, he learned that the offender's activities were correctly reported by the investigating probation officer. In the Women's Division in Detroit, it is customary for the supervisor and the investigating officer to confer on the

62 See Chapter 3.

matter of recommendation and to agree upon a single, departmental recommendation.

In Milwaukee the Deputy Chief Probation Officer and another probation officer do not supervise probationers but conduct almost all presentence investigations assigned to the department. All presentence reports must be approved by the Chief Probation Officer and submitted over his signature. He does not read each report in its entirety but does look over every report. He calls a conference with the investigating probation officer if he wishes to question the content of the report or suggest changes. All changes, particularly in recommendations, are agreed upon between them if the report is submitted over both signatures. If differences cannot be resolved, the report goes to the judge either not approved by the Chief Probation Officer or, if he required a change, without the signature of the investigating officer.

(2) *Criteria used to make the recommendation.* In making its recommendation, the probation department is concerned primarily about whether the defendant should be placed on probation or sentenced to a term of incarceration. The judge, in making that decision, considers a number of factors in addition to the probability that the defendant will succeed on probation — factors such as the seriousness of the offense and community sentiment toward the offense and the offender. The probation department, although it is aware of the necessity for the judge to take all these factors into account in making the probation decision, bases its recommendation almost exclusively on its assessment of the defendant's probable adjustment on probation. Most probation departments feel that their expertise lies in making this judgment and prefer not to express their opinions on factors that they consider to lie properly within the province of the judge alone. A probation department's concern with probable success on probation is modified in cases in which it knows that a particular judge wishes to make a decision on some basis other than probable probation success. In some of these situations, it may modify its recommendation in anticipation of the wishes of the judge.

(a) *Probable success on probation.* In general, the considerations that the probation department uses to arrive at its assessment of probable success on probation are the same as those used by a parole board to assess probable parole success.[63] In Detroit a recommendation for probation is almost routine in the case of a first offender. One supervisor said, "Every man deserves one break and that is the policy of the probation department." Repeating offenders may or may not receive a favorable probation recommendation

[63] See Chapter 11.

depending upon other factors. One supervisor stated that a man's attitude toward society, how he viewed his offense, and whether or not there was any real "remorse" are the principal criteria. Many offenders are given probation for a second or even third offense. This is especially true if an offender has successfully completed a prior period of probation.

The fact that the offender is addicted to narcotics or is a chronic alcoholic is likely to result in a recommendation against probation, while steady employment weighs in favor of a recommendation for probation. Probation officers in Milwaukee noted that similar factors were considered in assessing probable success on probation and, hence, in making their recommendations.

(b) *Anticipation of the judge's preference.* Probation officers in Detroit readily acknowledged that judicial preference was a factor in making their recommendations. Two probation officers stated that certain judges have pet peeves. One judge will not place a narcotics offender on probation, and he also has an abhorrence of bad check charges. Another judge usually places defendants in vice cases on probation. Each judge has his own private kind of case that he does not consider serious. In some instances probation officers are required to give the court the type of recommendation it expects — the judges want to hear and read only certain types of information. Another probation officer summed it up with "you have to take into consideration which judge you are writing a report for."

Certain judges in Detroit prefer not to have recommendations submitted with presentence reports, although most of them do wish to have recommendations included. One judge stated that he did not want recommendations and, more particularly, did not want the opinion or recommendation of a probation officer on whether or not an individual should make probation. He felt that it was his decision to make and his prerogative. What he wanted from the psychopathic clinic and the probation department were the facts and an adequate evaluation of the personality involved on which he could base his own decision and arrive at his own conclusions as to what the disposition should be.

A similar pattern occurred in Milwaukee. In several cases involving relatively minor offenses, the body of the presentence report indicated that, in terms of probable success on probation, the defendant should be incarcerated. However, the departmental recommendation was for probation. One probation officer explained that the judge would not incarcerate defendants for certain offenses he considered minor even though the probation department's estimate of probable probation success was unfavorable. On some occasions the judge has even been successful in persuading the investigating probation officer to change his recommendation from incarceration to probation. On the other hand, the probation department does not hesitate to recommend probation based on probable probation success when it knows the judge is likely to consider the offense serious enough to warrant incarceration. One possible explanation of this practice is that the judge may not feel a need for support to incarcerate a defendant but that he may feel a need for support to give probation. A sentencing judge is seldom publicly criticized for sending a defendant to prison but sometimes is for granting probation.

C. The Psychiatric Examination

The psychiatric examination is an important method of obtaining presentence information. It is normally used to supplement information obtained by the postplea of guilty hearing or presentence investigation. Because the demand for psychiatric services is much greater than the supply in most communities, the problem of selecting cases in which the offender is to undergo psychiatric examination is particularly acute. It is, therefore, important to understand the criteria used to select offenders for psychiatric examination. Psychiatric examinations are also used for a number of purposes other than to supply presentence information. They are used to determine competency to stand trial and to determine whether a criminal defendant can be committed as a criminal sexual psychopath. What use, if any, can the judge make of psychiatric examination reports or testimony presented for these other purposes when later he is sentencing the convicted offender? This question is obviously related to the problem of making the most efficient use of limited psychiatric resources.

There is also a problem of communication. The psychiatrist speaks in a language difficult for the sentencing judge to understand. Unless care is taken to translate the language used, the resources expended upon the examination may go for naught and the defendant may be prejudiced by misunderstanding. Related to this is the problem of reporting an adequate factual basis for the psychiatric evaluation and recommendation. If the experience in Detroit is representative, many judges feel that insufficient facts are provided in the psychiatric examination report. Depending upon the individual judge, these difficulties of communication often result in either blind reliance upon the psychiatric recommendation or complete disregard of it. In either event, the opportunity for erroneous interpretation of the information is great.

Finally, there is the problem of confidentiality of the psychiatric examination report.[64] In one respect there would seem to be less need for preventing disclosure of the psychiatric examination report than of the presentence report. In the former, the defendant himself is virtually the sole source of the information obtained, while in the presentence investigation he is only the principal source. There may be less likelihood of revealing confidential information and inhibiting future examinations than in the case of presentence examinations. But it can be argued that disclosure of the report could be injurious to the defendant, because the psychiatrist's evaluation of his personality, if revealed to him, would inhibit subsequent treatment. A related problem is whether the report can be revealed to defense counsel but not to the defendant himself, and the proper procedure if the defendant chooses not to have counsel.

1. *The availability of psychiatric examinations as presentence information.* Both Detroit and Milwaukee have well established procedures for obtaining psychiatric information to aid the trial judge in sentencing, and they apparently are used with some frequency. There is no indication that, at the time of the field survey, psychiatric resources were available in Wichita for presentence information purposes; if they were available, there is no evidence they were used.

a. *Detroit.* In Detroit there are two resources for psychiatric examinations which are used regularly by judges of Recorder's Court for presentence information. One is the Psychopathic Clinic, which is a court-supervised agency; the other is the Narcotics Clinic, which is part of the City of Detroit Department of Health.

(1) *The Psychopathic Clinic.* At the time of the field survey, the staff of the Psychopathic Clinic consisted of the Executive Director (who was also Director of the Probation Department for Recorder's Court), three full-time psychiatrists, a physician who conducted physical examinations, and ten clinical psychologists.[65] About 10 per cent of all cases processed through Recorder's Court were sent to the clinic for presentence examination, examination to determine competency to stand trial, or examination to determine commitability as a sexual psychopath. Most were examined for purposes of sentencing.

There are no legal requirements or limitations concerning selection of convicted offenders for presentence psychiatric examina-

[64] This problem is considered in more detail in Chapter 2.

[65] For a discussion of the history and operation of the Psychopathic Clinic, see Canty, The Structure and Function of the Psychopathic Clinic, Recorder's Court, Detroit, Michigan, 14 Ohio St. L.J. 142 (1953).

tion by the Psychopathic Clinic. Because selection of offenders for referral is a matter of discretion of the sentencing judge, there are great differences among the ten judges of Recorder's Court in cases referred. One judge refers almost all his cases for presentence psychiatric examination, while another judge refers only a very limited group of cases.

Despite this disparity, generalization about the kind of case likely to be referred to the clinic is possible. Murder cases are routinely referred to the clinic for presentence examination. All serious sex cases are referred. Sex offenses of a consensual nature, such as statutory rape, are usually not referred, although in some instances referral is made apparently for the purpose of assuring the judge there is no serious psychiatric problem or emotional illness involved. Prostitution cases are only occasionally referred.

Offenders between the ages of seventeen and twenty-one are routinely referred by some judges and usually by others. The reason for referral is to aid the judge in ascertaining the likelihood of rehabilitation if the youthful offender is released under supervision. The typical case involves a youth with a substantial prior record. One judge stated his objectives in referring sexual and youthful offenders. He said he sent all first offenders, sex offenders, and youthful offenders to the clinic for evaluation. He wanted to determine whether the subject could use psychiatric help, and should the subject later be placed on probation, the clinic's report would give the supervising probation officer some insight into the probationer's problem. However, the clinic itself is not equipped to give psychiatric help, and there is some doubt as to how much its report is used by the supervising probation officer.

According to the director of the clinic, the chronic offender with an extensive criminal record may be referred because the court may suspect the presence of serious intellectual or emotional deficiency associated with his recidivism. In cases involving a serious assault or those in which firearms are used, there is often a referral to the clinic for the purpose of assuring the judge that the defendant is not likely to repeat the serious offense if released on probation. All offenses involving cruelty to children are referred, as are all arson cases and a large number of narcotics cases.

The clinic's examination process occurs in several stages and takes two to five hours. The offender is required to complete a detailed social history form. He is then interviewed by a clinical psychologist, who explores relationships between the offender and his relatives, employers, teachers, and other persons in comparable relationships to him.

The clinic has the offender's prior criminal record available but not the arrest report prepared by the police department. Information on the offense is obtained from the offender himself or, sometimes, from the investigating probation officer. It is not customary for clinic personnel to conduct interviews of the offender's friends, relatives, or employer.

The offender is given a physical examination, including a blood test for venereal disease. The Wechsler-Bellevue Intelligence Test is the only psychological test routinely administered. The Rorschach and Thematic Apperception tests are given only when it is suspected the offender is psychotic or feigning psychosis. The latter tests are more likely to be given when the offender is referred to the clinic for pretrial sanity examination than when the referral is for presentence diagnosis.

When these steps are completed, a staff psychiatrist conducts a short psychiatric examination of the offender, primarily oriented to diagnosis of insanity and evaluation of personality characteristics. When this examination is completed, the psychiatrist prepares a report for the judge. The following report was submitted in a case involving a man who murdered his girl friend:

> To Judge ______:
> Date — February 15, 1957
> This is a fifty-three-year-old white man who was born in Yugoslavia and who has been a resident of Detroit for thirty-three years.
> *Physical Examination:* He is 5′8″ tall and weighs 147 lbs. The physical examinations reveal mild hypertension and defective vision. There is a history of arrested pulmonary tuberculosis.
> *Psychological Evaluation:* He has an adult normal intelligence and states that he completed the sixth grade.
> *Social Evaluation:* This patient is the youngest of three children. The father owned a small farm in Yugoslavia. He died when the patient was seven months old and the mother remarried about six years later. The step-father was alcoholic, abusive, and rejected the children, which resulted in the patient and his two older brothers living in a separate house on the farm where they were given little supervision. At eighteen, the patient came to Detroit, his older brother having arrived here earlier. He worked nine years at the Ford Motor Company and for the past twenty-two years he has been employed at Chevrolet. In 1947, he was hospitalized for hyperthyroidism, tuberculosis, and central nervous system syphilis and was confined for three years. He has lived in a hotel for the past five years and spent his money on alcohol and gambling.
> At eighteen the patient married a sixteen-year-old girl in Yugoslavia. She had tuberculosis at the time and after a few months he left her to come to this country. She died in 1931. He has had

a number of casual affairs but has not remarried. In 1943, he began an affair with the deceased, although she continued to live with her husband who has been aware of and apparently tolerant of the relationship. For the past two years he has tried to disentangle himself from her. She was quite critical of his excessive drinking and there was much conflict as a result.

Psychiatric Evaluation: This man is of an inadequate personality. He is unstable, alcoholic, nomadic and there is a history of psychotic episodes.

Recommendation: Because of the nature of the offense, we will recommend a period of institutionalization.

The Psychopathic Clinic recommendation is limited to its opinion between probation and incarceration. It makes no recommendation on the length of incarceration; if the granting of probation is prohibited by statute, the clinic makes no recommendation. One judge strongly felt that the clinic's evaluation and recommendation should relate to the judge's selection of the length of the sentence, if one is imposed, as well as to the choice between incarceration and probation. The same judge felt that the clinic, in its report, does not reveal all the information it has concerning the personality of the offender. The judge was confident the clinic had sufficent information upon which to base its evaluation and recommendation, but felt that so little of it was revealed in the report as to prevent him from making an independent judgment concerning the offender's personality.

Even though the probation department and the clinic are under the direction of the same person, the presentence report and the clinic report are prepared independently of each other. Information is seldom shared between the probation department and the clinic, although ordinarily both units elicit the same basic information from the offender. The probation department is principally concerned with developing factual data to identify the defendant and his social status, while the clinic attempts to determine the attitudes and responses of the offender to the experiences he has gone through in relation to his family, the community, or other situations which he has confronted. Often, the clinic report contains a much more brief statement of the social history of the offender than does the presentence report.

The probation department ordinarily does not refrain from making a recommendation concerning disposition even when the case involves apparent psychiatric difficulties and it knows the clinic is doing a workup. In a substantial number of cases these recommendations conflict. When a judge receives conflicting recommendations, he may remand the case to both agencies for further investigation, especially if he feels neither report contains sufficient substantiating data for the recommendation. One group of judges indicated that, when faced with conflicting recommendations, it usually follows the recommendation of the Psychopathic Clinic. Another group usually follows the recommendation of the probation department. These judges said they preferred the probation department recommendations because they typically include clearly understandable statements of the factual basis for recommendation, making possible the exercise of some independent judgment. The report of the clinic contains a limited amount of factual information, and it is often written in terms likely to be confusing to a person not acquainted with psychiatry.

(2) *The Narcotics Clinic.* In 1952 the City of Detroit established a Narcotics Clinic within the Department of Health. At the time of the field survey, the staff of the Narcotics Clinic consisted of one part-time psychiatrist, a full-time psychiatric social worker, and a clerk. The principal function of this facility is the treatment of drug addicts on a voluntary, outpatient basis. Occasionally, however, a case is referred to the clinic by Recorder's Court to determine if the offender is addicted and, if so, whether there is any prospect of treatment either in an institution or on an outpatient basis. The report of the clinic psychiatrist is an evaluation of the offender's prospects for successful treatment if he is addicted and contains no recommendation concerning the disposition of the case.[66]

b. *Milwaukee.* Psychiatric resources are available to the probation department by simple referral procedure. Sometimes the investigating probation officer discovers the need for a psychiatric examination from information obtained during the presentence investigation. At other times, the need for such an examination is revealed in the postplea of guilty hearing and will appear on the transcript of that hearing provided to the probation department when the defendant is referred for presentence investigation. At the hearing, the judge may note for the record that the defendant appears in need of psychiatric examination and may state that he is ordering a presentence investigation to permit such an examination.

The probation department can refer defendants for a psychiatric workup by the Neurology Clinic of the Milwaukee County Dispensary. If the defendant is in custody, arrangements are made

[66] Recorder's Court judges sometimes refer narcotic offenders, including suspected addicts, to the Psychopathic Clinic for examination. The data revealed no basis for determining which cases are likely to be referred to the Narcotics Clinic and which to the Psychopathic Clinic.

with the sheriff to transport the defendant to the clinic. If he is not in custody, the defendant is given instructions by the probation officer to report.[67] The clinic's report is given to the probation department, which forwards it to the judge with its presentence report.

The Milwaukee County Hospital of Mental Diseases is also available for psychiatric examinations. Commitment is by court order, usually for thirty days. Sometimes, the Neurology Clinic report to the probation department recommends a commitment for further study and examination. In such cases, the department returns the case to court to seek the commitment to the hospital. When the examination is completed, the hospital's report is sent directly to the judge.

2. *The use as presentence information of psychiatric examinations conducted for other purposes.* When a doubt is raised concerning the competency of the defendant to stand trial, a psychiatric examination is likely to be conducted to assist the court in resolving that issue. If the defendant is found incompetent to stand trial, he is committed to a mental hospital until competency is restored; but if he is found to be competent, the adjudication and sentencing of his case proceed in the usual fashion. In the latter instance, a question raised is whether any use can be made of the competency psychiatric examination to assist the court in sentencing.

Psychiatric examinations are also usually conducted when invocation of so-called criminal sexual psychopath statutes is sought. Statutes are common which permit an indeterminate commitment of a defendant who has committed one of several specified sex offenses and who, upon psychiatric examination, is found to have a defined mental condition. When the defendant is found not to be within the scope of the applicable sexual psychopath statute, he must be sentenced under the usual criminal provisions. The psychiatric examination report made for the sexual psychopathy inquiry may, under some circumstances, be helpful to the judge in making the sentencing decision.

a. *Determination of competency to stand trial.* Psychiatric examinations to determine competency are conducted frequently in Detroit and Milwaukee.[68] Although many defendants are found competent to stand trial, and later plead guilty or are found guilty,

[67] According to a probation officer who devotes full time to presentence investigations, no offender has ever refused to report to the clinic for a psychiatric workup. Should this occur, the probation officer would simply note in his presentence report to the court that the offender has failed to cooperate by refusing a request to report for psychiatric examination.

[68] No competency examinations or hearings were observed in Kansas.

the competency psychiatric examination is rarely, or never, helpful in sentencing. There are several reasons for this.

First, the applicable statutory definition of incompetency to stand trial restricts the purpose of the psychiatric examination and the testimony of the examining physicians. In Michigan, a criminal defendant is incompetent to stand trial if he is incapable of "understanding the nature and object of the proceedings against him and of comprehending his own condition in reference to such proceedings and of assisting in his defense in a rational or reasonable manner." [69] Wisconsin statutes provide that criminal proceedings must be suspended if the defendant is "insane or feebleminded." [70] Either definition of incompetency restricts the psychiatric examination and competency hearing to a scope much narrower than the general inquiry into the defendant's mental condition that is useful for sentencing purposes. In practice, the testimony or report of the examining physicians is limited to rendering an opinion on whether the defendant's mental condition meets the statutory definition of incompetency. No attempt is made to use either the examination or hearing to probe for the more general kind of information useful for sentencing; indeed, since the competency hearing normally precedes the guilty plea or trial, such a general inquiry might be inappropriate.

Second, the results of the psychiatric examination, or even the fact that one was conducted, are often unknown to the sentencing judge. In Detroit, the competency hearing is likely to be conducted before a different judge than the one who later makes the sentencing decisions and no attempt is made to communicate the results of the examination to the latter. In Milwaukee at the time of the field survey, a single judge conducted competency hearings and made sentencing decisions. It may be assumed, therefore, that in some cases he remembered the substance of competency proceedings at the time of sentencing, but there were no procedures for assuring that this information was regularly available. Notwithstanding that he knew he might later be making sentencing decisions, the Milwaukee judge made no attempt to use the competency hearing to gather more general psychiatric information about the defendant. The hearings were very brief and limited strictly to testimony on whether the defendant's mental condition was within the statutory definition of incompetency.

Thus, despite the fact that a competency examination is pre-

[69] Mich. Stat. Ann. §28.967 (1954).

[70] Wis. Stat. Ann. §957.13 (1958). Wis. Laws 1965, ch. 132, §1, changed the test to whether the defendant "as a result of mental illness or deficiency lacks capacity to understand the proceedings against him or to assist in his own defense. . . ." Wis. Stat. Ann. §957.13(2) (Supp. 1967).

mised on a suspicion of the defendant's mental abnormality and despite the fact that a finding of competency in no way precludes the possibility that psychiatric information may be useful for sentencing, in practice the psychiatric examination conducted to determine competency does not to any appreciable extent serve as a source of presentence information.

b. *The sexual psychopath examination.* Kansas, Michigan, and Wisconsin, as well as many other states, have so-called sexual psychopath statutes. A psychiatric examination is a usual step in the invocation of such statutes. While the results of that examination are used to determine whether the offender should be committed as a sexual psychopath or sentenced under the criminal law, they may be used as well to assist the judge in selecting the proper sentence from among the choices available under the criminal code. In Kansas and Wisconsin the psychiatric examination is used in that manner, while in Michigan it is not. This difference is a result of procedural differences in the statutory schemes.

Although the Kansas and Wisconsin sexual psychopath laws differ in many significant respects,[71] they are alike in that they cannot be invoked until after the defendant has been convicted of one of the sex offenses specified by statute. The Kansas statute authorizes the trial judge to commit any person convicted of certain sex offenses[72] to a mental hospital for psychiatric observation and a report, to aid him in disposing of the case. Depending on the findings and recommendations of the report, the judge may commit the defendant to a mental hospital or may sentence him under the criminal law.[73] The misdemeanor court judge in Sedgwick County is the only Kansas judge observed to use the statute to any substantial extent.[74] He routinely commits persons convicted of the offenses specified in the statute for psychiatric examination and almost always follows the recommendation of the psychiatrist. The report typically recommends probation, sometimes with special condi-

[71] For example, the Kansas statute permits an indeterminate civil commitment to a mental hospital, while the Wisconsin provision permits a criminal commitment for the duration of the maximum sentence specified in the statute violated, subject to an unlimited number of five-year extensions of the maximum sentence by the trial court. This and other details of the provisions in the three states are discussed in Chapter 7.

[72] Kan. Stat. Ann. §62-1534 (1964) permits observational commitment of any person convicted of "any offense against public morals and decency, as relating to crimes pertaining to sex, in which perversion or mental aberration, appears to be or is involved, or where the defendant appears to be mentally ill. . . ."

[73] Kan. Stat. Ann. §62-1536 (1964).

[74] Virtually all of the sex cases are processed through the misdemeanor court in Sedgwick County (the Court of Common Pleas) even though many of them involve felonious conduct, because of the practice of reducing charges from felonies to misdemeanors in exchange for guilty pleas.

tions such as non-association with persons under the age of twenty-one or out-patient psychiatric treatment. In Kansas City, Kansas, the judge disposes of similar cases without the statutory observational commitment and psychiatric report and usually places the defendant on probation.

The Wisconsin statute requires commitment for sixty days to the State Department of Public Welfare for observation and study of those persons convicted of certain sex offenses[75] and permits a commitment of persons convicted of other sex offenses.[76] A report much broader in scope than that submitted under the Kansas statute is made to the court. The Wisconsin report includes a complete social investigation of the defendant as well as a psychiatric examination: It is a combined presentence investigation report and psychiatric examination report. If the report concludes that the defendant is in need of specialized treatment,[77] the judge may commit him as a sexual deviant to the state prison or may place him on probation on condition that he receive treatment. Otherwise, he must sentence him under the criminal code.[78] The felony court judge in Milwaukee relies upon the report as a substitute for a presentence investigation report to decide upon probation or incarceration (and the length of the sentence) when the case must be disposed of under the criminal code.

In contrast to the Kansas and Wisconsin statutes, the Michigan provisions may be invoked before adjudication or after conviction.[79] In Detroit, practically all instances of invocation occur be-

[75] Forcible rape, sexual intercourse by consent obtained by fraud or as a result of mental deficiency, and indecent behavior with a child are the offenses for which commitment is required. Wis. Stat. Ann. §959.15(1) (1958).

[76] Wis. Stat. Ann. §959.15(2) (1958) defines these other offenses as "any crime except homicide or attempted homicide if the court finds that the defendant was probably directly motivated by a desire for sexual excitement in the commission of the crime. . . ."

[77] The precise statutory language is "if it appears from said report that the department recommends specialized treatment for his mental or physical aberrations. . . ." Wis. Stat. Ann. §959.15(6) (1958). The criteria currently used by the department of public welfare are: (1) that the defendant has a sexual pathology *and* either (2) he will be helped by available specialized treatment *or* (3) he is dangerous.

[78] Wis. Stat. Ann. §959.15 (5) (1958). A recent decision of the Wisconsin Supreme Court invalidates that portion of the statute that gives the state department the power to determine whether the defendant is sexually deviant with the resulting limitations upon the trial court's dispositional powers. The court held that due process of law requires a judicial hearing on the question of sexual deviancy and that the trial judge, not the state department, must make the determination. Huebner v. State, 33 Wis.2d 505, 147 N.W.2d 646 (1967). Several months later, in Specht v. Patterson, 386 U.S. 605, 87 Sup. Ct. 1209, 18 L. Ed. 2d 326 (1967), the United States Supreme Court reached virtually the same conclusion about the Colorado sexual offenders statute. Neither case affects the usefulness in sentencing of investigations and examinations made under these statutes.

[79] Mich. Stat. Ann. §28.967(1) (1954) defines a criminal sexual psychopath as "any person who is suffering from a mental disorder and is not feeble-minded, which

fore trial. The psychiatric examination is sought by petition of the prosecutor; in practice the procedure is initiated by an assistant prosecutor specializing in that area.[80] If, after examination and hearing, the defendant is committed under the sexual psychopath law, the criminal case is dismissed by the prosecutor. As a result of the assistant prosecutor's cautious approach in requesting psychiatric examination,[81] the vast majority of examinations result in commitment. In those that do not, the defendant is prosecuted and, if convicted, is likely to be sentenced by a different judge than the one who conducted the sexual psychopath hearing. No effort is made to bring the psychiatric report to the attention of the sentencing judge. As a result, the report is rarely used for sentencing purposes.

D. The Sentence Hearing

Whatever devices were used for obtaining presentence information — the postplea of guilty hearing, the presentence investigation, the psychiatric examination, or some combination — the court also holds a sentence hearing. When only a postplea hearing is used, as it sometimes is in Milwaukee, the sentence hearing is simply the concluding phase of a single proceeding. When a presentence investigation is used, as in Detroit, the sentence hearing is an additional day in court for the defendant. In Kansas at the time of the field survey, the sentence hearing was the only device for obtaining presentence information that was routinely available to trial judges.

The sentence hearing can perform several important functions. (1) It can give the sentencing judge an opportunity to discuss the case with the police, prosecutor, defense attorney, and the defendant himself and to combine these views with recommendations contained in the presentence report and psychiatric examination report. (2) If the judge discloses the presentence report to the defendant or his attorney, the sentence hearing can be used to give the defense an opportunity to question its reliability.[82] (3) It may satisfy a requirement of statute or common law that the judge give the defendant an opportunity to speak before sentence is im-

---

mental disorder is coupled with criminal propensities to the commission of sex offenses."

[80] The initiation procedures are discussed in detail in Miller, Prosecution (forthcoming).

[81] For example, the assistant prosecutor insists upon at least one prior conviction for an offense that was clearly sexually motivated, although such a limitation is not required by statute.

[82] This function of the sentence hearing is discussed in Chapter 2.

posed.[83] In practice, the defendant is present during at least part of the sentence hearing and is invited to make a statement.

1. *Detroit.* The form of the sentence hearing varies depending upon which Recorder's Court judge is conducting it. Some judges simply call the defendant and his attorney before the bench, permit them to make any statements they wish, and formally announce the sentence with little or no explanation. At least one judge uses a different technique. He sentences 95 per cent of all cases which come before him in chambers. The reason for this, he stated, is that it gives the defendant and his attorney a chance to relax and also gives the attorney an opportunity to express his full view, which he could not do in open court. Frequently, this judge discusses the case at length with the defense attorney, and sometimes with the investigating probation officer as well, in his chambers without the defendant. He then permits the defendant to enter and to make any statement he may wish to make, or he may question the defendant about specific aspects of the case. He informs the defendant of the sentence he is going to impose and later in open court formally announces the decision and sentences the defendant.

In Detroit sentence hearings, the role of the police is limited. Usually they are not represented at the sentence hearing and make no recommendation on sentencing, either directly to the judge or indirectly through the presentence report. Narcotics cases are an exception to this pattern. The Narcotics Bureau of the Detroit Police Department makes a sentence recommendation in its arrest and investigation report, which is incorporated into the presentence report.[84] In addition, one of the Recorder's Court judges routinely confers with a police representative in narcotics cases at the sentence hearing. He says that in narcotics cases he always calls the inspector of the Narcotics Bureau into chambers to give him background on the defendant that might not appear in the presentence report. For example, the fact that some defendants are actually in-

[83] Allocution, the defendant's right to speak before sentence is imposed, was recognized in at least some types of cases at common law and has been preserved by statute or court rule in a number of jurisdictions. For a discussion of the common law right to allocution and its modern equivalent under the Federal Rules of Criminal Procedure, see Green v. United States, 365 U.S. 301, 81 Sup. Ct. 653, 5 L. Ed. 2d 670 (1961).

[84] In one case a woman was found concealing a large quantity of marijuana (sufficient to lead most trial judges to an inference of intent to sell), and she later jumped bond. The following police recommendation was attached to the arrest report and incorporated into the presentence report: "In view of the above facts and circumstances and the fact that this subject left the jurisdiction of the court, forfeiting her bond and necessitating her extradition from Philadelphia, Pa., it is recommended that she be given a substantial confinement sentence for possession of marijuana."

volved in selling narcotics may not be reflected in the police reports forwarded to the probation department. This judge makes up his mind the night before as to what the disposition should be. He then asks the inspector's opinion without the inspector knowing that he has made up his mind. He concludes that their opinions in many cases are surprisingly close. Another judge expressed the view that the recommendations of the Narcotics Bureau are of no value because they invariably favor incarceration.

Recorder's Court judges almost never ask for sentence recommendations from the prosecuting attorney.[85] The prosecuting attorney who conducts plea bargaining and represents the state at the arraignment on the information frequently states to the judge those circumstances of the case which, in his judgment, support a reduction in the charge. Although this information might be useful in sentencing, it is doubtful if it is in fact available, since at least a two-week interval[86] separates the arraignment on the information from the sentence hearing.

In all three states, the defendant typically assumed a very limited role in the sentence hearing. If he was represented by counsel, he usually made no statement or only a very short statement in response to the formal invitation to speak, apparently relying upon his attorney to speak for him.[87] If he was unrepresented, his role might be more substantial, but it was unusual even in those circumstances for him to make a lengthy statement; it normally consisted of a short plea for mercy from the court.[88]

2. *Milwaukee.* The character of the sentence hearing in Milwaukee depends upon whether a presentence investigation was conducted. If the judge has not ordered a presentence investiga-

[85] On one occasion at which a judge requested such a recommendation, the prosecuting attorney refused to express an opinion because he was not familiar with the facts of the case or the background of the defendant.

[86] A minimum period of two weeks is necessary to conduct the presentence investigation in Detroit, made mandatory in all felony cases by Michigan law.

[87] The role of defense counsel at the sentence hearing is discussed in Chapter 16, in the context of the role of the attorney in the entire correctional process.

[88] Occasionally, the court specifically asks the defendant for his opinion on what sentence should be imposed. One Detroit judge stated that when probation is out of question, he tells the defendant so and asks him what minimum sentence he thinks should be imposed. The typical answer is that that decision is for the judge to make. The judge stated that when given that answer he simply asks the question again. If the defendant's opinion is close to that held by the judge, he sentences the defendant to the term which he recommended.

In Milwaukee, the judge is frequently confronted by defendants who seek a prison sentence to enable them to "dry out" from extended periods of drunkenness. In such cases, the judge states to the defendant that he seems to recognize his problem and asks him what amount of time he thinks he needs. He and the defendant then discuss available alternatives, and the judge gives the defendant the sentence he requests after assuring himself that it will result in release of the defendant when the weather is good. For a discussion of these cases, see Chapter 7.

tion at the conclusion of the postplea of guilty hearing, he proceeds directly with the sentence hearing. He asks the defendant to make a statement and requests statements and recommendations from the defense attorney. He then asks the assistant prosecuting attorney for a statement and recommendation.[89] The judge then states his view of the case, announces his decision, and briefly states the reasons for it, sometimes questioning the defendant to assure himself that he understands those reasons. Sentence is then formally imposed.

In those cases in which a presentence investigation is ordered, the case is adjourned at the conclusion of the postplea of guilty hearing to permit time for conducting the investigation. When the report is submitted to the judge, he discusses the case in chambers with the assistant prosecutor, the probation officer who conducted the investigation, and the defense attorney. The defendant is not present. The assistant prosecutor and the defense attorney are permitted to read copies of the presentence report, and the probation officer is available to answer questions concerning the case or to clarify ambiguous statements contained in the report. After discussing the case, the judge announces a tentative decision. The participants then convene in open court, in the presence of the defendant, and the sentence hearing proceeds as in those cases in which no presentence investigation was conducted.[90]

3. *Wichita.* At the time of the field survey, the sentence hearing was virtually the only device for gathering presentence information available to Kansas trial judges. Presentence investigations or postplea of guilty hearings were not used and psychiatric examinations were observed only in connection with the sexual psychopath statute.[91] After conviction following guilty plea or trial, the Kansas trial judge imposed the sentence specified by law for the offense. Immediately thereafter, the defense attorney would make an oral motion for probation, or "bench parole" as it was termed locally. The court would then hold a brief "parole hearing" in which it heard arguments from defense counsel, defendant, prosecuting attorney and, occasionally, other persons as to why the defendant should or should not be given probation. The motion for probation would then be granted or denied.

[89] Police officers play no role in the Milwaukee sentence hearing, nor is a police sentencing recommendation contained in the presentence report.

[90] When a presentence investigation has been conducted, the assistant prosecutor normally concurs in the recommendation contained in the presentence report. When the judge announces his sentencing decision in cases in which a presentence investigation has been conducted, he normally reads the "Summary and Recommendations" portion of the report into the record to support his decision.

[91] See pages 49-50.

A variation on this practice was to hold the sentence hearing prior to adjudication. Some Kansas judges held an informal conference before the defendant had entered a plea to the information. It was exactly the same as the post-adjudication "parole hearing" except the trial judge indicated whether he would give probation if the defendant pleaded guilty. It was an attempt to formalize the plea bargaining process,[92] to provide the trial judge with a modicum of information before deciding upon sentence, and to give the defendant an authoritative statement of the sentence he will receive if he pleads guilty.

[92] See Newman, Conviction 85-86 (1966).

CHAPTER 2

Assuring Accuracy of Presentence Information

The major problem in presentence information is often considered to be presenting the court with sufficient information — information going beyond the facts of the immediate offense and extending to the offender's prior record, background, and so on. But the accuracy of the information is also an object of concern. As a practical matter, the greater the amount of presentence information, the greater the risk of inaccurate information. Conversely, the more restricted the scope and the more simplified the data, the smaller the risk of error. Therefore, as efforts are made to increase the amount and sophistication of presentence information, the task of assuring accuracy of that information becomes increasingly difficult.

Public discussion of the problem of assuring accuracy of presentence information has focused almost exclusively upon the issue of whether the presentence report should be disclosed to the defendant or his attorney. Proponents argue that disclosure is necessary in order to assure that the information used by the judge in sentencing is accurate, while opponents assert that disclosure would "dry up" sources of information and eventually decrease the usefulness of presentence reports.[1]

Important as the issue of disclosure is, it is only one aspect of the total problem of assuring accuracy of presentence information. There are many facets of this problem that have received little public discussion because of the concern with disclosure. The most important have been isolated for discussion in this chapter: (1) What efforts should be made by the presentence investigatory staff to assure accuracy in their reporting and to what extent can these efforts be fostered by formal legal devices? (2) Should the trial

[1] See Higgins, Confidentiality of Presentence Reports, 28 Albany L. Rev. 12 (1964); Roche, The Position for Confidentiality of the Presentence Investigation Report, 29 Albany L. Rev. 206 (1965); Higgins, In Response to Roche, 29 Albany L. Rev. 225 (1965).

judge take steps to assure accuracy of presentence information apart from simply disclosing the presentence report to the defendant or his attorney? (3) Is the accuracy of presentence information affected by the methods used to obtain that information? The presentence investigation and the postplea of guilty hearing may be viewed as alternative methods of obtaining basic presentence information. If one generally produces more reliable information than the other, is there a corresponding sacrifice in the adequacy of the information produced? (4) What opportunities should be afforded the defendant or his attorney to determine the accuracy of presentence information? In addition to disclosure of the presentence report, this involves questions about the opportunity of the defense to determine reliability at the postplea of guilty hearing and at the sentence hearing.

A. Accuracy as a Concern in Conducting Presentence Investigations

Both probation departments and individual investigating probation officers seek to prevent the inclusion of factually inaccurate or misleading information in presentence reports. This effort raises questions in several areas: Should the investigating probation officer attempt to verify all factual data obtained from the police or the defendant? If it is assumed that verification is not practical or necessary for all data, what criteria should be used to select the information to be verified? What procedures should be used to assure that verification occurs in appropriate instances?

When information has not been shown to be either true or false, even though an attempt at verification has been made, should it be included in the presentence report? It can be argued that, when information is important enough to require an effort at verification, it should not be included in the presentence report unless it has been verified. On the other hand, it can be argued that such information should be included for what it is worth, perhaps with a caveat that it is unverified. A relevant question certainly is whether the risk of prejudicial inaccuracy is serious enough to outweigh the probable usefulness of the information if it is included in the report.

In addition to factual data, the presentence report normally contains the probation officer's interpretation of the data, evaluation of the defendant's potential for beneficial use of probation, and recommendation for or against probation. What should the probation department's policy be with respect to using unverified data in making the evaluation and recommendation? This is critical if the suspicion that some judges read only the evaluation and recommendation is correct.

Should the investigating officer's responsibility for accuracy be different when the presentence report is made available to defense counsel? It can be argued that disclosure should relieve the probation officer of some of the responsibility for assuring factual accuracy of the report because defense has an opportunity to do so. On the other hand, it can be argued that both assurances of accuracy are necessary. One effect of disclosure may be to restrict the contents of the presentence report because the probation officer wants to avoid a court contest over the accuracy of his report. It may also result in excluding information that the probation officer views as confidential.

1. *Detroit.* The process used in conducting presentence investigations in Detroit reflects concern with various aspects of the problem of accuracy of the presentence report. This concern is clearly demonstrated by the routine practice in the Men's Felony Division of having the supervisor reinterview the defendant to verify information about the offense, his prior criminal record, and various social data, after the investigating officer has completed his report and given it to the supervisor. This practice apparently began as a result of court encounters with many inaccurate reports, and the court established the policy of having supervisors check the accuracy of the reports. Although there seems little doubt that the procedure does eliminate some inaccuracies, it does so at a price. The Men's Felony Division supervisor indicated that, although his reinterviews last not more than five to ten minutes each, he nevertheless spends 80 to 90 per cent of his time conducting them. He felt that recent improvements in the training of probation officers, resulting in increased accuracy of their reports, make the continued usefulness of the reinterview procedure questionable.[2]

The evaluation and recommendation portions of the presentence report are likewise the subject of administrative concern. In some divisions of the probation department the investigating officer prepares the report, including the evaluation and recommendation. His supervisor then prepares a summary of the report in the form of a covering letter, in which he reevaluates the defendant and makes his own recommendation. Normally the two recommendations are the same, although sometimes this procedure results in contradictory recommendations. In other divisions, the

[2] The practice of reinterviewing the defendant occurs only in the Men's Felony Division of the Probation Department. The other three divisions that conduct presentence investigations use, instead, a conference between the investigating officer and his supervisor to check upon the accuracy of the investigation.

presentence report is prepared by the supervisor from data supplied by the investigating officer, and the supervisor and the officer discuss the case to arrive at an evaluation and recommendation. In any case, there is a strong desire to have a consistent departmental recommendation for every defendant. The department is not well regarded, nor is the judiciary comforted, when contradictory suggestions are tendered by case analysts presumed to be knowledgable and experienced.

Several of the probation officers in the Detroit office indicated that their reports were limited to "provable facts." Although it is not entirely clear what that term was intended to mean, it doubtless does not mean evidence which would be admissible in a jury trial upon a not guilty plea, since the reports contain many statements that would be excluded as hearsay. It may mean facts that have been proved to the satisfaction of the probation officer. In one case, for example, the probation officer did not include in his report his suspicion that the defendant was using narcotics because he had been unable to check it with the narcotics bureau of the police department. It is possible that the probation officer himself might not have been convinced that the defendant was using narcotics.[3]

In other instances, there was less concern about including unverified or inadequately verified information in the report. Such is the case with respect to much of the social information — personal history, present family status, present employment — that the defendant gives the probation officer. It seems clear that some probation officers require verification of only some information, notably that which does not come from the defendant or which could be extremely damaging to him.[4]

2. *Milwaukee.* The Chief Probation Officer of the Milwaukee County Municipal and District Court Probation Department routinely reviews all presentence reports submitted by officers on his staff. Although he does not read each report in detail, he surveys each and reads with particular attention the officer's summary and recommendation. If he doubts the adequacy of the report, especially with regard to the recommended disposition, he discusses it with the officer. It is likely that most conferences on reports concern the recommendations. The extent to which the Chief Proba-

[3] It is also possible that probation officers who indicated that their reports were limited to statements of "provable facts" might not have distinguished between presentence reports and reports prepared for a probation revocation hearing. In the later proceedings, some judges do require liberalized application of the rules of evidence. See Chapter 5.

[4] Compare with the director's statement on page 37 supra that in-service training had resulted in verification of social data by investigating probation officers.

tion Officer concerns himself with the accuracy of statements of fact made by the investigating officer in the body of the report is less clear, however. Some evidence suggests that he regards that as a matter to be reserved to the professional competency of the investigating officer.

It was noted earlier that presentence investigations in Milwaukee are discretionary with the judge, that they are usually ordered for specific reasons, and that the investigating probation officer usually has a copy of the transcript of the postplea of guilty hearing that led to the order for the investigation.[5] The presentence investigation is thus usually aimed at a particular problem that concerns the judge, and this guides not only the emphasis of the investigation but also the verification procedures. On some occasions the trial judge may feel that he has sufficient information to sentence without a presentence investigation but orders one anyway because the defense attorney insists on it. Under such circumstances the investigating officer usually conducts only a short, cursory investigation, making little effort to verify information he obtains. Although the report may in some respects be inaccurate and inadequate, the probation officer seems unconcerned and confident that his errors — indeed, his report as a whole, erroneous or not — are unlikely to influence the judge in his sentencing decision, and perhaps also that the defense attorney will not seriously attack the report because he, too, knows that it will have little significant effect on the outcome of the case.

The judge of the Milwaukee Municipal Court usually discloses the contents of the presentence report to the defense attorney. One probation officer stated that he generally agreed with the policy of disclosure because it made the officers more objective in writing reports and gave the defense counsel an opportunity to object to any hearsay that the report might contain. However, probation officers seem very reluctant to become involved in a court contest over the accuracy of the report. Consequently, if important information obtained during the investigation cannot be verified, the officer is likely to omit it from the report to avoid the possibility of a contest over its accuracy.[6] In addition, if the investigating officer believes there is a risk that confidential information will be revealed to the defendant by the trial judge, he is likely to exclude that information from the report. In one case, for example, the investigating officer indicated he would exclude psychiatric infor-

[5] See pages 25-26.

[6] Whether as a result of this practice or not, court contests over presentence reports are virtually unknown in Milwaukee.

mation from the report because he felt the judge would read it into the record in order to support his sentencing decision.

B. Judicial Concern with Accuracy

The trial judge is concerned with the accuracy of presentence information for a variety of reasons — fairness to the defendant, protection of society, and preservation of the reputation of the probation department and himself. In addition to exercising a strong influence on the presentence investigating and reporting process,[7] the trial judge can influence the accuracy of presentence information by permitting at least limited disclosure of that information to the defendant or his attorney, a decision that is usually within his discretion.[8]

The further question is what steps ought he to take beyond standard-setting for the probation department and affording the defense an opportunity to test the accuracy of the information. The routine use of postplea of guilty hearings in Milwaukee is suggestive. The hearing yields a body of presentence information that is highly accurate because the defendant and his attorney are present during the entire hearing and have the opportunity to cross-examine prosecution witnesses and to present evidence on the defendant's behalf. It is not clear, however, whether the postplea hearing reflects judicial concern for accuracy of presentence information or whether that is simply a by-product of concern for the accuracy of the guilty plea.

The trial judge's concern with the accuracy of the information presented at the postplea hearing goes somewhat beyond simply affording the defense an opportunity to test the accuracy of prosecution evidence and to present evidence of its own. On many occasions, the judge will interrupt the interrogation of witnesses by the prosecutor in order to clear up a point of ambiguity or to pursue more completely a line of questioning begun by the prosecutor. Again, the extent to which this reflects concern with the accuracy of the presentence information aspects of the testimony or only with its plea verification aspects is not clear. The Milwaukee trial judge also routinely interrogates the defendant to determine the accuracy of his criminal record. He describes each offense on the record and asks the defendant whether he was in fact arrested for or convicted of that offense.

[7] For example, the Detroit practice of reinterviewing defendants by division supervisors originated with complaints from the trial judiciary about the inaccuracy of some information contained in presentence reports.

[8] See pages 63-65.

Existing legal standards concerning the trial judge's responsibility for assuring accuracy of presentence information are, at best, uncertain. There are few statutory standards beyond those regulating the matter of disclosure. *Townsend v. Burke,*[9] in which a trial judge used an inaccurate prior criminal record in sentencing, imposes federal due process standards, but their scope is unclear. The fact that the defendant in that case was unrepresented at sentencing, a circumstance improbable in felony cases since *Gideon v. Wainwright*[10] and, more recently, *Mempa v. Rhay,*[11] was manifestly influential:

> We believe that on the record before us, it is evident that this uncounseled defendant was either overreached by the prosecution's submission of misinformation to the court or was prejudiced by the court's own misreading of the record. Counsel, had any been present, would have been under a duty to prevent the court from proceeding on such false assumptions and perhaps under a duty to seek remedy elsewhere if they persisted. Consequently, on this record we conclude that, while disadvantaged by lack of counsel, this prisoner was sentenced on the basis of assumptions concerning his criminal record which were materially untrue. Such a result, whether caused by carelessness or design, is inconsistent with due process of law, and such a conviction cannot stand.[12]

The more difficult question is what responsibility, if any, the trial judge has to assure accuracy of presentence information in cases in which the defendant is represented by counsel at the sentencing stage. *Townsend* implies, for example, that there might be an obligation on the trial judge to avoid hasty and undeliberative sentencing procedures regardless of counsel's acquiescence.

C. Opportunity for the Defense to Determine Accuracy

Even in a system characterized by great concern on the part of the trial judiciary and probation service for the accuracy of presentence information, it would still remain important to face the problem of the extent to which the defendant and his attorney should be given an opportunity to determine the accuracy of that information. Indeed, current discussion of the accuracy problem usually assumes that the real issue is the extent to which the de-

9 334 U.S. 736, 68 Sup. Ct. 1252, 92 L. Ed. 1690 (1948).
10 372 U.S. 335, 83 Sup. Ct. 792, 9 L. Ed. 2d 799 (1963).
11 389 U.S. 128, 88 Sup. Ct. 254, 19 L. Ed. 2d 336 (1967).
12 334 U.S. 736, 740-741, 68 Sup. Ct. 1252, 1255, 92 L. Ed. 1690, 1693 (1948).

fense should have the opportunity to determine accuracy. Discussion is typically limited to whether the presentence report should be disclosed to defendant or his attorney, with very little discussion of the opportunity of the defense to determine the accuracy of other kinds of presentence information. In practice, opportunities to determine accuracy occur at the postplea of guilty hearing and at the sentence hearing, in addition to the opportunity to test the accuracy of the presentence and psychiatric reports.

1. *At the postplea of guilty hearing.* The defense has full opportunity to determine the accuracy of presentence information obtained through use of the Milwaukee postplea of guilty hearing. The defendant is normally represented by counsel, often assigned by the court. He and his attorney are present during the entire hearing and are given the opportunity to cross-examine witnesses testifying for the state. The defendant typically testifies as to the circumstances of the offense and may be cross-examined by the prosecutor. In those instances in which the defendant does not wish an attorney, the trial judge assumes some of the role of defense counsel by cross-examining the state's witnesses and examining the defendant if he wishes to testify.

While the postplea of guilty hearing is adversary in structure, it is not in mood. The defendant and his attorney apparently wish to create an image of cooperation with the trial judge.[13] Certainly, this is consistent with the guilty plea and the rationale of the trial judge in granting leniency to defendants who plead guilty.[14] To engage in prolonged cross-examination of witnesses would be inconsistent with this general posture of cooperation, and it may be for that reason that very few factual disputes actually occur at such hearings. But if the information about which the defense has doubts seems important enough, there will be an effort to test its accuracy, despite a general desire to expedite the proceeding.

2. *Of the presentence report and psychiatric report.* In Michigan, presentence reports are by statute declared to be confidential documents:

> All records and reports of investigations made by probation officers, whether state or local, for courts of criminal jurisdiction in cases referred for such investigation by such courts, and all case histories of probationers are hereby declared to be privileged or confidential communications not open to public inspection. Judges and probation officers shall have access to such records, reports and case histories. The probation officer or the assistant director

[13] The "posture of cooperation" function of counsel is discussed in Chapter 16 in the context of the role of counsel in the correctional process.

[14] See Chapter 6.

> of probation, or his representative, shall permit the attorney general, the auditor general, and law enforcement agencies to have such access. The legislative intent is that the relation of confidence between the probation officer and the probationer or defendant under investigation shall remain inviolate.[15]

Detroit judges interpret this statute to preclude disclosure of the presentence report to the defendant or his attorney. Although by its terms the statute does not include the psychiatric report prepared by the Psychopathic Clinic, Detroit trial judges also refuse to disclose it.

The Detroit trial judges seemed generally in favor of nondisclosure and it is not unreasonable to assume that their practices would remain the same even if the statute were amended to give them discretion to permit disclosure. Commenting on proposed legislation which, if enacted, would have required disclosure, one Detroit trial judge stated that it would dry up sources of information now available to the probation department and as a consequence effectively prevent the court from having information at its disposal to assist in intelligent sentencing. He stated that the entire bench of Recorder's Court is violently opposed to any such legislation. Although another judge expressed a preference for disclosure to assure accuracy of the defendant's criminal record as it appears in the report,[16] he felt that he was probably alone in his opinion among the Recorder's Court judges. Despite a uniform practice of nondisclosure, defense attorneys sometimes obtain access to the report, or at least learn something of its contents, from the investigating probation officer. One trial judge acknowledged that this sometimes occurred, but he felt that it was entirely proper if the probation officer conducting the investigation consented.

In Wisconsin, the trial judge has discretion to disclose presentence and psychiatric reports to the defendant or his attorney. The Milwaukee trial judge regularly provides the defense attorney with a copy of the presentence or psychiatric report at the conference in his chambers prior to sentencing in open court. The defendant is not permitted to see either report. The time interval between disclosure of the report to the defense attorney and the sentencing is, however, only a matter of minutes and the attorney normally has little opportunity to confer with his client concerning the contents of the report prior to sentencing. On the basis of the data available, it is not possible to discuss what differences, if any, between the

[15] Mich. Stat. Ann. §28.2299 (1954).

[16] This judge felt the defendant should know his record is being taken into account in sentencing and should have an opportunity to admit or deny that the record is accurate.

sentencing processes in Detroit and Milwaukee might reasonably be attributable to differences in disclosure practices. It is clear, however, that disclosure is less important to the defendant in Milwaukee because much of the information contained in the presentence report is based on information obtained at the postplea of guilty hearing.

3. *At the sentence hearing*. The defendant and his attorney are given an opportunity to speak to the issue of sentencing, including the accuracy of presentence information, at sentence hearings in Detroit and Milwaukee. Very little new information is revealed to the defense at the sentence hearing. Most of the time is spent in discussing information already obtained.

There is, however, a limited type of disclosure of presentence and psychiatric reports at the sentence hearings in Detroit and Milwaukee. The Milwaukee trial judge frequently reads into the record the summary and recommendation portions of the presentence and psychiatric reports. It seems clear the reasons for this are to have something in the record to support the sentencing decision, not to provide the defense with an opportunity to test the accuracy of any factual statements that may be contained in those portions of the reports. It is also clear that such limited disclosure is of little benefit to the defense because no time is usually available for consultation between defendant and his attorney concerning the revealed portions of the report.

In Detroit, where a uniform practice of nondisclosure of presentence and psychiatric reports is followed, the trial judge may nevertheless make comments or ask questions of the defendant at the sentence hearing that reveal portions of the report. Like the practice of reading portions of the reports into the record, however, this affords the defense little opportunity to test the accuracy of such information.

PART II

The Probation System

> Probation officers work much more closely with courts than parole officers do. This is primarily because probation is in itself a legal or judicial function while parole is an administrative function. Probation officers are arms of the court. They are usually appointed by the court and serve at its pleasure. Most probation officers make frequent appearances in court and are engaged daily in carrying out its written and verbal orders.
>
> Clegg, *Probation and Parole* 7 (1964)

> In most major cities . . . the probation department is a complex organization requiring continuous and intensive administrative attention by professional, full-time managers. . . . To manage so widely dispersed an operation requires specialized expertise and close control which are almost impossible for a judge whose career investment is not in administration. Moreover, organizational effectiveness and continuity of policy are apt to be seriously impaired in an agency subject to detailed administrative direction by both a judge and a chief probation officer.
>
> The President's Commission on Law Enforcement and Administration of Justice, *Task Force Report: Corrections* 35 (1967)

In legal theory, and in the view of many commentators, probation is a judicial function. The trial judge has exclusive legal authority to place offenders on probation, to set probation conditions, to determine the length of the probation term, and to revoke probation. While it is recognized that many of these functions are carried out through probation officers, it is often assumed they are merely executing relatively specific judicial orders. That view, illustrated by the quotation from Clegg, may have reflected reality when probation was in its infancy and the probation staff consisted of a few court-attached persons who may in fact have been volunteers or court bailiffs. However, with the advent of the large, metropolitan probation staff, the influence of the trial judge over probation has decreased and that of the probation staff has increased. As the quotation from the Crime Commission report suggests, in the large cities the details of probation administration are no longer under direct judicial control. What originated as a judicial process has become in large part an administrative process and this fact has an important bearing upon the kinds of decisions which are made, the criteria applied, and the methods used to review the decisions which are made.

The role of the large city professional staff in administering the probation system is even more substantial than the Crime Commission report indicates. The probation department determines important supervision policies and techniques, often without judicial control or even knowledge. Although the trial judge usually has exclusive authority to set probation conditions, in practice the conditions are often formulated by the probation staff and imposed by the trial judge on a routine basis. In many courts, the probation staff plays a substantial role in the decision whether to place a defendant on probation because its recommendation is usually followed by the trial judge. And the probation revocation decision is, in large part, made by the probation staff, which may overlook known violations and, in some jurisdictions, may revoke probation without returning the probationer to court.

There are several explanations for the change from judicial to administrative responsibility for probation: (1) the trial judge is occupied with numerous civil and other criminal matters, responsibility for which cannot be delegated and he is, therefore, likely to delegate (deliberately or by default) responsibility for probation because of the availability of staff in that area; (2) the trial judge is likely to consider the probation staff as experts particularly as to whether an individual will respond favorably to supervision if placed on probation or if continued under supervision despite a violation, and is, therefore, likely to defer to the judgment of the probation officer; (3) in many urban courts, trial judges rotate from civil to criminal work and find it difficult to exercise continuing close supervision of the probation system; and (4) in many geographical areas, he probation staff is not selected by the trial judge but is supplied by a central state agency, and the trial judge has less control over their activities than with respect to most personnel attached to the court.

Understanding the probation system as it functions today requires an understanding of the relationship between administrative decisions made by the probation staff and judicial decisions made by the trial judge. This is particularly important in a day when there is increasing attention given to correctional decision making and to the question of whether it is desirable to have important correctional decisions made administratively without possibility of effective challenge.

Chapter 3 discusses the decision to grant or deny probation; Chapter 4 deals with probation conditions and supervision; and Chapter 5 treats revocation of probation. In each chapter an attempt is made to delineate as carefully as possible the roles played in practice by the trial judiciary and the probation staff.

CHAPTER 3

The Decision to Grant or Deny Probation

Sentencing alternatives open to the court in current practice are probation, sentence to prison, and fines. Fines are of very limited significance in the disposition of felonies and serious misdemeanors, the subject under consideration here. Dispositional alternatives more sophisticated than prison sentences and probation are, of course, well known to the literature of corrections. But such alternatives were unavailable in fact in the communities surveyed in this study; nor are they available in significant numbers in any but a few American jurisdictions today. The sentencing judge's basic choice, therefore, comes down to that between probation and prison.

The decision to grant or deny probation is obviously important to the defendant, since it means the difference between almost total freedom in the community and almost total control in the typical maximum security prison. Its importance to society is also obvious, since interests of immediate and long-range security are vitally affected. But the decision to grant or deny probation also has importance for the criminal justice system. Whether the probation system can be successful in rehabilitating offenders while protecting society depends in part upon how probationers are selected. Furthermore, basic administrative needs of the criminal justice system, such as the need for guilty pleas, may be met or frustrated by the process used to select offenders to be placed on probation.

Three aspects of that decision have been isolated for discussion here. The first is the allocation of discretion to make the decision. Although legislatures have created certain categories of nonprobationable offenses, in practice these provisions have little limiting effect on the probation decision. The second is the locus of responsibility in practice for the decision. Although formal responsibility for the decision is placed exclusively with the trial judiciary, in practice it is often shared to one degree or another with other officials, principally the probation staff. The third aspect is the criteria used to make the decision. Although formal law and correctional literature concentrate on probable recidivism as virtually the only probation criterion, in practice a number of other criteria influence the decision as well. Common to all these aspects is the fact that judicial and administrative agencies operate to modify sharply, and in certain respects to nullify, legislative directions and restrictions concerning authority and responsibility in making the probation decision.

A. Allocation of Discretion to Grant or Deny Probation

Legislatures have delegated discretion to grant or deny probation to the trial judiciary. This power is usually limited by statute. One typical limitation requires the trial judge to believe that the defendant merits probation; for example, a Michigan statute authorizes probation when "it appears to the satisfaction of the court that the defendant is not likely again to engage in an offensive or criminal course of conduct and that the public good does not require that the defendant shall suffer the penalty imposed by law. . . ." [1] Provisions of this type do not in practice impose substantial limitations upon discretion to grant probation[2] and even by their terms they do not limit discretion to deny probation.[3]

By contrast, statutes which limit eligibility for probation do have impact on the practice. It is common for legislatures to provide that persons convicted of specified offenses are not eligible for proba-

[1] Mich. Stat. Ann. §28.1131 (1954). Kansas statutes authorized probation "when it shall appear to the satisfaction of the court that the ends of justice and the best interests of the public, as well as the defendant, will be subserved thereby. . . ." Kan. Gen. Stat. §62-2203 (1949), repealed by Kan. Laws 1957, Ch. 331, §37. The present Kansas statute contains no criteria for the decision to grant or deny probation. Kan. Stat. Ann. §62-2239 (1964). Wisconsin statutes authorize granting probation to a defendant when "it appears to the court from his character and the circumstances of the case that he is not likely again to commit crime and that the public welfare does not require that he shall suffer the penalty of the law. . . ." Wis. Stat. Ann. §57.01(1) (1957).

[2] See pages 79-99.

[3] Compare Model Penal Code §7.01(1) (Proposed Official Draft, 1962): "The Court shall deal with a person who has been convicted of a crime without imposing sentence of imprisonment unless, having regard to the nature and circumstances of the crime and the history, character and condition of the defendant, it is of the opinion that his imprisonment is necessary for the protection of the public because: (a) there is undue risk that during the period of a suspended sentence or probation the defendant will commit another crime; or (b) the defendant is in need of correctional treatment that can be provided most effectively by his commitment to an institution; or (c) a lesser sentence will depreciate the seriousness of the defendant's crime."

tion.[4] Kansas statutes prohibit probation of persons convicted of offenses "punishable by death or life imprisonment." [5] In Michigan, persons convicted of "murder, treason, robbery while armed, and breaking and entering an occupied dwelling house in the night time" are not eligible for probation.[6] In Wisconsin, on the other

[4] See the chart of statutory provisions that appears in Model Penal Code §6.02, Comment (Tent. Draft No. 2, 1954). The Comment also notes: "Unlike the practice in many states, suspension or probation is authorized in any case except, of course, if sentence of death or life imprisonment is . . . prescribed. This provision rests on the view that no legislative definition or classification of offenses can take account of all contingencies. However right it may be to take the gravest view of an offense in general, there will be cases comprehended in the definition where the circumstances were so unusual, or the mitigations so extreme, that a suspended sentence or probation would be proper. We see no reason to distrust the courts upon this matter or to fear that such authority will be abused." Id. at 13-14.

[5] Kan. Gen. Stat. §62-2203 (1949), repealed by Kan. Laws 1957, Ch. 331, §37. The present Kansas statute does not exclude any person from probation eligibility. Kan. Stat. Ann. §62-2239 (1964).

Kan. Stat. Ann. §21-445 (1964) authorizes probation prior to conviction in desertion and nonsupport cases with the consent of the defendant. In paternity proceedings, if the court finds the defendant is the father of the child, it may order payment of support and require security for compliance with the order. The defendant may be imprisoned only if he is unable to provide adequate security or fails to comply with the court order. In the latter situation, the term of imprisonment may not exceed one year. Kan. Stat. Ann. §§62-2313, 62-2314 (1964). The analogy to probation in criminal cases is clear, but in paternity proceedings the trial judge has no authority to imprison the defendant in lieu of probation but only for failure to obtain security or comply with the support order. Compare the practice of using probation to obtain support for illegitimate children after the father has been convicted of nonsupport. See Chapter 4.

[6] Mich. Stat. Ann. §28.1131 (1954). Mich. Pub. Acts 1961, No. 185 gave probation eligibility to persons convicted of breaking and entering an occupied dwelling house in the nighttime. See Mich. Stat. Ann. §28.1131 (Supp. 1965).

Mich. Stat. Ann. §18.1122 (1957) punishes possession of narcotics without a prior narcotics conviction with a maximum sentence of ten years; possession by a person with a prior narcotics conviction with a maximum sentence of twenty years; and possession by a person with two or more narcotics convictions with a sentence of not less than twenty or more than forty years. Mich. Stat. Ann. §18.1123 (1957) specifically authorizes probation of the person convicted of narcotics possession who has not had a prior narcotics violation. Probation is not specifically authorized for sale of narcotics or for possession by a prior narcotics offender; presumably, persons convicted under these circumstances may not be placed on probation.

The Michigan habitual criminal act apparently prohibits probation of persons convicted as third or fourth felony offenders. It expressly authorizes probation of a person convicted as a second felony offender. Mich. Stat. Ann. §28.1082 (1954). No such provision appears in the sections relating to third and fourth felony offenders. Mich. Stat. Ann. §§28.1083, 28.1084 (1954). The habitual criminal statute can be invoked only by allegations of the prior convictions in an information filed with the court, a step the statute expressly places in the discretion of the prosecuting attorney. Mich. Stat. Ann. §28.1085 (1954). The practice in Detroit is that the prosecuting attorney does not allege prior convictions unless specifically requested to do so by the sentencing judge in a particular case. This occurs rarely and only when the sentencing judge wishes to impose a longer prison sentence than that permitted for conviction of the current offense alone. He would never request invocation of the statute if he wished to place the defendant on probation. In practice, then, the habitual criminal statute has no effect on probation eligibility. For a

hand, virtually all convicted offenders are eligible for probation.[7] Experience, particularly in Michigan, demonstrates that, in day to day administration, effort will be made to avoid the legislative limitations and to grant probation in cases which are thought appropriate for probation. So widespread is this that the legislative limitations are likely to be completely nullified in practice.

In Michigan, armed robbery and breaking and entering an occupied dwelling house in the nighttime are nonprobationable offenses.[8] Offenses originally charged as armed robbery are almost always reduced to charges of unarmed robbery or assault with intent to rob, both probationable offenses, and original charges of breaking and entering an occupied dwelling house in the nighttime are almost always reduced to breaking and entering in the daytime, or to entering without breaking, which are also probationable.

In Wisconsin, where virtually all offenses are probationable,[9] there is no necessity to reduce charges to create probation eligibility and in practice reductions are much less common. In Kansas, probation is not available for any offense punishable by death or life imprisonment,[10] but the only offenses found punishable in that manner are first degree murder,[11] treason,[12] and first degree kidnap-

---

discussion of the experience at sentencing with habitual criminal statutes in the three states, see Chapter 7. The statutes are discussed in detail in Miller, Prosecution: The Decision to Charge a Suspect With a Crime (forthcoming).

7 Wis. Stat. Ann. §57.01 (1) (1957). By Wis. Laws 1961, Ch. 477, §5, persons convicted of violating laws relating to narcotic drugs or marijuana who have previously been convicted "of any violation of the laws of the United States or of any state, territory or district thereof, relating to narcotic drugs or marijuana" are not eligible for probation. Wis. Stat. Ann. §161.28(1) (Supp. 1967). The decision whether to invoke these provisions by alleging prior convictions rests in the discretion of the prosecuting attorney. Wis. Stat. Ann. §161.28(3) (Supp. 1967) and Wis. Stat. Ann. §959.12(1) (1958).

Wis. Stat. Ann. §52.05(4) (1957) authorizes probation for the offense of abandonment or nonsupport "before the trial, with the consent of the defendant, or at the trial, on entry of a plea of guilty, or after conviction, instead of imposing the penalty hereinbefore provided. . . ."

8 Mich. Stat. Ann. §28.1131 (1954). After the field survey, the statute was amended to permit probation for the latter offense. See note 6 *supra*.

9 In 1961 the Wisconsin legislature denied probation eligibility to persons convicted of naroctics violations who had previously been convicted of a narcotics violation. Although the implementation of this statute is unknown, since the amendment was made after the field survey, it is unlikely that charges are reduced to create probation eligibility in these cases, for two reasons: First, the limitation of ineligibility to persons with prior narcotics convictions makes the probability of probation small in any event, and, second, the statute gives the prosecutor discretion not to invoke its provisions by not alleging the prior conviction. See note 7 *supra*.

10 Kan. Gen. Stat. §62-2203 (1949) repealed by Kan. Laws 1957, Ch. 331, §37. Under present Kansas law all offenses are probationable. Kan. Stat. Ann. §62-2239 (1964).

11 Kan. Stat. Ann. §21-403 (1964) (death or life imprisonment).

12 Kan. Stat. Ann. §21-201 (1964) (death).

ing.[13] These offenses are charged with such infrequency that the limitation has no great impact on the practice.

The primary reason for reducing charges of nonprobationable offenses in Michigan seems simply to permit the trial judge to place the defendant on probation if the presentence report indicates that probation would be appropriate. The Michigan prosecutors appear to make no attempt themselves to judge the likelihood that the defendant will be given probation; rather they reduce the charge routinely in virtually all cases.[14] The trial judges appear to encourage routine charge reduction in nonprobationable cases.[15] Instances were observed in which trial judges refused to accept pleas of guilty to nonprobationable offenses from young, inexperienced defendants and appointed counsel for them with instructions to work out a charge reduction with the prosecutor.

There are, of course, other reasons for charge reductions particularly when, if a prison term is imposed, the judge must impose a high, mandatory maximum.[16] One Michigan prosecutor explained that when a person is charged with armed robbery, which is nonprobationable and carries a maximum sentence that may be as long as life imprisonment,[17] the defendant has no incentive to plead guilty rather than stand trial. However, if the charge is reduced to one that is probationable and carries a shorter maximum sentence, he is much more likely to plead guilty.

The precise effect of the statutory limitation upon eligibility for probation is difficult to assess because charges are often reduced when the original one was probationable, and even when the original charge is nonprobationable it is likely to be reduced despite the fact that probation seems extremely unlikely.[18] In these cases the

[13] Kan. Stat. Ann. §21-449 (1964) (death or life imprisonment).

[14] In Michigan two persons were charged as co-defendants with armed robbery. At the arraignment on the information, they pleaded not guilty. Later, both charges were reduced to assault with intent to rob, and they pleaded guilty to them. After presentence investigation, one defendant received a prison sentence of two to fifteen years and the other received probation.

[15] A Michigan assistant proscuting attorney stated one reason he reduced charges of nonprobationable offenses was that the trial judge wanted it that way in order to permit him to place the defendant on probation if he wished.

[16] For a detailed discussion of guilty plea bargaining in the three states, see Newman, Conviction: The Determination of Guilt or Innocence Without Trial 76-130 (1966).

[17] Mich. Stat. Ann. §28.797 (1954).

[18] An example of this is first degree murder. A defendant charged with this offense is usually permitted to enter an "open plea" — a plea of guilty to some degree of homicide less serious than murder first, to be determined by the court. After hearing testimony and studying the presentence report, the trial judge finds the defendant guilty of second degree murder or of manslaughter depending upon how serious he views the episode. Neither degree of murder is probationable but manslaughter is. Mich. Stat. Ann. §28.1131 (1954). It is extremely rare for a defendant originally charged with first degree murder to be placed on probation, even

major objective of a defendant is to decrease the length of the sentence which will be imposed if he is imprisoned.[19]

Charge reduction, in practice, also makes it easier for a trial judge to give probation to a defendant. Even though the judge is aware of the reduction and is convinced the defendant is guilty of the original charge, he seems to feel better — and perhaps believes he will look better — if the probationer is officially recorded as being convicted of a less serious offense. In Wichita, Kansas trial judges refuse to consider probation for defendants convicted of murder, rape, or armed robbery, even though probation was precluded by statute only for first degree murder. If these charges are reduced, the judges are willing to consider probation for first offenders and sometimes actually grant probation. An assistant prosecutor indicated that, for this reason, charge reductions from these three offenses are easy to obtain.

Legislative probation eligibility requirements do not in practice preclude defendants from receiving probation. Like statutory limits on sentencing discretion[20] and parole eligibility requirements,[21] these limitations are nullified in their implementation.

---

when he is found guilty of manslaughter. Nevertheless, almost all persons charged with first degree murder are permitted to enter the open plea. The reason appears to be the differences in the length of the maximum sentences. First degree murder is punishable by a sentence of life imprisonment. Mich. Stat. Ann. §28.548 (1954). Second degree murder is punishable by life imprisonment or any term of years in the discretion of the trial judge. Mich. Stat. Ann. §28.549 (1954). Manslaughter is punishable by a statutory maximum sentence of fifteen years. Mich. Stat. Ann. §28.533 (1954).

[19] The standard reduction of armed robbery to unarmed robbery or to assault with intent to rob affects the maximum sentence in this way: Armed robbery is punishable by life imprisonment or any term of years in the discretion of the court. Mich. Stat. Ann. §28.797 (1954). Unarmed robbery is punishable by a statutory maximum of 15 years and so is assault with intent to rob. Mich. Stat. Ann. §28.798 (1954) and Mich. Stat. Ann. §28.283 (1962). Breaking and entering in the nighttime carries a maximum sentence of 15 years. Mich. Stat. Ann. §28.305 (1962). Breaking and entering in the daytime and entering without breaking carry maxima of five years. Mich. Stat. Ann. §28.306 (1962). The daytime and nighttime distinction has since been abolished and the maximum sentence for breaking and entering other than an occupied dwelling house has been reduced to ten years. Mich. Stat. Ann. §§28.305, 28.306 (Supp. 1965).

Sale of narcotics carries a maximum sentence of life imprisonment, a twenty-year mandatory minimum sentence, and is not probationable. Mich. Stat. Ann. §18.1122 (1957). This is usually reduced to possession of narcotics, which carries a maximum sentence of ten years and, if the defendant does not have a prior narcotics conviction, is probationable. Mich. Stat. Ann. §18.1123 (1957).

[20] For a discussion of the responses in practice to legislative limitations on trial judge sentencing discretion, see Chapter 6.

[21] For a discussion of evasion of legislative parole eligibility requirements, see Chapter 9.

B. Locus of Responsibility for the Probation Decision

Legal responsibility for the probation decision rests on the individual trial judge. By contrast, legislatures have placed responsibility for the parole decision on parole boards consisting of several members who are expected to exercise discretion as a group. In terms of formal allocation of discretion, the parole decision is the product of group decision-making while the probation decision is the product of a single decision maker — the trial judge.

In practice, however, many trial judges share with others the responsibility for making probation decisions. The tendency to do so varies among judges, and the processes by which sharing is accomplished are informal and often subtle. One trial judge is content to make the probation decision without consulting other persons; indeed, he may feel that advice and recommendations are an interference with judicial prerogative. Another trial judge actively seeks advice from others and, although he may not always follow the advice, he reaches a contrary decision only after very careful reconsideration of the sentence which seems to him to be appropriate. Even among the trial judges who rely upon the advice of others, there are differences as to which officials are drawn into the decision-making process: Some judges seek the advice of police officials in certain cases; some judges regularly seek the advice of the prosecuting attorney; some judges give great weight to the recommendations of the probation department.

These differences are highly informal and, indeed, personal to different trial judges. There may be a number of reasons for the differences. Some judges may feel more of a need than others to seek advice to assure themselves they are making proper decisions. In such cases the advice of others may do no more than give the trial judge needed psychological assurance. Other judges, however, may feel that the advice of other officials is helpful in insulating themselves from possible public criticism of their decisions.

1. *Detroit.* The differences in judicial reliance on the opinions of other officials are most apparent among the various trial judges in Detroit's multi-judge Recorder's Court. The same officials are available to all the judges, but greatly different use is made of them. One trial judge very clearly indicated that he does not wish to receive recommendations from the probation department or Psychopathic Clinic.[22] Another judge displayed considerable am-

[22] A probation officer stated that all the judges except this one want a probation department recommendation in the presentence report. He stated that all the proba-

bivalence in his attitude toward the weight that should be given to probation department recommendations:

> If both the probation officer investigating the case and the supervisor submit a recommendation to the court and both concur, he is quite likely to give this considerable weight and follow it. However, he indicated that he does not let the recommendation of the probation department influence him very much. Usually, he has a tendency to rely on his own judgment, particularly in cases that have gone to trial where he is quite familiar with the facts. These facts that come out at the trial have a tendency to convince the judge as to the proper kind of disposition. In 90 percent of the cases the recommendation of the department will usually agree with the judge's own opinion. The judge just simply happens to agree with that recommendation. He believes that the department should be required, or at least permitted, to include recommendations with their presentence report. The judge does not have to agree with the recommendation, but most of the men in the department are college men and their opinions are to be respected. Probation work is their profession and their opinion should at least be considered.

A third judge stated simply that as a general rule he follows the recommendations of the probation department.

In many cases, the trial judge has a report from the Psychopathic Clinic as well as a presentence report. Because these reports are prepared independently, their recommendations sometimes conflict. Several judges indicated that, when this occurs, their tendency is to follow the recommendation of the probation department because their report contains more factual data to substantiate the recommendation. One judge indicated, however, that, when recommendations conflict, he follows that of the Psychopathic Clinic. In sex cases the judges are concerned about whether the defendant is sexually deviant, and there is a stronger tendency to rely upon the Psychopathic Clinic report.[23]

The same judge who wants no recommendations in presentence reports always consults the inspector of the police department narcotics bureau when sentencing narcotic violation cases. Other judges indicated that the recommendations of the narcotics bureau

---

tion officers must be careful not to include recommendations when writing reports for this judge unless he specifically asks for one; the judge has stated on numerous occasions that he considers such recommendations an invasion on his sentencing prerogatives.

[23] One judge indicated, however, that he frequently disagrees with the recommendations of the Psychopathic Clinic in sex cases. Because he considers homosexuals and prostitutes to be pathetic people, he has a tendency to place them on probation despite clinic recommendations for incarceration.

are of little value to them because they invariably favor incarceration.

Recommendations from the probation department and the Psychopathic Clinic are in part designed to be supportive of the decision which it is believed the judge wishes to make. If the person writing the report knows that the judge has definite views on the type of case involved, he is likely to make his recommendation conform to those views, even though he may really feel otherwise and, indeed, even though the body of the report may suggest a contrary recommendation. In one case involving forgery, the probation department recommended incarceration. At the sentence hearing, it became obvious the trial judge wished to place the defendant on probation. When specifically questioned about his recommendation by the trial judge, the probation officer reluctantly changed it.[24]

2. *Milwaukee.* The trial judge disposes of many cases immediately following the postplea of guilty hearing without referring them for a presentence investigation. Generally, reference of a case for a presentence investigation reflects a decision that the offense was not so serious as to preclude probation and that he wants more information about the background of the defendant.[25]

When a presentence report has been prepared, the trial judge discusses it in chambers prior to sentencing with the prosecuting attorney, the defense attorney, and the probation officer who prepared the report. He seeks the advice and opinions of each of them as to the proper disposition.

The probation department's recommendation in Milwaukee, as in Detroit, is influenced by known preferences of the trial judge in particular kinds of cases. In one minor larceny case in which the defendant had been released from a federal correctional institution only two weeks before his arrest on the current offense, the probation department recommended probation. Although the body of the presentence report indicated incarceration, the probation officer said he recommended probation because he knew the judge would not want to incarcerate a person with recent prison experience for a minor larceny. The judge placed the defendant on pro-

[24] In another case, involving a bad check, both the investigating probation officer and the division supervisor felt that the defendant was not probation material. However, when the question was put directly to them by the judge, both refused to state their opinion, because they both knew the judge desired to put the offender on probation.

[25] In some cases, he makes a presentence referral simply to satisfy a persistent defense attorney. When the probation department is aware of this, it conducts a quick investigation. The report is returned to court and the defendant is almost always sentenced to prison.

bation. Other instances were observed in which the probation department recommended probation despite its opinion that the defendant was not a good risk.

The trial judge seems much more likely to sentence a defendant to incarceration against the probation department's recommendation than to grant probation when it is not recommended. If both the prosecuting attorney and the probation department concur in their recommendations, the trial judge is extremely reluctant to select a different position. The area of disagreement between the trial judge and the probation department is small; officials estimated that departmental recommendations were followed in at least 95 percent of the cases.

C. Criteria for Granting or Denying Probation

In correctional literature[26] and in statutes[27] primary emphasis is placed upon the rehabilitative function of probation and upon the difficulties of determining whether the defendant will succeed on probation. In practice, this is an important aspect of the probation decision, one that causes great concern to trial judges and, especially, to probation officers who make probation recommendations.[28] However, rehabilitation is not the only concern of persons who make probation decisions. Trial judges reflect their assessment of the seriousness of the offense in probation decisions. Offenses they view as very serious are likely to result in a prison sentence despite the fact the defendant's potential for rehabilitation seems good; conversely, persons who commit offenses viewed as minor are likely to be placed on probation without regard to their prospects for rehabilitation.[29] In part, this attitude doubtless reflects concern over the seriousness of the offense the defendant may commit if he

[26] See, for example, the discussion of probation criteria in National Probation and Parole Association, Guides for Sentencing 33-47 (1957). The book discusses the deterrent effect of sentencing but concludes that "the deterrent force of severe penalty alone for major crimes has been highly overrated and belief in its value is unrealistic." Id. at 2. It continues: "Far more effective than deterrence as an objective of sentencing is rehabilitation, the satisfactory adjustment of the offender to law-abiding society. Whether it takes the form of probation — proved to be the most practical approach where circumstances warrant its use — or of commitment and ultimately parole, it is based on the principle that the best way to protect society is to change convicted offenders into law-abiding citizens." Id. at 3-4.

[27] See note 1 *supra* and accompanying text.

[28] See Chapter 1.

[29] Many statutes recognize the seriousness of the offense as a proper criterion for the probation decision. Statutes also frequently preclude probation of persons convicted of very serious offenses. See note 4 *supra*.

is released on probation. But it also reflects a judgment that probation is leniency, and some offenses are so serious they require full community condemnation — a prison sentence.

In addition, the probation decision is used to accomplish some objectives that cannot be achieved by incarceration. The probation decision is sometimes used to relieve court congestion by encouraging the disposition of cases by guilty pleas. It may be used to support police efforts to detect crime and apprehend offenders through informants by rewarding their services with probation. The probation decision is often influenced by a desire to secure restitution to the victim of the offense or support for the offender's family — goals that cannot be achieved by a prison sentence.

1. *Criteria related to probable adjustment on probation.* One of the central concerns of trial judges and probation officers is assessing the likelihood that a defendant will successfully adjust to community living under probation supervision. The focus is primarily upon the likelihood that the defendant will violate the criminal law if placed on probation,[30] and the question is whether the defendant will be able to lead a law-abiding life if he is given the assistance of probation supervision. In practice, a number of indicia of probable adjustment are used: criminal record, personal characteristics of the offender, sexual deviancy, narcotics addiction, and professional criminality.

a. *Criminal record.*

> *Illustration No. 1:* The defendant had been charged with armed robbery but was permitted to plead guilty to the less serious offense of larceny from the person. The presentence report indicated that the nineteen-year-old defendant's record consisted only of an arrest without prosecution and a bad conduct discharge from the army. Probation was recommended because of his age, absence of criminal record, the fact that his family was respectable and interested in him, and the willingness of his employer to rehire him. The court placed him on probation for two years on condition that he pay restitution to the victim and court costs.

[30] In this respect, the probation decision closely resembles the parole decision. See Chapter 11. There are major differences, however, in the data to which the decision maker looks to assess the probability of recidivism. These differences stem from the fact that the parole decision is made after a period of institutional treatment, whereas the probation decision maker functions at the very beginning of the treatment process. Much parole board emphasis is placed upon the response of the inmate to the institutional program — whether he exhibits changes in attitudes, whether he has participated in institutional programs, whether he has conformed to institutional disciplinary rules, and whether he has formulated a plan for his release. The probation decision maker is unable to use response to treatment efforts as a guide; the probation decision, therefore, tends to be based more on the status of the offender, such as age and criminal record, and less upon psychological factors.

The defendant's criminal record is one of the most important factors influencing the probation decision. In Kansas, the trial judges place almost all first offenders on probation except those convicted of murder, first degree robbery, or forcible rape.[31] In Michigan, the trial judges stated there is a great likelihood of probation if the defendant has no prior felony convictions, provided the present conviction is for an offense other than an extremely serious one.[32] They also indicated it was unusual for a second or third felony offender to receive probation. A major exception to this occurs in the case of a person who has previously been convicted of a felony but who has no recent conviction. One judge stated that when he would place a two or three time loser on probation it would be in a situation in which the defendant might have had his previous conviction ten years before his present appearance in court but then only if the present offense was not of great seriousness and the defendant was not vicious or a professional criminal.[33] In Milwaukee, there is a strong presumption that a defendant without a prior felony conviction will be given probation.[34]

Attention is directed primarily at prior felony convictions. A defendant who has several misdemeanor convictions on his record[35]

31 A prosecuting attorney in Sedgwick County, Kansas, stated that trial judges there will consider probation for a first offender who commits one of these offenses if the charge is reduced, which it often is.

32 A supervisor in the Detroit probation department stated that Recorder's Court judges are very liberal in granting probation. He said that for those offenses that allow probation, it is almost certain a first offender will receive probation.

33 Another judge, stating essentially the same principle, indicated he would consider probation even if the defendant caused personal injury to another but only if it occurred in a fight in which the defendant simply lost his temper. In the fight situation, however, probation would be denied if the defendant had a recent felony conviction.

34 In both Detroit and Milwaukee, there is a strong policy against incarceration of the habitual nonsupport violator; they will be placed on probation even with a record of several felony nonsupport convictions. A Detroit trial judge explained that the family cannot be supported if the father is in jail and the entire purpose of the nonsupport law is to obtain support for the family. Further, if the nonsupport violator is incarcerated parole boards release him as soon as possible. However, on very rare occasions, the nonsupport violator will be incarcerated. The criterion used, according to the judge, is whether the defendant has a very bad record and, after investigation of the case, it appears that he will never support his family and needs to be taught a lesson. See pages 98-99 for further discussion of the use of probation in nonsupport cases.

35 In one case in Detroit, a woman was sentenced to prison although she had no prior felony convictions. She was a prostitute and was charged with armed robbery of a client but pleaded guilty to larceny from the person. The presentence report noted that she had been arrested sixty-eight times and had been convicted of misdemeanors involving prostitution fifteen times. All of the misdemeanor convictions resulted in probation, short jail sentences, or fines. The presentence report recommended a denial of probation on the ground her record indicated she did not respond well to leniency. The court imposed a prison sentence of one to ten years,

or several arrests not followed by conviction[36] is regarded as a first offender for these purposes. A defendant whose record consists only of violations of the juvenile code is also likely to be regarded as a first offender, but a number of serious juvenile violations may result in incarceration even on the defendant's first appearance in criminal court.[37]

If a defendant has seriously violated probation previously, it is unlikely he will be placed on probation again, and a defendant who has served a felony prison sentence, whether as a result of probation revocation or a direct commitment, is unlikely to be given probation upon a subsequent felony conviction.

In Detroit, the trial judge is informed of the defendant's record in the presentence report prepared for him in all felony and serious misdemeanor cases.[38] In Milwaukee, the trial judge is informed of the defendant's record at the postplea of guilty hearing and in the presentence report in those cases in which an investigation is conducted.[39] Because of the prevalence of pleading guilty to reduced charges in Detroit, the trial judges must interpret the defendant's record in light of the plea bargaining process to arrive at an accurate judgment about the seriousness of the conduct involved in the prior convictions.[40]

In both Detroit and Milwaukee, an offender arrested for one offense is interrogated to determine whether he has committed other offenses. He is told that he will not be charged with other

---

indicating that by permitting her to plead to larceny from the person he had shown her as much leniency as possible.

36 Although arrests that do not result in conviction are usually ignored in making the probation decision, they are taken into consideration if they form a pattern that clearly indicates the defendant is guilty of the offense for which he was arrested. This is the case when the arrests fall within the scope of cases in which the police usually do not seek prosecution even when they have sufficient evidence. See LaFave, Arrest: The Decision to Take a Suspect into Custody 437-489 (1965). In the case discussed in note 35 *supra,* the presentence report indicated that most of the sixty-eight arrests did not result in convictions because the victims refused to prosecute.

37 In one case, the juvenile court waived jurisdiction over a sixteen-year-old boy who was charged with unlawfully driving away an automobile. He had been awaiting transportation to the juvenile training school when the offense occurred. His record consisted of adjudications of delinquency for breaking and entering a business place in the nighttime, breaking and entering an automobile, drunkenness, escape from juvenile detention twice, and four previous car thefts. He pleaded guilty to the offense as charged and, although this was his first appearance in criminal court, he was sentenced to a prison term of two to five years.

38 See Chapter 1.

39 See Chapter 1. In cases tried upon a not guilty plea, the court is given the defendant's record after conviction but before sentencing.

40 A Detroit prosecutor stated he has heard every trial judge in Detroit say to a defendant at one time or another: "I see in 1955 you were given a break by the prosecutor's office when they permitted you to plead guilty to a lesser offense. I see that the same thing happened last year."

offenses he admits, that they are "free offenses." He is not in fact charged with admitted offenses[41] but they are brought to the attention of the sentencing judge,[42] who is expected to take them into account in disposing of the case. The admitted but uncharged offenses do affect the disposition, but apparently not to the extent that prior convictions of the same offenses would.[43] One or two admitted felonies does not preclude probation for the defendant without a prior felony conviction unless the admitted offenses are extremely serious. However, a large number of admitted offenses will preclude probation.[44]

While there is a tendency to use the defendant's record in a rather mechanical fashion in making probation decisions — probation for almost all first felony offenders, no probation for almost all defendants with prior felony convictions — in reality, the defendant's record is closely related to other considerations used to make probation decisions. As the illustration case suggests, the absence of prior felony convictions may reflect the fact the defendant is a youth who simply hasn't had time to accumulate prior convictions or that his family has been effective in controlling his behavior before the present offense. Yet, the defendant's age and his family relationships are factors that, independently of the criminal record, may be sufficient indication of good rehabilitation potential to result in probation.[45]

b. *Age, family relationship, and similar considerations.*

> *Illustration No. 2:* The defendant, age seventeen, pleaded guilty to carrying a concealed weapon. He admitted his intention to use the gun in a hold-up. He had spent six weeks in jail awaiting disposition. He had no record other than an arrest for investigation of larceny. Defense counsel stated the

41 For discussion of the details of this practice, see Miller, Prosecution (forthcoming).

42 In Detroit, the trial judge is informed of the admitted but uncharged offenses in the presentence report, while in Milwaukee, evidence concerning them is introduced at the postplea of guilty hearing by stipulation of the parties. See Chapter 1.

43 Perhaps the reason for this is that a felony conviction followed by a new felony means the defendant failed to respond to prior probation, even though the present offense may not have been committed until after discharge from probation supervision. When the prior offenses have not led to conviction, however, and the rehabilitative measures of the court have not been utilized, the court may have more reason to believe that probation will be successful.

44 In one case, a defendant was reported in the presentence report to have admitted twelve burglaries in addition to the one for which he was prosecuted. Upon questioning by the court, the defendant denied commission of seven of the offenses but admitted the other five. The court sentenced him to prison, although he had no prior felony convictions, stating that the large number of offenses finally admitted by the defendant precluded probation.

45 Indeed, the illustration case fits the popular conception of the purpose of probation as the furtherance of the rehabilitation of the young, first offender from a stable family.

defendant's mother was ill and his father was unemployed and they were depending upon him for support. The judge stated, "I don't like to send a boy of seventeen to prison if there's any chance for him" and placed him on probation.

As the illustration case suggests, one of the prime considerations in sentencing a youthful offender is the anticipated negative effect of exposing a young defendant to the environment of an adult prison; if at all possible, a prison sentence is avoided. One judge stated he places all young offenders on probation who appear in adult court for the first time unless the offense is extremely serious or the defendant has an extensive juvenile record.[46] But beyond the negative effects of a prison sentence, trial judges view young defendants as possessing capabilities for rehabilitation. Several judges tell young defendants whom they place on probation that this is their last chance to become law-abiding citizens and that they had better take advantage of it.[47]

Although age is the most conspicuous and frequently encountered personal characteristic that influences the probation decision, other similar considerations may be important in a particular case. The aggregate of these characteristics is sometimes referred to by trial judges as the defendant's rehabilitation potential. They include: family stability and whether the family is attempting to control the defendant's conduct; if the defendant is married, whether he supports his family and has a sense of responsibility for them; employment stability and performance; and school attendance and conduct.

c. *Sexual deviancy.* Judges express concern over whether the defendant is a sexual deviate. One Michigan trial judge stated he always orders a psychiatric examination in sex cases to determine whether the offense was an isolated act or reflects mental deviancy of a sort that indicates recidivism. In one case, a Michigan trial judge gave probation to a defendant who had pleaded guilty to gross indecency but imposed the condition that the first sixty days must be served in the house of corrections. He stated if the defendant was able to secure private treatment for his problem, he would

[46] Age is also a factor in the recommendations made in presentence reports and psychiatric examination reports. In one case in Detroit, both the probation department and the Psychopathic Clinic recommended probation because of the defendant's youth.

[47] One judge told two co-defendants whom he placed on probation that they were only nineteen years of age and that in the future they would have to be very careful. He told them if they continued to be wise-guys thinking they could fool the police, they would be back in court on other charges. He told them they were at the crossroads; it would be one way or the other, and only they could make up their minds to be respectable — that one road led to misery and prison and the other would bring decency and happiness to them.

revise the probation order to permit him to enter a hospital; if private treatment were not obtained, he would then revoke probation or, at least, give serious consideration to it. In Wisconsin, offenders convicted of certain sex crimes must undergo psychiatric and social examinations. Until 1967, if the Department of Public Welfare recommended specialized treatment, the trial judge had to sentence the offender to incarceration for the maximum term prescribed in the statute or place him on probation on condition that he receive treatment. In 1967, the Wisconsin Supreme Court held that the decision whether to incarcerate must be made by the trial judge rather than by the correctional agency.[48]

d. *Narcotics addiction.*

> *Illustration No. 3:* The defendant, a youth, pleaded guilty to breaking and entering an automobile with intent to commit larceny. The defendant admitted he committed the present offense to obtain money to purchase narcotics. He admitted he had used narcotics for seven years and, although he had voluntarily committed himself to the federal narcotics hospital at Lexington, Kentucky, he had not stayed long enough to complete the course of treatment. The judge told the defendant he needed a jail sentence to break his dependency on narcotics and that after his release from prison he could decide whether he wished to continue using narcotics. He sentenced the defendant to a term of two and one-half to ten years in Michigan State Prison at Jackson.

Addiction to narcotics is regarded as a strong indication the defendant will violate the criminal law if placed on probation. Trial judges in Detroit[49] unanimously regard the narcotics addict as a poor risk for probation. One judge stated that he has very little faith or confidence that addicts will ever be rehabilitated. His understanding of the experience of the Detroit Narcotics Clinic[50] is that there is no reasonable hope for the eventual rehabilitation of any narcotics addict and as a consequence the best thing that can be done is to protect the community by removing them and preventing the unlawful activity that they must pursue in order to afford the habit.[51] The same judge indicated he is willing to place

[48] Wis. Stat. Ann. §959.15 (1958). In practice, the Michigan sex psychopath law is almost always invoked prior to conviction. Only those cases that slip through the pretrial screen present sentencing problems in Detroit. See Miller, Prosecution (forthcoming).

[49] Little is known about the attitudes of trial judges in Milwaukee or Wichita concerning the narcotics addict. Relatively few narcotics addicts appear in court in those cities compared to Detroit, where the problem appears to be much greater.

[50] See Chapter 1.

[51] A supervisor in the Detroit probation department who makes recommendations in large numbers of cases indicated he did not consider alcoholics and narcotics ad-

an addict on probation if there is a plan for hospitalization or outpatient treatment for the addiction, but even under such circumstances he has little hope for rehabilitaion. Another judge indicated the same reluctance to place addicts on probation and stated the only time he considers probation is when the addict has performed informant services for the police.[52] A third judge stated the only time he even considers probation for a narcotics addict is when he is convinced the addict is not selling narcotics or is selling only enough to support his habit.[53]

The practice of reducing the nonprobationable charge of sale of narcotics to the probationable one of narcotics possession[54] does not seem to reflect a desire to place such defendants on probation. The principal motives appear to be a desire to avoid the twenty-year mandatory minimum sentence for sale and to encourage guilty pleas. A Detroit prosecutor stated the only time a reduction from sale to possession is likely to result in probation is when the defendant has given valuable information to the police.

When sentencing narcotics addicts to prison, judges frequently state they are doing so to permit the addict to break his dependency on narcotics. In one typical case, the judge told the defendant, whom he had sentenced to a prison term of one to five years, "For your own protection I am forced to sentence you to a period of confinement so you will be able to lose the habit of taking narcotics. You may then become a worthwhile citizen." Other trial judge statements reveal very little faith in the curative effects of prison on addicts.[55]

e. *Professional criminality.*

Illustration No. 4: The defendants, husband and wife, pleaded guilty to check forgery. They had no previous felony convictions. The presentence report stated they had passed a number of bogus checks in several states and appeared to be making their living in that manner. The report continued

---

dicts to be good probation risks. He would sometimes recommend probation despite this factor, but usually a prison sentence was recommended.

52 See page 96.

53 For a discussion of professional criminality as a probation criterion, see pages 86-88. Detroit judges were observed to interrogate narcotics offenders at length to determine whether they were selling narcotics as well as using it. In large part this determination is based upon the amount of narcotics the defendant has in his possession when he is apprehended. The fact the addict sells narcotics influences the judges to set a higher minimum prison sentence as well as to deny probation. The nonaddicted seller is even more likely to be denied probation and to receive a long minimum sentence.

54 See pages 74-75.

55 Detroit trial judges appear not to differentiate between heroin users and marijuana users in terms of the likelihood of rehabilitation and, acordingly, treat them the same at sentencing.

that the husband was the instigator of these operations and that the wife was in some degree coerced by him. The trial judge sentenced the husband to prison and placed the wife on probation on condition she make restitution for all of the checks.

A distinction is made between the person who does not receive financial benefits from his criminal acts, or only occasional financial benefit, and one who derives his livelihood from crime. In the latter case, a prison sentence is likely even if the trial judge might not normally view the offense as a serious one. To some extent, this is simply a special application of the concern with the defendant's criminal record as an indication of his probable future conduct. There is reason to believe, however, that some judges distinguish between the professional and the nonprofessional recidivist. One judge stated that some of these check writers are really experts and they make their living at this type of antisocial behavior. He considers such check artists as dangerous individuals with conniving and scheming minds. They are usually shrewd con men and he is not inclined to be particularly lenient with the professional check writer. However, he does not consider a person who writes bad checks when he is drunk particularly dangerous. Whether he will consider this kind of individual for probation depends upon his past record.[56] Another judge stated that he usually placed young defendants convicted of auto theft on probation, but if the defendant has stolen several automobiles or has been involved in stripping automobiles as a commercial operation or has done damage to the automobile, he is less likely to grant probation. Another judge distinguishes between the professional and nonprofessional thief, stating that he has absolutely no time for a con man who plays on the weakness of others. In his opinion this is the lowest type of crime that can be committed by an individual. Similarly, he has a strong aversion to pickpockets and shoplifters. He stated that all these people simply live by their wits and actually know what they are doing. On the other hand, there are women who shoplift when they have the money to buy the goods. When they come into court, they are often crying and quite upset and it is usually their first offense. In such cases, he indicated that those kind of shoplifters are good probation material.[57]

[56] A Kansas prosecuting attorney stated that check forging cases are normally disposed of by placing the defendant on probation on condition he pay restitution; however, if he has reason to believe the defendant is a professional check writer he will inform the judge of this belief and recommend a prison sentence, which is normally imposed.

[57] A Michigan judge stated that the methods used in burglary are often important considerations in making the probation decision. If the burglary involves safecracking or dynamiting or if the defendant was apprehended with burglary tools

In Detroit, persons convicted of misdemeanors for engaging in the numbers racket or a dice or poker game are usually given suspended sentences or fines. Persons convicted of the felony of conspiracy to gamble are usually higher up in the numbers racket. Even they are not dealt with as severely as the law permits. It is apparent that the judicial attitude is that gambling is not the most serious kind of criminal activity even when engaged in for profit. One judge said that in cases involving conspiracy to gamble, which is a felony, it is the policy to sentence the ring leaders. In most cases, gambling is not a serious or vicious crime as compared to such offenses as murder and rape and he frankly does not consider that the ordinary violation of the state gambling laws, which usually involve some limited numbers writing by Negro defendants or card gambling, is serious or vicious. Even persons convicted of conspiracy to gamble who are the leaders or operators of lottery games are not considered to be in the same class as the seriously assaultive criminal.

2. *Criteria related to the seriousness of the offense.* The probation decision also reflects the seriousness with which the offense is viewed. In part, this is related to concern about the seriousness of the offense the defendant may commit if placed on probation, but more is involved than simply this. Some offenses are regarded by the judges as too serious to permit the use of probation no matter how great the defendant's prospects for rehabilitation may seem: They require full condemnation, and that means imprisonment. The seriousness with which the community views the offense, reflected largely in newspaper articles and editorials, also influences the probation decision. So does the lack of moral blameworthiness of the defendant, as for example, when the offense is committed under strong provocation or by a mentally defective person.

a. *Crimes involving violence or its possibility.*

Illustration No. 5: The defendant pleaded guilty to assault with intent to do great bodily harm. One night, he had stabbed his wife in the left side of her chest with a butcher knife while she was lying in bed asleep. The wounds required hospitalization and the victim remained in critical condition for two weeks. Apart from apparently unfounded suspicions that his wife was having an affair, the attack was unprovoked. A prearraignment mental examination resulted in the conclusion that the defendant was not of unsound mind. He had no prior felony convictions. The presentence report recom-

---

in his possession, in this judge's opinion he must be an expert and has probably committed other offenses but has simply not been caught until the present offense. In that situation, he stated he would definitely impose a prison sentence.

mended incarceration because of the seriousness of the offense. The court imposed a prison term of one to three years.

In all three states, the possibility of probation is slight if the defendant has committed a crime involving serious injury to the person of another. Probation is a realistic possibility in non-negligent homicide cases only when the defendant acted as a result of strong provocation.[58] Other factors that normally weigh heavily in favor of probation have little impact in homicide cases.[59]

Trial judges in all three states indicated that defendants convicted of robbery perpetrated with a gun are almost never placed on probation. Even when the robbery with a weapon has not actually involved violence, the risk of violence is always present; one judge stated he regards all armed robberies as potential murders. In Detroit, armed robbery charges are usually reduced to robbery unarmed or assault with intent to rob, but the presentence report carefully notes whether a weapon was used. For purposes of the probation decision the trial judges treat them as armed robbery cases despite the reduction in charge. Similarly, in Detroit, many cases in which juvenile court jurisdiction is waived to permit trial in adult court involve crimes of violence.[60] In most of these cases, prison sentences are imposed.

[58] Only one non-negligent homicide case was discovered in which the defendant was placed on probation. He was originally charged with first degree murder, but in accordance with the Detroit practice was permitted to enter a plea of guilty to some degree of homicide less than murder first. The presentence report stated that the defendent and victim engaged in a dispute during a card game. The defendant left the place of the game and was followed by the victim. The victim had previously threatened the defendant with a knife and had told the defendant that he owned a gun. The victim approached the defendant with one hand in his pocket under such circumstances that it was not unreasonable for the defendant to believe that the victim was armed with a gun. When the victim approached, the defendant shot him. The defendant had a good reputation in the community and a history of steady employment. The trial judge found the defendant guilty of manslaughter and placed him on probation for five years on condition he contribute to the support of the victim's family during that period.

[59] In Wisconsin, a traveling jewelry salesman from a neighboring state became intoxicated while celebrating his birthday. While in that condition, he drove his car and crashed it into another car, killing all its occupants, a husband and wife and several children. He was convicted of negligent homicide amid considerable newspaper publicity. He had an excellent reputation in his home town, was respected by his business acquaintances, and was a family man. He had no prior felony or misdemeanor convictions. Despite these favorable indications, he was given a prison sentence.

In Milwaukee, a woman pleaded guilty to second degree murder. She had stabbed her brother to death for no apparent reason, an act she willingly admitted with considerable contrition. She had one prior conviction for disorderly conduct resulting in a suspended sentence. She was thirty-five years of age and had nine children, seven of them living with her. She was separated from her husband and was receiving financial assistance from Aid to Dependent Children. The trial judge sentenced her to prison.

[60] Public pressure has considerable impact on the waiver decision in such cases.

In assault cases, the extent of injuries suffered by the victim is an important factor. In the illustration case, the fact the victim suffered extensive injuries made the crime serious and took it out of the category of a routine spousal stabbing. In another Detroit case, the defendant pleaded guilty to the misdemeanor of aggravated assault, a charge which had been reduced from the original charge of felonious assault. He had engaged in a barroom fight, not entirely unprovoked by the victim, and had stabbed him several times with a broken beer bottle. Forty-eight stitches were required to close the wounds. The defendant had a large number of misdemeanor arrests and convictions. The presentence report characterized him as "brutal mad man when drunk" and the trial judge imposed the maximum jail sentence of one year. In Milwaukee, the trial judge always questions the police officer at the postplea of guilty hearing in robbery and assault cases to determine precisely the extent of personal injuries to the victim. If the offense involved extensive injuries, the defendant is very unlikely to receive probation.

b. *Community attitudes toward the offense.*

Illustration No. 6: The defendant had pleaded guilty to a felony involving homosexual activity. After receiving the presentence report, the trial judge placed him on probation for five years. A local newspaper began criticizing the trial judge for placing the defendant on probation. During the two months of newspaper criticism, the trial judge received hundreds of letters from various citizens criticizing his sentencing practices. The newspaper criticism ended one month before the judge ran for re-election.[61]

The attitude of the community toward particular offenses is an important consideration in the probation decision. All the trial judges seemed aware of this and some acknowledged that community sentiment has an impact on their sentencing. One judge stated that there are certain types of offenses in which the community interest is involved. As an example, he stated that everybody gets quite excited about sex offenses involving attacks on young girls.

A juvenile court judge in Detroit explained that in very serious crimes such as murder, manslaughter, armed robbery, rape, and various crimes for which the penalty is many years in the penitentiary, public pressure forces him to waive jurisdiction. This is particularly true if the defendant, although between the ages of fifteen and seventeen, acts, thinks, and displays the general characteristics of an adult. The judge said that if he constantly went on record as refusing to grant a waiver in such cases, the various civic organizations, the prosecutor's office, and the newspapers would severely criticize him.

[61] He won the election, but in his opinion only because the newspaper criticism ended when a group of ministers called a press conference and expressed strong support for the judge.

In these cases, the offender may well not be considered for probation. Another observed that sex cases involving children are "frequently the most touchy." He always refers defendants in such cases to the Detroit Psychopathic Clinic for examination and recommendation and finds their support most helpful. He indicated that even with a Psychopathic Clinic examination, sex cases can cause considerable difficulty if the newspapers follow the case and disagree with the sentence imposed.[62]

c. *Circumstances of aggravation or mitigation.*

Illustration No. 7: The defendant entered a plea of guilty to a charge of assault with intent to commit carnal knowledge on a female child. The defendant was thirty-eight years old, married and the father of eight children. The victim had spent considerable time at the site of a construction project where the defendant worked as a city inspector. The defendant stated she invited his advances but when he responded she became frightened and he did not persist. He further stated the victim's family offered to settle the case for $1500. When he refused, they called the police. The defendant's wife testified at the postplea of guilty hearing that she was willing to continue living with the defendant and that he was a good husband and father. The trial judge stated he would place the defendant on probation.

In a number of cases, the circumstances of the offense, while not affecting the defendant's guilt or innocence of the charge, do have a significant impact on the probation decision, because they affect the seriousness with which the offense is viewed. The extent to which the victim of a sex crime was the initiator or willing participant in the offense is important for this reason. Probation is the likely disposition of statutory rape cases in which the age difference between the male and female is not great and she was clearly a willing participant.[63] The same is true when the female in statutory rape cases has previously engaged in sexual intercourse.[64]

62 See note 60 *supra* for an indication of the effect of publicity on the juvenile court judge's decision whether to waive juvenile court jurisdiction in cases involving violence.

63 A Kansas judge, after stating that he is lenient as possible on statutory rape defendants who are only a few years older than the victim, noted that the situation is different if the girl has what he termed a "marked mental disability." He said that although she might have a chronological age of seventeen she may actually be eleven or twelve mentally. In these cases, he indicated that he shows the defendant little mercy.

64 In a Wisconsin case, the defendant pleaded guilty to statutory rape. He had been living with a girl who was under the age of consent. This was done with the knowledge and consent of her parents. She had lived with other men before meeting the defendant. The trial judge placed him on probation, noting that the defendant was not inducing a young girl of previous chaste character into an illicit relation-

The trial judge's view of the sexual standards of the racial or cultural group to which the parties to a statutory rape belong is also important to the probation decision. One trial judge stated that in deciding upon probation in certain kinds of sex cases he must take into consideration the social standards of the persons involved. For example, he cited the case of statutory rape involving a young man who might be above legal age and a girl below the legal age. Particularly among Negroes, the judge said, there is usually mutual consent of the two persons involved. Also he said that among the Negro group this type of sexual behavior is not particularly frowned upon. Considering the morals of this group, he said, probation may be an appropriate disposition. The same judge indicated, however, that, although he believed that incest might be normal behavior among a group he identified as "hillbillies," he would not grant probation in those cases. He considers incest a serious offense and usually imposes a prison sentence.

The conduct of the victim is also important in assault cases. If the assault occurred in a fight in which the victim probably was an aggressor, the likelihood of probation is great. Similarly, if the victim provoked the attack, especially by prior assaults, probation is likely.[65]

If the defendant has engaged in, or is likely to engage in, offenses involving particularly vulnerable victims, probation is unlikely. In Detroit, trial judges differentiate between possession of narcotics for one's own use and possession with intent to sell.[66] The concern, especially in marijuana cases, is that the defendant has been selling to juveniles. If the defendant has been arrested while selling to juveniles, a prison sentence is almost certain.[67]

---

ship. The probation officer who prepared the presentence report indicated that a prison sentence would have been imposed if the victim had had no sexual experience prior to her relationship with the defendant.

65 In a Detroit case, a defendant who stabbed his girlfriend in the stomach with a knife was convicted of felonious assault. During the presentence investigation it was disclosed that the victim was entertaining another man in her room and without warning physically attacked the defendant. It was also learned she had attacked him on previous occasions and had cut him with a knife. The investigating probation officer recommended probation, which was granted, because in his view the conduct of the victim was worse than that of the defendant.

66 The distinction is usually based on the amount of narcotics the defendant had in his possession at the time he was arrested. In one case, the trial judge stated the defendant was arrested with sixteen marijuana cigarettes in his possession and another 7.56 grains in an envelope, commenting, "Now, no one has that much except to sell." The defendant denied intent to sell, but the trial judge imposed a prison sentence.

67 In one such case, the trial judge, after remarking that sale of narcotics to juveniles is about the worst crime that anyone can commit, said, "To induce juveniles to become addicted to narcotics. I see nothing at all for this man. The sentence of the court is that you be confined to Michigan State Prison for Southern Michigan at Jackson for a period of four to ten years."

d. *The mentally defective offender.*

Illustration No. 8: The defendant pleaded guilty to a charge of accosting and soliciting for immoral purposes, which had been reduced from an original charge of gross indecency. The defendant had accosted two thirteen-year-old boys and played with their genitals. He was married and had four children. He was forty-one years old, illiterate, and of very low intelligence. His criminal record consisted of two arrests for discharging firearms. The Psychopathic Clinic reported that the defendant was not sexually deviant and that psychotherapy would be useless because of his low intelligence and verbal ability. The Clinic recommended probation with close supervision. The probation department also recommended probation with close supervision, noting the defendant's extremely low intelligence. The trial judge said the defendant wasn't able to understand the offense or what was happening to him. He placed the defendant on probation and very carefully explained the meaning of probation and what the defendant must do to keep it.

There is obvious reluctance to incarcerate a mentally defective person whose condition is not sufficiently acute to warrant a civil commitment. This attitude may result in part from the hardship that would result for the individual and, in part, from the view that mental defectives are only partially responsible for their conduct. One judge said that probably the most difficult type of individual to deal with is the feeble-minded person — particularly when the individual who is feeble-minded is quite young. The judge frankly stated that he is quite willing to play along as far as he possibly can with such individuals because of their obvious limitations. About the only thing that can be accomplished is to attempt to secure manual type of work for them and to keep them occupied. Quite a few such individuals whom he had placed on probation have worked out successfully. A probation officer, commenting on the sentencing policy of judges of Recorder's Court, confirmed the fact that this is a general policy but maintained that there are limitations. He stated that the courts are reluctant to sentence youthful individuals who have limited intelligence. However, a person with a long record for such offenses as assault or carrying dangerous weapons such as knives would receive sentences of incarceration from the court. Judges do not usually sentence feeble-minded boys unless they have patterns of serious antisocial behavior.

3. *Criteria related to particular uses of probation.* The probation decision is used to accomplish a number of objectives that can-

not be accomplished by incarceration. It may be used to encourage disposition of cases by plea of guilty, or to support the police use of informants, or to obtain restitution for the victim of a crime or support for the offender's family.

a. *To encourage guilty pleas.* Criminal justice administration is dependent upon the disposition of a large percentage of cases by guilty pleas. A decrease in the present high guilty plea rate would put the volume of trials beyond the capabilities of manpower presently available. Officials feel that guilty pleas must be rewarded to assure a sufficient number to permit the system to operate on present resources.[68] In the three states studied, reductions in charges and shorter prison sentences were both used to encourage guilty pleas.[69] Although trial judges are unlikely to announce that their policy is not to give probation to those who plead not guilty,[70] it is commonly assumed that most judges are more likely to give probation if there is a plea of guilty, and this prevalent assumption, whether accurate or not, serves to stimulate guilty pleas.

In Kansas one trial judge uses a pre-arraignment probation hearing to inform the defendant and his counsel whether he will place the defendant on probation if a plea of guilty is entered. The prosecuting attorney, defendant, defense attorney, and trial judge are present at the hearing. The defendant testifies to the circumstances which he believes are favorable to probation, and the case is discussed by all participants. The trial judge then makes a firm statement whether he will place the defendant on probation if he pleads guilty. There is no evidence that the judge invariably denies probation to defendants convicted on a not guilty plea, but it seems clear that in at least some cases probation is granted on a plea of guilty when it would not follow conviction upon a plea of not guilty.

In Michigan the principal inducement for a plea of guilty is a reduction of the charge to a less serious one. This has the effect of requiring a shorter maximum sentence if the defendant is incarcerated and it may eliminate the necessity for a high, mandatory minimum sentence. In addition, there is considerable evidence that trial judges in Detroit also use their discretion in setting minmum sentences to encourage guilty pleas.[71] In some cases, the charge is reduced from an offense that is by statute not probationable to one that is.[72] In some of these cases, the defendant is placed

68 See Newman, Conviction 76 (1966).

69 See Chapter 6.

70 According to the appellate court, this was done by the trial judge in United States v. Wiley, 267 F.2d 453, 455 (1959).

71 See Chapter 6.

72 See pages 71-75.

on probation, but in others he is not. There is no evidence that defendants who are convicted following a not-guilty plea are regularly denied probation. There is, in sum, no evidence that whether the defendant pleads guilty has any effect on the probation decision in Detroit. It is possible that the use of charge reductions and low judicially set minimum sentences is sufficient inducement; in addition, when a defendant pleads guilty in exchange for a reduction from a nonprobationable to a probationable charge he at least creates the possibility of probation even though he may not receive it.

In Wisconsin the Milwaukee trial judge holds the view that "probation and perjury do not mix." By this he means that, if a defendant on a plea of not guilty has testified as to his innocence at his trial and is ultimately convicted, the trial judge regards him as having perjured himself. The judge almost always refuses probation.[73] There is also some evidence that he regularly denies probation to defendants convicted upon a not guilty plea. A court reporter stated that in several years the judge has placed on probation only one defendant convicted in a jury trial.[74] It is very clear that the trial judge reduces the maximum sentence if he incarcerates a defendant who has pleaded guilty and refuses to do so for one who has pleaded not guilty.[75] Whether the trial judge intends it or

[73] In one case, the defendant pleaded not guilty to carnal knowledge and assault. He requested a jury trial, testified in his own behalf and was found guilty. He then requested probation. The judge referred him for presentence investigation but warned him to tell the probation officer the truth about everything because "probation and perjury do not mix." He told the probation officer that he pleaded not guilty because of shame and humiliation about what he had done and a desire to avoid stigma for his children. The probation department recommended probation. At the time of sentencing, the defense attorney said, "If it pleases the court, the defendant would like to make a statement." The judge replied:

"You had better make a truthful one for a change. He gambled, but he could not pull the wool over the eyes of the jury. He didn't fool me, but he thought that he might outwit our jury system; the system invested in our Constitution where twelve men are required to listen to this evidence and hear his perjured testimony. He gambled with our judgment and gambled with the truth. He gambled with loaded dice since he was applying for probation when he lost and hoped that though he did lose, he still might win. The bad thing here is not the misstep so much, but the perjury. You didn't fool me; I was convinced of your guilt. But you were trying to fool the jury and might have done so, gambling again with the common sense of the jury of twelve men under which our American system of jurisprudence operates. I am certain you fooled the defense attorney and forced a long jury trial, inconvenienced the district attorney, the jury, and the witnesses. You deserve absolutely no consideration on that account."

In this case, the trial judge did place the defendant on probation. He imposed a long probation period (five years) and imposed as a condition of probation payment of jury costs, a condition he stated he had never imposed before.

[74] The case referred to by the court reporter is the one discussed in note 73 *supra.*

[75] See Chapter 6. When announcing the sentence, the judge states he is giving the defendant "guilty plea credit" on the maximum.

not, defense attorneys experienced in his court are convinced there is little chance of probation after a not guilty plea, and they inform their clients of this when discussing whether they should plead guilty.[76]

b. *To reward informants for their services.* Police make widespread use of informants. Since most informants are persons who have engaged in criminal activity themselves, frequently the most persuasive inducement to assuming informant duties is lenient treatment of their own criminality. They may be promised immunity from arrest for certain offenses,[77] or they may not be charged with a crime they committed or charged with a less serious crime than the one they committed.[78] In addition, if a prison sentence is imposed, the term may be decreased because of cooperation with the police.[79] In some situations, informant services may be rewarded with probation despite trial judge opinion that the defendant is not a good probation risk. One judge claimed that narcotics cases were not good probation material. The only time he would consider probation in such cases is when the individual has been cooperative with the police by being an informer or helping the police contact and make a case on a seller. However, even with these individuals he would not trust an addict "as far as he could throw him." He might consider probation in a case where, while not good probation material, the individual had cooperated with the police and it was known that it might be dangerous to commit him to prison along with other prisoners on whom he may have informed. The same judge indicated that it is sometimes necessary to grant probation to one defendant in exchange for testimony that will convict his co-defendants. In such situations, he stated he is willing to sacrifice one case to convict the other defendants.

c. *To obtain restitution for the victim.*

Illustration No. 9: The defendant pleaded guilty to check forgery. He was thirty-nine years of age, divorced, and a plumber, although he had not worked for three months prior to the offense. His criminal record included two felony convictions for check forgery, one of which resulted in probation which was later revoked, the other resulting in a prison sentence. He was a heavy drinker, perhaps alcoholic. His sister offered to permit him to live with her if he were placed on

[76] At least one defense attorney indicated that he told his client the trial judge would be more favorably disposed toward probation if the defendant pleaded guilty.

[77] See LaFave, Arrest 132-137 (1965).

[78] This is discussed in Miller, Prosecution (forthcoming).

[79] See Chapter 6. In addition, parole boards sometimes grant parole to an inmate who has performed valuable informant functions for the officials of the correctional institution. See Chapter 11.

probation. Although he was charged with only one forgery, the presentence report indicated that he admitted passing eight other checks, totaling $243. The presentence report recommended a prison sentence. The trial judge noted that the defendant could earn fifteen dollars a day as a plumber and that his sister's home seemed a proper place for him to live. He placed the defendant on probation on condition he make restitution for all nine checks, the precise amount to be determined by the probation department.

Obtaining restitution for the victim of the offense is an important consideration in many bad check, forgery, and minor larceny cases. Normally, if the offender is able and willing to pay restitution, the prosecutor will not charge him with an offense and the case will not even reach court.[80] If the case reaches court, the likelihood of probation is great if the defendant seems able to make restitution. If a prison sentence were imposed, the victim would be put to his civil remedies to obtain restitution; in most cases the amounts are so small and the defendant so insolvent that a civil suit is not a profitable undertaking. A prison sentence may be imposed, however, if the defendant has a long record or if he makes his living by passing checks or stealing.[81]

Usually, these defendants have committed more than one offense. They are charged with one or two offenses and the remainder are brought to the attention of the trial judge in the presentence report or during the postplea of guilty hearing.[82] The restitution order almost always includes all offenses the defendant admits committing.[83] Trial judges recognize that many check forgers, especially the alcoholic ones, are not good probation risks. On the other hand, they are unlikely to commit serious offenses. One trial judge said that when he places such an individual on probation he always considers restitution to the victim and will usually include restitution of all checks passed by the defendant that come to the attention of the court through police reports and probation department reports. As a general rule, even though probation might be granted, the judge stated that these offenders are not usually good probation risks.

In the illustration case, the probation officer who prepared the presentence report predicted that the defendant would violate pro-

80 This is discussed in Miller, Prosecution (forthcoming).

81 See pages 86-88.

82 See Chapter 1.

83 One Kansas trial judge refuses to order probation on offenses for which the defendant has not been prosecuted. The reason, he said, is that he does not wish to turn his court into a collection agency; if the victim wishes restitution, he can sign a complaint and express a willingness to prosecute the defendant.

bation within three months. However, he stated he did not strongly oppose probation because the trial judge obviously wished to grant it.

d. *To obtain support for the offender's family.*

Illustration No. 10: The defendant entered a plea of guilty to a charge of child and wife desertion. He had been returned from Oklahoma to Kansas on his waiver of extradition. Although his wife originally complained against him, she now wished a reconciliation. The prosecuting attorney recommended that the defendant be placed on probation. The trial judge placed him on probation on condition he support his wife and child.

Throughout the criminal justice system, officials recognize that the purpose of nonsupport, desertion, and abandonment laws is to obtain support for the family. Effort is made to accomplish that objective with as little expenditure of resources as possible. When a complaint of nonsupport is made to the prosecuting attorney, the defendant is contacted and an attempt is made to arrange with him an informal program of support payments made through the prosecutor's office. If the program is accepted, the defendant is not prosecuted. Even if he fails several times to abide by his agreement to support, effort is made to obtain support without prosecution.[84] If these efforts fail, the defendant may be prosecuted for misdemeanor nonsupport and placed on probation. Only if all these efforts fail does the case reach court on a charge of felony nonsupport.[85]

When a defendant is convicted of felony nonsupport, he is almost certain to receive probation. Judges in all three states expressed great reluctance to sentence nonsupport violators to prison. With regard to such cases, one judge declared that he would go a long way before he would place such individuals in a prison. He would go as far as to make individuals convicted of nonsupport bring their paychecks into the probation department. His primary interest is keeping the family together, insuring their support and keeping them off the welfare rolls if at all possible. Nonsupport offenders are, of course, sometimes sentenced to prison but only in the most aggravated cases. A prison sentence is normally not im-

[84] This is discussed in Miller, Prosecution (forthcoming). In Detroit attempts to obtain support without prosecution are made by a division of the probation department, the Adjustment Division, specially established for that purpose.

[85] In Kansas and Wisconsin statutes specifically authorize formal deferral of prosecution in nonsupport cases. Kan. Stat. Ann. §21-445 (1964); Wis. Stat. Ann. §52.05(4) (1957). These statutes require trial judge participation. They are not often used, because they accomplish nothing that cannot be more easily accomplished through informal methods in the prosecutor's office.

posed unless the defendant has several felony nonsupport convictions on his record.[86]

[86] A Michigan trial judge explained the circumstances under which he will sentence a nonsupport violator to prison: "On very rare occasions, the defendant will be incarcerated. The criterion used is whether the defendant has a very bad record and, after investigation of the case, it appears that he will never support his family and needs to be taught a lesson."

CHAPTER 4

Probation Conditions and Supervision

The effectiveness of probation depends in significant measure upon what is done with the offender after he has been selected for supervision in the community. Probation may be an effective means of control and treatment of some convicted offenders, or a system of hurried and arbitrary decision-making by overworked probation officers, or a mere bookkeeping system for offenders who are permitted to live in the community without real supervision. Which of these or other possibilities a probation system becomes depends in part upon the resources devoted to probation. But it also depends upon the thought and care devoted to the processes of selecting probation conditions, determining supervision policies within existing resource limitations, and deciding which probationers should be regarded as failures and sentenced to prison. This chapter deals with two aspects of the probation system: probation conditions and probation supervision. Because probation revocation raises a somewhat distinct set of issues, it is discussed separately in the following chapter.

The theme, introduced earlier, of the shared authority between the trial judiciary and the probation staff is especially applicable here. While probation officers play important roles in virtually all probation decisions, their part is particularly significant in selecting probation conditions and determining supervision policies and practices. Judicial guidance and control of this segment of the probation system varies greatly from judge to judge and, even with respect to the same judge, is more likely to be in the form of crisis intervention than systematic policy-making and control. Furthermore, administrative control within the large, urban probation department is also uneven and far from systematic; indeed, in many situations administrative and judicial guidance and control are totally lacking and final authority rests with individual probation officers.

A. Probation Conditions

The conduct of a probationer is closely regulated by probation conditions. In theory, probation is revocable for even a single violation of a probation condition, although in practice minor violations are usually excused and even serious ones may be handled by action less drastic than revocation. The threat of revocation is present to deter noncompliance.

Probation conditions also regulate the behavior of the supervising probation officer, limiting the right which the agent has to intervene in the life of the probationer. Because the conditions imposed by a judge may express the expectations of the court concerning the type of supervision that is to be given in particular cases, conditions may also affect the nature and intensity of the probation supervision. If the court imposes a condition that is not routinely imposed, the probation officer normally responds by taking extra care to require the probationer to comply with it.

Statutes typically grant the trial judge broad discretion in formulating probation conditions. Usually, a set of conditions is formulated that is imposed routinely in every case. In addition, trial judges often impose special conditions of probation upon selected defendants. The specification of probation conditions is not necessarily complete when supervision begins because the probation officer often has authority to waive the necessity for complying with judicially imposed probation conditions or to impose new probation conditions himself.

In practice, both the trial judge and the probation officer usually take steps to assure themselves that the probationer understands the conditions applicable in his case and their importance.

1. *Legal authority to impose probation conditions.* Statutes in the three states authorize the imposition of probation conditions. Kansas statutes in force during the field survey authorized probation "upon such terms and conditions as it [the court] may deem best." [1] They also authorized as conditions of probation that "the defendant may be required to pay in one or several sums a fine imposed at the time of being placed on parole [probation] and may also be required to make restitution or reparation to the aggrieved party or parties for actual damages or loss caused by the offense for which conviction was had, and may also be required to provide for the support of any person or persons for whose support he is legally responsible. . . ." [2]

[1] Kan. Gen. Stat. §62-2203 (1949), repealed by Kan. Laws 1957, Ch. 331, §37.

[2] Ibid. Kan. Stat. Ann. §62-2241 (1964), the present law, provides:

Michigan statutes make certain probation conditions mandatory:

> The conditions of probation shall include the following:
> (1) That the probationer shall not, during the term of his probation, violate any criminal law of the state of Michigan, or any ordinance of any municipality in said state;
> (2) That he shall not, during the term of his probation, leave the state without the consent of the court granting his application for probation;
> (3) That he shall make a report to the probation officer, either in person or in writing, monthly, or as often as the latter may require.[3]

The statute authorizes as conditions of probation the payment of a fine or service of a jail term in a local correctional facility.[4] It also authorizes the court to impose "such other lawful conditions of probation . . . as the circumstances of the case may require or warrant, or as in its judgment may be meet and proper" including, specifically, payment of restitution and court costs.[5]

In Milwaukee County, Wisconsin, probation supervision is the responsibility of the county probation department, while in the remainder of the state it is the responsibility of the State Depart-

---

"The board [of probation and parole] may adopt general rules or regulations concerning the conditions of probation or suspension of sentence. The conditions shall apply in the absence of any specific or inconsistent conditions imposed by the court. Nothing herein contained shall limit the authority of the court to impose or modify any general or specific conditions of probation or of suspension of sentence.

"The probation officer may recommend and by order duly entered the court may impose and may at any time modify any conditions of probation or suspension of sentence. Due notice shall be given to the probation officer before any such conditions are modified and he shall be given an opportunity to be heard thereon. The court shall cause a copy of any such order to be delivered to the probation officer and the probationer.

"The court may include among the conditions of probation the following, or any other: That the defendant shall (a) avoid injurious or vicious habits; (b) avoid persons or places of disreputable or harmful character; (c) report to the probation officer as directed; (d) permit the probation officer to visit him at his home or elsewhere; (e) work faithfully at suitable employment as far as possible; (f) remain within a specified area; (g) pay a fine or costs, applicable to the offense, in one or several sums as directed by the court; (h) make reparation or restitution to the aggrieved party for the damage or loss caused by his offense in an amount to be determined by the court; (i) support his dependents."

[3] Mich. Stat. Ann. §28.1133 (1954).

[4] Ibid. By Mich. Pub. Acts 1957, No. 72, the period of imprisonment authorized as a condition of probation was increased from sixty days to six months. Mich. Stat. Ann. §28.1133 (Supp. 1965). Mich. Pub. Acts 1955, No. 154, authorized as a condition of probation service a period of one year in a probation camp. Mich. Stat. Ann. §28.1133(1) (Supp. 1965). For a detailed discussion of this provision and the use made of it, see page 116.

[5] Mich. Stat. Ann. §28.1133 (1954).

ment of Public Welfare. Courts in Milwaukee County have "authority to impose any conditions which may in their discretion appear to be reasonable and appropriate in granting probation. . . ." [6] In the remainder of the state, trial courts have authority to require payment of restitution and court costs as conditions of probation,[7] but the State Department of Public Welfare has authority to impose all other conditions of probation.[8]

2. *Conditions routinely imposed prior to supervision.* In each of the states, certain probation conditions are imposed in all cases at the time the defendant is placed on probation by the court. In Detroit, the form which, when signed by the trial judge, constitutes the court order of probation imposes four sets of conditions:

A. Probationer shall not violate any criminal law of the State of Michigan or any ordinance of any municipality of the State, nor attempt to do so, nor make any preparation leading to the same.[9]

B. During the term of probation, probationer shall not leave the State without the consent of the Court granting probation.[10]

C. Probationer shall make a report to the probation officer, either in person or in writing, weekly, or as often as the Court may require.[11]

D. Probationer shall cooperate at all times with the probation officer and conform to the following regulations and suggestions: To keep regular and reasonable hours; To avoid questionable associates and places; To seek and retain regular employment; To endeavor to accumulate some savings; To take advantage, if possible, of educational and other facilities for self-improvement. In case of doubt, consult the probation officer.

[6] Wis. Stat. Ann. §57.025(3) (1957).

[7] Wis. Stat. Ann. §57.01(1) (1957). Wis. Laws 1965, Ch. 394, §2, gave trial courts outside of Milwaukee County authority to require confinement in a local jail as a probation condition under some circumstances. Wis. Stat. Ann. §57.01(6) (Supp. 1967).

[8] Wis. Stat. Ann. §57.02 (1957) provides that "every probationer in the custody of the department [State Department of Public Welfare] shall be subject to the control of the department under regulations applicable to paroled persons." Wis. Stat. Ann. §57.01(5) (1957) provides: "The department shall furnish to the several courts forms setting forth the requirements and conditions applicable to probation."

[9] This condition is substantially the same as that required in all cases by Mich. Stat. Ann. §28.1133 (1954) except the statute does not include attempts to commit crimes nor preparation to commit crimes. See text accompanying note 3 *supra.*

[10] This condition is substantially the same as that required in all cases by Mich. Stat. Ann. §28.1133 (1954). See text accompanying note 3 *supra.*

[11] This condition is substantially the same as that required in all cases by Mich. Stat. Ann. §28.1133 (1954) except that the statute requires monthly instead of weekly reports. The statute authorizes the probation officer to determine reporting frequency, while the standard conditions keep that authority with the trial court. See text accompanying note 3 *supra.*

In addition, the form provides space for the court to order payment of court costs or fines, restitution, family support, or to impose other special conditions.[12]

In Milwaukee the trial judge imposes probation conditions orally from the bench. A verbatim transcript of the proceedings is given to the probation department, which relies on the transcript to determine what conditions were imposed. The trial judge routinely imposes seven probation conditions. The first states the objectives of probation, encourages the probationer to discuss problems with his officer, and advises him that the officer is available for assistance in securing employment. The second requires the probationer to report in person each month to the department's office until discharged from probation, unless he is instructed otherwise by his officer. The third states that he must conduct himself honestly and properly, not engage in criminal practices, and avoid evil companions and improper associates; it admonishes him to obey the laws and to abstain from the use of intoxicating liquors. The fourth rule imposes the condition that the probationer file with the department a monthly report written on standard forms, unless otherwise instructed by his officer. Rule five prohibits him from leaving the state without permission from his probation officer. Rule six states that the probationer must follow such additional instructions and rules as his supervising officer finds desirable or necessary. The seventh rule instructs the probationer that his officer keep the court informed about contacts during the probationary period and, at expiration, makes a final report to the court on his general conduct and conformity to rules and instructions; it suggests that the court is guided by the officer's report in its decision to discharge the probationer from supervision.[13]

In Wichita the trial judge orally imposes conditions. Three are routinely imposed: prohibition against violating the laws of Kansas or any municipal ordinance, or any federal law or the laws of any other state; requirement that the probationer register with and report to his probation officer as often as the latter requires;

[12] Conditions imposed in fewer than all cases at the time of granting probation are discussed in the following section.

[13] In Wisconsin, elsewhere than in Milwaukee County, the State Department of Public Welfare has authority to impose probation conditions. The trial courts have authority to impose conditions requiring payment of restitution or court costs. See Wis. Stat. Ann. §§57.01, 57.02 (1957) and notes 7 and 8 *supra* and accompanying text. The State Department has developed a Probation and Parole Agreement that specifies the conditions routinely imposed on every parole from a Wisconsin correctional institution and every probationer from a court outside of Milwaukee County. The complete agreement is reproduced in Chapter 13 as part of a discussion of parole conditions in Wisconsin.

and a statement that the probationer is subject to the payment of certain probation fees and expenses. If the court wishes to impose payment of probation fees, it simply specifies the amount.

3. *Conditions selectively imposed prior to supervision.* In practice, some probation conditions are imposed frequently, though not in every case. Since selection is involved, it is important to understand the bases upon which these conditions are imposed. Conditions frequently imposed are payment of restitution, court costs, or family support; provisions for leaving the state or changing place of residence; and particular requirements as to treatment or incarceration.

a. *Restitution.*

> *Illustration No. 1:* Two defendants each pleaded guilty to a charge of check forgery. Although they had admitted passing a number of checks, they were charged with only one violation. One defendant was given a prison sentence because of his extensive criminal record. The other defendant was placed on probation on condition he make restitution for all checks passed by the pair, the amount to be determined by the probation department.

In practice, it is usual to impose as a condition of probation the requirement that the defendant make restitution to the victim of his offense. The restitution condition can be viewed as a means of assisting the defendant in his rehabilitation by impressing upon him responsibility for his acts, or it can be viewed as a means of compensating victims for losses due to criminal offenses. While these purposes are usually compatible, they sometimes conflict. When restitution seems to conflict with rehabilitation goals, for example, when extreme financial hardships might result to a defendant who has not obtained financial gain from the offense,[14] some officials would argue that restitution should not be ordered. Many probation officers would take this position, arguing that rehabilitation must take precedence over restitution and that effective probation supervision is impossible when they must perform extensive collection agency functions.[15] Others would argue that

[14] This might be the case, for example, in negligent homicide or manslaughter or assault cases, when restitution is ordered for the expenses of hospitalization, for compensation for wage loss, and, in the event of death of the victim, for payment of funeral expenses and support payments to the surviving members of the victim's family.

[15] A probation and parole agent in the Wisconsin State Department of Public Welfare stated that he thought restitution orders frequently interfered with the rehabilitation of probationers. He said that probation was in danger of becoming a form of collection for victims rather than a period of rehabilitation for probationers.

the victim is too often forgotten in criminal justice administration and that restitution should be ordered even when it may interfere with the rehabilitation of the defendant.[16]

Restitution may be ordered in any case in which the victim has suffered a loss. Probably the most frequent are bad check and forgery cases and larceny cases in which the stolen property has not been recovered. In burglary cases, restitution may be ordered for damage to the building as well as unrecovered stolen property. Joyriding may result in a restitution order if the automobile is damaged. In assault cases, the court may order restitution to compensate the victim for hospital expenses and loss of earnings.[17] In negligent homicide or manslaughter cases, the restitution order may encompass hospital expenses, property damages, funeral expenses, and support for the deceased's dependents.[18]

The amount of restitution required of the defendant is usually determined by the probation department. In Detroit, the probation officer conducting the presentence investigation determines the extent of the victim's loss from the police report and interviews with the defendant. If the court places the defendant on probation with a restitution order, the amount is unspecified. The probation officer then verifies the restitution amount with the victim and again with the defendant. The court then specifies that amount in the restitution order. In Milwaukee a similar procedure is followed.[19]

16 If a prison sentence is imposed, the victim is relegated to his civil remedies to obtain restitution for the loss. Unless the defendant has an estate, there is little chance of receiving compensation while he is serving the prison sentence. Restitution is rarely, if ever, ordered as a condition of parole in the three states studied.

17 There apparently is no attempt in assault cases to compensate the victim for items of damages that in a civil case would be denominated "pain and suffering." Perhaps the reasons are the difficulty in determining the extent of such injuries and the trouble most defendants would have in making payments if such damages were included in the order. If the victim has obtained a civil verdict or a settlement of a civil case, the amount of the verdict or settlement may be used to determine the amount of the restitution order in the criminal case. Then, of course, the order is likely to encompass pain and suffering.

18 In one case the defendant, while intoxicated, crashed his car into another, killing both occupants, married men. He was originally charged with manslaughter with an automobile but pleaded guilty to negligent homicide. He was placed on probation for five years on condition he surrender his driver's license for that period and pay each widow $5 per week for five years. A check of supervision files four years later revealed that the defendant had complied with the restitution order with no difficulties.

19 A manual prepared for the Milwaukee County Probation Department which, although not officially adopted, reflects many of the practices observed during the field survey states: "1) When a court has ordered restitution, a form letter is sent to the person who incurred the loss, requesting verification of the amount. Also asked for is the name and address of the claims agent if the loss was paid by an insurance company. 2) When determination of the amount of restitution is made by the supervising officer, he must exercise caution. Itemized statements are to be

If the victim has filed or intends to file a civil suit to recover damages for the loss caused by the defendant's criminal conduct, the trial judge is likely to use the civil claim as a basis for ordering restitution. He may order restitution but leave the amount unspecified until the civil case is settled or a verdict returned [20] or he may even incorporate into the restitution order the amount of any civil verdict that later may be obtained. When no civil suit is involved and the restitution amount is determined by the criminal court, there is, of course, an increased possibility of error,[21] even to the extent that restitution may be ordered under circumstances that would not give rise to civil liability.[22] If the defendant believes the probation department's determination of the victim's loss is excessive, he will normally have an opportunity to inform the trial judge of the reasons for his belief.[23]

---

obtained where possible. These are checked with the probationer to eliminate errors, establish validity, and secure his acknowledgment in writing." A survey of one probation officer's supervision file indicated that when restitution is ordered the victim is contacted by letter to verify the extent of loss.

[20] In one case in which the defendant had pleaded guilty to felonious assault, the judge placed the defendant on probation and ordered restitution but did not specify the amount because the defendant's attorney informed him that the victim's civil suit would probably be settled for the costs of hospitalization. The judge instructed the attorney to inform the probation department of the amount of the settlement and stated that a restitution order for that amount would be entered.

A Michigan trial judge stated that in cases of negligent homicide and manslaughter with an automobile he orders restitution in the amount of any civil verdict or settlement which has occurred or may occur. He said further that if he believed the civil settlement did not adequately provide for the wife and the children of the deceased, he might require additional restitution for them.

[21] One trial judge reported a case in which the defendants had pleaded guilty to robbery unarmed. They were apprehended within hours of the offense and turned $600 over to the police, which they claimed was the full amount stolen. The victim alleged that $1300 was stolen and claimed the remainder from his insurance company. The company paid $700 and requested a restitution order for that amount. The trial judge said he refused to enter such an order unless the victim could prove that in excess of $600 had been stolen. The judge said that the victim did not attempt to prove the loss and it was his opinion that in fact only $600 was stolen.

[22] In a Michigan State Bar Association committee meeting a case was discussed in which the defendant pleaded guilty to leaving the scene of an accident. He was placed on probation on condition he make restitution to the victim of the automobile accident. He complied with the restitution order. The victim then instituted a civil suit against the defendant for losses occurring in the automobile accident, including pain and suffering, which were not included in the restitution order. The jury returned a verdict in favor of the defendant because they found the plaintiff had been contributorily negligent.

[23] In one Michigan case, the defendant had pleaded guilty to felonious assault. The defendant had injured the victim in a drunken fray. The presentence report assessed the victim's injuries at a certain amount, which included loss of earnings. The defendant and his attorney informed the court that the manufacturing concern for which both defendant and victim worked had not been operating for six weeks because of a strike. The judge then reduced the restitution amount to take account of the strike.

As observed earlier, if the defendant has admitted to the police that he has committed a number of offenses, he may be charged with only one or two of them; the remainder are brought to the attention of the court in the presentence report (Detroit), by stipulation of the parties in the postplea of guilty hearing (Milwaukee), or informally by the prosecutor prior to sentencing (Wichita). If the defendant is placed on probation, restitution is usually ordered for the offenses the defendant admits committing as well as the one or two offenses of which he was convicted. The probation department contacts each victim and attempts to obtain information to substantiate the loss claimed. One Kansas trial judge refuses to include uncharged offenses in the restitution order on the ground he is not running a collection agency: If the victim wants restitution he can prosecute the offense committed against him.[24]

If more than one person is convicted of an offense and all are placed on probation, each defendant is usually required to pay an equal amount in restitution; no attempt is made to apportion the restitution burden on the basis of degree of culpability or other factors. The problem becomes more difficult when one co-defendant is sentenced to prison and the other is placed on probation. As a practical matter, there is little hope of obtaining restitution from the one sentenced. The question then becomes whether the defendant placed on probation should be required to make full or partial restitution. The trial judge in Milwaukee regularly requires the defendant placed on probation to make full restitution. In the only case of this kind observed in Detroit, two of three co-defendants were sentenced and the third was placed on probation on condition he make restitution of one-third of the victim's loss.[25]

[24] There is support in the Kansas probation statutes for the position taken by this judge. The statute in force at the time of the field survey authorized a restitution order "for actual damages or loss caused by the offense for which conviction was had. . . ." Kan. Gen. Stat. §62-2203 (1949) repealed by Kan. Laws 1957, Ch. 331, §37. The present Kansas statute authorizes an order to the defendant to "make reparation or restitution to the aggrieved party for the damage or loss caused by his offense in an amount to be determined by the court. . . ." Kan. Stat. Ann. §62-2241 (1964).

[25] In one Milwaukee case, two defendants were convicted of robbery unarmed. One was on active duty in the Navy and had gone AWOL before committing the offense. He was placed on probation on condition he pay court costs and submit himself to the Navy's custody. A Navy representative had informed the court that he would probably be court-martialed. The other defendant was placed on probation on condition he make full restitution. The judge explained that normally he places the restitution burden equally on co-defendants. In this case, however, there was little likelihood the other defendant would be able to make restitution payments as a result of discipline anticipated from the Navy. The other defendant, however, would be in the community working and could make the payments. Although full responsibility was placed on one defendant, the court instructed the probation department to attempt to secure payment of one-half the loss from the

The financial ability of the defendant to make restitution is sometimes taken into account at the time he is placed on probation and always throughout the supervision process. A Michigan trial judge recalled a case in which he would have required restitution but for the fact the defendant was attempting to support his wife and five children on a limited income; requiring restitution would have imposed a useless hardship on the defendant and his family. There is some indication that if the defendant is supported in whole or part by public welfare benefits, restitution will not be required.[26] The restitution order normally requires the full payment to be made before the end of the probation period. In almost all cases, the payments are made in installments, accumulated in special probation department accounts, and paid to the victim when the full amount has been collected. If the defendant's probation period is almost over and full restitution has not been made, supervision may be extended if it appears the probationer can make full restitution if given additional time. If it appears unlikely the defendant will be able to make full restitution, the probation officer will often ask the court to waive the restitution requirement and discharge the defendant from probation. Because of the availability of this waiver device, there is little concern over ability to pay at the time the defendant is placed on probation except in dramatic cases; it is contemplated that adjustments will be made if it later appears the defendant is unable to meet the obligation. Probation is virtually never revoked solely because the defendant has failed to pay restitution.

b. *Court costs.*

> *Illustration No. 2:* The defendant pleaded guilty to embezzlement. The trial judge said to the defendant, "I understand you and your husband will restore this money and that you won't embezzle further. I'll place you on probation for two years to make restitution and waive the costs in this case because of the large amount of money you'll have to make restitution on. The probation officer will work out the arrangements with you as to restitution."

In each of the three states, it is typical for a probationer to be required to pay court costs as a condition of probation. In Wichita,

---

other defendant. If that failed, the defendant remaining in Milwaukee could be held responsible for the full amount.

26 The proposed handbook for the Milwaukee County Probation Department, discussed in note 19 *supra,* makes the following statement: "No payments on court obligations are accepted from probationers, either single or married, who are receiving full or partial public assistance. These grants are based upon need, and to require payment of these obligations would cause financial hardship, and would involve the use of public funds for such payment."

court costs of $30 to $35 are imposed in virtually every case; in addition, a probation fee of $3 per year is required of every probationer.[27] Court costs and probation fees are not waived even when it appears the defendant is financially unable to pay them.[28] In Milwaukee, court costs of $50 to $60 are imposed in almost every case.[29] If it later appears the probationer is financially unable to pay costs, probation may be extended and, if it appears further extensions will not be useful, the requirement will be waived and the defendant discharged from probation.[30]

In Detroit, court costs are imposed in all cases except those in which the defendant is financially unable to make payment.[31] By act of the judges of Recorder's Court *en banc,* a uniform assessment of $50 per year for felony cases and $25 per year for misdemeanor cases is made.[32] This is intended to cover the costs of supervision. In addition, if the defendant was represented by court-appointed

27 This is intended to cover the full costs of probation supervision. The full probation fee at the rate of $3 per each year of the probation period must be paid as soon as the defendant is placed on probation. One probation officer stated he has little difficulty collecting probation fees since the defendants fear they will not be placed on probation unless they are paid.

28 One probation officer stated that, although court costs and probation fees are never waived, restitution may be waived if the probationer has paid costs and is financially unable to pay restitution. Probation will be extended if court costs have not been paid at the expiration of the supervision period. The total probation period cannot exceed five years, however. Kan. Gen. Stat. §62-2203 (1949), repealed by Kan. Laws 1957, Ch. 331, §37. Under present law, the probation period cannot extend beyond the maximum sentence permitted for the offense of which the defendant was convicted. Kan. Stat. Ann. §62-2243 (1964).

29 In one rural Wisconsin county, the trial judge regularly required of probationers payment of the costs of pretrial detention in the county jail. In one case, this order required a payment in excess of $130. The State Department of Public Welfare sought an opinion from the Attorney General, who declared this an invalid condition.

30 A proposed handbook for the Milwaukee County Probation Department states: "Priority in collection of financial obligations is given to court costs and fines, unless payment of restitution is ordered within a certain period of time, or in abandonment cases where the probationer's earnings are sufficient to meet only support payments."

31 A check of supervision records in the Men's Felony Division of the Detroit Probation Department revealed that court costs were imposed in 82 percent of the cases placed on probation to that division in 1956. Costs are not imposed when the defendant is financially unable to pay them, as in the illustration case. In a second case, the defendant was ill and unemployed, so costs were not required. In a third case, the defendant was old and blind and for that reason costs were not imposed.

32 Mich. Stat. Ann. §28.1133 (1954) seems to authorize this method of taxing costs: "in case it requires the probationer to pay any costs it shall not be confined to or governed by the laws or rules governing the taxation of costs in ordinary criminal procedure, but may summarily tax and determine such costs without regard to the items ordinarily included in taxing costs in criminal cases and may include therein all such expenses, direct and indirect, as the public has been or may be put to in connection with the apprehension, examination, trial and probationary oversight of the probationer."

counsel, a condition may be imposed requiring reimbursement to the county of the amount it paid the attorney.[33]

If the defendant was returned from another state to stand trial, court costs in the event of probation will normally include the costs of bringing him to the place of trial, which, in some cases, may amount to several hundred dollars.[34] Greater than usual court costs may also be imposed as a punitive measure.[35] Normally, however, they are regarded as simply a way of minimizing the expense to the public of operating the probation system. In addition, some judges regard the payment of court costs as a helpful rehabilitative device.[36]

c. *Family support.* A defendant who is convicted of nonsupport, desertion, or abandonment is usually placed on probation on condition he support his family.[37] This is not surprising since the apparent reason for making nonsupport a criminal offense is to create the leverage often necessary to persuade husbands to support their families. Probation is an effective way of accomplishing this. A special probation condition requiring family support may also be imposed upon a defendant convicted of other offenses if he is known not to have supported his family.

If the defendant is living with the family, the condition requires no implementation other than the probation officer assuring himself that the defendant is employed or actually seeking employment and adequately supporting his family with his earnings. Reliance is placed on routine interrogation of the defendant at the office and an expectation that members of the probationer's family will complain to the probation officer if support is not provided. When the defendant is separated or divorced from his wife, or

[33] The payment for assigned counsel in the routine felony guilty plea case is $75.

[34] In one Wisconsin case a girl was returned from Florida. She was convicted and placed on probation on condition she pay $250 restitution and $500 for expenses incurred in returning her to Wisconsin. In one Kansas case the defendant's return from Seattle, Washington, to Wichita added about $500 to his court costs.

[35] In a Michigan case a defendant was convicted of operating a gambling establishment and placed on probation for two years. Normal costs would have been $100. He was fined $100 and costs of $250 were assessed. In a Wisconsin case the defendant was convicted after a jury trial in which he testified to his innocence. With great reluctance, the trial court judge placed him on probation. He required as a condition of probation that the defendant pay the jury expenses in his case because he had committed perjury in his defense and had attempted to perpetrate a fraud upon the jury. The judge stated he had never imposed such a condition before this case.

[36] Two Michigan judges stated they believed that requiring payment of court costs was a helpful rehabilitative technique in cases of young offenders on the ground it makes them accept responsibility for their offense and making the payments is a good device to teach them discipline. In addition, one of the judges stated that with young offenders he tells the parents not to pay the costs for the defendant; he admitted, however, that such an order is difficult to enforce.

[37] See Chapter 3.

when the support of an illegitimate child with whom he is not living is involved, the support order normally requires the probationer to make the support payment to the probation officer. The officer, in turn, remits the payments to the probationer's family, or to the public welfare agency if the family is receiving public assistance. If support has been ordered in a divorce, separation, or paternity decree, the probation condition requires support in that amount. In the absence of such a decree, the amount of support is determined by the probation department and depends primarily upon the probationer's income and number of dependents. Probation is virtually never revoked solely for failure to comply with the family support condition.

d. *Leave the state or change place of residence.*

Illustration No. 3: The defendant pleaded guilty to check forgery. He was a resident of Indiana but wished to seek employment in Chicago, Illinois. The probation department recommended probation on condition the defendant leave the State of Wisconsin and not return. The trial court placed the defendant on probation for one year on condition he return to Indiana or Chicago, Illinois, that the probation department should make sure he leaves Wisconsin, and that he is not to return to Wisconsin without the permission of the probation department.

Every major metropolitan area receives its share of transient criminal offenders. Such a person is likely to be regarded as "belonging" to some other state. If he is placed on probation, a condition will often be attached requiring him to leave the state and not return. Usually the defendant consents to the condition, perhaps because he may view the alternatives as those of leaving the state or being sentenced to prison. This practice was observed in Milwaukee but not in Wichita[38] or Detroit.[39]

The Milwaukee practice is not the simple dumping of undesir-

[38] In misdemeanor cases and ordinance violations, Wichita courts sometimes place the defendant on "sundown probation," which simply requires him to leave the city or county within twenty-four hours or a jail sentence will be imposed. This is simply banishment; there is no attempt to supervise the defendant or even to determine where he is going. No cases were observed in which sundown probation was used in felony cases.

[39] A Detroit judge stated that Michigan law prohibits the imposition of a probation condition requiring the probationer to leave the state. He cited People v. Smith, 252 Mich. 4, 232 N.W. 397 (1930), holding that requiring a probationer in a case of disturbing the peace to move from his neighborhood is an invalid probation condition. However, the judge continued that when it seems desirable for the defendant to return to his home, whether it is in Michigan or another state, he will "suggest" to him that he do so during the probation period. He stated the suggestion is most likely to be used when a transient comes to Detroit and commits an offense but has neither employment nor relatives in the city. However, a formal condition requiring such conduct is not imposed.

ables upon other states. The probation department attempts to secure real supervision over the defendant in the state to which he is returning. If the probation department views the probation system in the other state as adequate, it attempts to secure supervision over the defendant under the Interstate Compact.[40] If the system is viewed as inadequate, the probation department will avoid the delays involved in securing Compact supervision and simply supervise the case directly by requiring the defendant to submit regular reports by mail.[41]

Cases were observed in which there were unusual pressures to remove the defendant from the neighborhood in which he resided. Especially in cases involving taking indecent liberties with a child, the offender's neighbors may become very anxious to secure his removal to prevent further offenses against children living in the area. In these cases, the court may be faced with choosing between sentencing the defendant to prison or placing him on probation on condition he move from the neighborhood to an area with no children.[42]

[40] The Interstate Compact for the Supervision of Parolees and Probationers, a product of the Council of State Governments, sets up machinery for the supervision of probationers and parolees in states other than where they were given probation or parole. The Compact has been adopted by all fifty states. See Council of State Governments, The Handbook on Interstate Crime Control 4 (1966). The provisions of the Compact have been summarized as follows:

"1. Any state will accept supervision of a parolee or probationer if he has the proper residence and employment qualifications. . . . If he is not qualified in this regard the state has a choice as to whether or not to accept him, and he may not be sent there without its consent.

"2. The supervising state . . . must use the same standards of supervision for cases sent from other states as it does for its own parolees and probationers. . . .

"3. The sentencing state . . . may retake a person being supervised under the compact at any time without formalities. . . . All legal requirements to obtain extradition of fugitives from justice are expressly waived by the states under the compact and by the individual parolee or probationer who signs a waiver of extradition before he leaves the sending state." Id. at 5.

[41] See page 132. A probation condition similar to leaving the state may be imposed in other cases. For example, in one Wisconsin case the defendant was AWOL from the Navy when he committed an offense. A Navy officer informed the court that he would be court-martialed when the Navy obtained custody of him. He was placed on probation on condition he submit himself to the custody of the Navy for disciplinary action.

In a number of cases probation is used to assist in the disposition of the multiple offender. When, during its investigation, the probation department discovers a detainer against the defendant, it may suggest to the court that he be placed on probation on condition he submit himself to the custody of the authority lodging the detainer. The court may then place him on probation on that condition and order him to be held in custody until the jurisdiction filing the detainer picks him up. If he is not taken to the other jurisdiction within a reasonable time, the trial court then considers the question whether to sentence the defendant to prison or place him on probation in the community.

[42] In a Milwaukee case the defendant, sixty-six years of age, was convicted of taking indecent liberties with two children living next door to him. The presentence

e. *Treatment.*

Illustration No. 4: The defendant pleaded guilty to incest and taking indecent liberties with a minor. A presentence psychiatric examination was conducted and the report recommended that the defendant be committed to a mental hospital. The trial court placed the defendant on probation on condition his wife apply to the probate court immediately for his commitment to a public mental hospital.

In sex cases, trial courts frequently require treatment as a special condition of probation. In Detroit, a condition requiring outpatient treatment is almost always imposed in cases involving indecent liberties with a child or homosexual behavior between adults. However, unless the defendant is financially capable of obtaining private treatment, the condition is not complied with because of the difficulty of obtaining psychiatric treatment for the indigent.[43]

Each of the three states has sexual psychopath statutes permitting lengthy incarceration for inpatient treatment.[44] Although incarceration may seem necessary, the court sometimes prefers the more permissive atmosphere of a civil commitment to a public mental hospital over the more secure custody imposed on persons held under sexual psychopath commitments; in such cases, civil commitment may be made a condition of probation.[45] If the defendant's family is able to afford private inpatient psychiatric care, that may be made a condition of probation.[46]

---

examination required by the Wisconsin Sex Crimes Act was conducted and probation was recommended. See Wis. Stat. Ann. §959.15 (1958). The entire neighborhood was quite upset over the offense and the parents of the victims made arrangements to move from the neighborhood. A plan was finally devised in which the defendant agreed to sell his house and buy one in a rural part of the state with which he was familiar. Probation was granted on condition he move to that particular location immediately and not return to Milwaukee County.

[43] The Chief Probation Officer in Detroit stated the outpatient treatment condition is not implemented unless the defendant can afford private psychiatric care. He could not recall a case in which probation was revoked for failure to obtain the required psychiatric care.

Several probation officers voiced the opinion that it is useless to impose an outpatient treatment condition on homosexuals even if psychiatric resources are available because the psychiatrist will simply help the defendant accept his problem and confine his homosexual activities to adults. The probation officers further said they tell homosexuals simply to confine their sexual activities to consenting adults, and most of them do; in terms of cooperation with the department and regular reporting they clearly are the best probationers.

[44] See Chapter 7 for a discussion of these statutes and their administration in the three states.

[45] This was the situation in the illustration case. There was no evidence the defendant had engaged in indecent behavior with anyone except his two daughters. Before the sentence hearing, they had both been taken from the custody of their parents by juvenile authorities and placed in detention.

[46] In Detroit, a defendant pleaded guilty to gross indecency. A presentence psychiatric examination was conducted by the Psychopathic Clinic and the report

Under the Wisconsin Sex Crimes Act[47] persons convicted of specified sex offenses must be examined by the State Department of Public Welfare prior to sentence. If the department's report recommends specialized treatment of the defendant under the Sex Crimes Act, the court may either commit him to the custody of the department or place him on probation "with the requirement as a condition of such probation, that he receive outpatient treatment in such manner as the court shall prescribe. . . ." [48] Although the statutory condition is regularly imposed when required by law, there is evidence that in some cases the court and the probation service make no effort to secure compliance with it.[49]

f. *Incarceration.*

> *Illustration No. 5:* The defendant entered a plea of guilty to larceny from a building, a felony. He had stolen a canister set from a muscular dystrophy clinic. His record consisted of sixteen arrests, seven traffic violations, and convictions of two misdemeanors and one felony. The trial judge told the defendant he had done "the lowest of lowest things." The defendant had no explanation for his conduct and stated he would do anything to rectify his mistake. The judge said, "I should throw the book at you, but after reading both the clinic and probation department reports, I will place you on probation for two years. The first sixty days of this probation, however, are to be spent in the House of Correction."

---

recommended proceedings to commit the defendant as a criminal sexual psychopath. The trial judge indicated that the defendant came from a good family who expressed interest in securing private psychiatric care for him and he wished to give the family an opportunity to secure such treatment if they could. He placed the defendant on probation for two years, on condition he spend the first sixty days in the Detroit House of Correction. He said further that if the family secured care in a private psychiatric hospital, he would release him from jail. If such care were not secured within sixty days, he would reconsider the entire situation and, perhaps, sentence him to prison or initiate proceedings to have him declared a criminal sexual psychopath. A third alternative, mentioned by the judge because the defendant seemed of unsound mind, was to seek a probate court commitment as a mentally ill person.

47 Wis. Stat. Ann. §959.15 (1958).

48 Wis. Stat. Ann. §959.15(6) (1958). Wis. Laws 1961, Ch. 169, amended this provision to permit the trial judge to require either inpatient or outpatient treatment as a condition of probation. Under present law, the trial judge must require one or the other.

49 In a Milwaukee case the psychiatrist who conducted the presentence examination expressed his opinion that psychiatric treatment would be of no help to the defendant. When the trial court placed the defendant on probation, he imposed the mandatory outpatient treatment condition. There was little expectation the condition would be enforced since the defendant was moving to a place in rural Wisconsin where psychiatric resources were scarce, he had insufficient funds to obtain private treatment, and a psychiatrist had expressed his view that psychiatric treatment would not help him.

Michigan law authorizes the trial judge to impose as a condition of probation a term in a local correctional institution for a period not to exceed sixty days.[50] It is not clear how frequently this provision is invoked. One judge stated he almost never uses it because a defendant who has been humiliated by being placed in jail cannot be rehabilitated by a subsequent period of probation supervision. Other judges appear to use the provision when they cannot decide whether to sentence the defendant to prison or place him on probation.[51] Still other judges sometimes invoke the provision to keep the defendant in secure custody while awaiting the completion of arrangements for other dispositions.[52]

[50] Mich. Stat. Ann. §28.1133 (1954) provides: "As a condition of probation, the court may require the probationer to be immediately imprisoned in the county jail for not more than sixty [60] days. . . ." Mich. Pub. Acts 1957, No. 72, amended this provision to read: "As a condition of probation, the court may require the probationer to be imprisoned in the county jail or the house of correction for not more than 6 months, at such time or intervals, which may be consecutive or non-consecutive, within the probation period as the court in its discretion may determine. . . . But the period of confinement shall not exceed the maximum period of imprisonment provided for the offense charged if such maximum period is less than 6 months." Mich. Stat. Ann. §28.1133 (Supp. 1965). The primary purpose of the amendment was apparently to authorize a work release or Huber Law type of procedure in which the defendant spends nights and weekends in jail and works in the community under probation supervision the remainder of the time.

[51] This appears to be the situation in the illustration case. In another case, three defendants pleaded guilty to breaking and entering. They had been apprehended in the process of removing a safe from a business establishment. Two of them were sentenced to prison, one because he had a long criminal record, the other because he used narcotics. The probation department and the Psychopathic Clinic recommended probation for the third defendant. The trial judge said, "What worries me is that anybody breaking into a building and caught in the process of moving a safe out of it has tendencies to be a hardened and habitual criminal." He placed the defendant on probation for three years on condition he serve the first sixty days in the Detroit House of Correction.

[52] See the case discussed in note 46 *supra*. In 1955 the Michigan legislature authorized the establishment and use of a probation camp to provide a healthy environment and work experience for young adult offenders who have neither adequate homes nor employment opportunities. A camp was actually established by the Department of Correction over 100 miles from Detroit. The program consisted of conservation work, group discussion sessions, and maintenance work. Mich. Stat. Ann. §28.1133(1) (Supp. 1965) provides:

"Any person under the age of 22 years who shall be convicted of a crime in this state for which a sentence in the state prison may be imposed may be required, under and pursuant to a probation order of the court, to spend such part of the probation period, not exceeding 1 year, as the court may direct, in such probation camp as may be made available to the court by the department of correction, provided that admission to such camp will be made with the prior consent of the department of correction. The department shall have custody of the person of such probationer for such period as the court may direct. Any probationer fleeing the custody of the department may be pursued and recaptured as if he had been regularly committed to a penal institution and had escaped therefrom. A violation by the probationer of the rules and regulations of the department shall constitute sufficient grounds for the revocation by the court of its probation order in such case and for the sentencing of the probationer for the offense for which he was originally convicted and placed on probation."

Under Wisconsin's Huber Law, the trial court may sentence a defendant to a local correctional institution under conditions that permit him to leave the institution to perform work or other approved activities in the community.[53] A Huber Law offender is not on probation while in the community, but he is subject to similar controls since the Huber sentence can be changed at any time into an ordinary jail sentence.[54] Although the statute is applicable to persons convicted of felonies,[55] it has been used in Milwaukee County almost exclusively for misdemeanants.[56]

g. *Other special conditions.*

> *Illustration No. 6:* The defendant, age seventeen, pleaded guilty to carrying a concealed weapon. He had admitted to the police that he and another youth planned to use the gun in a holdup. Because the defendant had no serious criminal or juvenile record, the judge placed him on probation for two years, saying, "I'm going to require you to stay off the streets after 12:00 midnight. Now, if you can't do this, tell me. There'll be no monkey business about it; you either do it or you don't." The defendant indicated he would do it and left the room.

The latitude afforded the trial judge to devise and impose probation conditions on a case-by-case basis is virtually unlimited, because statutes typically grant him broad discretion to impose any probation conditions he thinks proper.[57] Although the exercise of

[53] Wis. Stat. Ann. §56.08 (1957). The present law provides: "Any person sentenced to a county jail for crime . . . may be granted the privilege of leaving the jail during necessary and reasonable hours for any of the following purposes . . . : (a) Seeking employment; (b) Working at his employment; (c) Conducting his own business or other self-employed occupation including, in the case of a woman, housekeeping and attending the needs of her family; (d) Attendance at an educational institution; or (e) Medical treatment. Wis. Stat. Ann. §56.08(1) (Supp. 1967).

[54] Wis. Stat. Ann. §56.08(6) (1957) provides: "In case of the violation of the conditions laid down for his conduct, custody and employment, he shall be returned to the court; and it may then require that the balance of his sentence be spent in actual confinement and may cancel any earned diminution of his term." For the present law, unchanged in substance, see Wis. Stat. Ann. §56.08 (2) (Supp. 1967).

[55] The heading of the statute in force during the field survey was "Employment of misdemeanants," but its body spoke of "Any person sentenced to the county jail. . . ." Wis. Stat. Ann. §56.08 (1957). Since persons convicted of many felonies can be sentenced to a county jail or a state correctional institution, it was the opinion of the felony court judge in Milwaukee that the law is applicable to felonies despite its heading. In a subsequent revision of the statute a new heading was provided: "'Huber law'; employment of county jail prisoners," which would support the view that the provisions are available to persons convicted of felonies who are sentenced to the county jail. Wis. Stat. Ann. §56.08 (Supp. 1967).

[56] During 1955, 412 prisoners were accepted in the Milwaukee County Jail under the Huber Law. All of them had been convicted of misdemeanors except one, who had been convicted of negligent homicide.

[57] See notes 1, 5, and 6 *supra* and accompanying text. In Wisconsin outside of

this discretion tends to become routinized into standard probation conditions that are imposed in every case,[58] there still remains a considerable amount of individualization in formulating and imposing conditions.

In Detroit several trial judges indicated that they impose a curfew on youthful offenders placed on probation.[59] In the absence of a curfew, the probationer's conduct is regulated by a condition imposed in every case that he "keep regular and reasonable hours." [60] Although the standard probation conditions require the probationer to "avoid questionable associates and places," [61] several trial judges indicated that, if a youthful offender engages in criminal conduct as a member of a gang, they were likely specifically to prohibit the offender from associating with any members of that gang.

When the criminal offense involves the use of an automobile, trial judges in both Detroit and Milwaukee were observed to require the defendant to surrender his motor vehicle operator's license as a condition of probation.[62] Some trial judges in Detroit frequently prohibit adults from using intoxicants to excess and prohibit youthful offenders from using them at all. If there appears to be a close relationship between the defendant's drinking and his criminal activity, the trial judge may prohibit an adult from using any intoxicants.

In Detroit a probation condition required of each probationer is that he "endeavor to accumulate some savings." [63] One Detroit trial judge requires the probationer to place in an escrow account in the probation department a specified amount of money each

---

Milwaukee County, the trial court is limited to imposing conditions concerning restitution and court costs, but the State Department of Public Welfare has discretion to impose any conditions it thinks proper. See notes 7 and 8 *supra* and accompanying text.

The draftsmen of the Model Penal Code attempted to limit judicial discretion to devise and impose probation conditions on the grounds that current practice often results in the imposition of conditions that unnecessarily interfere with the defendant's liberty. After authorizing a large number of conditions, however, the Code permits the trial judge to require the defendant "to satisfy any other conditions reasonably related to the rehabilitation of the defendant and not unduly restrictive of his liberty or incompatible with his freedom of conscience." Model Penal Code §301.1 (Proposed Official Draft, 1962).

[58] See notes 9-13 *supra* and accompanying text.

[59] If the trial court does not impose a curfew, the supervising probation officer sometimes does. See page 119.

[60] See text accompanying notes 9-11 *supra*.

[61] Ibid.

[62] In Detroit, a defendant pleaded guilty to negligent homicide. While drunk, he had crashed his car into another, killing its two occupants. He was placed on probation for five years on condition he surrender his motor vehicle operator's license for the entire probation period.

[63] See text accompanying notes 9-11 *supra*.

week, to be accumulated and returned to him when he is discharged from probation.[64]

4. *Conditions imposed or waived after supervision has begun.*

Illustration No. 7: A sixteen-year-old defendant was placed on probation on condition the first sixty days be spent in the house of correction. The trial court imposed no other special probation conditions. After the probationer was released from confinement, the Youth Division of the probation department imposed special probation conditions requiring an 11:00 P.M. curfew, residence with the probationer's parents, and nonassociation with the co-defendant in the case.

The probation department has broad supervising powers over a probationer. The probation officer interprets to the probationer the conditions of probation imposed by the trial court, some of which are sufficiently vague to permit considerable latitude in construction.[65] In each of the three states, the probation officer is expressly delegated the authority to determine how frequently the probationer must report.[66] Often, the trial court imposes conditions of probation that the probationer must observe unless the supervising probation officer consents to noncomplying conduct in advance.[67]

[64] In one misdemeanor case the defendant was placed on probation for two years for simple assault on condition he pay $20 per week into an escrow account in the probation department. After the expiration of the two-year period, the probation officer returned the case to court requesting the defendant's discharge from probation and a court order paying the defendant the $2080 in the escrow account. There is some evidence that failure to comply with this condition is a very strong factor in the judge's decision whether to revoke probation, should the case be returned to court for a revocation hearing. Probation officers frequently tell their clients that the judge means business and that failure to save may result in revocation.

[65] In Detroit, a probation condition imposed in every case instructs the probationer to "avoid questionable associates." The Detroit probation department interprets this condition to prohibit association with ex-convicts. The probation officers stress this condition when supervising a probationer with a record of addiction to or trafficking in narcotics and repeatedly warn against associating with known addicts or peddlers.

[66] A Milwaukee condition requires monthly reporting unless otherwise instructed by the probation officer and a Wichita condition requires the probationer to report as often as the probation officer directs. Mich. Stat. Ann. §28.1133 (1954) requires reporting once monthly or as often as the probation officer requires, but the standard probation conditions used in Detroit require weekly reporting unless otherwise ordered by the court. See text accompanying note 11 *supra*. In practice the supervising probation officer determines reporting frequency without consulting the trial court.

[67] Milwaukee probation conditions prohibit the probationer from leaving the state without the consent of the probation officer. The Probation and Parole Agreement used by the State Department of Public Welfare in Wisconsin outside Milwaukee County provides:

"I will secure advance approval from the Probation and Parole Officer in writing, if practicable, if at any time I wish to:

"a. Purchase or operate a motor vehicle.

The standard probation conditions often grant general authority to the probation officer to impose any probation conditions he considers appropriate.[68] Moreover, the power of the probation officer to request or not request revocation in the event of a violation of conditions[69] gives considerable sanction to any suggestions he may make to the probationer concerning his behavior. In general, the probationer is under an obligation to "cooperate" [70] with his

---

"b. Incur debts whether by borrowing money or installment buying.
"c. Take on additional responsibilities, such as marrying.
"d. Change employment or place of residence.
"e. Leave the state.
"f. Own or carry firearms or other weapons."

In Detroit probationers at one time were prohibited from marrying without obtaining the consent of their probation officer.

[68] A Milwaukee condition states that the probationer must follow such additional instructions and rules as his supervising officer finds desirable or necessary. In practice the Milwaukee probation department does not impose additional probation conditions on a routine basis, but they are imposed in individual cases.

The Probation and Parole Agreement in effect in Wisconsin outside Milwaukee County provides: "I will be guided by such specific instructions as may be issued by the Probation and Parole Officer with regard to companions, hours, intoxicants, medical attention, family responsibilities and support of self, court obligations or other special restrictions listed below."

In Detroit each probationer is given a booklet in which to record his earnings and expenditures. The statutory probation conditions are set out along with any special conditions imposed by the court. Then follows a statement titled "What Your Probation Officer Expects" as follows:

"That you will call on him whenever in need of advice. That if you are laid off notify office. That you will mark your time page daily. That you will be strictly honest in your record of time put in and wages earned. That you will avoid such employment that will bring you in relation with questionable characters. That you will not change employment without taking up the matter of the proposed change with him before you leave your present work. That proposed changes of residence will be taken up with him before the removal is made. That if you are ill or meet with an accident you will request that the probation officer be informed of the fact. That in case of an arrest you will ask the desk sergeant to notify your probation officer. That you will not engage in any illegal activity and will avoid association with questionable characters. That you will avoid association with other probationers and paroled men, and very particularly of such men as would engage with you in the same offense." In addition, the court order of probation lists the probation conditions, standard and special, imposed by the court.

[69] In practice, the probation officer exercises considerable discretion in deciding whether to request probation revocation when a violation becomes known to him. In fact, most violations known to the supervising officer do not result in a request for revocation. See the discussion of probation officer discretion not to seek revocation in Chapter 5. In addition, the probation officer has discretion to request the court to waive any special conditions it may have imposed on the probationer. This is done frequently in cases in which the probationer is financially unable to comply with conditions requiring payment of court costs or restitution.

[70] A condition imposed in every case in Detroit provides that the "probationer shall cooperate at all times with the probation officer" and instructs the probationer that "in case of doubt, consult the probation officer." A Milwaukee condition imposed in every case instructs the probationer that his officer keeps the court informed about contacts during the probation period and, at the expiration, makes a final report to the court on his general conduct and conformity to rules and

probation officer and the threat of revocation always exists when there is a failure of cooperation.[71]

5. *Communicating conditions to probationers.* In practice, care is taken that the probationer understands the conditions of his probation. In Detroit, when a defendant is placed on probation he is taken to the probation department office, where he is briefly interviewed to gather basic information about him for departmental files. He is given a copy of the court order of probation which sets out the conditions, standard and special, imposed by the court.[72] He is required to read these conditions in the presence of the interviewer and is given an opportunity to ask questions about them. If there is reason to believe he may not understand any of them, the interviewing officer carefully explains them. In Milwaukee, in a similar interview, the probationer is required to sign a document that sets out the probation conditions and is given a copy to retain. If he is illiterate, the conditions are read to him and carefully explained.

The probationer thereafter has his initial interview with the officer who will supervise him, and the probation conditions are usually discussed again. The officer explains to the probationer which conditions he thinks are most important in his case. The process of communicating the conditions to the probationer continues throughout the probation period, because whenever the probationer becomes involved in a possible breach of a condition, the probation officer will frequently respond with an interview in which he emphasizes the importance to the probationer of the violated condition and threatens revocation if further violations occur.

B. Probation Supervision

Probation statutes are based upon the assumption that probationers are given meaningful supervision, an assumption that may often be contrary to fact. Probation is one thing if supervision involves frequent contacts with a probation officer who has the time,

---

instructions and suggests that the court is guided by the officer's report in making its decision whether to discharge the probationer from supervision. The Probation and Parole Agreement in effect in Wisconsin outside Milwaukee County requires the probationer to promise: "I will, to the best of my ability, take advantage of the opportunities offered me by probation," and "If I prove myself unsuited to supervision, I will hold myself ready to be . . . returned to the court which placed me on probation. . . ."

[71] Later discussion will make clear the extent to which failure to cooperate with the probation officer is a factor in decisions to extend probation, discharge the probationer, or revoke probation.

[72] For a description of the departmental conditions in Detroit, see note 68 *supra.*

ability, and inclination to work with the probationer's problems; it is quite another when supervision involves only a few perfunctory reports per year to a probation officer burdened with a large caseload. Which type of supervision prevails depends in part upon forces outside the control of the individual probation officer or even the probation department. It depends upon the level of appropriations that legislative bodies are willing to make, upon the willingness of trial judges to place defendants on probation, and upon the availability of resources to handle special cases — such as nonsupport — which otherwise would find their way into the probation caseload. It also depends upon the availability of able personnel.

But within these limitations, the probation department and the individual probation officer make decisions that vitally affect the nature of the supervision including its objectives, the techniques used, the intensity of supervision, and its duration. It is upon these decisions that this discussion focuses.

1. *The objectives of probation supervision.* Within resource limitations and subject to an occasional specific instruction from a trial judge, the probation department is free to define its function in carrying out its probation supervision responsibilities. One of the important policy questions a probation department must face is what it conceives to be the objectives or purposes of probation supervision: The way it discharges its supervision responsibility depends in part upon the answer to that question.

One important source of information about probation department policy is the published statements of the department — reports to the trial judiciary, the legislative bodies, and the public; operational manuals for its probation officers; and handbooks explaining probation to probationers. Other sources are the informal statements of individual probation officers and observations of the supervisory process in action. Often, these sources lead to contradictory conclusions. In part, this may be because the probation department wishes to obtain a particular response from the reader of its published statements — the trial judiciary or the legislative body controlling appropriations. But the published statements, and even the statements of individual probation officers, may express not so much an accurate reflection of current supervision practice but rather an ideal or goal that probation department personnel are striving to attain.

It is convenient to think in terms of three major objectives of probation supervision. One major purpose is to control the probationer — to make him conform his behavior to the requirements of the law and the probation conditions during the time he is under supervision. This objective is achieved if the probationer makes it through the supervision period without a serious violation of the criminal law or the probation conditions. A second major objective of probation supervision is treatment — to attempt to achieve through counselling or referral to other resources a permanent change in the probationer's antisocial behavior. This objective is accomplished if the probationer is discharged from supervision with an improvement in his willingness and ability to live a law-abiding existence in the free community. A third objective is service to the probationer or to others in his behalf — assisting the probationer and his family to overcome problems, such as obtaining and keeping employment. This objective is accomplished if the probation officer is able to solve the problems presented by the probationer.

These objectives are closely interrelated. The policies and practices of virtually every probation department would lead to the conclusion that all three objectives are sought in at least some situations. Which objective receives emphasis may depend upon the facts of individual cases, the background and attitudes of the particular probation officer or of supervisory personnel, or upon official positions of the department. In official documents, the treatment or rehabilitation objective of probation supervision receives primary attention. In practice, however, the control objective receives the major expenditure of manpower.

a. *Control.* A major purpose of probation supervision in Michigan and Wisconsin is control of the probationer's behavior in such a way as to prevent conduct which constitutes either a serious violation of the criminal law or a serious violation of a condition of probation. However, important differences exist among probation officers concerning (1) what constitutes a serious violation and (2) what measures a probation officer should use to avoid serious violations. It is difficult to regard probation supervision in Kansas as serving a control purpose because caseload sizes permit only minimal contact between probation officer and probationer.[73] The only control purpose served is attempting to secure compliance with probation conditions requiring the payment of court costs, restitution, or family support.[74] Even this effort is minimal and, with the exception of collecting court costs,[75] successful only to a limited ex-

[73] A typical probationer might see his probation officer five or six times a year. Virtually all contacts occur in the probation office; the interviews are short and perfunctory in nature. Many probationers are permitted to report by mail, and it is likely that once court-imposed financial obligations are satisfied personal contact between the probation officer and his client ceases. For a detailed discussion of the intensity of probation supervision in each of the three states, see pages 133-135.

[74] See pages 105-112.

[75] A real effort is made to collect court costs, which are imposed as a condition

tent. Enforcing financial obligations imposed by the trial court is an important control objective in the other two states but there are other objectives. Furthermore, the more intensive supervision in those states increases the likelihood that all control objectives will be achieved.

Enforcing conditions imposing financial obligations is an important control objective in some divisions of the Detroit Recorder's Court Probation Department. In the Men's Felony Division and the Youth Division, heavy emphasis is placed upon collecting financial obligations. The initial interview, as well as subsequent office and field interviews, are dominated by discussion of the probationer's financial obligations and his progress, or lack of it, in satisfying them. The frequency of office interviews is determined by some probation officers on the basis of the probationer's progress in meeting his financial obligations.[76] If financial obligations remain unsatisfied at the end of the probation period, probation is likely to be extended and efforts to secure payment increased.[77] Threats of revocation are made against probationers who fail to respond to other enforcement techniques, although revocations seldom occur solely for nonpayment of financial obligations.[78] The Women's Division places much less emphasis upon collecting financial obligations and is much more willing to request the trial court to waive the probation condition when there is doubt about the financial ability of the probationer to make the payments.[79]

---

of probation in virtually every case. When restitution is ordered, it may not be enforced if the probationer has difficulty making the payments. Court costs are never waived, however, and in some cases they must be paid before the defendant is placed on probation supervision.

[76] Many probation officers require weekly office interviews until the probationer has paid court costs in full. Then only monthly, or at most semi-monthly, interviews are required. One probation officer explained that many officers do this to provide some inducement for payment of court costs as quickly as possible.

[77] The most frequent reason for extension of the probation period is nonpayment of financial obligations. See pages 136-138.

[78] Although probation is seldom, if ever, revoked for failure to pay financial obligations, one probation officer explained that most probation officers place great emphasis upon the collection of court costs and restitution because it is in this area, along with reporting, that they can prove lack of progress or irresponsibility on the part of the probationer when and if they want to have a probation case revoked.

[79] The Supervisor of the Women's Division explained that probation conditions requiring payment of court costs or restitution create problems. "Most women have little or no income. Either they are married and have no income of their own, or only have part time jobs. Also, in many instances when they are working, the women are contributing a great amount of their income to the support of their families." She further pointed out that she has serious reservations with regard to the purposes served by imposing court costs on female probationers. She would much rather not see them imposed at all. An additional danger in imposing court costs is that some probationers are inclined to take probation as a monetary ob-

A special division of the Recorder's Court Probation Department — the Domestic Relations Division — supervises probationers convicted of nonsupport. The entire purpose of the nonsupport law and its enforcement, and of the Domestic Relations Division's supervision in these cases, is to secure payment of family support obligations.[80]

In both Detroit and Milwaukee, the control objective dominates the supervision process. In the routine office interview, little is done other than to permit the probation officer to determine progress in meeting financial obligations and to keep current on the probationer's residence and employment arrangements. The home visit, when it is used, is primarily a control device.[81] If the probationer is interviewed at his home, he is reminded of his financial obligations and other restrictions and urged to contact the probation officer when a problem arises. If a relative of the probationer is contacted in the home, the probation officer may urge that person to report problems to him. If no person is at home when a visit is made, the probation officer usually leaves his business card to indicate to the probationer that a home visit was attempted.

Some probation officers feel very strongly that control is best accomplished through active surveillance of probationers. These officers emphasize the necessity of going into the field to find out "what actually is going on." Like the police, they seek to enhance their control function by making their "presence" felt, by making

---

ligation and look upon supervision only in this light, rather than as a period of adjustment which requires a rehabilitative effort on their part.

80 A probation officer in the Domestic Relations Division asked his client what he thought probation was all about. The man fumbled for a reply; the officer interjected that the man was expected to pay $20 a week and that if he was going to live in the home, he was going to have to pay more. The client was then instructed to pay $20 per week and report regularly. Many nonsupport cases are settled before they reach court. A special division of the probation department, the Adjustment Division, has as its sole responsibility settling nonsupport cases before they reach court and supervising defendants to enforce the terms of the settlement agreement. For a detailed discussion of the operations of this Division, see Miller, Prosecution: The Decision to Charge a Suspect With a Crime (forthcoming).

Persons placed on probation following conviction for a misdemeanor in Detroit are supervised by the Misdemeanant Division of the probation department. Supervision is less intense than in felony cases and virtually the sole supervision goals are to enforce conditions requiring financial payments and to secure regular reporting.

The Domestic Relations Division also supervises clients convicted of assaulting members of their family, usually wives or children. These cases often involve extensive family counselling, either directly by the probation officer or by referral to a counselling agency.

81 Although some probation officers make routine home visits, most home visits are made when a particular control problem, such as failure to report or failure to meet financial obligations, arises. The home visit is made in an attempt to correct the problem. The home visit is discussed in more detail at pages 129-132.

their clients feel that they are being watched carefully. One probation officer who supervises young adult offenders said he usually makes home visits during the late evening hours because that "gives an opportunity to visit neighborhood hangouts where much of the difficulties start." He continued that his moving throughout the district, dropping in at all the various hangouts, lets the probationers know that he is out and around keeping an eye on their activities. He feels that this type of procedure is a necessary part of his work. He said that many of his probationers need this type of surveillance. Other probation officers feel just as strongly that surveillance is not an appropriate part of their job. They emphasize that their function is to assist the probationer in his rehabilitation and that surveillance interferes with that objective.[82]

b. *Treatment.* In the probation services of both Detroit and Milwaukee, treatment is often stated as a primary goal of the supervision process. A manual proposed for adoption by the Milwaukee department defines probation as "a process of treatment prescribed by the court for persons convicted of offenses against the law during which the individual on probation lives in the community and regulates his own life under the conditions imposed by the court (or other constituted authority) and is subject to supervision by a probation officer." It lists two objectives of probation supervision:

> (1) Rehabilitation of the offender.
> The alternate aim of probation is to assist the probationer toward a more normal social adjustment by developing him to his fullest capacity for self maintenance in keeping with the approved standards of social behavior.
>
> (2) The protection of society.
> The supervising officer must be constantly aware of the responsibility for the protection of society. When a probationer's behavior affects the safety of persons or property the probation officer must not hesitate in using authority. However, society can be best protected by rehabilitation of the offender.

Despite the manual's emphasis, the recruitment of persons trained in social work, and the interest of some staff members in implementing casework skills learned in graduate schools of social work, treatment appears to be limited. Departmental employees stated

[82] One probation officer, when asked if he considered surveillance a part of his job, replied that he was not a detective and that as a caseworker he did not feel that he should go around spying on his men. He believed that this would make probationers lose confidence in him and feel he could not be trusted. He said he thought he could accomplish more by getting the client's confidence in this manner than by surveillance. The attitude of probation officers toward surveillance is in part a function of their formal training. Most probation officers with formal training in social work do not use surveillance, while many without the training do.

that little treatment in the sense of psychologically oriented therapy is attempted. The press of social investigations and of major problems in many cases — health, residence, employment, and other economic problems — consumes available time.[83] When counselling is attempted, it usually concerns probationers' marital problems. Occasionally a probationer is referred to an outside agency such as Alcoholics Anonymous.[84] Referrals to psychiatric resources apparently are rare.

In Detroit the large majority of probationers are handled in a routine, businesslike manner. Treatment is attempted only in cases presenting unusual problems. In part, this may be because psychiatric resources are limited. The Psychopathic Clinic is designed primarily for conducting presentence psychiatric examinations and can accept very few referrals from the probation department for diagnosis and treatment.[85] Most probation officers attempt very little counselling themselves. In the Women's Division, however, the officers attempt to provide clients with counsel for psychological or social problems.[86] One woman probation officer, the only one trained in psychiatric social work, is given responsibility for all cases involving serious psychiatric problems.

Two resources are used for the treatment of narcotic addicts: the federal hospital in Lexington, Kentucky and the Narcotics Clinic of the Detroit Department of Health. Usually, the probation officer attempts to persuade his client to use one of these resources, but sometimes the trial court may impose treatment as a condition of probation. In the latter situation, probation is likely to be revoked if the addict refuses to comply with the treatment condition.

Most treatment efforts are aimed at domestic problems. Some probation officers attempt extended counselling with the probationer and his spouse when marital problems are apparent. Refer-

83 Records kept on supervision of individual cases reflect the lack of time. They reveal only changes in basic facts such as employment or residence, rather than statements of casework planning and treatment.

84 The probation department received a complaint from the local chapter of Alcoholics Anonymous that probationers were being forced to contact the chapter by their probation officers. The chapter representative claimed that when interviewed the probationers stated they did not come voluntarily and did not want to join the treatment program. He felt that a genuine desire to seek help was a prerequisite to effective treatment in Alcoholics Anonymous.

85 The probation officer who seeks psychiatric services for an indigent client faces a difficult task. In one case, an officer referred a client to a psychiatric clinic in a local university hospital. At first, the referral was refused. By contacting the director of the clinic, the officer was finally able to secure acceptance. The clinic conducted an examination and recommended that the client be civilly committed to a public mental hospital.

86 Perhaps the reason counselling is attempted by officers in the Women's Division is that their caseloads are lighter than in most of the other divisions. See pages 133-135.

rals to private marriage counselling agencies or to social workers in the welfare department occur frequently.

c. *Services.* One probation officer expressed the view that in many cases providing services is about all that can be done for a probationer. "There is no deep psychotherapy involved in most probation work. The probation officer does casework in selected cases — most cases are minor and you are 'manipulative': helping them with their kids, seeing that the children have shoes to get them to school, helping them to manage their budget, and some other types of problems. This is particularly important with married probationers and teenagers." Probation officers devote considerable time to assisting their clients overcome a wide variety of problems of the kind many law-abiding persons encounter. Obtaining and keeping employment is a particularly difficult problem because of a general low level of marketable skills among probationers and the added difficulty that a felony conviction creates.[87] Although some probation officers are able themselves to develop employment opportunities, the routine response to probationer unemployment is a referral to the public employment service.[88] Probation officers often assist clients in applying for public assistance, either emergency or long-term, and sometimes must make temporary residence arrangements for those with no place to stay. Clients with medical problems are referred to public clinics.

Many probationers have financial problems created by heavy installment purchasing. Because a garnishment proceeding may endanger the probationer's employment, resort is often made to a wage assignment device to avoid garnishment. Under the wage assignment agreement, the probationer's wages are paid directly to the probation department which disburses the fund to provide living expenses for the probationer and his family and to pay creditors.

For many young probationers, a felony conviction is a bar to enlistment in the military service. The Detroit Recorder's Court

[87] Most probation officers do not disclose the status of clients as probationers to their employers. In their view, probationers have enough difficulty obtaining and keeping employment without this added handicap. Some probation officers indicated that, when an employer learns of the probationary status of an employee, he is likely to discharge him. If the particular criminal conduct of a probationer creates an unusual risk for an employer, a probation officer may suggest that his client disclose his status and may himself do so if the client does not.

[88] The Detroit office of the Michigan State Employment Service has designated a particular employment counsellor to handle the employment needs of all probationers and parolees referred to the Service. Probationers are referred directly to this person, who has apparently accumulated considerable experience in locating the best employment prospects for probationers. Probation officers in Detroit report considerable success in obtaining employment through this person.

Probation Department and local recruiting officers devised a system for expunging the conviction record when a probationer is otherwise eligible for enlistment. The probation officer returns the case to court and moves that it be re-opened and a new trial granted. That is done and the defendant is acquitted, thus making him eligible for military service.[89]

2. *The techniques of probation supervision.* Major differences exist among the three states in the nature of the contact between probationer and probation officer. These differences are, in part, the result of differing purposes in the contacts and of differences in caseload sizes. Primary concern is with the use of office interviews and home visits as supervision techniques.

a. *Office interviews.* In each of the three states the principal form of contact with probationers is the routine office interview. In Detroit, probationers are required to report for office interviews weekly until they have satisfied conditions of probation requiring payment of court costs and restitution; they are then permitted to report once or twice each month.[90] The interviews are brief, the longest not exceeding ten minutes. Their content consists of routine questions by the probation officer about payment of costs and restitution,[91] changes in residence or employment, and, when time permits, friendly inquiries as to the probationer's general welfare. With the exception of the Women's Division, little attempt is made to counsel probationers about their problems. In Milwaukee monthly office interviews are required; they are similar in nature to those held in Detroit.

In Wichita probationers are required to report directly to the trial judges three times each year. The interviews are quite brief[92] and consist of little more than a progress report by the probationer on the status of court cost payments and warnings by the trial judge to obey the law. In addition, probationers must report to their probation officers. Usually five or six such office interviews are held with a probationer each year.

b. *Home visits.* In addition to routine office interviews, proba-

89 Since this system also shortens the probation period, it is discussed in detail in that connection at pages 138-141.

90 Office hours are kept for night reporting by probationers who find it difficult to report during normal business hours. Each probation officer remains at the office until 7-8 P.M. one night each week to receive reports from his clients.

91 A probation officer in Recorder's Court Probation Department said, "The office reporting procedure is of a strictly perfunctory nature; men simply come in and are checked off on the record for the sole purpose of providing an opportunity for the collection of court costs."

92 In one two-hour session, fifty-two probationers reported to the trial judges sitting *en banc.*

tion officers in Detroit and Milwaukee conduct interviews in the homes of probationers, but their frequency and purpose vary. In Wichita home visits are virtually never used.[93] In Detroit there is no departmental policy concerning the number of home visits an officer must make. That is left to the supervisor of each division[94] or, more often, to the individual probation officer.[95] Most probation officers make a home visit on new cases to verify the residence reported by the probationer. The visits consist of brief interviews with the probationer or anybody else found at the address to verify the probationer's residence, employment, the hours he is keeping, or to remind him that payments of court costs or restitution are due. A home visit is frequently made when an officer discovers that a probationer has failed to report for an office interview or is behind in court costs or restitution payments. Most probation officers attempt no counselling in connection with home visits.[96]

The probation department in Milwaukee has established no policy concerning home visits.[97] Consequently, the frequency and uses of home visits are decisions within the discretion of each probation officer. There is sharp disagreement among the officers in the department about the usefulness of home visits.[98] One probation officer summarized the position held by himself and several other officers.

93 A field observer was told that home visits are used when the probationer has failed to report for a long period of time and efforts to contact him by mail and telephone have failed. In these cases, the effort is not so much to interview the probationer as to locate him. The only other time home visits are used is when they are requested by probationers who are unable to go to the office for an interview.

94 The supervisor of the Women's Division said the only requirement she imposes is that at least one home visit per year must be made. The supervisor of the Domestic Relations Division requires a home visit each three months.

95 One probation officer said he attempts to see felony cases once a month, although he admitted this is not always possible. Most probation officers are probably not able to visit the homes of each probationer more than once each two months.

96 A probation officer in the Women's Division stated that she found it difficult to counsel clients in their homes because of interruptions by small children. Also, she said, some probationers are embarrassed about their inadequate housekeeping and would spend most of the interview offering excuses. This interfered with the comfortableness of the relationship and the ability of the probation officer to develop the necessary rapport with the probationer. But by the same token, she said, some individuals were ill at ease at the probation office and found it more comfortable to be interviewed at home.

97 The manual proposed for adoption by the department suggests, but does not require, a home visit once a month.

98 The disagreement appears to be based mostly upon the background and training of the officers. Six of the eight probation officers with degrees in social work make little or no use of home visits, while the other two use them selectively for counselling purposes. All of the nine probation officers without graduate training in social work make extensive use of routine home visits to increase their control over the behavior of the probationers.

> A requirement of one home visit a month is silly. In most cases you simply would arrive at a home and, finding no one there, leave your calling card at the mail box to let the probationer know he is "over the barrel." As for collateral visits to probationers' employers, over 50 percent of the employers of my probationers would fire them if they knew the man was on probation. Such visits are desirable if they are not a serious threat to steady employment of probationers. The probation department needs some sort of employment service providing employers who know individuals are on probation and who will cooperate with the probation department.

A second group of probation officers makes extensive use of routine home visits, some spending as much as 50 percent of their time in the field making home visits and conducting presentence investigations. They place strong emphasis on finding out "what actually is going on" in the home of a probationer. They believe they may be "conned" by their probationers if they are not in the home to observe actual conditions. The home visits of these officers have the characteristics of a friendly visit. In the content of most interviews no specific objective in making the call was evident beyond letting the probationer or his family know of the officer's continuing interest. No efforts at casework were observed in these calls, but in several of them the officer gave a word of advice.[99]

A third group neither rejects home visits entirely nor makes use of them as a routine control device, but uses them selectively. These officers make home visits only to accomplish specific objectives.[100] They are careful to avoid using the home visit as a surveil-

[99] For example, in one case a probation officer advised an unemployed probationer that he should make himself useful by repairing things about the house; in another case, the officer advised a probationer and his wife who had just moved into public housing that they should make a special effort to keep their apartment clean since it was probably the best living facility they had ever had.

A woman probation officer who makes considerable use of home visits in supervising women probationers stated that with women, home calls are absolutely essential, particularly to married women with children. To have women with small children visit the office makes an impossible interview situation, with small children crying and running all over the office. Going into the home is much more natural. It also gives an opportunity to observe the conditions of the home. Seeing the physical condition can give strong indications about the probationer; if it is dirty and ill-kept, it may suggest a problem with the probationer. Contrast the position of a woman probation officer in Detroit on the value of home visits in supervising women. See note 96 *supra*.

[100] Some of these purposes are to locate possible absconders, to encourage the wife of a probationer involved in a marital dispute to contact the officer if further difficulties arise, to ascertain whether a probationer, injured in an accident, has been discharged from the hospital, to inform a probationer's wife that her husband's probation is likely to be revoked if his behavior does not improve, and to encourage the wife of an alcoholic probationer to endure his behavior when drunk.

lance device.[101] Indeed, some of them feel that home visits are essential to effective counselling in some cases.[102]

c. *Mail supervision.* In some cases, probation supervision may involve no face-to-face contact with the probationer. This happens in many cases in which probationers are permitted to leave the state in search of employment or to live with relatives. Sometimes, probation supervision may be assumed by the probation service of the state where the probationer will work and reside under the terms of the Interstate Compact for the Supervision of Parolees and Probationers.[103] The Compact is not always used, however, and in many instances probation supervision is conducted by mail. In Kansas at the time of the field survey, the Compact was not used, although enacted by the Kansas legislature.[104] All Kansas probationers permitted to live out of the state were supervised by mail.[105] In addition, many probationers who lived in the local area reported by mail.

In Detroit most probationers permitted to live out of state are continued under the supervision of the Recorder's Court Probation Department and are required to report by mailing in monthly report forms. The Interstate Compact is used only when the trial judge believes closer supervision is necessary and directly requests it. Adult probationers who request permission to leave the state are usually in pursuit of better employment opportunities. The typical reason for a young offender to leave the state is to join his family. The probationer must provide evidence of good faith by presenting letters from parents or the prospective employer, the authenticity of which the officer verifies. The probationer given per-

101 One probation officer who makes selective use of home visits stated that he is careful to make an appointment before visiting the home to avoid the impression he is spying on the probationer and his family. Another probation officer indicated that home visits minimize his control image in the eyes of the probationer. "Home visits hasten the feeling on the part of some probationers that you are not a 'copper.' If a probation officer goes into a home, discusses the problems with the probationer, and meets the family, the probationer and the entire family begin to feel that the probation officer is not simply a police officer checking up or investigating or trying to get something on the probationer."

102 One probation officer stated that "Before you can do casework, in many instances, the probation officer must ascertain what the facts are, what the problem is that the probationer is facing. Many times, for obvious reasons, the probationer is not discussing his problems and giving the officer the facts. In order to help through casework, the probation officer must go out into the community and ascertain the problems."

On the other hand, another probation officer indicated that home visits do not help in the casework or counselling aspects of supervision but are useful on a selective basis in providing services to the probationer and his family.

103 See note 40 *supra*.

104 Kan. Stat. Ann §62-2503 (1964).

105 A probation officer in Wichita indicated that 8 to 10 percent of his caseload lived outside of Kansas and reported by mail.

mission to move must sign a "waiver of extradition." He is given a number of report forms and instructed to fill one out and mail it to the department each month.[106]

In Milwaukee, out-of-state probationers are either transferred through the Interstate Compact or supervised by mail. The decision to retain or transfer responsibility for supervision depends upon the availability of local services and the department's opinion of them. For example, a probationer living in a midwestern state was supervised by mail because the department believed local services were inadequate; another probationer residing in New York City was transferred to local supervision because the department believed supervision in that city to be of excellent quality.[107]

3. *The intensity of probation supervision.* One measure of the quality of probation supervision is its intensity. Intensity of case supervision depends both upon the work load of each probation officer — caseload size and number of presentence investigations conducted — and upon the ability of the officer to classify cases into those requiring more and those less intense supervision. In Wichita, Kansas at the time of the field survey, the bailiff for each of the six judges of the District Court served as probation officer for persons placed on probation by his judge. Approximately 30 to 40 percent of the bailiff's time was devoted to probation supervision, although the time required varied depending upon whether a par-

[106] The monthly report form used by all divisions of the department for out-of-state probationers is a single sheet of paper on one side of which are questions the probationer is expected to answer:

Name of employer
Address of employment
Kind of work
Number of days worked
Reasons for lost time, if any
Are you avoiding habits, practices or places which led you into difficulty?
In what ways have you made improvements under probation?
Are you studying or going to night school?
Are you reading any good books?
Have you gone to a public library?
Have you attended church?
Have you attended any other public meetings?
What do you do for recreation?
Have you had any trouble or misunderstanding of any kind?
If so, what?
Are you making the most of your job?
Are you keeping up restitution payments?
What wages have you received during month?
Have you saved any money?
Have you a bank account?
Have you paid debts?

[107] The department does not attempt to utilize the Interstate Compact for probationers who move to some southern states. It was indicated that in the past these states have given little or no cooperation. For example, a narcotics user was given permission to go to a southern state and to report by mail.

ticular bailiff's judge was or was not assigned to the criminal division of the Court. One bailiff, whose judge was then in the criminal division, had a current caseload of ninety-five to one hundred. Two other bailiffs, whose judges were at the same time handling civil cases, had caseloads of sixty-five and forty-seven. Since no presentence investigations were at that time conducted in Kansas, caseload supervision was the sole probation function of the bailiffs. The only classification of cases attempted was to permit some probationers to report by mail and to require others to report personally.[108]

In Detroit the average caseload size for probation officers in Recorder's Court Probation Department was ninety-nine probationers. The caseload size varied from an average of 156 in the Men's Division to 55 in both the Women's and Youth Divisions.[109] In addition, each probation officer conducted an average of five presentence investigations per month. No attempt was made to systematically classify cases in terms of intensity of supervision needed.[110]

In Milwaukee thirteen of the fourteen male probation officers who supervised probationers had caseloads in excess of ninety-five. Of these, six had caseloads greater than 102, the highest 105. In addition, two male probation officers conducted most presentence investigations. The fourteen supervising officers conducted an average of only one and one-half presentence investigations per month. Three women probation officers who supervised probationers had caseloads of under eighty cases and conducted an average of five and one-half presentence investigations per month.

The manual proposed for adoption by the probation department in Milwaukee recommends that officers classify their cases in terms of the kind of supervision needed:

> Effective management of caseloads requires classification of probationers according to: kinds and degree of help needed; intensity of supervision required; amount of self-direction of which they are capable. Additional classification of cases might be according to

[108] The one with the caseload of sixty-five stated that he permitted all but fifteen of them to report by mail. Most of the fifty so reporting were living in the local area.

[109] In the Domestic Relations Division the average caseload size was 109.

[110] The only distinction of this kind noted being used consistently was in the Domestic Relations Division where officers attempted to contact felony nonsupport offenders once each month and misdemeanant nonsupport offenders once each three months.

Some cases doubtless require virtually no supervision. Nevertheless, little use was made of suspended sentence without probation supervision in felony cases. In the only case observed, a judge in the Wayne County Circuit Court gave a suspended sentence to a man convicted of carrying a concealed weapon who had no prior record, was a substantial citizen, and who convinced the judge he carried the weapon solely for self-protection.

> the offender's attitudes, "cooperativeness, evasive, resistive, having good insight," or with respect to the supervising officer's role, "supportive, father substitute, confidant." It is essential that the supervising officer make a workable classification to suit his design for rendering differential service.

While classification of cases is not made in advance of supervision, officers do devote different amounts of work to different probationers.[111] Some of the social work trained officers rejected a conception of classification of cases according to the intensity of control needed on the ground that it is more appropriate to police work than probation supervision.

4. *The duration of probation supervision.* The duration of probation supervision defines the period of time in which rehabilitation efforts must occur and during which the probationer is subject to the controls and possible incarceration incident to probation. In practice, the duration is fixed by three separate decisions: at the time the defendant is placed on probation; extending the probation period after supervision has begun; and by granting discharge from probation prior to the expiration of the period originally set. A fourth decision that determines the duration of probation supervision — the revocation of probation — is discussed in the following chapter.

a. *Setting the initial probation period.* Kansas statutes grant the trial judge discretion to determine the length of the probation period with the limitation that the period "together with any extension thereof, shall not exceed five years." [112] In most cases, Wichita trial judges set a two year probation period. Michigan statutes grant the trial judge discretion to "fix and determine the period . . . of probation" at any time not in excess of five years.[113] As in Wichita, most Detroit trial judges select a two-year probation pe-

[111] One probation officer discussed a state tax evader who needed no supervision. The offender was an independent oil refiner who was being pushed out of business by a gas war instigated by larger oil companies. The only way this refiner could survive was through an effort to evade state income taxes in order to compete in price. However, he was caught and placed on probation. He was a good family man who was generally respected in the community. In the officer's opinion, this man needed no supervision and, therefore, was given none.

[112] Kan. Gen. Stat. §62-2203 (1949), repealed by Kan. Laws 1957, Ch. 331, §37. This provision is unclear because Kan. Gen. Stat. §62-2209 (1949) provides that the probation period cannot continue for a period longer than ten years. The shorter time limitation is relied upon here because, presumably, it would govern. The present law, Kan. Stat. Ann. §62-2243 (1964), provides: "The period of probation . . . shall be fixed by the court at not more than five years, subject to renewals by the court for fixed periods not exceeding five years, but in no event shall the total period of probation . . . for a felony exceed the maximum term provided by law for the offense. . . ."

[113] Mich. Stat. Ann. §28.1132 (1954). The probation period for a misdemeanor cannot exceed two years. Ibid.

riod. Wisconsin statutes authorize the trial judge to place a defendant on probation for "a stated period" with the limitation that "the original term of probation shall not be less than one year nor more than the statutory maximum term of imprisonment for the crime." [114] If the defendant is convicted of more than one offense, multiple probation terms can be imposed and they can be made to run consecutively.[115] In Milwaukee the most typical probation period is two years, although in unusual cases shorter[116] or longer[117] periods may be imposed. In all cases observed involving multiple convictions, concurrent rather than consecutive probation periods were imposed.

b. *Extending the initial probation period.* Under some circumstances, the initial probation period set by the trial court is extended. This occurs frequently in Detroit and Milwaukee; no extensions were observed in Wichita, although legal authority for extension exists in Kansas.[118] Michigan statutes provide that the trial court is to set the length of the probation period and that it "shall be at all times alterable and amendable, both in form and in substance, in the court's discretion." [119] The statutes also provide

[114] Wis. Stat. Ann. §57.01 (1957) (applicable to Wisconsin outside of Milwaukee County). Wis. Stat. Ann. §57.025 (1957) appears to incorporate these provisions for Milwaukee County. Wis. Laws 1965, Ch. 394, §1, set the maximum probation period at the maximum for the offense or three years, whichever is greater. Wis. Stat. Ann. §57.01(3) (Supp. 1967).

[115] Wis. Stat. Ann. §57.01(1) (1957) provides in part: "The period of probation may be made consecutive to a sentence of imprisonment on a different charge, whether imposed at the same time or previously. Consecutive periods of probation may be imposed. In case the conditions of probation are violated, the current probation and all subsequent consecutive probations shall be revoked."

[116] In one case, for example, the trial court granted probation for one year to a defendant on condition he leave Wisconsin and not return. It is reasonable to suppose that since mail supervision was contemplated in this case, the trial court saw little reason to extend the probation period beyond one year. The major purpose of the probation grant — to have the defendant leave the state — would be accomplished almost immediately.

[117] In one case a defendant was convicted by a jury in a trial in which he testified to his innocence. The trial judge regarded the defendant's testimony as perjury and would not have granted probation but for the urging of the other officials involved in the case. He granted probation for a five year period and imposed as a condition the requirement that the defendant pay the costs of the jury trial.

[118] Kan. Gen. Stat. §62-2203 (1949) provides in part: "The court may revoke or modify any condition of parole, or may change the period of parole. The period of parole, together with any extension thereof, shall not exceed five years." The context of the statute makes clear that "parole" means "probation." The fact that one district court probation officer doubted whether legal authority exists for extension of probation indicates that extensions were rarely sought. The present Kansas law, Kan. Stat. Ann. §62-2243 (1964), provides: "The period of probation or suspension of sentence shall be fixed by the court at not more than five years, subject to renewals by the court for fixed periods not exceeding five years, but in no event shall the total period of probation or suspension of sentence for a felony exceed the maximum term provided by law for the offense. . . ."

[119] Mich. Stat. Ann. §28.1132 (1954). Mich. Stat. Ann. §28.1135 (1954) also pro-

that the probation period for a felony cannot exceed five years.[120] The Michigan Supreme Court has indicated that the probation period can be extended by the trial court as long as the total probation period (including extension) does not exceed five years.[121]

In Detroit virtually all extensions of probation are made because of failure to make restitution or court cost payments ordered by the trial court.[122] Extensions are made informally by the trial court and the probationer is often not notified in advance of the decision. Sometimes probationers are kept under supervision beyond the initial probation period without securing a formal extension of probation from the trial court. One probation officer who did this stated correctly that he could return the case to the trial court at any time within the five year statutory period for a retroactive extension of probation if he needed authority to revoke.[123] Some probationers are retained under supervision after the expiration of the statutory five-year term. They are required to sign a waiver of their right to the statutory limitation. One trial judge stated that probation supervision beyond the five-year period was a "bluff" but acknowledged that it was sometimes done.

Wisconsin statutes require that "the original term of probation shall not be less than one year nor more than the statutory maximum term of imprisonment for the crime" [124] but provide that "prior to the expiration of any probation period the court may by order extend his probation for a stated period." [125] In Milwaukee

---

vides: "Upon the termination of the probation period, the probation officer shall report the fact to the court and also the conduct of the probationer during the period of probation, and the court may thereupon discharge the probationer from further supervision and enter a judgment of suspended sentence, or extend the probation period, as the circumstances may require; Provided, That the maximum period or [of] probation herein limited shall not be exceeded."

120 Mich. Stat. Ann. §28.1132 (1954).

121 In People v. Marks, 340 Mich. 495, 65 N.W.2d 698 (1954) the defendant was placed on probation for three years upon conviction of felonious operation of an automobile. Some four months after the three-year probation period had expired, the trial court, upon petition of the probation officer, extended the probation period for two years from the date of expiration. When probation was later revoked, the Michigan Supreme Court upheld the extension because the total probation period did not exceed the statutory five-year limitation.

122 In one case, the defendant was given two years' probation on a plea of guilty to breaking and entering in the daytime and ordered to make restitution of $636. Since full restitution had not been paid at the end of the two-year period, probation was extended for one year. In another case, the defendant received probation for two years for attempted larceny. He was ordered to pay $100 court costs, but by the end of two years he had paid only $30. Probation was extended for one year.

123 See *supra* note 121.

124 Wis. Stat. Ann. §57.01(3) (1957).

125 Wis. Stat. Ann. §57.01(2) (1957). In State *ex rel* Vanderhei v. Murphy, 246 Wis. 168, 16 N.W.2d 413 (1944) the defendant was convicted of embezzling more than $100 and less than $1000. He was placed on probation for five years, the statutory maximum sentence for the offense of which he was convicted. Approxi-

most extensions of the probation period occur because the probationer has failed to pay restitution as ordered by the trial court.[126] When expiration of the probation period is near and full restitution has not been made, the probation officer must decide whether to request the court to waive the restitution condition and discharge the probationer or to request an extension of probation.[127] In almost all cases the court grants the request of the probation officer. If extension is sought, the probation officer contacts his client to inform him of his decision and to determine whether the probationer wishes to appear in court to contest the extension. If the probationer does not wish to appear, he signs a waiver of appearance. The probation officer then informally presents his request for extension together with his reasons to the trial judge. If the probationer wishes to appear, a formal hearing is held at which the probation officer, under oath, presents the facts he believes support his request for extension and the probationer is given an opportunity to speak.

c. *Discharge from probation.* In each of the three states a person is routinely discharged from probation when he has completed his probation period with any extensions and has substantially complied with the probation conditions. In some cases discharge may be granted even though all conditions were not complied with if the probation officer and court believe the violations were not serious and little would be gained by extending the probation period.[128] When a person is discharged from probation he is given a copy of the court order discharging him as proof that he completed his probation period.

---

mately one month before the five-year probation period expired, the trial court extended probation for one year from the expiration date. During this one-year extension, probation was revoked. The Wisconsin Supreme Court upheld this procedure and denied the petition for *habeas corpus*. Nothing in the statute or this case imposes any limitation on the ability of the trial court to keep a person on probation indefinitely by a series of extensions of the probation period.

126 The manual proposed for the probation department states: "[Extension of probation] occurs when court obligations are not paid in full and it is felt that more time is needed for payments; when a new offense, which is in violation of the conditions of probation, has not been disposed of by the probation expiration date; or when it is felt that the probationer will benefit by further supervision."

127 One probation officer stated that when probation is near expiration and restitution has not been paid in full, he sometimes contacts the victim to determine whether strong objection would be made if the probationer were to be discharged without making full payment. He said further that he is not too worried if insurance companies do not receive full payment, but he will expend considerable effort to obtain restitution and will readily seek extension if the victim is some individual who cannot afford the loss.

128 For example, probationers are often discharged from probation at the end of the period even though they still owe payments on court costs or restitution if the probationer has made a good faith effort to make the payments but has been financially unable to do so.

Legal authority exists in each of the three states to discharge persons from probation before the probation period expires. Kansas statutes give the trial court discretion to grant early discharge from probation after two years of supervision.[129] The probation officer appears before the court and states his reasons for requesting an early discharge from probation. The court then grants or denies the officer's request. The court proceedings appear to be only a formality, the probation officer's recommendation being followed in each case.[130] The probationer himself is usually not present.[131]

In Michigan, legal authority exists for the early discharge of a probationer from supervision in the discretion of the trial court.[132] In Detroit, early discharges are granted when a probationer has conformed to the conditions of probation, especially those impos-

129 Kan. Gen. Stat. §62-2209 (1949) sets the two-year minimum probation term. Kan. Gen. Stat. §62-2208 (1949) provides that after two years on probation if "the court granting the parole [probation] shall be satisfied that the reformation of such person is complete and that he will not again violate the law, such court may, in its discretion, by order of record, grant his absolute discharge. Such order of discharge shall recite the fact that such person has earned his discharge by good behavior, and such order shall operate as a complete satisfaction of the original judgment by which the fine or jail sentence or imprisonment in the penitentiary or reformatory was imposed."

Kan. Gen. Stat. §62-2213 (1949) provides: "Any person who shall receive his final discharge under the provisions of this law shall be restored to all the rights and privileges of citizenship."

The present Kansas law, Kan. Stat. Ann. §62-2243 (1964), provides: "Probation or suspension of sentence may be terminated by the court at any time and upon such termination, or upon termination by expiration of the term of probation or suspension of sentence, an order to this effect shall be entered by the court."

130 In one proceeding, the probation officer recommended early discharge in five cases and in each of them it was granted. In one case, the probationer had been placed on supervision for five years for manslaughter of her husband, an habitual drunkard. She had successfully completed two years and was now remarried. The probation officer reported to the court that the home conditions provided by her new husband seemed adequate and that the probationer and her five children seemed well cared for. In another case, the probationer had been placed on probation for burglary and larceny on condition he pay $1200 in restitution. He secured employment with the victim of the offense and in the two years of probation paid the $1200. The victim-employer wrote the probation officer a letter requesting early discharge of the probationer, which the officer displayed to the court. In each case, early discharge was quickly granted.

131 The probation officer stated he tells probationers whom he has decided to recommend for early discharge that there is no need for them to appear in court since discharge is a certainty.

132 Mich. Stat. Ann. §28.1132 (1954) provides: "The court shall by order, to be filed or entered in the cause as the court may direct by general rule or in each case fix and determine the period and conditions of probation and such order, whether it is filed or entered, shall be considered as part of the record in the cause and shall be at all times alterable and amendable, both in form and in substance, in the court's discretion." Mich. Stat. Ann. §28.1136 (1954) provides: "When a probationer is discharged upon the expiration of the probation period, or upon its earlier termination by order of the court, entry of the discharge shall be made in the records of the court, and the probationer shall be entitled to a certified copy thereof."

ing financial obligations, and further supervision does not appear useful. The court proceeding is a formality in which the probation officer presents documents requesting an early discharge and giving reasons. The requests are almost always granted by the court.

Another method of early discharge — a motion for a new trial — is used in certain cases. The practice began in the Recorder's Court Probation Department as a device for expunging the criminal record of probationers with excellent adjustment when the conviction record interfered with employment or enlistment in the armed services. It is used almost exclusively by the Youth Division of the probation department[133] and only with respect to probationers with a single felony conviction. The youth's probation officer petitions the trial court for a new trial [134] stating the reasons for the request.[135] The prosecuting attorney formally moves the court for a new trial, which the court grants and immediately dismisses the case. A copy of the dismissal order is given to the ex-probationer and a copy is sent by the Youth Division to the Detroit Police Department, which returns the youth's fingerprint records to the probation department. Thereafter, a search of the police records by an employer or army recuiter will reveal no convictions.[136] In one and one-half years of using the new trial device, almost one hundred new trials and dismissals were granted.[137]

133 The Youth Division supervises probationers aged seventeen through twenty-one.

134 See Mich. Stat. Ann. §§28.1098, 28.1099 (1954) for the statutory provision authorizing motions for new trials in criminal cases.

135 A form entitled "Order for New Trial and Dismissal" is used. On it, the probation officer states the date of conviction and the offense and the granting of probation. The officer then briefly states the reasons for requesting the new trial. In one case, for example, the following statement of reasons was provided:

"Defendant was placed on probation by Your Honor for a period of three years on the above charge. He was assessed costs of $100.

"During his probation period, he completed high school, paid costs of supervision in full as ordered, and has been steadily employed.

"He was accepted by [a nationwide company's] sales and maintenance training program. The company, having subjected the defendant to extensive tests of ability and personality fitness, indicated in employing him considerable confidence.

"In view of this fact, coupled with his excellent response to probation supervision, it is recommended he be given consideration for a new trial and subsequent dismissal."

136 Apparently, most employers of probationers given a new trial and dismissal are aware of the conviction record. Expungement of the record probably does little more than create a more attractive personnel file for them. It may also, of course, be of significance if new employment is later sought. Expungement also serves as a substantial reward for excellent adjustment by probationers.

It is clear the armed services recruiting officers are aware of the probationers' status. Indeed, a recruiter was given use of a room in the probation office to interview probationers once a week. Only after a probationer indicated desire to enlist and passed his physical and mental examination was the new trial and dismissal procedure initiated.

137 Approximately half of these cases involved enlistment in the armed services.

Wisconsin statutes authorize early discharge from probation. In Milwaukee County authority to grant early discharge rests with the trial court, while in outstate Wisconsin it rests with the State Department of Public Welfare.[138] The proposed manual for the probation department in Milwaukee County states the grounds for discharge:

> Regular discharges are accomplished on satisfactory completion of the probation period with Court obligations paid, or with a balance set aside. A premature discharge may be recommended when the probationer has been making an unusually good adjustment, or Court obligations have been paid, and he has received the maximum benefit of probation treatment. It is recommended chiefly when the probation period is longer than two years. It may also be recommended when a probationer volunteers for induction or enlistment in the armed forces and is accepted.

Discharge proceedings are informal. The probation officer presents a petition for discharge with supporting facts to the trial judge, who signs a court order discharging the probationer. A copy of the discharge order is mailed to the ex-probationer.

[138] See Wis. Stat. Ann. §§57.025, 57.03 (1957).

CHAPTER 5

Probation Revocation

Legal authority to revoke probation usually rests exclusively with the trial court. In practice, however, responsibility for the decision is shared between the trial court and the probation staff, and there is no clear delineation of function between the court and staff. As a result, the decision-making process is a complex one based mainly on personal interaction between various trial judges and individual probation officers. Individual probation officers make the initial decision whether to seek revocation and negative decisions are not reviewed; some negative decisions are made because the probation officer believes the trial judge would refuse to revoke if presented with the case; some cases are returned to the court not for revocation but to obtain judicial reprimand of the probationer's conduct; probation officers sometimes conform their revocation recommendations to expected judicial preferences; and some trial judges make revocation decisions at least in part upon their impression of what the supervising probation officer desires.

In the metropolitan courts and probation departments under study, there is no system of administrative review of revocation decisions made by individual probation officers. Opportunity is thus created for wide disparity in revocation practices: Revocation in many cases may depend upon which combination of probation officer and trial judge has responsibility for supervising the case.

Three major aspects of probation revocation practice have been isolated for discussion: sufficiency of the evidence to revoke probation; the decision to revoke probation because of the probationer's proved or suspected criminal conduct; and the decision not to revoke probation despite sufficient evidence for revocation.

A. Sufficiency of the Evidence to Revoke Probation

Most correctional decisions do not involve questions of evidence sufficiency in the sense that certain findings must be made before the decision maker can act. It is true that all correctional decisions depend in part upon fact finding, thus presenting evidentiary problems for correctional decision makers, but seldom is it essential that particular facts be found. Probation revocation is an exception.[1] Although the matter is left somewhat in doubt by the law, officials in practice invariably insist that a violation of a probation condition must be proved to justify revocation.

1. *What constitutes grounds for revocation.* The Kansas statutes in force during the field survey authorized the trial judge to revoke probation "at any time without notice" to the probationer "by merely directing the clerk of the court to make out and deliver to the sheriff or other proper officer a certified copy of the sentence. . . ."[2] No judicial finding of any kind was required. The Michigan statute requires a judicial finding to authorize revocation, but it does not require proof of a violation of a probation condition:

> It is the intent of the legislature that the granting of probation to one convicted shall be a matter of grace conferring no vested right to its continuance, if, during the period of probation it shall appear to the satisfaction of the sentencing court that the probationer is likely again to engage in an offensive or criminal course of conduct, or that the public good requires revocation or termination of probation previously granted. All probation orders, therefore, shall be revocable or terminable in any manner which the court which imposed probation shall deem applicable, either for any violation, or attempted violation of any condition of probation, or for any other type of anti-social conduct or action on the part of the probationer which shall satisfy such court that revocation is proper and in the public interest.[3]

Wisconsin statutes authorize revocation if a probationer "violates the conditions of his probation."[4]

Although only Wisconsin of the three states requires by statute a finding of violation of a probation condition as a prerequisite to revocation, it is the uniform practice in all three states to revoke only upon proof of a probation condition violation. There may be several reasons why the broader statutory authority is not used.

[1] Parole revocation is another exception. See Chapter 14.

[2] Kan. Gen. Stat. §62-2204 (1949), repealed by Kan. Laws 1957, Ch. 331, §37. Present Kansas statutes require a probation violation hearing that "may be informal or summary." The court is authorized to revoke probation only if a violation of probation conditions is "established" at that hearing. See Kan. Stat. Ann. §62-2244 (1964).

[3] Mich. Stat. Ann. §28.1134 (1954).

[4] Wis. Stat. Ann. §57.03 (1957). In Wisconsin, outside of Milwaukee County, authority to revoke rests with the State Department of Public Welfare. Ibid. In Milwaukee County it rests with the trial court that granted probation. See Wis. Stat. Ann. §57.025 (1957).

The number and kind of probation conditions employed in practice make proof of violation relatively easy.[5] There is some feeling that revocation without proof of violation would be unfair to the probationer or at least would appear to him to be unfair. Finally, there may be doubt of the validity of the broader authorization and a desire to avoid litigation of the issue. Whatever the reason, it is clear that probation officers and trial judges in the three states behave as if the statutes required proof of violation of a probation condition for revocation.

2. *Degree of certainty there has been a violation.* Since, in practice, proof that the probationer violated a condition is required for revocation, an issue is raised regarding how certain the trial judge must be that there has been a violation. Statutes do not speak to this issue. Nor is the question often raised in practice, for several reasons. In probation violation hearings, in Detroit at least, the alleged violations are read to the probationer and he is required to plead guilty or not guilty. Since most probationers plead guilty, proof of a violation is not needed and the question of "degree of certainty" normally does not arise. In almost all cases returned to court for a violation hearing, a number of probation violations are alleged. In most Detroit hearings, for example, failure to report regularly and pay all court costs are alleged in addition to other violations. In these cases there is little doubt that these conditions were violated.

The issue arises in practice, then, only when the probationer pleads not guilty and only when the trial judge is unwilling to revoke on the basis of irregular reporting and nonpayment of court-imposed financial obligations. This does not occur often, in part because probation officers are alert to such problems and are unlikely to seek revocation when a proof problem is anticipated. When the issue arises, trial judges in Detroit refuse to accept hearsay evidence as a basis for determining that the violation in question occurred.[6] Beyond this, it is not possible to state what degree of certainty is required in practice. One trial judge was able to state that he does not require proof beyond a reasonable doubt but was unable to verbalize his standard.

3. *Sources of information concerning probation violations.*

a. *Observation of the probation officer.* Many requests for probation revocation cite failure to report regularly and failure to pay required court costs or restitution among the violations alleged. Evidence of these two violations is gathered by the probation offi-

[5] For a discussion of probation conditions used in practice, see Chapter 4.

[6] Proof problems are discussed in detail in the treatment of probation violation hearings at pages 148-151.

cer from his own records. Although revocation is rarely, if ever, sought simply for irregular reporting and nonpayment of financial obligations, they do constitute important formal grounds for supporting revocation in addition to more serious violations that probably move the officer to seek revocation. Absconding is sometimes discovered as a result of a check of reporting records by the probation officers. When the records reveal several consecutive instances of failure to report, the officer normally attempts to contact the probationer; if he is unable to do so, he will initiate proceedings for revocation on the ground of absconding.

As previous discussion has indicated, probation officers are in sharp disagreement among themselves concerning whether they should actively seek to detect probation violations through surveillance. Those officers who use surveillance clearly discover violations (such as deliberate unemployment, violation of curfew, and association with prohibited companions) that are missed by officers who do not use this technique. They also encourage reports of violations from persons in contact with the probationer, such as his spouse or parents.

Even those officers who use surveillance function more as the recipient of information on violations than as sources of information themselves. Perhaps heavy caseloads dictate that probation officers are often unable to do little more than receive and investigate violation reports made by other persons. It also seems clear that probation officers do not themselves frequently discover serious violations. Except for absconding, the violations they discover are rarely sufficient alone to lead to revocation.

b. *Police reports.* The police are an important source of information about new offenses committed by probationers. The Detroit Police Department provides Recorder's Court Probation Department with a daily list of persons arrested who are known to be on probation. If the arrest is for a serious offense and the probationer is not quickly released, the probation officer may interview him to determine whether revocation proceedings should be initiated. If the arrest is for a misdemeanor or other offense not regarded as serious, the probation officer would simply note the arrest in his records for possible use later as a ground for revocation.

c. *Reports from other persons.* Probation officers receive many complaints from persons who have contact with probationers, particularly from relatives. Wives frequently complain that their husbands are drinking, causing family trouble, or running around with other women. For example, a wife informed the officer that, as a result of a family dispute, she had called the police to arrest her husband for drunkenness. Persons other than relatives also provide information, although this happens less frequently. For example, a priest told a probation officer that a probationer was living with a woman and had a wife in another state.

Many reports from other persons concern minor violations of probation that will not lead to initiation of revocation proceedings. The role of the probation officer is limited to accepting the complaint, thanking the complainant, assuring him that action will be taken, recording the complaint and verifying it with the probationer, and perhaps reprimanding him for the conduct that resulted in the complaint.

4. *Measures designed to assure that revocations occur only upon sufficient evidence.* Certain precautionary steps are followed as a matter of practice when a probation officer discovers a possible violation of probation. First, if he has doubt about whether there was actually a probation violation, or how serious it was or whether he can prove it to the satisfaction of the trial court, he may undertake an investigation to determine the necessary facts. Second, he may sometimes confer with a supervisor in the probation department about whether revocation should be sought. Third, if he seeks revocation he must present the facts which he believes constitute a ground for revocation to the trial court in a probation violation hearing.

a. *Investigating reported violations.* Some types of probation violations require little or no investigation to verify them. This is true of violations that appear from the records of the probation department — such as nonreporting or failure to pay court-imposed financial obligations. Other reports of probation violations require considerable investigation if they are to be used as a basis for initiating revocation proceedings. Some investigations stem from the probation officer's understanding of court evidentiary requirements at the probation violation hearing. It is clear, for example, that probation officers in Detroit who suspect a probationer may be using narcotics refuse to initiate revocation proceedings unless witnesses to the use are available and willing to testify at the violation hearing. This position results from experiences some of the officers have had with trial judges who refuse to revoke on the basis of hearsay evidence of use or even of extra-judicial admission of use by the probationer to the probation officer. If the probation officer is unable to verify a suspected violation, he may nevertheless seek revocation on other grounds, such as nonreporting or failure to pay financial obligations. No mention is made of the unverified suspected violation in the probation violation report or at the hearing.[7]

[7] In one case, a probationer was accused by his employer of failing to deposit

Officers frequently exercise discretion not to investigate violation reports. This very often happens when the violations alleged, if they actually occurred, would be regarded as minor or when the officer suspects that the person making the report may not be truthful.[8] Some probation officers limit investigation to questioning the probationer about the reported violation. In one case, for example, an officer asked a probationer about a report that he had possessed a pistol, and the probationer replied that he had but had thrown it away in an abandoned quarry. Other officers are reluctant to use information obtained in interviews with probationers as grounds for revocation. One officer said: "If you try to get a probationer to tell the probation officer all and then turn around and use this against him, you are doing the very thing that made the probationer what he is."

b. *Administrative review of the decision to seek revocation.* Parole officers in Michigan and Wisconsin are required to obtain the concurrence of their immediate supervisor before sending a revocation request to central headquarters. By contrast, no requirement or practice of administrative review by department supervisors of requests for probation revocation was observed. If a probation officer confers with his supervisor before taking a probationer into court for revocation, it is usually because he is unable to decide whether revocation should be sought. The Women's Division of Recorder's Court Probation Department is a possible exception to this pattern. The supervisor of the Division herself appears in court at the violation hearing. She must, therefore, approve all requests for revocation before they are filed in court. It is doubtful, however, whether she gives careful attention to the merits of the revocation request. She stated the major reason for her appearing in court, instead of the probation officer, was to preserve the relationship between the probationer and the supervising officer in the event the probationer is continued on supervision by the trial

---

$285 in a night depository for the employer. The probationer denied taking the money and insisted that he deposited it as instructed. No criminal charges were brought. Probation was revoked on the grounds the probationer failed to report financial transactions in which he had engaged, sold a mortgaged automobile without disclosing the mortgage to the purchaser, and failed to report a $400 loan he had obtained. The suspected theft of $285 was not mentioned in the violation report or at the hearing, but it seems clear it was a consideration in the decision to seek revocation.

[8] One probation officer recalled a case in which a probationer's wife had complained that he was drinking excessively and going out with another woman. The man was on probation for abandoning his wife and child and was not then living with them. The officer did not attempt to investigate the wife's report because it would be difficult to verify it and he was concerned about the possibility of vindictive claims by a scorned wife.

court. There was no indication she was concerned about probation officers making revocation requests in inappropriate cases.

c. *Probation violation hearings.* Neither Kansas[9] nor Wisconsin[10] statutes require a probation violation hearing before the trial court as a prerequisite to revocation. A hearing is required by statute in Michigan.[11] Nevertheless, in each of the three states, it is an almost [12] unvarying practice to hold a probation violation hearing before revocation. However, the characteristics of the hearings vary considerably among the three states.

In Wichita, Kansas, revocation is virtually never sought except when a probationer has been arrested for or convicted of a new offense. The prosecuting attorney, not the supervising probation officer, initiates the revocation proceedings. A hearing is held in which the prosecutor states that there has been a conviction or that the probationer was arrested for a new offense. A brief description of the offense is provided by the prosecutor from the police report. The trial judge asks the probationer whether he wishes to make a statement and then decides whether to revoke probation.[13] The supervising probation officer is usually present during the hearing but normally does not participate.[14]

In Milwaukee, violation hearings are more formal. The violations alleged are reduced to writing and the probation officer,

[9] Kan. Gen. Stat. §62-2204 (1949), repealed by Kan. Laws 1957, Ch. 331, §37. Present Kansas law requires a hearing. Kan. Stat. Ann. §62-2244 (1964).

[10] Wis. Stat. Ann. §57.03 (1957), applicable outside Milwaukee County, provides: "If a probationer in its charge violates the conditions of his probation, the [State Department of Public Welfare] may order him brought before the court for sentence which shall then be imposed without further stay or if already sentenced may order him to prison. . . ." There is no provision regulating probation revocation in the statute applicable to Milwaukee County. See Wis. Stat. Ann. §57.025 (1957).

[11] Mich Stat. Ann. §28.1134 (1954).

[12] On some occasions outside Milwaukee County if the trial court imposed a sentence and stayed its execution when placing the defendant on probation, the State Department of Welfare could, by statute, take him to prison on probation revocation without returning the case to court. See note 10 *supra.* If the imposition of sentence was stayed, the State Department of Public Welfare must return the probationer to court for imposition of a sentence to be selected by the trial judge.

[13] In one probation violation hearing the prosecuting attorney informed the court that the probationer, a woman, was arrested by the police for being drunk in a hotel. He requested the court to revoke probation. The trial judge asked the probationer where she worked. When she stated that she worked as a waitress in a particular cafe, he replied, "Your probation is revoked" and terminated the hearing.

[14] In Wyandotte County (Kansas City), Kansas, the District Court meets *en banc* twice per month to conduct probation violation hearings and other business related to probation. Cases are presented to the judges by a full-time probation officer—probation officers in Wichita double as bailiffs. The hearings are informal. A member of the prosecuting attorney's staff is present but does not participate. The only instances observed in which probation revocation was sought were cases in which the probationer was convicted of a new offense in another jurisdiction and was returned to Wyandotte County for revocation.

under oath, testifies concerning them and the probationer's adjustment under supervision in general. Unlike Detroit, no plea is required, but the probationer is usually asked whether he wishes to make a statement or produce witnesses in defense of the allegations. Apparently, the rules of evidence are not followed to the extent they are in Detroit. The probation officer makes a recommendation to the trial judge that is often but not always followed.

The Michigan statute requiring a probation violation hearing provides: "Hearings on such revocation shall be summary and informal and not subject to the rules of evidence or of pleadings applicable in criminal trials. . . . The method of hearing and presentation of charges accorded shall lie entirely within the discretion of the court which granted probation; Provided however, that the probationer shall be entitled to a written copy of the charges against him which constitute the claim that he violated his probation, and shall be entitled to a hearing thereon." [15]

A probation violation hearing in Detroit is initiated by the probation officer informally contacting the trial judge who originally granted the probation or his clerk to arrange for a hearing time. At the designated time, the probation officer brings the probationer into court and presents to the trial judge a "Notice of Probation Violation" which lists the probation conditions imposed and the violations of those conditions alleged to have occurred.[16] Although the probationer is already in custody by virtue of a probation "hold," the probation officer also requests issuance of a bench warrant from the trial judge.[17] In addition, the trial judge is provided

[15] Mich. Stat. Ann. §28.1134 (1954).

[16] One Notice of Probation Violation, after listing all the probation conditions which had been imposed, alleged the following violations:

"1. On 8/31/56 defendant convicted of simple larceny and sentenced to 30 days in the Detroit House of Correction by Hon. Judge X.

"2. On 1/7/57 defendant sentenced to three days in Wayne County Jail by Hon. Judge Y for ordinance violation.

"3. Defendant has failed to secure employment or discharge his costs and restitution as ordered.

"4. His parents advised he is repeatedly absent from home for periods in the extent of 24 hours, whereabouts unknown."

The Notice of Probation Violation is usually served on the probationer by the probation officer several hours before the hearing.

[17] Few probationers are actually taken into custody under the authority of a probation violation bench warrant. Many of them are arrested by police without an arrest warrant for commission of new offenses. When that occurs, the probation officer is notified, and the probationer is retained in custody on authority of a probation hold, a document authorizing custody of the probationer for investigation of probation violation. If a probation officer wishes to take a probationer into custody to initiate revocation proceedings, he usually simply phones the police to have them make the arrest. A probation hold is then issued to authorize continuance of custody. In either event, the probationer is continued in custody under

with a copy of the presentence report that was prepared before the probationer was placed on supervision.

A formal record is made of the hearing. Besides the trial judge and court reporter, only the probation officer and probationer are usually present. Occasionally, the probationer may retain an attorney[18] or have witnesses present to testify for him; in some cases, witnesses may be called by the probation officer. The hearing is opened by the judge asking the probation officer to state the case against the probationer. This usually consists of a recitation of the violations alleged in the Notice of Probation Violation. The judge then asks the probationer for a plea to the charges. If he pleads guilty, further proof of the allegations is not required and the trial judge questions the probation officer and probationer preliminary to deciding whether to revoke.

If the probationer pleads not guilty, the trial judge requires the probation officer to prove the allegations. Although the statute seems to require the trial judge to admit evidence that might be excluded in a criminal jury trial, trial judges in Detroit uniformly refuse to find a probation violation solely upon the basis of inadmissible evidence. The following hypothetical case was put to several trial judges: A probation officer testifies in a violation hearing that the probationer's mother told him she saw the probationer (previously convicted of narcotics use and possession) injecting something into his arm by a hypodermic needle. All the trial judges replied they would not accept this evidence as proof the probationer used narcotics. If the witness testified to what she saw, the judges said they would consider that proof of narcotics use and, in addition, would probably revoke.[19]

---

authority of the hold until the trial judge signs the bench warrant at the probation violation hearing. The only time a bench warrant for probation violation is issued prior to apprehension of the probationer is when his whereabouts is unknown and it is desirable to alert the police to the fact that he is wanted.

18 At the time the survey was conducted, appointment of counsel for the indigent at probation revocation proceedings was not required as a matter of federal constitutional law. It was not the practice in any of the three states to appoint counsel for the indigent at this stage of the correctional process nor to notify probationers of their right to the presence and services of retained counsel. However, if a probationer appeared at a probation violation hearing with an attorney, counsel was permitted to represent his client at that proceeding. Chapter 16 discusses the role of counsel in the entire correctional process, including probation revocation. In Mempa v. Rhay, 329 U.S. 128, 88 Sup. Ct. 254, 336 L. Ed. 2d 19 (1967), the United States Supreme Court held that the federal constitutional right to counsel extends to probation revocation proceedings.

19 The proof problem on narcotics use allegations is made more difficult by additional factors. Although the probation department can refer probationers to the Detroit Narcotics Clinic for a medical determination whether they are addicted to narcotics, the Clinic refuses to permit this information to be used in violation hearings on the ground that would violate confidentiality. One trial judge even requires

In most violation hearings on not guilty pleas, the probation officer is able to prove the violations alleged.[20] One reason for this is that probation officers do not request a violation hearing unless they feel able to prove violations sufficiently serious to warrant revocation.[21] There is considerable evidence the probation officers screen out cases on the basis of anticipated failure of proof under circumstances when adequate proof exists. For example, a number of probation officers stated that, if a probationer admitted to them he used narcotics but denied that admission in a violation hearing, the trial judge would refuse to revoke. Several trial judges, however, stated that they would consider the probation officer's testimony as proof of use despite the later denial by the probationer.[22]

B. The Decision to Revoke Probation Because of the Probationer's Criminal Conduct

Although legal authority exists for revocation on the basis of noncriminal rules infractions, in practice revocations are ordinar-

---

probation officers who seek to prove use by needle marks to prove they are recent marks. Other trial judges, however, expressed willingness to consider the officer's opinion on whether needle marks indicate use during the probation period, but did not indicate whether that alone would be sufficient proof of use to permit revocation.

20 One trial judge recalled a case in which the probation officer testified the probationer's mother told him she saw her son using narcotics. When the mother testified in court, she denied making the statement or ever seeing her son using narcotics. The trial judge stated he refused to revoke probation because the use had not been proved. In another case, failure to report and pay costs, associating with questionable persons, and intimidating a fifteen-year-old boy were the allegations. The probationer pleaded not guilty. The fifteen-year-old boy testified, under questioning by the trial judge, that he could not be certain the probationer was among the gang of boys that harassed him. The probationer stated he had formerly been with the gang that evening but had gone home before the event in question. The trial judge refused to revoke probation on the ground that the crucial allegation had not been proved. This obviously placed the probation officer in the difficult position of continuing to supervise a probationer he had attempted to revoke. He handled the situation by telling the probationer he had not really wanted him revoked but only wanted to scare him, and further, that he could have put on a stronger case if he had desired revocation. He later confided to the field observer that he had, indeed, desired revocation.

21 On some occasions, however, they bring cases into court for a violation hearing to scare the probationer, but not to seek revocation. On these occasions, they inform the trial judge in private before the hearing of their purpose and secure his cooperation.

22 In one case, a probation officer stated a probationer admitted to him that he lived with a fifteen-year-old girl and used her as a prostitute. The officer further stated that he would not seek revocation because he possessed only hearsay rather than direct knowledge and, therefore, would be unable to prove a violation. In another case, a probation officer stated that if he were later to submit a violation request to the court, the fact that the probationer was arrested for investigation by the police and had admitted to him that he was using drugs would have to be withheld from the court.

ily sought only when the probationer has engaged in serious criminal conduct. In the three states, this was invariably true except for absconding and repeated, flagrant rules violations. This is not to imply, however, that all criminal conduct or even all serious criminal conduct results in revocation. Discretion not to revoke is exercised when the violation is criminal as well as when it is noncriminal.

1. *Probation revocation following conviction.* The effect of conviction of a criminal offense on the offender's probation status varies with the seriousness of the offense and how the case happens to arise. In all three states, conviction of an ordinance violation or a misdemeanor does not itself normally result in revocation. The probationer is continued on supervision even if the new conviction results in a sentence to a local correctional institution. The probation officer notes the conviction for possible later use as a ground for revocation, if he has been informed of it; he may also interview the probationer to determine the circumstances of the new offense and to warn him of its possible effect on his probation status. If revocation is later sought, the conviction, together with noncriminal rules violations, will be used as grounds.[23] Most misdemeanor convictions are regarded as no more serious than rules violations.

If the probationer is convicted of a felony, however, the consequences are far more serious. The fact the defendant is on probation makes it unlikely he will be given probation for the new conviction and also is likely to increase the length of the prison sentence if the trial judge has discretion in sentence selection. In Kansas and Wisconsin when a probationer is sentenced to prison for a felony, his probation is usually revoked. Although trial judges in those states have authority to impose consecutive sentences in that situation,[24] normally concurrent sentences are imposed. If the trial judge who granted probation hears the new felony case, the probation violation hearing is likely to be combined with the sentence hearing on the new offense and the entire matter disposed of at one time. When different trial judges are involved, revocation is sought following sentence as a separate step in the proceedings.

In Detroit the pattern of practice is not so uniform. Conviction

[23] In one Detroit case, the process was accelerated. The individual was placed on probation for breaking and entering an automobile. Four months later, he pleaded guilty to simple larceny (a misdemeanor) and was given a suspended sentence and turned over to the probation department. Revocation was requested on the ground of the larceny conviction, failure to pay court costs and restitution, and admitted use of narcotics. Probation was revoked and the probationer was sentenced to a term of eighteen months to five years in prison.

[24] See Chapter 7 for a discussion of authority to sentence the multiple offender in the three states.

of a felony by a probationer can have different consequences, depending upon the circumstances. It is very unlikely that probation will be revoked. Several trial judges in Detroit stated that revocation under these circumstances accomplishes little because Michigan law requires that concurrent sentences be imposed.[25] One trial judge stated he would revoke probation only if the new felony offense was considerably less serious than the original one and he believed the probationer needed a longer maximum sentence than permitted by the new offense. It is clear, however, that if the new offense is processed in the same court that originally granted probation, revocation would probably occur before the new offense reaches trial stage and prosecution would be dismissed.

The most typical consequence of conviction of a new felony while on probation is to discharge the defendant from probation "without improvement." This removes the case from probation department supervision and the defendant enters prison sentenced for the new offense alone. Another practice is to continue the defendant on probation despite the fact he has been sentenced to prison for the new felony conviction. This is done when he has not fully paid court costs or restitution. Probation officers wish to continue him on supervision to collect these obligations when he is released on parole or upon service of sentence.[26]

2. *Probation revocation without conviction.* In practice, probation revocation is frequently used as an alternative to prosecution for serious offenses committed by probationers. If the probationer is clearly convictable of the new offense, there is little need both to prosecute him for it and revoke his probation. Often, the choice between prosecution and revocation is a fortuitous one. Greater problems arise, however, when there is doubt about the probationer's convictability of the new offense. Revocation is used without conviction in both Kansas and Michigan. In Milwaukee, the trial judge has apparently required that prosecution be instituted and that revocation occur only after conviction.[27]

[25] See Ex parte Allison, 322 Mich. 491, 33 N.W.2d 917 (1948).

[26] In one case, the defendant had been placed on probation for two years for breaking and entering an automobile. Five months later he was sentenced by a different court to a term of two and a half to five years for receiving stolen property. At the time of his sentence he still owed restitution on the original offense. He was continued on probation, and supervision was resumed when he was released from prison on parole.

[27] A probationer was under supervision for check forgery. He had failed to report for several months and was presently in jail on a new forgery charge. The probation officer filed a petition seeking revocation of probation. Although he stated he had sufficient grounds for revocation, he obtained adjournment of the violation hearing until after conviction on the new forgery charge. He stated that the trial judge prefers to adjourn violation hearings until after conviction and handle sentencing in both cases at the same time.

In Kansas revocation without conviction occurs frequently. A Deputy County Attorney in Sedgwick County indicated this is used when the new crime is not more serious than the original one. He stated revocation saves the county the expense of a new trial and usually serves the same purpose; it is also handled very easily since it is entirely within the discretion of the trial judge. There is some concern over whether the probationer is convictable of the new offense. A trial judge in Sedgwick County stated that one of his major problems in deciding whether probation should be revoked is the constant requests by police officers, the county attorney's office, and the F.B.I. to have probation revoked when a probationer is suspected of a crime. He said he refuses to revoke probation merely because a law enforcement officer or prosecutor suspects the probationer of committing an offense, but when he is presented with evidence which in his judgment would result in a jury verdict of guilty, he is willing to revoke.[28]

Revocation without conviction is also used in Detroit. The supervisor of the Women's Division of Recorder's Court Probation Department stated: "If probationers are again arrested on a new felony while under supervision the prosecutor will ask the probation department to return the case to court as a probation violation rather than go through the time, effort, and expense of a new trial." Apparently, the major motive for this procedure is saving the effort of a trial. Despite the fact that the case would probably be adjudicated by plea of guilty, officials are apparently unwilling to assume that a trial will not be demanded. This is clear at least in cases in which the probationer is convictable of the new offense.[29]

Revocation is also used when there is doubt as to the convictability of the probationer. In one case, the probation officer agreed to seek revocation when the police admitted they were unable to prove a charge of statutory rape because the victim was unable to testify. In this case and others in which there is doubt of convictability, the probationer has usually been uncooperative with the probation department to such an extent that they, as well as the

[28] In one case, a deputy county attorney brought before the court the case of a probationer found drunk in a hotel. He asked the district court to revoke after he informed the court of the circumstances of the offense as they appeared from the police report. Probation was revoked.

[29] In one case, a probationer was charged with breaking and entering. The prosecutor and probation officer agreed to seek revocation instead of prosecuting for the new offense. The probationer freely admitted his guilt to the probation officer. Revocation was sought on the grounds of (1) a charge of breaking and entering which was admitted by the probationer and (2) associating with a prohibited person, his partner in the new offense. The probationer pleaded guilty to the violations, but he was continued on probation on condition he spend the next sixty days in the House of Correction.

police, are seeking a reason to secure his incarceration.[30] The only indication of an evidentiary limitation upon this type of proceedings was the statement by the supervisor of the Women's Division that when police request revocation for a new offense she requires the investigating police officer to be present in court and to testify to the facts which constitute the basis for revocation.

C. The Decision Not to Revoke Probation Despite Sufficient Evidence

Most probationers violate their probation conditions at least once during the supervisory period. This occurs in part because the conditions typically imposed are quite broad and numerous. Moreover, they are applicable to persons who have in the past demonstrated inability to conform to conduct requirements. Although many of these violations do not come to official attention, those which do and can be proved would probably permit almost every probationer to be revoked at one time or another during the supervision period. In practice, however, only a small percentage of known, provable violations result in revocation.

The decisions analyzed in this section involve probation violations that can be proved to the satisfaction of both the supervising probation officer and the trial judge responsible for revocation. There is no doubt, therefore, about the authority of these officials to revoke probation if they desire to do so. Focus is upon the reasons this authority is not exercised in individual cases.

Discretion may be exercised at either of two stages in the revocation decision-making process: The trial judge, when presented with evidence of violations at a probation violation hearing, may decide not to revoke despite the fact the violations were proved to his satisfaction; the probation officer, when presented with evidence of a probation violation, may decide not to return the probationer to court for a violation hearing despite his ability to prove the violations to the satisfaction of the trial judge.

There is an interrelation between these two stages. On some occasions, the trial judge may not revoke, despite adequate proof of

[30] In this case, the probationer was originally convicted of larceny of $160 and was placed on probation for two years. Because he had failed to pay court costs and restitution, his probation period was extended for two years. At the time of the revocation, the extension was to expire shortly. The violation report alleged nonpayment of court costs and restitution, living with a fifteen-year-old girl for the past six months, irregular reporting, and receiving a thirty-day sentence for aiding and abetting prostitution. The police were convinced the probationer was guilty of statutory rape and of using the fifteen-year-old girl as a prostitute, but felt they were unable to prove these charges since the girl had just been committed to a mental hospital and could not be used as a witness.

violations, because he believes the probation officer does not desire revocation but has returned the case to court to secure judicial reprimand of the probationer or to ask for other judicial action short of revocation. Conversely, sometimes a probation officer may not return a case to court despite a provable violation because he believes the trial judge would not be willing to revoke probation due to the minor nature of the violations, or for some other reason.

Finally, in most cases in which provable violations do not lead to revocation, officials take other action: an extension of the probation period, imposition of new probation conditions, a short stay in a local correctional institution, or a reprimand of the probationer and a warning that further violations may result in revocation. At each of the two stages, therefore, decisions are analyzed in the following terms: (1) the reasons for the exercise of discretion, (2) the impact of other officials on the decision and (3) the alternatives to revocation employed.

1. *Trial judge discretion not to revoke probation.* In practice, trial judges exercise broad discretion not to revoke probation despite sufficient proof of a violation. Statutes in Kansas[31] and Wisconsin[32] provide no guidelines for the exercise of this discretion, and the Michigan statute merely requires the trial judge to consider whether "the probationer is likely again to engage in an offensive or criminal course of conduct" or whether "the public good requires revocation. . . ."[33] Within these broad statutory limitations, the trial judge is free to make the revocation decision.

Discretion exercised by the trial judge not only determines the outcome of the specific case involved but also influences which cases will be brought to court in the future. The process of communication is not formalized, so there is opportunity for misunderstanding. Nevertheless, probation officers feel they have rather good impressions of the decision-making criteria of particular trial judges and this impression clearly influences their decisions.

a. *The criteria used.*

Illustration No. 1: In a probation violation hearing in the judge's chambers, the supervising officer alleged that the probationer had not reported for three months and had been convicted of a misdemeanor in another court. He was placed on probation in the misdemeanor case, the officer stated, in anticipation of the action the judge might take in this violation hearing. The officer stated the probationer had refused to co-

[31] Kans. Gen. Stat. §62-2204 (1949), repealed by Kan. Laws 1957, Ch. 331, §37.
[32] Wis. Stat. Ann. §§57.025, 57.03 (1957).
[33] Mich. Stat. Ann. §28.1134 (1954).

operate with him and had given false addresses to the department. The probationer stated he had not reported because of an injury he had sustained in a fight. The judge indicated he intended to revoke probation, but when the probationer stressed his intention to cooperate in the future, he decided to continue him on supervision and extended the probation period one year.

The most important criteria in the decision whether to revoke probation are the number and seriousness of the violations. In determining the seriousness of a violation of probation, trial judges tend to separate felony offenses from misdemeanor offenses and technical violations.[34] Most instances of probation revocation involve the commission of a felony by the probationer; however, not all new felony offenses result in a probation violation hearing[35] and not all probation violation hearings for new felonies result in revocation.[36] In most instances, nevertheless, a new felony offense will result in revocation; an important question remaining, therefore, is what violations less serious than a felony offense are likely to result in revocation.

In Sedgwick County, Kansas, there are virtually no probation revocations for misdemeanors or technical violations. According to an assistant in the county attorney's office, probation supervision is so minimal that virtually no technical violations are discovered. Revocation proceedings are instituted by the prosecuting attorney, rather than the probation officer, and almost invariably involve commission of a new felony offense by the probationer.[37]

[34] Technical violations are violations of probation conditions that are not also violations of the criminal law; the usage is unclear on the question whether a municipal ordnance violation is a technical violation.

[35] The probation officer's decision whether to return a known violator to court for a violation hearing is discussed later in this chapter.

[36] In one case, the defendant was charged with felonious assault (while drunk) but pleaded guilty to a misdemeanor charge of assault and battery. He was placed on probation. Later, he was arrested again and charged with felonious assault (also while drunk) but again pleaded guilty to assault and battery, for which he served a ninety day sentence in a local correctional institution. His probation case was returned to court for a violation hearing but the trial judge refused to revoke on the ground that the ninety-day sentence was sufficient punishment.

[37] The assistant county attorney continued that even absconding does not usually result in revocation. In the first place, there is very little absconding because reporting is made extremely easy; for example, probationers are permitted to report by mail. Even if a probation officer returned a case to court for absconding, it would be very unlikely to result in revocation. The assistant county attorney felt that one reason for this was that the prisons and jails are extremely overcrowded and most judges feel that prison facilities should not be taxed with persons who can function fairly well outside of prison. On the other hand a district court judge in Sedgwick County indicated that he is willing to revoke probation for repeated technical violations, such as arrests for violations of public drunkenness ordinances or complete failure to pay restitution.

In Detroit trial judges emphasized the seriousness of the violation as the key criterion. They indicated that a new felony offense is very likely to result in revocation, but that revocations might occur in other cases as well.[38] Each judge provided several examples of violations that he would normally consider not to be serious enough to warrant revocation: drinking to excess or arrest and conviction for public intoxication; failure to report to the probation officer;[39] failure to pay court costs or restitution; associating with persons prohibited by probation conditions; violation of curfew imposed by probation conditions; possession of marijuana; and most misdemeanors. Several of them, on the other hand, provided situations in which they would seriously consider revocation despite their view that the violation itself was minor: revocation for drunkenness would be considered if drinking was an important factor in the original offense or if the court had imposed a special probation condition prohibiting any drinking; a misdemeanor conviction might result in revocation if it was the same kind of offense as the original one; and repeated, minor violations clearly indicating a refusal by the probationer to accept the authority of the court and probation officer might result in revocation. The same kinds of considerations appear to affect the revocation decision in Milwaukee.[40]

Another important criterion in the revocation decision is the impact revocation would have upon the probationer's family. If the probationer has been supporting his dependents, even sporadically, trial judges are very reluctant to revoke because the family would be denied support entirely and, in many cases, would have to apply for public assistance.[41] This consideration is especially ap-

[38] On the other hand, several probation officers in Detroit stated that in order to effect revocation there has to be a new felony offense. If there is one, and it is pressed by the probation officer, it will usually result in either revocation or conviction for the new offense and a sentence for it.

[39] Several of the judges indicated that in many cases of failure to report, the probationer is financially unable to make his payment on court costs or restitution and does not report for that reason.

[40] For example, a probation officer indicated that even several arrests and convictions for public intoxication would not result in revocation if the case were returned to court.

[41] In one case, the defendant had been placed on one year's probation for a misdemeanor assault and battery upon his wife. Three days later, his wife reported that the probationer had been drunk the entire time since he was placed on probation, had kicked in the door of the house after his wife had locked him out, had sworn in front of the children, and had generally created a disturbance. The probation officer immediately telephoned the police to arrest the probationer on a probation violation hold. The police brought him to the probation officer; he was still somewhat intoxicated. The officer filed a probation violation notice with the court and arranged for a hearing. He contacted the judge informally and expressed his opinion that revocation was proper since the probationer had grossly violated probation almost immediately after leaving the court hearing in which he was

plicable to probationers under supervision for criminal nonsupport because the purpose of the statutes and of officials administering them is to obtain support for the family. Family support orders in nonsupport cases are frequently violated, but revocation very rarely occurs; instead, compliance is attempted through revocation threats made by the probation officer or through returning the case to court for a stern judicial lecture. The circumstances in which revocation is regarded as a possibility in nonsupport cases are those in which the probationer absolutely refuses to ever pay support because of hostility toward his wife, or in which almost continuous drunkenness precludes gainful employment altogether.

Trial judges often consider the impact of revocation upon the probationer himself. There is a general reluctance to revoke probation because of the presence of overcrowded, inadequate prison facilities. Trial judges are especially reluctant to revoke youthful offenders because they fear prison may have an adverse effect upon them. Trial judges are also reluctant to revoke feeble-minded probationers despite repeated violations, perhaps as a result of sympathy for them or a feeling that they are not completely responsible for their conduct.[42]

b. *The probation officer's recommendation.*

Illustration No. 2: The probationer had been placed on supervision for felony nonsupport. He had a long history of failure to provide adequate support and had been placed on probation three times before for misdemeanor nonsupport. Recently, he had been arrested on his wife's complaint, for being drunk and disorderly. The notice of probation violation alleged that the probationer had been drinking to excess, had created a disturbance in his home, and had demanded money from his wife for alcohol. Before the violation hearing, the probation officer contacted the judge in private and explained that, although the probationer was constantly in trouble, his wife and three children needed his support; he recommended a few days in jail for him to "dry out." At the violation hearing, after the evidence of violation was presented, the trial judge turned to the probationer and in a very gruff

---

given probation. The judge responded simply, "Well, I like that check coming in." He did not change his position when the probation officer explained that the probationer worked only occasionally and that the wife had to work in order to support the children. At the violation hearing, the judge refused to revoke probation and warned the probationer to support his family by paying $20 per week to the Domestic Relations Division.

42 One trial judge stated he tended to be quite lenient toward youthful, feeble-minded probationers and would tolerate almost any conduct that does not involve violence.

voice said, "You are going to prison." He continued by saying that the probationer needed a long stay in prison to straighten him out. However, he then told the probationer he was deferring sentence for a few days and instructed the police to hold him in custody until the time set for sentencing. After the hearing, the judge explained that this was a little scheme he and the probation officer had devised and that the probationer would be released in a few days and continued on probation.

At probation violation hearings, most trial judges ask the probation officer for his recommendation on the disposition of the case. In some cases, the officer's recommendation is part of the notice of probation violation. One probation officer indicated that the trial judges follow the supervising officer's recommendation in most cases: "Most of the judges understand that the probation department does not bring the probationer into court unless they have exhausted all means of effecting the subject's rehabilitation. In the vast majority of cases, they realize that returning a subject to court is the last resort used by the probation department and, therefore, the judges usually follow the recommendations of the department." It is clear, however, that departmental recommendations are not uniformly followed by trial judges. Several cases were observed in which the probation officer recommended revocation but the trial judge continued the probationer on supervision.[43] When this occurs, probation officers may take steps to reestablish the position of authority over the probationer which they may feel was undermined by the trial judge's decision.[44] In the majority of cases,

[43] In one case, for example, the probation officer recommended revocation of probation in a nonsupport case. The judge refused on the ground that his family needed whatever support he could provide. Some trial judges are more willing than others to rely upon the probation officer's recommendations in revocation matters. Before one probation violation hearing, the officer stated that although he was going to recommend revocation he couldn't tell what the judge would do since he had his own opinions and one had to be careful with him. On the other hand, another judge was described as being quite willing to follow virtually all probation department recommendations.

Revocation recommendations, unlike recommendations at sentencing, are made by the individual probation officer supervising the case without review by case supervisors within the department. The informal manual used in the Milwaukee probation department states: "The recommendation for or against continuance of probation to be made when probationer is charged with a new offense while on probation is according to the type of offense, extenuating circumstances, adjustment on probation (including payment of support and other financial obligations) possibilities for further constructive probation supervision, etc."

[44] In one case, the probation officer recommended revocation but the trial judge continued the probationer on supervision. After the hearing was over, the probation officer instructed the probationer that he had not really wanted revocation but could have secured it by putting on a much stronger case. Some probation officers talk with the trial judge informally before the violation hearing to determine the judge's wishes in the case. One reason for this practice may be to avoid

nevertheless, the trial judge decides in accordance with the probation officer's recommendation; in part, this may result from the fact that some probation officers conform their recommendations to known preferences of the trial judge.[45]

The effect of the probation officer's recommendation is quite different in those cases in which the probationer is returned to court for reasons other than revocation. In these cases, the probation violation hearing is used as a disciplinary device to assist the officer in supervising the case. Violation hearings are frequently used this way in Detroit when the officer feels that the probationer has not responded to his lectures and reprimands but that he might respond to a threat of revocation made by the trial judge. It may also be used in situations in which the probation officer seeks an alternative to revocation — such as an extended stay in a local correctional institution or an extension of the probation period — that he is unable to impose without court authority. In either event, the probation officer in Detroit usually contacts the trial judge before the hearing to inform him of his purpose and to enlist his cooperation. The trial judges are normally willing to cooperate.[46] The same device is used in Milwaukee without informal arrangements between the trial judge and probation officer; one officer stated that the trial judge assumes that any time an officer does not recommend revocation he wants the judge to deliver a stern lecture to the probationer threatening revocation, and he always cooperates.[47]

c. *Alternatives to revocation.*

Illustration No. 3: The probationer was returned to court for a probation violation hearing. The violation report alleged (1) that he had failed to report regularly and kept irregular hours; (2) that he had paid nothing on his court

---

the problem of continuing to supervise an individual after recommending revocation.

45 See page 166.

46 It seems clear that in some of these cases the facts are such that the trial judge would be unwilling to revoke even if the probation officer recommended it. In other cases, however, the officer's recommendation is the controlling factor; one Detroit trial judge stated, for example, that he always tries to support probation officers with all probationers but particularly when the officer requests continued supervision to work further with the probationer.

47 In one case the trial judge extended the probation period for two years on recommendation of the probation officer. The officer had reported a disorderly conduct arrest (probable homosexual conduct) to the trial judge at the violation hearing but had not informed the trial judge that the probationer had not reported to him in three months. He stated that giving the trial judge the information on nonreporting would make the case appear too serious to permit extension rather than revocation. The officer stated that the trial judge knew information was sometimes withheld from him at violation hearings in cases like this, but he approved of the practice.

costs; and (3) that he had been sentenced in a justice of the peace court to ten days in the county jail for illegal possession of alcohol. The trial judge did not revoke probation but imposed a new condition requiring the probationer to serve sixty days in the house of correction.

Illustration No. 4: The probationer was returned to court for a probation violation hearing. He had failed to report for six weeks; he explained that he lived and worked outside of the county and that reporting was difficult. The judge said, "We have a reformatory available, and no reporting is necessary there. Maybe the reformatory would be easier for you." The probation officer stated that the probationer had reported regularly for the first five months of the twelve-month probation period and recommended an extension of probation for one year. He informed the judge that the probationer had been in jail for three days as a violator. The trial judge did not revoke probation but extended the probation period one year.

When the trial judge does not revoke probation despite proof of a violation, he usually does more than simply continue the probationer on supervision. In almost all cases the trial judge gives the probationer a stern reprimand for his conduct and threatens to revoke probation if another violation occurs. Furthermore, in almost all cases, the probationer has spent at least one day in jail under a probation violation hold awaiting his court hearing.[48]

In many cases, other alternatives to revocation are used. One of the most frequent is an extended stay in a local correctional institution. In Detroit, probation officers feel their authority to detain a probationer on a violation hold is limited to a few days at most. The trial judge, however, may impose a jail term of as long as sixty days as a condition of probation.[49] In many cases in which the conduct is not viewed by the trial judge as serious enough to warrant revocation, he may impose a sixty-day sentence as a condition of continuing the probationer on supervision.[50] In Milwaukee, proba-

[48] It is even more likely that he will have spent several days in jail awaiting court hearing. Probation officers use this as a disciplinary device and sometimes deliberately delay the court hearing to keep the probationer incarcerated. In an extreme case, the probation officer kept the probationer incarcerated under his probation violation hold for one month. He refused to respond to several requests from the probationer to talk with him about the violation. The officer explained that he intended to scare the probationer and would take the case to court and recommend continued supervision.

[49] Mich. Stat. Ann. §28.1133 (1954). Mich. Pub. Acts 1957, No. 72, increased the maximum permissible period of incarceration to six months. Mich. Stat. Ann. §28.1133 (Supp. 1965).

[50] Another technique is to continue the probation violation hearing for a brief

tion officers apparently do not believe their authority to detain the probationer is that limited. They are more likely to require extended stays in jail on authority of a probation violation hold without returning the case to court.

Extension of the probation period is also used by trial judges as an alternative to revocation of probation. This is very likely to occur when the violation is discovered near the end of the probation period. The probation officer normally has the alternative of discharging the probationer from supervision or returning him to court for an extension of the period. If the conduct is viewed as too serious to permit discharge or if the probationer has failed to pay the financial obligations imposed as conditions of probation, the officer is likely to seek extension.[51]

Specialized commitment procedures may be used as another alternative. The Michigan criminal sexual psychopath law can be invoked against a defendant at any time between formal charging and sentence to prison, including any time during a probation period.[52] Although the statute, if invoked at all, is normally used before conviction for the criminal offense,[53] occasionally facts are discovered after the defendant has been placed on probation that lead to its use against a probationer. In such cases, the probationer is returned to court as a probation violator and is detained as a violator while the sexual psychopath proceedings are initiated. A similar procedure may be used when a probationer manifests conduct justifying commitment to a state hospital as a mentally ill person.[54] Finally, one trial judge stated he often would not revoke the probation of a narcotics addict who is willing to seek help from the

---

period while the probationer remains detained in a local institution. See Illustration No. 2 *supra*.

51 The probation period is sometimes extended ex parte by the trial judge upon request by the probation officer. See Chapter 4. Whether probation is extended in this way or by returning the probationer to court for a violation hearing probably depends upon whether the officer believes a judicial reprimand would be helpful in supervising the case.

52 Mich. Stat. Ann. §28.967(3) (1954).

53 See Miller, Prosecution: The Decision to Charge a Suspect with a Crime (forthcoming).

54 Mich. Stat. Ann. §14.811 (1956). In one case, a woman probationer informed her supervising officer that her husband was plotting to murder her and was presently digging her grave in the basement. Furthermore, she stated he had already murdered their two children. The woman was detained for psychiatric examination under authority of a probation violation hold. The psychiatrist reported that she has a long history of alcoholism and diagnosed her as "schizophrenic, paranoid type, and delusional." He recommended a probate court civil commitment to a state mental hospital. The probation officer returned the case to court for a probation violation hearing and recommended a sixty-day sentence to the house of correction to give the psychopathic clinic an opportunity to initiate civil commitment proceedings in probate court.

Detroit Narcotics Clinic or to commit himself to a federal hospital for treatment.

2. *Probation officer discretion not to return a case to court.* In each of the three states studied, probation officers took the position they are not required to return all probation violation cases to court for judicial disposition. Discretion is exercised with respect to criminal offenses committed by probationers[55] as well as noncriminal (technical) violations. Some trial judges appear to insist that probation officers handle the great majority of probation violations without returning them to court.[56] Whether or not that is a widespread judicial attitude, observation of practice indicates that the great majority of violations are in fact handled by probation officers without judicial participation.

a. *The criteria used.*

> *Illustration No. 5:* The defendant, nineteen years old, had been convicted of larceny and was placed on probation for two years. After several months of supervision, he was convicted of simple larceny, for which he served a five-day jail sentence. In an interview with the probation officer, the probationer admitted his guilt of the simple larceny offense, stating merely that he needed the money. The probation officer made a notation of the conviction, reprimanded the probationer severely and advised him to discontinue his association with his co-defendant in the simple larceny case. He did not return the probationer to court.

Most probation violations coming to the attention of supervising officers are not regarded by them as sufficiently serious to warrant returning the probationer to court as a violator. Misdemeanor arrests or convictions are usually not regarded as serious enough to call for judicial decision-making and neither are technical violations, with the exception of absconding. Despite toleration for misdemeanor conduct and technical violations, probation officers may

[55] The unofficial manual for the probation department in Milwaukee states: "All offenses committed while on probation are violations of probation. Because of the great variability of the offenses, the supervising officer (usually in consultation with the chief probation officer) determines whether or not to return the probationer to court as a violator and, if returned to court, what recommendation to make."

The supervisor of the Women's Division of Recorder's Court Probation Department indicated that her officers rarely return a probationer to court on the basis of a misdemeanor violation or a technical violation, except absconding.

[56] A probation officer in the Wayne County Circuit Court Probation Department stated that revocation is used by the department only as a last resort. A probation officer who returns a case to court for revocation is admitting failure to the trial judge. When courts place defendants on probation they expect probation officers to rehabilitate them. Rather than admit failure, the department will carry a case on supervision until the last possible moment, unless the probationer becomes arrested for a new felony offense.

return such cases to court when the nonconforming conduct persists and the probationer shows little ability or willingness to reform.[57] However, it seems likely that even the persistent petty violator will be continued on supervision by the court, at least at his first violation hearing. Revocation is likely only when he has returned to court several times.[58]

A large number of probation violations involve domestic problems — failure to support, assaulting wife or children, drunkenness in the home, failure to seek employment. These almost never result in return to court or revocation; indeed, in many cases the probation officer may not even investigate the complaint to determine whether there actually was a violation of probation. When the probationer has been supporting his family at least occasionally, there is great reluctance to seek revocation because that would eliminate all support.[59]

When a probationer has failed to report for several successive office interviews, the supervising officer usually takes steps to locate him and discover the difficulty. If he is unable to find him, he will usually obtain a probation violation warrant for absconding. The police are notified of the existence of the warrant and alerted to apprehend the probationer if they find him. If the probationer is discovered in the metropolitan area, he is likely to be returned to court;[60] usually, the trial judge continues him on supervision. If he is discovered in another state, however, he may not be returned because of the expense involved.[61] If he is returned from the other state it is usually because he has a family living in the city he left; in that case, he will be returned to court and probably continued on probation to secure support for the family.

[57] The defendant had been placed on probation for two years on a conviction of unlawfully taking and using an automobile. The supervising officer returned him to court for a probation violation hearing, alleging three violations: (1) he resisted all efforts to aid himself in rehabilitation; (2) he refused to report even though notices were sent and his parents were requested to tell him to report; (3) he refused to pay court costs.

[58] See pages 156-159.

[59] Some probation officers reported that they are influenced not to return a violator to court because of expectations that the victim will complain if revocation deprives him of his restitution payments.

[60] One probation officer in Detroit stated that once a violation warrant is issued the officer must return the case to court even if he is certain the judge will continue the probationer on supervision. Normally, warrants are not obtained until the officer has decided to return the case to court, but in absconding cases warrants are issued as soon as the violation is discovered in order to alert the police to the fact the probationer is wanted for probation violation. In such cases, the probationer may be returned to court when he is found simply because the officer feels he has no discretion in the matter.

[61] This is especially likely if the probationer was a transient in the city in which he was placed on probation. In such cases, officers believe there is little purpose to returning him to a place where he has no ties.

b. *The effect of anticipated judicial decision making.*

Illustration No. 6: The nineteen-year-old probationer had been placed on probation for unlawfully taking and using an automobile. He was required to serve the first sixty days of his probation period in the House of Correction. Six months later, he served thirty days in jail for reckless driving. Two days after his release, he was arrested for investigation of statutory rape. He was released because the complainant refused to prosecute, but he freely admitted to the probation officer that he was responsible for the pregnancy of the thirteen-year-old complainant. Four days after his release he was arrested again for resisting an officer who intervened in a fight between the probationer and his father-in-law. He then failed to report for three months despite notices sent to him by the probation officer. The officer drafted a notice of probation violation, alleging (1) conviction and sentence for reckless driving; (2) failure to report; and (3) two arrests without convictions. The officer did not return the case to court, however, explaining simply that he did not feel the judge would revoke probation on these facts.

It is difficult to assess accurately the impact of anticipated judicial decision-making on the probation officer's decision whether to return a violator to court. It is clear that probation officers do not normally seek revocation unless they believe the trial judge will be willing to revoke. Since there are no formally promulgated criteria to guide the probation officer, he must rely upon his past experiences with various judges and upon reports and rumors of decisions made in cases handled by other officers. The process of communication, needless to say, is not precise and there is every reason to believe that misunderstandings occur. While probation officers may use the fact that the trial judge would not revoke as a convenient way of deciding cases or explaining decisions, it seems clear that their experiences in court do have a significant impact. Most officers were able to recall several cases in which they returned a violator to court recommending revocation only to have the trial judge continue him on supervision. On the basis of such experiences, several officers remarked that they regarded trial judges as too lenient on probationers and too slow to revoke when presented with grounds for revocation. On the other hand, no officer reported a case in which he recommended continuing a probationer on supervision and the judge revoked probation. In addition, several officers indicated that trial judges generally consider family support by the probationer a stronger reason for continuing supervision than do most probation officers.

c. *Alternatives to returning a case to court.*

Illustration No. 7: The probationer had been placed on supervision for nonsupport. He had failed to report for some time and had failed to make support payments. The officer was severely reprimanding the probationer for his conduct, stating, "How many breaks did you expect to get?" Finally, the probation officer stated this would be the last time he would permit the probationer to get away with this type of behavior. He dismissed the probationer, telling him to report regularly and make support payments. He did not return the case to court.

Illustration No. 8: The probation officer received a report from the probationer's wife that he was intoxicated and causing trouble in the home. The officer telephoned the police department to arrest the probationer as a probation violator. After the probationer had sobered up in jail, the wife came to the probation officer seeking his release. The officer released him and did not return the case to court.

Like trial judges, probation officers seldom take no action at all when a probation violation is discovered. They employ a wide range of alternative actions to returning the probationer to court as a violator. Which alternative is selected depends for the most part upon the officer's assessment of the seriousness of the situation. This, in turn, often depends upon the probationer's past conduct under supervision. The alternatives selected, then, tend to become more severe with each violation; only when violations persist does the officer return the case to court for a judicial reprimand and disposition. Except for a new felony offense, revocation is normally effected only after all these steps have been taken.

The most frequent, and least severe, alternative to returning the violator to court is a reprimand by the probation officer. This usually takes the form of a very stern lecture to the probationer with warnings that further violations will result in court action. Occasionally, the probation officer may accompany the reprimand with increased restrictions upon the probationer's freedom, such as requiring more frequent reporting[62] or imposing an earlier curfew upon a youthful probationer.[63]

[62] In one case an eighteen-year-old probationer had been required to report twice a month. When he became involved in gang activities in his neighborhood, the probation officer lectured him severely and threatened revocation, but, instead of returning the case to court, he required him to report weekly until his conduct showed improvement and he secured employment.

[63] In one case, a probation officer made a home visit late at night only to find his youthful client not at home. The boy's mother indicated that he frequently

Some alternatives to seeking court action involve a settlement of a controversy between the probationer and a third person. Thus, the probation officer may arrange for restitution to the victim of an offense committed by a probationer in lieu of returning the case to court.[64] Some probation officers handle domestic disputes between probationers and their spouses by having both of them come to the office to talk over their problems in the presence of the officer.[65]

The probation violation hold is also used as an alternative to returning a violator to court.[66] In cases in which the officer feels that a brief period of incarceration in a local jail may prevent recurrence of violations, he may order the probationer apprehended and detained until he orders his release.[67] The hold may also be used to solve a crisis situation, as in Illustration No. 8, or it may be used to prevent an anticipated violation of probation.[68]

---

stayed out very late at night. At the next office interview, the probation officer imposed an 11:00 P.M. curfew on the probationer.

64 In one case, the probationer had passed $52 in forged checks. The police informed the probation officer of the offense, but agreed not to arrest the probationer if the officer could secure restitution. The officer had an interview with the probationer in which the latter agreed to make restitution within thirty days. The officer sent a letter to the victim to verify the claim and did not return the case to court.

65 One probation officer stated that a typical violation report is one in which the wife tells the officer her husband is running around with other women. In most cases, the officer takes no action beyond, perhaps, referring the wife to the police department vice squad. In some cases, he might bring up the matter with the probationer if he had a good relationship with him. However, in cases in which both the probationer and the wife are unreliable, he would ask her to come into the office with the probationer and discuss the entire problem. He said that in such cases the office visit is a very good way of clearing the air and dissipates the tension between a husband and wife who can both air their feelings and problems in front of the probation officer. If the wife really doesn't want to clear up the problem, she will not come to the probation office nor go to the vice squad.

66 The probation violation hold is an informal device by which the probation officer vicariously exercises his power to arrest without a warrant for probation violations. He simply notifies the police to arrest the probationer and files a document with the jail to authorize his detention. The hold is used most frequently as an investigative device; when a probationer is arrested by the police and they notify the probation officer, he will frequently file a hold to assure the probationer's availability in jail for an interview. The hold is also used to apprehend a probation violator who has not already been arrested by the police.

67 Since the hold is an informal device, there are no very precise limits on its use. Most of the probation officers in Detroit felt that they could detain only for a limited time on authority of a hold. Some officers felt detention could not extend beyond twenty-four hours without securing a warrant from the court. Other officers felt they could detain a probationer under a hold for two or three days. In Milwaukee, there is apparently no feeling by probation officers that detention under the hold has very tight time limitations; in one case, the officer kept the probationer in detention for one month on authority of the hold before returning him to court.

68 One probation officer cited a case in which a youthful probationer was a member of a neighborhood gang. The officer received a report that the gang was going to involve itself in trouble with another gang over the weekend. The officer ordered the arrest of the probationer and held him in detention over the weekend to prevent his participation in any trouble that might develop.

PART III

Determining the Length of Incarceration

Even when aided by a competent presentence study and report, the court is poorly equipped at the time of sentence to make solid and decisive judgments on the period required for the process of correction to realize its optimum potentiality or for the risk of further criminality to reach a level where release of the offender appears reasonably safe. The organs of correction, on the other hand, are best equipped to make decisions of this order and to make them later on in time, in light of observation and experience within the institution. . . .

Furthermore, and certainly of prime importance, it is an abiding difficulty of judicial sentencing that different judges vary in their judgments, producing a disparity in the terms of commitments transcending any that can be attributed to the just individualization of each sentence. . . . The best approach to a solution lies in reducing the variety of commitments. This can be done with the least sacrifice of other values by employing a fixed maximum determined by the grade and degree of the offense.

WECHSLER, Sentencing, Correction, and the Model Penal Code, 109 *University of Pennsylvania Law Review* 465, 476-477 (1961)

To avert excessively long imprisonment, therefore, two things are necessary: First, the judge must have a discretion to fix a maximum term less than that prescribed under a statute. Second, the scale of punishments must be reduced substantially below its present levels.

TURNBLADH, A Critique of the Model Penal Code Sentencing Proposals, 23 *Law and Contemporary Problems* 544, 546 (1958)

If a convicted criminal offender is sentenced to prison, a determination of the length of his incarceration must be made. The manner in which that determination is made has great importance for the offender, for society, and for criminal justice administration. For the serious offender the determination is quite complex[1] and may involve decisions by a trial judge, a parole board, and parole officers and administrators. In addition, the prosecuting attorney and executive clemency authorities may become involved.

Like most correctional decisions, the determination of the length of incarceration is discretionary in nature: it raises basic issues relating to what agency of government should have responsibility for making the decision, the propriety of criteria used, equality of treatment, and guidance and control of discretion.

The question of responsibility for determining the length of incarceration has several aspects: Should the legislature attempt to control the length of sentence or should this responsibility be delegated to the trial judge and correctional agency? [2] If the legislature attempts to control the length of sentence, how successful is it likely to be in getting judges and correctional agencies to follow the legislative mandate? If there is delegation of responsibility, how should that responsibility be shared between trial judge and correctional agency? If the trial judge or correctional agency makes a decision, upon what criteria should they base their decision and what means are available to review that decision if the defendant thinks it an improper one?

Observed practices create serious doubt that eliminating judicial discretion to select the sentence will accomplish the objectives advanced in support of that proposal.[3] Trial judges in Kansas[4] and

[1] It is comparatively simple for petty offenders sentenced to local correctional institutions: The trial judge selects the sentence and the offender serves that term less allowances for good conduct within the institution. The complexities parole introduces into the determination for the serious offender are usually absent because release from jail on parole is still very uncommon. See The President's Commission on Law Enforcement and Administration of Justice, Task Force Report: Corrections 60 (1967).

[2] In most states the trial judge has discretion to select the maximum sentence within statutory limits. In a few states, and for certain offenses in many states, the trial judge is required to impose the maximum sentence provided by statute. An inmate must be released from prison when he has served his maximum sentence, which is usually reduced for good conduct within the institution. See Chapter 12. See also Note, Statutory Structures for Sentencing Felons to Prison, 60 Colum. L. Rev. 1134 (1960) for a helpful discussion of the various ways legislatures have allocated authority to determine the length of incarceration.

[3] Model Penal Code §6.06 (Proposed Official Draft, 1962) proposes that the trial judge be required to impose the maximum sentence provided by statute. As the quotation from Professor Wechsler's article indicates, two major objectives of that proposal are to delay individualizing the length of incarceration until more can be learned about the offender and to eliminate sentence disparity resulting from the judicially fixed maximum. Partly in response to that proposal, the National Council on Crime and Delinquency's Model Sentencing Act advocates judicial discretion in selecting the maximum sentence. Model Sentencing Act §9 (1963). As the statement by Turnbladh indicates, a major purpose of that proposal is to reduce the length

Michigan[5] are required to impose the maximum sentence specified by statute for the offense of which the defendant was convicted, while trial judges in Wisconsin[6] have discretion to impose shorter maximum sentences than those specified by statute for the various offenses. All three states have high plea of guilty rates, usually explained as a result of a willingness to reward a plea of guilty with a less severe sentence. The Wisconsin trial judge takes into account the defendant's plea of guilty in selecting the maximum sentence, giving a substantial reduction in the length of the maximum as "guilty plea credit." In Wisconsin bargaining with the prosecutor for a reduced charge is not prevalent. In Kansas and Michigan, however, where the trial judge does not have discretion in selecting the maximum sentence, bargaining for reduced charges is prevalent, and a shorter maximum sentence for the person who pleads guilty is effected through a reduction in the charge.

Practices in the three states indicate that when the trial judge has sentencing discretion he is likely to use it to reward guilty pleas and, when judicial sentencing discretion is eliminated, pressure to reward guilty pleas is directed toward the prosecutor rather than the trial judge. Thus, the legislatively fixed maximum sentence tends to place responsibility for determining length of incarceration with the prosecutor, rather than postponing it until the parole stage. This substitutes prosecutor disparity for judicial sentencing disparity.[7] Whatever the merit of the legislatively fixed maximum, it is difficult to implement in practice when pressure is heavy on the judge and prosecutor to adapt the sentence to the individual case.

Some sentencing criteria relate to such traditional criminal law objectives as rehabilitation and community protection. But others, such as a lesser sentence where there is a guilty plea, relate essentially to administrative considerations, i.e., the speed and efficiency of the criminal justice process. Closely related is concern for community attitude and the likelihood that a certain correctional deci-

---

of imprisonment. Responding to criticism of its original proposal, the American Law Institute drafted an alternate section that would provide judicial discretion to select the maximum sentence. Model Penal Code Alternate §6.06 (Proposed Official Draft, 1962).

[4] Kan. Stat. Ann. §62-2239 (1964).

[5] Mich. Stat. Ann §28.1080 (1954). For several offenses the trial judge is authorized to impose a sentence of life imprisonment, or a maximum sentence of any duration, in his discretion. Mich. Stat. Ann. §28.1081 (Supp. 1965).

[6] Wis. Stat. Ann. §959.05 (1958).

[7] For more detailed discussion of this thesis, see Ohlin and Remington, Sentencing Structure: Its Effect upon Systems for the Administration of Criminal Justice, 23 Law & Contemp. Prob. 495 (1958); Newman, Conviction: The Determination of Guilt or Innocence Without Trial 177-197 (1966).

sion will alienate the community and perhaps result in less support, including financial support, for the correctional system. These latter criteria, often reflected in practice, raise important and debatable policy questions.

Traditionally, most correctional decisions, including those relating to length of incarceration, were not subject to challenge or control. This is in process of change, with increasing attention being given to whether there should be opportunity for hearing and for appeal.[8]

Chapters in Part III discuss the procedures and criteria used in making the decisions that collectively determine the length of incarceration. Chapters 6 and 7 deal with the criteria used in selecting prison sentences, while Chapter 8 deals with the problem of sentence disparity. Chapters 9 and 10 deal, respectively, with parole eligibility and parole information. Chapter 11 deals with the decision to grant or deny parole and Chapter 12 with mandatory release from prison upon service of the maximum sentence. Chapter 13 discusses parole conditions and supervision; Chapter 14 deals with parole revocation.

[8] The problem of controlling discretion in determining the length of incarceration is considered in Part IV, where control of discretion in the entire correctional process is discussed.

CHAPTER 6

The Sentence as an Administrative Accommodation

A basic issue in criminal justice administration is whether a defendant who pleads guilty should receive a shorter sentence than one who stands trial and is found guilty. The practice of granting sentence leniency to defendants who plead guilty exists in a large number of state and federal courts, and its propriety has engendered considerable controversy. In practice, however, the guilty plea is not the only object of bargaining for leniency, although doubtless it is the most important. Jury waiver, cooperation during in-custody interrogation, agreement to serve as an informant, and any other cooperation by the defendant that enhances the efficiency of the system may result in sentencing leniency.

Sometimes sentencing leniency is the immediate result of face-to-face negotiation; in other situations, leniency at a later stage in the process reflects earlier cooperation by the defendant. A defendant may cooperate in the expectation that he will be rewarded later or because of a fear that failure to cooperate will later result in greater severity.

Leniency usually takes the form of a grant of probation or a shorter prison sentence. In Wisconsin, where the trial judge has considerable discretion in granting probation and in setting the maximum sentence, a defendant may plead guilty knowing that the trial judge will take his plea into account in deciding on probation or, if other reasons compel a prison term, in selecting the length of the maximum sentence. In Michigan and Kansas, where trial judges' sentencing authority is limited, leniency may take the form of a charge reduction from a nonprobationable to a probationable offense, from an offense that carries a high mandatory maximum sentence to one that carries a considerably lower one, or from an offense with a high mandatory minimum to one with a judicially fixed minimum or a lower mandatory minimum.

Major concern in this chapter is whether encouragement of

guilty pleas or other forms of cooperation that enhance the efficiency of the system is an appropriate criterion for setting the maximum or minimum sentence.[1] Whether it is proper to use the sentence in that way is doubtless a judgment that should not be made until consideration is given to the reasons for the practice and their variations. As with other issues in sentencing, the statutory sentencing structure has a major influence on the practices. Attention is given first to administrative accommodations when the trial judge has broad sentencing discretion and then to accommodations when that discretion is limited by the legislature.

A. The Judicial Sentencing Decision as an Administrative Accommodation

An important consideration in evaluating a sentence structure that delegates discretion to the trial judiciary is its effect on criminal justice administration. The position might be taken that the trial judge should have discretion to set the sentence because he will take into account the administrative need to encourage guilty pleas and other forms of cooperation by defendants. The soundness of this position depends in part upon whether in fact trial judges do use sentence discretion to encourage cooperation by criminal defendants. Trial judge attitudes toward using their discretion for these purposes are, therefore, of great importance.

Under Wisconsin law the trial judge has discretion to set the maximum sentence, and the minimum is set by statute,[2] usually at one year. In Milwaukee the judicially set maximum is used to encourage efficiency in the system by rewarding defendant cooperation, with the consequence that prosecutor reduction of charges is very rare.

Under Michigan law the trial judge commonly must impose the maximum sentence specified by statute but he has discretion in setting the minimum.[3] In Detroit, an important consideration in setting the minimum is administrative efficiency. The mandatory maximum appears to explain the prevalent practice by prosecutors of reducing charges.

1. *Judicial attitudes toward using sentencing discretion to encourage cooperation from criminal defendants.* There is a variety of opinion among trial judges on the propriety of giving a shorter sentence to a defendant because he pleaded guilty. An indication of difference in attitudes is apparent in the Federal Sentencing In-

[1] See Chapter 3 for a discussion of the relationship between guilty pleas and the decision to grant or deny probation.

[2] Wis. Stat. Ann. §959.05 (1958).

[3] Mich. Stat. Ann. §28.1080 (1954).

stitutes. In the Institutes the following question was usually raised: "Whether a defendant who is willing to plead guilty ought to receive a lighter sentence than he would receive if he pleads not guilty and puts the government to the expense of trial." [4]

On group of judges took the position that a plea of guilty should not be considered because granting sentence leniency for a plea of guilty amounts to imposing a penalty on a defendant for exercising his constitutional rights to a trial,[5] because a guilty plea entered under such circumstances might be regarded on appeal as involuntary and void,[6] and because such a policy might result in an innocent person pleading guilty from fear of a severe sentence if he demanded a trial.[7] Another view was that it is entirely proper for a trial judge to give a lighter sentence to a defendant who pleads guilty, because it is necessary to reward pleas of guilty in order to handle all the cases brought into court,[8] and because defendants who plead guilty are repentant and have taken the first step in rehabilitation; hence, they do not require as severe a sentence as a defendant who continues to deny his guilt in the face of overwhelming evidence.[9] Some judges took the position that it

[4] Pilot Institute on Sentencing, 26 F.R.D. 231, 285 (1959). For an excellent discussion of this problem, see American Bar Association Project on Minimum Standards for Criminal Justice, Standards Relating to Pleas of Guilty (Tent. Draft, 1967).

[5] Seminar and Institute on Disparity of Sentences for Sixth, Seventh and Eighth Judicial Circuits, 30 F.R.D. 401, 448 (1961): "Some judges expressed the view that an offender ought not be penalized for demanding a trial in the view that a defendant should not be penalized for insisting on his constitutional right to trial."

[6] Pilot Institute on Sentencing, 26 F.R.D. 231, 286-287 (1959): "I wonder what a court of appeals would do with the case where it appeared that a defendant, before he entered his plea, was told in substance that if he pleads guilty it will be easier on him, but if he pleads not guilty the court is going to give a more severe sentence. Could a conviction on such a plea of guilty be affirmed? Does it make any difference whether there is an implied threat or a direct threat by a sheriff or enforcement officer or someone else connected with the government? It seems to me that it amounts to exactly the same thing. I wonder whether we are going to continue to reverse convictions based upon promises of leniency made by law enforcement officers to induce a plea of guilty and not reverse convictions based upon an implied promise of leniency by a court if the defendant will plead guilty. It seems to me that this problem transcends the issue of practicality and is of basic importance."

[7] Seminar and Institute on Disparity of Sentences for Sixth, Seventh and Eighth Judicial Circuits, 30 F.R.D. 401, 448-449 (1961): "There was also concern expressed as to whether a general policy of leniency to those who plead guilty will cast doubt upon the trustworthiness of pleas of guilty and encourage such pleas from persons who are actually innocent of the offense charged but who feel that an assertion of their rights will be futile and merely bring a heavier sentence than might otherwise be assessed."

[8] Pilot Institute on Sentencing, 26 F.R.D. 231, 288 (1959): "In a large metropolitan court it would be impossible to keep abreast of the large number of criminal cases if it were not generally known among the practicing bar that consideration is given to those who are willing to plead guilty."

[9] Id. at 287: "I put the person who pleads guilty in one category and the person who pleads not guilty in another category, because the person who pleads guilty

was entirely proper for the court to give sentence leniency to those who plead guilty, but that a trial judge should not participate in bargaining for a plea, although it might be proper for police or prosecutor to bargain.[10] A third group of judges took the position that a person who pleads guilty should receive a shorter sentence than a person who stands trial and commits perjury in testifying to his innocence, or advances a frivolous defense.[11] Finally other judges said that guilty plea leniency is proper in complicated cases, such as income tax evasion, in which there is a greater likelihood of acquittal by a jury.[12]

In *United States v. Wiley*,[13] the trial judge, with unusual candor, indicated that the practice of giving guilty plea leniency is widely followed and that it is based on administrative necessity:

> I think that almost any trial judge in the United States will take into consideration a plea of guilty when imposing sentence and, in fact, most judges usually state for the record words to the effect that "since the defendant has saved the government the time and expense of trial, the sentence is less than it ordinarily would be. . . ."
>
> As Judge Lummus of the Supreme Judicial Court of Massachusetts has pointed out in his book, "The Trial Judge" at pages 46-47: "If all the defendants should combine to refuse to plead guilty, and should dare to hold out, they could break down the administration of criminal justice in any state in the Union. But they dare not hold out, for such as were tried and convicted could hope for no leniency. The prosecutor is like a man armed with a revolver who is cornered by a mob. A concerted rush would

---

realizes that he has done something wrong and is willing publicly to confess his crime. The man who demands all of his constitutional rights has a right to do so, of course. Most of these realize that they are guilty; but they want to take every opportunity to avoid conviction. I do not think you need to say that, because one exercises constitutional rights, he is entitled to do that without any reservation whatsoever. If, in exercising them, he indicates that he is not taking a step toward rehabilitation, I do not think he ought to be treated the same as the man who says in effect that he is wrong and wants to start over."

[10] Id. at 289: "I do not think the Court should ever bargain with defendants or counsel, nor should the United States Attorney be informed that any concession will be made to those who plead guilty. The Court's practice will soon be found out without the Court making a statement of policy."

[11] Id. at 287: "I do not think any judge here would hold it against the defendant if he demanded a trial and presented a reasonable defense, either on the government's failure of proof or otherwise. On the other hand, if the defendant presents a fraudulent defense, or adds perjury to his other crimes, I think it ought to be considered in determining his sentence."

[12] Id. at 288: "In relation to the income tax violator particularly, the opportunity to confuse the jury is great. Therefore, why should the defendant who runs the risk, takes his chances, gambles on a jury verdict, be given the same treatment as the defendant who does not gamble, who does not take his chance, who does not attempt to confuse the jury, but rather stands up and admits his guilt?"

[13] 184 F. Supp. 679 (N.D. Ill. 1960).

overwhelm him, but each individual in the mob fears that he might be one of those shot during the rush. When defendants plead guilty, they expect more leniency than when convicted by a jury, and must receive it, or there will be no such pleas. The truth is that a criminal court can operate only by inducing the great mass of actually guilty defendants to plead guilty, paying in leniency the price for the plea." [14]

Because trial judges differ on whether judicial sentencing discretion should be used to encourage cooperation from criminal defendants, granting broad sentencing discretion to the judiciary does not necessarily result in a uniform accommodation to the administrative need for defendant cooperation. For example, if a trial judge steadfastly refuses to take pleas of guilty into account in exercising sentencing discretion, pressures are created for the prosecutor to encourage guilty pleas by reducing charges. The resulting accommodation may not differ substantially from that which is likely to result from legislative elimination of judicial sentencing discretion.[15] Furthermore, some trial judges may prefer to have defendants bargain with prosecutors for charge reductions rather than themselves exercising sentencing discretion to encourage guilty pleas. Granting sentencing discretion permits, but does not require, the use of that power to reward defendant cooperation. The way that power is used varies from judge to judge.

2. *The judicial maximum sentence in Wisconsin.* The trial judge in Wisconsin has discretion to set the maximum sentence;[16] the minimum term is set by statute at a uniformly low level.[17]

In Milwaukee a single-judge felony court sentenced approximately 50 percent of the persons who were committed to the Wisconsin prison at the time of the field survey. A study was made of the transcripts of the postplea of guilty hearings used by this judge in guilty plea cases.[18] The results are indicative of the relationship between the guilty plea and the sentence in Milwaukee and are relied upon in describing practice in Wisconsin.

a. *Cooperation with police investigations.*

Illustration No. 1: The defendant pleaded guilty to control of and giving away of narcotic drugs, a charge that carries a

[14] Id. at 684.

[15] See pages 188-192.

[16] Wis. Stat. Ann. §959.05 (1958).

[17] Wis. Stat. Ann. §57.06 (1957) declares an inmate eligible for parole "when he has served the minimum term prescribed by statute for the offense (which shall be one year unless a greater minimum is prescribed by the statute defining the crime) or one-half of the maximum of an indeterminate term or 2 years, whichever is least, or when he has served 20 years of a life term, less the deduction earned for good conduct as provided in s. 53.11."

[18] See Chapter 1 for a discussion of the postplea of guilty hearing in Milwaukee.

possible maximum sentence of five years. At the sentence hearing, the district attorney said, "I just discussed with the police officer the question of disposition and he felt that this defendant was extremely honest and without such honesty and cooperation they would not have gotten very far. Because of that situation and because of the fact that he doesn't have a criminal record, they do not oppose probation." The trial judge responded that he could not place the defendant on probation, but he imposed a maximum sentence of thirteen months, commenting: "Now that's practically a minimum sentence, gentlemen, and I am doing that because of his frankness and honesty."

Many of the investigatory devices used by police depend upon the cooperation of the person being investigated. The goals of police in-custody investigation — confessions, identification of accomplices, admissions of offenses other than the one for which the defendant was arrested, full disclosure of the extent and location of stolen property — could not be realized without the cooperation of the person being questioned. Should a person who cooperates with the police in their investigation, and who is later convicted, receive sentencing leniency that is denied to one who refused to cooperate? Put differently, should a judge regard it as one of his functions in sentencing to support police investigatory devices by encouraging cooperation by defendants?

In Milwaukee one of the considerations entering into the sentence is the extent to which the defendant cooperated with the police, and a frequent inquiry at the postplea of guilty hearing is whether the defendant cooperated with the police after his arrest. Typically, this information is secured from the investigating police officer on cross-examination by the defendant's attorney.[19] It is not clear how important cooperation of this kind is in sentencing. In many cases, it seems likely it is simply another factor in mitigation of the sentence, not more important than some factors, such as the defendant's age, and frequently less important than other factors, such as his criminal record. In other cases, however, the defendant's cooperation may assume major importance. In the illustration case, the fact that the defendant cooperated fully with the police was perhaps the dominant factor in selection of the sentence.

[19] On one occasion, a defense attorney elicited from the police officer that the defendant had cooperated fully with the authorities, even to the extent of taking them to where he had discarded the stolen wallet and where he had placed the jacket he wore during the theft. When more than one person is involved in an offense, cooperation may involve identifying the other participants, and if such an identification is made, the cooperating defendant's attorney is likely to elicit that fact from the police officer on cross-examination.

b. *Cooperation in the guilty plea process.*

Illustration No. 2: Defendant pleaded guilty to three counts of auto theft, each carrying a possible sentence of ten years. After the postplea of guilty hearing and presentence investigation, the court said: "I am highly suspicious that the defendant, as stated in the presentence report and implied in the testimony of the investigating police officer, has been involved in a large number of similar operations involving cars — very clever, very difficult to track down, although he was finally tripped up. He doesn't admit any of these others and he reluctantly admits the three that are involved here. I am satisfied from what the district attorney has told me in chambers, in the presence of the defendant's attorney and the investigating probation officer, that the state would have been required to call a large number of witnesses—twenty-six, I believe he stated — upon a plea of not guilty; the trial would have been very lengthy, lasting, according to the district attorney's estimate, at least a week. I am going to give the defendant credit for his plea of guilty because that has made possible cutting through all of these matters to the provable situation that is now before the court and has saved the state a great deal of time and expense. I would be inclined had the situation not been resolved in a plea of guilty to give this defendant twice as much as I intend to give him now." The court then imposed a sentence of five years on each count, to run concurrently.

One of the important features of criminal justice administration in most states is the high percentage of cases disposed of by guilty pleas. Many police, prosecutors, and trial judges feel the system could not operate were there a substantial decrease in the number of guilty pleas, and many of them feel that some inducement to plead guilty is necessary and justified. Commonly, that inducement assumes the form of a shorter sentence, although probation[20] may be used as well. In some jurisdictions the trial judge takes the guilty plea into account as a factor favorable to the defendant in setting the sentence, while in other jurisdictions, because of statutory restrictions on judicial sentencing discretion or because of trial judge attitudes on this question, the sentence may be shortened indirectly by means of charge reductions.[21]

In Milwaukee both the probation decision and selection of the maximum sentence are affected by whether the defendant pleads guilty. Pleading guilty results in a shorter maximum sentence than

[20] See Chapter 3.
[21] See pages 188-192.

pleading not guilty, which also normally disqualifies the defendant from probation.

The guilty plea process in Milwaukee involves taking sworn testimony in court from state's witnesses and from the defendant — the postplea of guilty hearing. The postplea hearing is designed primarily to assure that defendants who plead guilty are in fact guilty, although it is also a source of presentence information about the circumstances of the offense and the defendant's background.[22] Because the guilty plea process involves testimony in court, the trial judge is concerned not only with maintaining an adequate flow of guilty pleas but also with the defendant's truthfulness in court during the postplea hearing. Complete cooperation in the guilty plea process in Milwaukee, then, involves both a guilty plea and the defendant's in-court frankness about the circumstances of the offense and his background. Defendants are not required to testify at the postplea hearing, but in fact almost all defendants do testify. There is no evidence that a defendant who refuses to testify is given an increased sentence for that reason.[23] It does seem clear, however, that defendant testimony which indicates to the judge that he is "covering up" some aspects of the case is met with an increased sentence.[24]

In many cases, the fact that defendant entered a guilty plea is expressly referred to by the court as a favorable factor in setting the sentence, such as, "I will give him credit for his plea of guilty and I will give him as light a sentence as the circumstances permit." There is no clear evidence in most cases of the extent to which the maximum is reduced as a result of a guilty plea. In many cases, the combination of a guilty plea and defendant's candor at the postplea hearing make it difficult to isolate the guilty plea factor. In some cases, credit on the sentence is given for a guilty plea entered after the trial is partially completed even though the resource savings may not be substantial. In other cases, such as the illustration case, the resource savings are substantial, and substantial credit may be given despite the defendant's unwillingness to speak fully about his suspected criminal episode.

The effect of a guilty plea on the judge's selection of the sentence is apparently well known to the local bar and, presumably, to defendants who have previously been before the court. Although

[22] See Chapter 1.

[23] No instances were observed of a defendant refusing to testify at a postplea of guilty hearing.

[24] This is consistent with the judge's position that "perjury and probation do not mix," that is, that a defendant who pleads not guilty and who is subsequently found guilty by a jury after testifying to his own innocence should be dealt with severely, on the ground he has committed perjury. See Chapter 3.

the judge's language of a credit due on the sentence might imply that the trial judge is simply performing the state's part of a sentence bargain made by the prosecutor and the defendant's attorney, this does not in fact seem to be the case. Apparently because the court's practices of rarely giving probation to a defendant who pleads not guilty and of giving sentence credit to a defendant who does is well known among the local bar, the prosecutor seems to find little need to persuade defendants that pleading guilty is in their interest. In fact, it is likely that the court's practice is most often communicated to the defendant through his counsel.[25]

c. *Cooperation in the trial.*

Illustration No. 3: Defendant was charged with operating his automobile in excess of the speed limit of 65 miles per hour, an offense carrying a fine of not less than $10 nor more than $200. He asked for a jury trial and, through his attorneys, secured several adjournments of the proceedings. Jury was then waived. The officer's testimony was that defendant was traveling 75 miles per hour. He was found guilty and fined $150 and costs.

Although most criminal cases are disposed of by plea of guilty, the question whether judicial sentencing discretion should be used to encourage cooperation in the conduct of a trial on a plea of not guilty remains an important one. In *United States v. Wiley,*[26] the trial court considered cooperation in the trial in selecting the maximum: "In view of the fact that the trial was expedited by waiving jury and by stipulation of the various items that expedited the proof I make the sentence less than I otherwise would." [27] In the Wisconsin case of *State v. Tuttle,*[28] abstracted in the illustration, the converse situation was presented — an increase in the normal sentence because the defendant and his attorneys were extremely uncooperative in the disposition of the case. The court first held it was within its power to review a sentence not in excess of the statutory limits. It then concluded that the conduct of the defendant's counsel was an inappropriate criterion for increasing the fine and remanded the case for resentencing:

> [The trial judge] was entirely justified in feeling that insufficient consideration was being shown the court. Whether the original demand for a jury was in good faith or not, counsel should have

25 One defense attorney said at the postplea of guilty hearing: "Just as late as two days ago, I said to the defendant, 'Now you have a chance of pleading guilty and if you do, I am sure the Court will give serious consideration to that plea in determining any sentence or probation.' "

26 267 F.2d 453 (7th Cir. 1959).

27 Id. at 458.

28 21 Wis. 2d 147, 124 N.W.2d 9 (1963).

> been prepared to proceed with trial on the adjourned date. Instead, they sought a second adjournment the evening before the trial, too late to have their client present when unsuccessful in obtaining it. At best, defendant's counsel were inconsiderate, at worst contemptuous.
>
> We conclude, however, that it was inappropriate to increase defendant's fine substantially beyond what would otherwise have been imposed because of the unsatisfactory conduct of his counsel. Other means are at hand for disciplining attorneys.[29]

The state often has as much interest in the efficient conduct of a criminal trial as it does in securing guilty pleas from persons who are in fact guilty. When a postplea of guilty hearing is used, the difference between a guilty plea and a trial without jury may not be as great, in terms of time and resource expenditures by the state, as the difference between a jury trial and a trial without jury. Whether the state's interest in jury waivers and other forms of cooperation during a trial is sufficient to justify use of the sentence as inducement poses problems as difficult as cooperation in police investigations and in the guilty plea process.

3. *The judicial minimum sentence in Michigan.* In Michigan the maximum sentence is fixed by statute and the minimum is set by the trial judge.[30] One way to analyze such a system is to determine the extent to which judicial discretion to set the minimum facilitates the administration of criminal justice. In Wisconsin the judicial maximum sentence is used to encourage various forms of cooperation from criminal defendants. Can the judicial minimum sentence be used by a trial judge to accomplish similar goals? Another way to ask the same question is to inquire whether it makes any difference in the day-to-day administration of criminal justice whether the minimum is set by the trial judge, whether there is any minimum at all, or whether it is set by statute at a uniformly low level. It is clear that it makes a great deal of difference whether there is a high, mandatory minimum.[31]

A study of judicial minimum sentences by the Michigan Department of Corrections indicated that, on the whole, they tend to be quite low. Of the cases analyzed, 67 percent received minima of two years or less, while only about 7 percent had minima of five years or longer, and the remainder, over 25 percent, had minima ranging between two and five years. Michigan parole board members have often noted not only that charge reductions occur more frequently in Detroit than elsewhere in Michigan but also that ju-

[29] Id. at 152, 124 N.W.2d at 12.
[30] Mich. Stat. Ann. §28.1080 (1954).
[31] See pages 190-191.

dicial minimum sentences tend to be substantially lower in Detroit. One explanation for this apparent disparity in minima between Detroit and outstate Michigan could be that shorter minima are necessary in Detroit to encourage guilty pleas because of the crowded dockets in the courts there.

a. *Supporting the police informant program.*

Illustration No. 4: Defendant was found guilty by a jury of the offense of possessing marijuana, which carries a statutory maximum sentence of ten years. The defense attorney insisted that defendant be placed on probation because she had cooperated with the police by testifying against three other defendants charged with sale of narcotics. The judge pointed out that, while defendant was at liberty on bond awaiting her arraignment on the present charge, she was arrested for possessing 21 grains of heroin. The judge said he contacted the inspector of the narcotics bureau and learned that the defendant had, in fact, cooperated with the police so as not to be charged with possession of the 21 grains of heroin. He said this did not place any moral obligation on him or the police department concerning sentencing her on the earlier offense of possessing marijuana. He sentenced the defendant to imprisonment for two to ten years.

One of the major investigatory devices in Detroit is the police department's informant program, designed primarily to aid discovery of narcotic law violators. Many persons arrested for narcotics violations become informants for the police, identifying other violators, making or arranging purchases from pushers under police supervision, or, sometimes, testifying against other violators in court. The informant program is designed to eliminate the major sources of supply by "trading the little ones for the big ones." When a narcotics violator is arrested, the most common inducements used to enlist his cooperation in performing informant duties are not to charge[32] him with the offense he committed and not to arrest[33] him for certain minor offenses he may commit later. In the illustration case, the defendant was not charged with the second possession offense because she testified against other narcotics offenders whom the officials had more desire to prosecute.

Sometimes, however, the cooperative offender is charged with the offense he committed, or with a less serious offense, in order to insure that he will perform his part of the agreement. Later, the

32 See Miller, Prosecution: The Decision to Charge a Suspect with a Crime (forthcoming).

33 See LaFave, Arrest: The Decision to Take a Suspect into Custody 132-137 (1965).

charges may be dropped, but sometimes the informant is convicted. Also, in many cases a defendant may testify against his co-defendant if the state would otherwise have difficulty proving its charges. In such cases, the question arises whether the trial judge should take the defendant's cooperation into account in sentencing him. One judge said:

> I am decidedly more lenient on a cooperative co-defendant than I would be if the cooperation were not present. This does not present a major problem, however, because it is a basic theory of all the judges of Recorder's Court that a cooperative co-defendant will probably spend as much time in prison as the other defendants. Assuming the charge against all the co-defendants was robbery armed and the cooperative co-defendant provided the testimony necessary to convict the other defendants in exchange for being permitted to plead to robbery unarmed, the only real advantage the defendant would have would be the possibility of probation. If the informant had a good record and all of the other factors that go to make up a good probation risk, then he would probably be placed on probation. If, however, the informant's record was bad and the elements of a "probation risk" were missing, then the informant would be sentenced to a term in prison with a minimum not too much less than the minimum set for the other defendants. All of the defendants, including the informant, if sentenced at all, would serve three to five years in the penitentiary.

Use of the minimum sentence as a reward for informant services or for testimony against a co-defendant raises many of the same questions raised by the Milwaukee practice of rewarding cooperation in the police investigation with a shorter maximum sentence. Whether this is an appropriate criterion for the minimum sentence may depend upon whether it is necessary to use the minimum to reward this kind of cooperation; whether the trial judge is doing nothing more than performing the state's part of an agreement which will be made whether a sentence concession is given or not; or whether the sentence concession really makes any difference in the time actually spent in prison. The primary inducements for informant services or for co-defendant testimony are immunity from prosecution or, less frequently, a charge reduction which reduces the mandatory maximum sentence. A sentencing structure that provides for no minimum term or a uniformly low minimum term would therefore not frustrate police informant efforts.

b. *The minimum sentence and the guilty plea process.* Officials in Detroit, like those in Milwaukee, depend upon the disposition of a high percentage of cases by guilty pleas and feel that inducements to plead guilty must be offered in order to maintain the flow of guilty pleas at the necessary level. The guilty plea process in Detroit, however, differs markedly from that in Milwaukee in its methods, if not in its aims. The primary difference is that in Detroit the trial judge's sentencing discretion is limited by statute, in the vast majority of cases, in the form of one or more of three types of provisions: a mandatory maximum sentence, a mandatory minimum sentence, or statutory probation ineligibility. The presence of one or more of these limitations on trial judge sentence discretion may, in a particular case, deter a defendant from pleading guilty because the trial judge is not in a position to reward the plea with sentence leniency. In such cases, defendants may feel they have nothing to lose by demanding a trial, while at the same time pleading not guilty preserves the possibility of an acquittal. One result of this sentencing structure is the extensive practice in Detroit of reducing the charge from one which accurately reflects the defendant's conduct to one carrying sufficiently lighter sentence consequences to persuade the defendant of the advantage of pleading guilty. When a defendant is unwilling to plead guilty to a charge carrying a high mandatory maximum sentence, a high mandatory minimum sentence, or statutory probation ineligibility, the difficulty is resolved by arranging a plea of guilty to a charge carrying a lower mandatory maximum sentence, no mandatory minimum sentence, or probation eligibility, or all three.

For the vast majority of cases, then, the relation between the sentence structure and the guilty plea process is clear: Limitations on trial judge probation or sentencing discretion that inhibit the flow of guilty pleas are likely to lead to a practice of charge reductions in exchange for guilty pleas. The relationship is somewhat more obscure with regard to the few offenses for which the trial judge has complete discretion to set both the maximum and the minimum sentence. For the approximately twenty offenses in the Michigan criminal code punishable by "life or any number of years" the trial judge has discretion to impose a life sentence or to impose a maximum and a minimum sentence of any length he chooses.[34] One might expect, therefore, that for these offenses pleas of guilty would be entered without charge reduction because the trial judge has ample discretion to reward the plea with sentence leniency. In fact, however, these offenses are the object of charge reduction to about the same degree as the offenses which carry high mandatory maximum or minimum sentences. There are several reasons for this. First, there is independent value in a charge reduction because it creates a less serious appearing criminal record than does conviction on the maximum charge. Second, by far the most

[34] Mich. Stat. Ann. §28.1081 (Supp. 1965).

frequently occurring offenses in this category — second degree murder and armed robbery — are nonprobationable.[35] Thus, even though the judge has complete discretion to set the maximum and the minimum, and presumably could handsomely reward pleas of guilty, some defendants may be unwilling to plead guilty to a non-probationable offense although, viewed objectively, there is little or no chance of probation for them. Third, because the vast majority of offenses carry one or more of the three types of limitations on sentencing discretion, it may just be simpler to use charge reductions to induce pleas of guilty in all cases, even though in a small percentage a charge reduction might not be the only way in which a plea could be rewarded.

How does the judicially set minimum sentence, authorized for all offenses except first degree murder[36] and sale of narcotics[37] fit into a system of reducing charges in exchange for guilty pleas? It could be argued that since guilty pleas are induced and rewarded by charge reductions, the guilty plea should have no independent significance in setting the minimum sentence. The guilty plea reward has already been made; there is no need to give a double reward. In fact the Detroit practice indicates that this is not the case.

There is no evidence in Detroit of a sentence promise practice, although it would certainly be possible for a prosecutor to agree to reduce the charge while at the same time giving the defendant some indication of his chances for probation or for a short minimum sentence if he pleads guilty to the reduced charge. Also there is no indication that the trial judges in Detroit announce that the minimum is lower than it otherwise would be because the defendant pleaded guilty. There is clear evidence, however, that the judge's general reputation for leniency or severity in granting probation or in setting the minimum is a significant factor to defendants contemplating pleading guilty to reduced charges. This is especially apparent in Detroit's multijudge Recorder's Court, where each month a different judge sentences virtually all defendants who plead guilty. An assistant prosecutor said that "one judge sometimes imposes too harsh a sentence during the beginning of his month's term as presiding judge thereby frightening all defendants out of pleading guilty with the possibility of a large sen-

[35] Mich. Stat. Ann. §28.1131 (1954).

[36] Mich. Stat. Ann. §28.548 (1954) requires a life sentence for first degree murder and Mich. Stat. Ann. §28.1081 (Supp. 1965) prohibits the trial judge from imposing a minimum sentence when a life sentence is required by statute. See Chapter 9 for discussion of the parole eligibility consequences of the mandatory life sentence for first degree murder.

[37] Mich. Stat. Ann. §18.1122 (1957) requires a life sentence and a minimum sentence of twenty years.

tence." Another assistant prosecutor mentioned one judge who is very liberal in his sentencing philosophy and practices, but whose gruff manner in talking and handling cases frightens defendants and defense attorneys. He noted that guilty pleas are not as frequent when this judge sits as presiding judge. He said it becomes his duty as the assistant prosecuting attorney in such cases to convince the defense counsel and the defendant that the judge is not really a tough judge and his gruff remarks made during the course of an assignment or acceptance of a plea are not really indicative of his sentencing policies.

The general conclusion seems possible that, while trial court discretion to set the minimum is not the subject of prosecutor sentence promises and while the trial judges make no particular effort to indicate that a guilty plea is a factor in setting the minimum, it is in fact a factor that tends to keep minimum sentences in guilty plea cases at a fairly uniformly low level. Persistently high minimum sentences would interfere with prosecutor efforts to encourage guilty pleas by charge reductions.

c. *The minimum sentence and jury waivers.* Although cooperation in the guilty plea process is doubtless of primary importance to the system, it is also true that of those cases in which not guilty pleas are entered it is far less expensive and time consuming to try the case to the court than to a jury. In Detroit, over 75 percent of the not guilty pleas are tried to the court. Just as the system depends upon a high level of guilty pleas it also depends upon a high percentage of jury waivers in pleas of not guilty cases. The issue is then raised whether the minimum sentence should be used to encourage jury waivers.

Detroit prosecutors perceive a need to encourage defendants who plead not guilty to waive their right to trial by jury, and one of the advantages they advocate for trials to the court is sentence leniency. One assistant prosecutor said that defense attorneys are constantly being interviewed by him for the purpose of having jury trials waived. He always points out that statistics show that there are just as many acquittals by the court as by juries. If, however, the case is tried to the court and a guilty verdict is rendered, the court will be more inclined to be lenient than if it were required to go to the inconvenience of impaneling a jury.

The proposition was phrased somewhat differently when it was presented to the judges of Recorder's Court for their comments. They were asked, "Is the court inclined to be more severe when sentencing a defendant who has insisted on a jury trial and has been convicted, thus putting the state to a great deal of expense and the court to the task of conducting a jury trial?" The judges unanimously replied that insistence upon a jury trial is not a factor in sentencing. Their attitude was that the right to a jury trial is so basic that to let it influence them in sentencing would be a violation of their duties as judges and a deprivation of the defendant's constitutional rights.

Thus, some prosecutors believe that trial judges definitely take jury waivers into account in sentencing, while trial judges insist that they do not. Defense attorneys had still a third view. Several defense attorneys stated they used jury waivers to maneuver their cases before judges with lenient sentencing practices. One defense counsel said that if a defense attorney informs the assignment clerk that he wants a particular judge to handle his case, and that the case would be tried to the court rather than to a jury because of the selection, then there would be little doubt that the request would be granted. The defense counsel feels that Judge X, because of his leniency in sentencing, receives a great many cases from the presiding judge because a request is made, either directly or by implication, to either the presiding judge or the assignment clerk.

The relationship in Detroit between the minimum sentence and jury waivers is unclear: Prosecutors insist that jury waivers are a factor in sentencing, while judges insist they are not. Defense attorneys insist that the combination of a multijudge court, sentencing disparity, and the need to dispose of as many cases as possible by trial to the court enables them to use the jury waiver to get their cases before a judge with lenient sentencing practices, but do not indicate that the same judge would sentence more leniently when a jury had been waived than he would after a jury trial.

B. Administrative Accommodation in Legislative Sentencing Systems

Although the focus of this chapter is upon use of judicial sentencing discretion to encourage defendant cooperation, discussion of that problem would be incomplete without considering alternative methods of achieving the same objectives. When judicial sentencing discretion is eliminated or curtailed by the legislature, pressures that would otherwise be directed to the trial judge to reward defendant cooperation do not cease; rather, they are directed to other officials, principally the prosecuting attorney. The same result is likely when the trial judge has discretion but does not regard defendant cooperation as a proper criterion for sentencing. It is somewhat surprising, therefore, that, when trial judges argue for the propriety of rewarding a plea of guilty by sentence leniency, they fail to assert that, if they refuse leniency, they may merely be forcing the prosecutor to provide it without judicial controls and scrutiny. Experiences in Michigan and Kansas are helpful in understanding what happens when judicial sentencing discretion is not used or cannot be used to reward cooperation by criminal defendants.

1. *Michigan.* In general, bargaining for charge reductions in Detroit takes the form of attempting to manipulate either a high, mandatory maximum sentence or a high, mandatory minimum sentence. Bargaining to avoid statutory probation ineligibility attaching to some offenses[38] and to avoid connotations which attach to records of convictions for certain offenses,[39] while clearly of importance, are not of immediate concern here.

Avoiding a high, mandatory maximum sentence is probably the most frequent motivation for a defendant entering a negotiated plea of guilty. The offense of breaking and entering in the nighttime carries a mandatory maximum sentence of fifteen years[40] and, in addition, under some circumstances is nonprobationable.[41] A common procedure in cases involving that charge is for the defendant and prosecutor to agree to a plea of guilty to breaking and entering in the daytime, which carries a mandatory maximum sentence of five years[42] and which in all cases is probationable.[43] The assistant prosecutor in Detroit who conducts the majority of negotiations for pleas indicated that it is the high, mandatory maximum sentence that most defendants fear and which makes them hesitate to plead guilty. He said that most of them are afraid they will be kept in prison until they have served the full sentence and that no amount of discussion about liberal parole policies will convince them to plead unless the maximum is reduced. The assistant prosecutor himself is convinced that it makes no difference, in terms of the time actually spent in prison, whether the defendant pleads to breaking and entering in the nighttime, with its fifteen-year maximum, or to breaking and entering in the daytime, with its five-year maximum. In either event, the assistant prosecutor believes the defendant will serve two or three years and be released on parole.

[38] See Chapter 3.

[39] The defendant's desire to avoid conviction on a charge that accurately describes his conduct is especially strong in sex cases. See Newman, Conviction: The Determination of Guilt or Innocence Without Trial 105-111 (1966).

[40] Mich. Stat. Ann. §28.305 (1962). The distinction between daytime and nighttime burglary has since been abolished. See Mich. Stat. Ann. §28.305 (Supp. 1968).

[41] At the time of the field survey, Mich Stat. Ann. §28.1131 (1954) made breaking and entering an occupied dwelling house in the nighttime a nonprobationable offense. Subsequent amendment has eliminated that offense from the nonprobationable list. Mich. Stat. Ann. §28.1131 (Supp. 1965).

[42] Mich. Stat. Ann. §28.306 (1962). See note 40 *supra.*

[43] Mich. Stat. Ann. §28.1131 (1954).

First degree murder carries a maximum sentence of life[44] and an effective minimum sentence of fifteen years.[45] Sale of narcotics carries a maximum sentence of life and a mandatory minimum sentence of twenty years.[46] Neither offense is probationable.[47] These two offenses present the most pressure for accommodation to induce pleas of guilty, for in these cases all three types of sentencing limitations are present in fairly severe form. The murder accommodation is accomplished by the "open plea," in which the defendant agrees to plead guilty to some degree of homicide less than murder first. It is reasonably clear that determination of the degree of homicide depends more on what the court wishes to do with the person than upon evidence of the degree of homicide. Virtually all narcotics sales cases are reduced to possession,[48] which carries a maximum of ten years, a judicial minimum, and is probationable, or to use of narcotics, which carries a maximum of one year.[49] All of the judges and prosecutors interviewed agreed that the twenty-year mandatory minimum sentence is much too severe, places a serious limitation on judicial sentence discretion, and renders the law ineffective.

In Detroit almost all charge reduction negotiations are handled by one member of the prosecutor's office, who has authority to negotiate in virtually all cases without securing approval from the prosecutor or another assistant. The prosecutor's primary motive in granting charge reductions in exchange for guilty pleas is that a large number of pleas are necessary in order to dispose of pending cases with the manpower available to him. In many cases there may also be the feeling that the mandatory maximum or minimum or statutory probation ineligibility is inappropriate to the circumstances of the case. The trial judges generally favor the charge reductions, although they do not participate in the negotiations. Most of them cooperate to the extent of taking the guilty plea into consideration in setting the minimum sentence, thereby avoiding frustrating the prosecutor's effort to encourage guilty pleas by reducing the charges.[50] Occasionally, a trial judge may indicate displeasure with the arrangement worked out by the parties and may take the plea "under advisement," but normally the plea will be accepted later on the basis of the same arrangement. In some cases involving a charge of narcotics sale, which carries a mandatory

44 Mich. Stat. Ann. §28.548 (1954).
45 See Chapter 9.
46 Mich. Stat. Ann. §18.1122 (1957).
47 Mich. Stat. Ann. §28.1131 (1954).
48 Mich. Stat. Ann. §18.1123 (1957).
49 Mich. Stat. Ann. §18.1124 (1957).
50 See pages 184-187.

twenty-year minimum, trial judges have refused to accept pleas of guilty to that charge entered by young defendants, continuing the case and assigning counsel with instructions to work out a deal with the prosecutor.

The police attitude is unclear. On the one hand, individual police officers assigned to particular cases have been observed in agreement with arrangements worked out by the prosecutor and defense counsel. Formally, however, the police department takes the position that it should refuse to concur in all charge reductions on the theory that concurrence would be an admission that the original charge (and, by inference, the police request for that charge) should not have been brought in the first place. One prosecutor summed up all these views:

> By reducing a charge everybody seems to be happy: The defendant and his attorney feel that they have accomplished something by being able to plead to an offense less severe than that for which there was actual guilt; the prosecutor is happy because he does not have to try the case; society is happy because the defendant, if sentenced, is put away for the same amount of time as if he had pleaded to the original charge; the courts are happy because the dockets do not become congested; the police are happy if the defendant is sentenced, but if he is not, they are alone in their unhappiness.

2. *Kansas.* For virtually all offenses, the Kansas trial judge has no discretion to set either the maximum or the minimum sentence.[51] Each offense in the criminal code is given a maximum and a minimum, and the trial court, if a prison sentence is to be imposed, must impose the terms specified in the statutes.[52] The legislative maximum and minimum sentences are manipulated by charge reductions in order to induce guilty pleas. In addition, there is indication that the prosecutor often promises not to invoke the habitual criminal statute, which provides for mandatory increases in the prison terms,[53] in exchange for a defendant's promise to plead guilty. The accommodation in Kansas, then, resembles that in Michigan.

In Wichita, Kansas, the prosecuting attorney has authorized his assistants to arrange charge reductions in exchange for guilty pleas

[51] Kan. Gen. Stat. §62-1521 (1949), repealed by Kan. Laws 1957, Chap. 331, §37. See Kan. Stat. Ann. §62-2239 (1964).

[52] The trial court has discretion to place defendants on probation, limited only in that persons convicted of offenses punishable by life imprisonment may not be placed on probation. Probation is frequently used as an inducement to plead guilty; indeed, some Kansas judges have a probation hearing before pleading in which they indicate to the defendant whether he will be placed on probation if he pleads guilty. See Chapter 3.

[53] Kan. Stat. Ann. §21-107a (1964).

without his prior approval in all cases except those which are unusually serious, such as armed robbery, murder, and rape, or in which there has been substantial publicity. There are some cases, however, in which the prosecuting attorney's office will refuse to negotiate at all with defense attorneys; normally these involve extremely serious offenses in which there has been a great deal of publicity. The practice of bargaining with defendants for pleas of guilty is usually justified by the prosecuting attorney's office on the ground that any effort to try all cases on the original charge would require a prosecuting attorney's staff of at least three times its present size. The trial judges clearly approve of the prosecutor's practice of exchanging charge reductions for guilty pleas. Indeed, in many cases in which the prosecutor and defense attorney have been unable to arrive at a satisfactory arrangement, the trial judge holds a pretrial conference in which he may indicate that he will place the defendant on probation if he pleads guilty or suggest a charge reduction in exchange for a guilty plea. The police attitude toward the charge reduction practices seems generally to be one of approval. Indeed, in some cases they initiate the negotiations, knowing that the prosecuting attorney will follow their recommendation that a defendant be allowed to plead guilty to a reduced charge when he has cooperated with the police. In one such case the defendant agreed to confess to a crime in exchange for the police officer's promise to "get him off easier," a promise honored by the prosecutor by permitting the defendant to plead guilty to a reduced charge. This is in contrast to Detroit, where the police are officially opposed to, or at least have mixed feelings about, the charge reduction system.

C H A P T E R 7

The Sentence as an Individualization of Justice

In the preceding chapter, use of the sentence to encourage cooperation by defendants was examined. As such it is of considerable significance to police, prosecutor, and trial judge, who share responsibility for the efficient disposition of criminal cases. In this chapter the sentencing decision is examined as an indivdualization of justice — a reflection of the circumstances of the offense and the characteristics of the offender. As such it is of considerable importance to prison and parole authorities, who share responsibility for determining the length of incarceration.

Primary concern is with the function of sentencing discretion in relationship to the parole system and with devices for increasing the sentence because of offender characteristics — habitual offender statutes, consecutive sentences, and sex deviancy legislation.[1]

A. Sentencing Discretion and Parole

If the length of incarceration were determined solely by the sentence, there would doubtless be a consensus of opinion that sentencing should reflect the circumstances of the offense and the characteristics of the offender. In almost all misdemeanor cases, judges have discretion to set the length of sentences; release by operation of law upon serving the sentence or the sentence less good time is the norm, and release on parole is the exception.[2] Although misdemeanor sentences are often routinely imposed on the basis of offense categories and may not really be individualized, a proposal

[1] Almost all of the criteria affecting the decision to grant or deny probation also affect the selection of the length of the prison sentence. A full discussion here of sentencing criteria would, therefore, be largely repetitive of much of the discussion in Chapter 3.

[2] A report of the President's Crime Commission indicates that parole for misdemeanants is "extremely limited." The President's Commission on Law Enforcement and Administration of Justice, Task Force Report: Corrections 76 (1967).

to eliminate judicial sentence discretion in misdemeanor cases would be met with serious objection. And the ground of objection would be the felt need to individualize sentences. In commitments of serious offenders to state institutions, however, the situation is quite different because parole authorities ordinarily determine the actual length of incarceration.[3] In Wisconsin, for example, approximately two-thirds of all inmates released from adult correctional institutions are released on parole,[4] while in Michigan about 80 percent are released on parole. The purpose of the parole decision is normally viewed as the individualization of the length of incarceration.[5] But conferring sentencing discretion on trial judges is based on the assumption that the circumstances of the offense and the characteristics of the offender are to be considered in the sentencing decision as well as at the time of the parole decision. This, in turn, raises the problem of "meshing" the two decisions.

One alternative is for the trial judge to give the parole board the broadest possible range of discretion by imposing the shortest minimum and longest maximum sentences consistent with rewarding guilty pleas in cases where that is viewed as appropriate. This position was taken by a federal district judge at the Pilot Institute on Sentencing with regard to using the federal provision giving the trial judge discretion to permit immediate parole eligibility:

> In the seven months following its enactment, the writer has used the law in every case except those where mandatory sentences were required under the narcotics laws or where sentences imposed were a year or less. It has been my practice to impose sentence for a substantial period, often the maximum set out in the statutes, and then append to the sentence the proviso that the defendant shall be "eligible for parole at such time as the Board of Parole may determine," quoting from the statute. The writer has used this authority in every kind of case, including interstate transportation of stolen cars, white slave, bankruptcy fraud, mail theft, interstate transportation of forged securities, narcotics cases where the mandatory provisions are not applicable and even selective service violations. Recently I employed it, I am not sure if prudently, in a contempt of court sentence.[6]

[3] The President's Commission estimates that two-thirds of all releases from state prisons are on parole or conditional release. Id. at 186.

[4] See state-by-state chart in Model Penal Code §6.09A, Comment (Tent. Draft No. 5, 1956). In Wisconsin those inmates not released upon parole must be released conditionally and under supervision when they have served their maximum sentence less allowances for good time. See Chapter 12.

[5] See Chapter 11 for a discussion of the extent to which the parole decision, like the sentencing decision, is responsive to administrative needs.

[6] Pilot Institute on Sentencing, 26 F.R.D. 231, 317 (1959).

A second alternative is for the judge to fix the maximum sentence at a length thought appropriate in the individual case, leaving to the parole board discretion to release earlier if progress in the correctional program makes this seem appropriate. This position was also expressed at the Pilot Institute:

> Judge Kaufman indicated the view that the judge still has the responsibility for setting the maximum within the statutory limits, on the basis of a determination by the judge of the maximum time which he thinks the offender should be required to serve. Judge Kaufman added that the issue cannot be resolved until judges know more about how the Parole Board operates. He indicated that judges do not now know how the Parole Board operates and complete knowledge of its practices and procedures, and confidence in them, is essential if the indeterminate sentence is to be effectively implemented. It will make a great deal of difference, in his view, whether the Board has a practice of typically retaining an offender in the institution for a long period or whether its practice is to grant early release when it has power to do so.[7]

1. *Wisconsin.* Judicial discretion to set the maximum sentence is used in Milwaukee both as an administrative accommodation and as an individualization of justice. In many cases, imposition of sentence is preceded by expression of the considerations intended to be reflected in the sentence, such as guilty plea, criminal record, extent of economic loss or personal injury to the victim, and the defendant's motive in committing the offense. It is unusual, however, for the judge to indicate whether any particular consideration is more important than others mentioned or to state the precise effect on the sentence of any particular consideration. The problem of isolating sentence motives is complicated somewhat more because giving a shorter maximum sentence to defendants who plead guilty is regarded partly as a matter of sentence individualization in that a guilty plea is viewed as a willingness on the defendant's part to admit his guilt and attempt rehabilitation. Part of the difficulty in isolating sentencing motives is that there is an attempt to make the maximum sentence reflect the total circumstances of the case,[8] which is largely an impressionistic determination.

[7] Id. at 376-377.

[8] In one case, the court responded to defense counsel's plea for leniency with this statement: "Every case stands on its own facts. There are, then, many different dispositions involved in many different crimes. In other words, a disposition cannot necessarily be the same in all cases involving the same offense, because it depends upon the individual and also upon the facts involved.

"In imposing sentence, the Court considers what didn't happen as well as what did happen. . . . I will attempt to interpret the entire picture, as I see it, in the sentence."

It is difficult to determine the judge's view of the function of his sentencing decisions in relation to parole decisions. In many cases, the parole decision seems ignored and the sentence set as if it alone would determine the length of incarceration — hence, the attempt to reflect all the circumstances of the case in the sentence. In other cases, the judge expresses his awareness of the parole function. When he finds it necessary to impose a relatively high maximum sentence he may remind the defendant that he may be paroled long before the maximum has been served. In virtually all cases he follows statement of the sentence with an admonition that "if you behave yourself you'll get out sooner than that."

In still other cases the trial judge has a definite view of the likely parole decision and in such cases he has a very specific idea of the relation of his decision to that which he anticipates the parole board will make. Three such situations can be identified: (1) the maximum may be increased to prolong the parole supervision period when the trial court anticipates that the defendant will be paroled as soon as he reaches eligibility, or shortly thereafter, but feels that the defendant needs a longer period of parole supervision; (2) the maximum may be increased to give the parole board flexibility in timing release in cases in which there may be a danger to the community, or where it is uncertain how long incarceration should be in order to accomplish treatment objectives: (3) the maximum may be decreased in cases in which it is anticipated that the defendant will not be paroled.

a. *Use of maximum sentence to prolong parole supervision.*

Illustration No. 1: Defendant pleaded guilty to burglary, use of narcotics, and possession of narcotics. He had been stealing narcotics out of medical bags in doctors' cars parked in their garages. Earlier that year he had spent ten months in a state mental hospital for his narcotics addiction. He was sentenced to four years for burglary, two years for use of narcotics, and four years for possession of narcotics, all terms to run concurrently.

The maximum may be increased in cases in which the trial court anticipates that the defendant will be paroled as soon as he becomes eligible, or shortly thereafter. A high maximum is set in order to increase the period of parole supervision, if the judge feels that the defendant will need a longer than usual parole period in order to have the best chance of readjustment. This appears to be the situation in Illustration No. 1, in which the court stated:

> What I am going to do isn't particularly with any idea of punishing this defendant because, outside of the larceny of these vari-

ous narcotics and paraphernalia from physicians, nobody has been damaged except himself. It becomes my function now, as a last resort, to protect him against himself and that is only going to be temporary. Even if I added all these various counts up — they would amount to a substantial term because the burglary alone carries ten years — if I added them all up it would still enable this defendant to get out at some reasonably foreseeable time. Then, of course, it is up to him.

I want to make the commitments here for a reasonable length of time so that he has some time on his feet and some reasonable supervision after that. There is a point beyond which segregation isn't going to be too helpful.

b. *Use of maximum sentence to permit flexibility in timing release on parole.*

Illustration No. 2: Defendant pleaded guilty to burglary, which carries a possible maximum sentence of ten years. He had broken into a YMCA room and had stolen $16. His prior criminal record and available psychiatric evidence indicated that he was homosexual. At the time of the offense, he was on probation for a misdemeanor involving sodomy. Defendant received a sentence of three years.

If there is some question about the danger which the defendant poses to the community or some doubt about the length of time that will be required to accomplish treatment objectives, the maximum may be increased to permit flexibility in the timing of release on parole. The trial court thus attempts to enable the parole board to keep the defendant institutionalized longer than usual should his institutional experience indicate that this would be desirable.

In Illustration No. 2 the court committed the defendant to the state prison, which is also the sex crimes facility.[9] The court said:

The only question is, for how long should I commit you? Now, I am indicating in the record that the only reason that I am committing this defendant to the state prison is so the District Court may be able to use the same facility if it desires to in connection with the sex deviate commitment. I am making the term three years, not particularly because of this instant offense, but because of his general past history and the fact that he is on probation, and particularly to give them some elasticity so if they need more than the minimum time, they may keep him longer.

[9] Wis. Stat. Ann. §959.15 (1958), the Sex Crimes Law, authorizes the State Department of Public Welfare to establish a facility for the custody and treatment of offenders committed under the act. The Department has established such a facility in the Wisconsin State Prison.

c. *Use of maximum sentence to control release dates when parole is not anticipated.*

Illustration No. 3: Defendant pleaded guilty to forging a welfare voucher by increasing the amount from $3 to $8. He had a record of fifty arrests for drunkenness. The following colloquy occurred between the court and the defendant:

Q. Are you asking that I sentence you to two years?
A. Yes, Sir.
Q. Two years with time off, when will that get you out?
A. I don't know, about eighteen months, I guess, or nineteen.
Q. Do you think you need that much time?
A. I could get by with fifteen months.
Q. I am asking you these questions because you apparently appreciate your problem at this time and you have been up there before.

A. Well, Your Honor, this time I have intentions of quitting drinking for good and I figure just to get myself straightened out. It is up to you. If I do fifteen months, I will do it all without parole because they refused me parole on account of my drinking. I know I could get straightened out if you gave me fifteen months.
Q. You would get about three months off for good behavior?
A. Yes.
Q. That will get you out when the weather will be all right?
A. Yes, Sir.

The court imposed a prison sentence of fifteen months.

In any city of considerable size there is likely to be an appreciable number of habitual drunks who inhabit the skid row areas. Although their most frequent contacts with enforcement agencies involve misdemeanor violations arising out of habitual intoxication, they sometimes appear in felony court charged with crimes against property committed in an attempt to secure money for alcohol. When this occurs, they present an unusual problem in selection of the maximum sentence.

Officials do not expect them to be paroled because of their alcoholism. Rather, it is anticipated that unless an unusually long maximum is imposed they will be held until they have served the sentence. This seems to have two consequences. First, because parole is not seriously anticipated, the maximum may be set lower than usual. Second, because most of these persons live on the streets, the maximum may be set in such a way as to secure their release in warm weather.

Since most of these persons are not viewed as dangerous, probation might seem the appropriate disposition, unless the property crimes become too serious. One reason it may not be used is, of course, the virtual certainty that they will return to alcohol and violate probation. But another reason is that the commission of a felony presents the opportunity to separate the man from alcohol, not necessarily in the expectation of permanent abstinence thereafter, but at least to provide him with regular meals, a warm place to sleep, and an opportunity to return to good physical health. Sometimes probation is not granted, partly, at least, because the defendant says he does not want it. Some of the habitual drunks who have pleaded guilty to forgery or similar offenses have requested imprisonment in the hope of "cure." When a prison term is imposed, the court attempts to use the maximum sentence to assure sufficient time for physical health to return and to secure the release of the defendant when the weather is warm.

2. *Michigan.* Sentence individualization in Michigan assumes two forms. Judicial discretion to set the minimum sentence is used to reflect the individualization factors, and to a more limited extent, so is the judicial maximum sentence. Those offenses punishable by a high, mandatory minimum or maximum sentence are apparently precluded from any attempt at individualization. In practice, however, charge reductions are often motivated in part by a desire to avoid imposition of mandatory sentences that seem disproportionately high in relation to the circumstances of the case.

a. *Judicial sentencing discretion.* For most offenses the trial judge has discretion to set the minimum sentence. The minimum less allowances for good time determines the defendant's parole eligibility date, although release earlier than that date is permitted with the written consent of the sentencing judge.[10] One alternative would be for the judge to set the minimum uniformly low to permit the fullest possible exercise of discretion by the parole board. This view is clearly rejected by Michigan trial judges. It was one judge's reasoning that, at the time he sets the minimum, he is provided with a great deal of information by the probation department and the psychopathic clinic, and, in addition, he has observed the defendant in court and is sometimes able to judge from his demeanor the possibility of rehabilitation if placed on probation. At this point in the disposition of the case, the judge feels that he, and he alone, is qualified to determine the minimum. He considers it his duty to make this determination, notwithstanding any future decision that may be made by the parole board. Another judge stated that he would not think of sentencing an armed robber from one to twenty years and relying on the parole board to release the prisoner when they feel in their discretion that he is qualified to enter society again. On the contrary, the trial judges uniformly hold the view that the minimum sentence will determine the ac-

[10] This procedure is termed "special consideration" and is discussed in Chapter 9.

tual period of incarceration. Their premise is that, because of prison population pressures, the defendant will be released by the parole board at the expiration of the minimum term set by them, less good time allowances. While they are clearly aware that some prisoners are retained by the parole board for a period considerably beyond the minimum, and while they consider this a proper exercise of parole board discretion, nevertheless, as a working assumption, they set the minimum as if it alone determined the date of release.

Trial judges in Michigan attempt to make the minimum sentence reflect the total circumstances of the case. One judge, asked what factors he took into account in fixing the minimum, replied: "Such matters as the convict's criminal record, family situation, circumstances of the crime in question, etc., are always taken into account by the court in fixing the minimum." Although there is an attempt to individualize the minimum sentence, the extent to which this is possible is limited by the necessity for disposing of a large number of cases by pleas of guilty. Most of the minima are set at one or two years and those judges who set higher sentences find they discourage guilty pleas by doing so. Within the limits imposed by the guilty plea system, however, the minimum reflects the judge's view of the case.

Approximately twenty of the most serious felonies are punishable under Michigan law by imprisonment "for life or for any number of years." If the trial judge elects to incarcerate the defendant, he is authorized either to impose a life sentence or to set both a minimum and a maximum sentence.[11] If a life sentence is imposed, the offender is eligible for parole under the "lifer law" at the expiration of ten years.[12] If a minimum and a maximum sentence are imposed, parole eligibility attaches at the expiration of the minimum sentence less deductions for good time or at the expiration of ten years, whichever is shorter.[13]

The minimum sentence is regarded as the crucial determination. The maximum sentence is usually set in such a way as to provide a wide range of parole board discretion to retain the defendant beyond the expiration of the minimum. In one case, the trial judge imposed a sentence of twenty-two and a half to forty-five years. The judge remarked that he simply wanted to get the defendant out of circulation for a long time. He said that the twenty-

[11] Mich. Stat. Ann. §28.1081 (Supp. 1965).

[12] Mich. Stat. Ann. §28.2304 (1954). The "lifer law" does not apply to inmates serving life sentences for first degree murder. Ibid. The operation of this statute is discussed in Chapter 9.

[13] Ibid.

two and a half years was simply an opinion based on all of the circumstances of the case. In setting the maximum sentence, he said he simply doubled the minimum term. He said he had no explanation for this other than that he used this simple little formula which seemed to be equitable. Doubtless, one reason for this attitude toward the maximum is a belief that it makes little difference because the defendant will be released upon expiration of the minimum no matter how high the maximum is set. This view is logically inconsistent, however, with the trial judge's attitude toward the mandatory maximum sentence.

b. *Mandatory sentences.* Judicial resistance to the twenty year mandatory minimum sentence for sale of narcotics[14] is very strong. All the judges of Recorder's Court, in registering their dislike for the provision, cited the hypothetical case of a young man having no criminal record being given a twenty-year minimum sentence for selling a single marijuana cigarette. Charge reductions from sale to possession or use are routine.[15] Indeed, in some cases judges have refused to accept guilty pleas to sale of narcotics, but have continued the case and appointed counsel with instructions to negotiate a charge reduction.

The effect of the twenty-year mandatory minimum is to postpone parole eligibility; it restricts the parole board's discretion as well as that of the trial judge. However, the high mandatory maximum sentence does not affect the board's ability to grant early parole and increases its authority to retain custody of the defendant. Nevertheless, there is judicial resistance to imposition of mandatory maximum sentences that seem unduly long in relation to the circumstances of the case. One of the justifications offered for the charge reduction–guilty plea practice is that the resulting reduction in the length of the mandatory maximum makes no difference in the time actually served because prison population pressures force release long before the maximum, and thus the person is kept incarcerated for the same length of time whether he is convicted of the more serious or less serious offense. The value of the reduction in charge is that it does induce guilty pleas, probably because it relieves the particular defendant of the worry that he may be the exceptional case which is held to the long maximum. Inmates, for obvious reasons, feel more comfortable when they know they *must* be released in this relatively short time.

3. *Kansas.* The sentencing structure in Kansas requires imposition of both the statutory maximum and minimum sentences in all

14 Mich. Stat. Ann. §18.1122 (1957).

15 See Chapter 6.

cases of commitment to the state prison system.[16] Judicial sentence discretion is not available, then, either to reward guilty pleas or to individualize the sentence, although probation is used for both purposes. Most cases disposed of by bargained guilty pleas are preceded by charge reductions, although bargaining may also involve promises not to invoke the habitual offender statute or promises of probation. There were no clear cases observed in Kansas of charge reductions motivated solely by a desire to individualize the sentence. These considerations doubtless enter into plea bargaining, which may, in fact, be couched in terms of individualization factors. One assistant prosecutor indicated that he feels that he has to balance two things in coming to a decision about reducing a charge: The first consideration is the duty of the county attorney, both to the county and society, and the second consideration is self-respect or the fact that "you have to sleep with yourself." He indicated that he was a sucker for a sob story and very often reduces a charge when he feels sorry for the defendant. Cases are quite common in which felonies are reduced to misdemeanors in order to avoid giving youthful offenders a felony conviction record.[17] There is no doubt that factors of youth, respectability, and lack of serious prior record influence the prosecutor in making his charge reduction decisions in the guilty plea bargaining process.

B. Extended Terms

Legislatures have authorized longer periods of incarceration to be imposed on certain offenders because of characteristics that differentiate them from the "typical" offender. The most obvious example is the habitual criminal statute. On a more mechanical level, provisions permitting consecutive sentences have similar aims. More recently, attention has been focused on the dangerous offender reflected in the legislative enactment of so-called "sex deviate" provisions designed to enable sex offenders to be incarcerated longer and to afford them specialized treatment.

The problem of identifying persons who should be sentenced for extended terms is being given increasing attention. The Model Sentencing Act and the Model Penal Code[18] provide extended

[16] See Chapter 6.

[17] In one case, a charge of forcible rape was reduced to contributing to the delinquency of a minor. The defendant was of quite low mentality and, although force had been used, it was obvious that the victim had not been greatly corrupted by the event since she was pregnant by her uncle at the time of the offense.

[18] See Model Sentencing Act §§5, 6 (1963); Model Penal Code §§6.07, 7.03 (Proposed Official Draft, 1962).

terms and criteria to control the impositions of such terms. As techniques for diagnosis and treatment improve, it seems likely that legislation of this kind will become even more common.

1. *Habitual Offenders.* Most jurisdictions have habitual offender statutes that provide for increased sentences when it is proved or admitted that the defendant has been convicted of one or more offenses prior to the present conviction. Some habitual offender statutes make the increase in sentence mandatory upon proof of prior convictions; others authorize but do not require a longer sentence in such circumstances. The experience under the Michigan mandatory statute supports the general observation[19] that trial judges resist mandatory increases in sentences for recidivists. On the other hand, Kansas has a mandatory statute and there was no evidence of trial judge resistance there, although perhaps part of the reason is that the mandatory provisions do not restrict otherwise unfettered trial judge sentencing discretion because Kansas trial judges have no such discretion. Perhaps, also, the reasons for invoking the statute — to support its use as a bargaining device by invoking it against defendants who refuse to plead guilty — are approved by the trial judiciary. In any event, the experience in Wisconsin, where the statute is discretionary, and in Michigan after the statute was amended to make it discretionary, has been an almost complete nonuse of the provisions. Thus, neither mandatory or discretionary provisions are likely to be used very much in practice, except perhaps in the exceptional case or when a defendant refuses to plead guilty. The reason for this appears to be that, in the opinion of many prosecutors and trial judges, the present statutory levels of sentences are sufficiently high to adequately handle recidivists without the necessity of an increased term.

a. *Kansas.*

Illustration No. 4: Defendant was charged with passing a bad check over $20 in value, which, if imprisonment is imposed, carries a mandatory one-year minimum and five-year maximum. The deputy prosecuting attorney bargained with the defendant's attorney, promising not to invoke the habitual offender statute in exchange for a guilty plea, but the latter refused the deal. The defendant was convicted of the

19 Model Penal Code §7.03 (Proposed Official Draft, 1962) authorizes, but does not require, the trial judge to increase the sentence for habitual offenders. Model Penal Code §7.03, Comment (Tent. Draft No. 2, 1954): "Experience has shown that sanctions of this kind [habitual offender laws] are more effective when they are both flexible and moderate; highly afflictive, mandatory punishment provisions become nullified in practice. . . . The draft proposes, therefore, that the use of the extended term should not in any case be mandatory on the court."

check charge and the deputy prosecuting attorney then invoked the habitual offender statute and proved the prior felony conviction, which automatically doubled the sentence.

The Kansas habitual offender statute requires an increase in the already mandatory minimum and maximum sentences. If a person convicted of a felony has a record of one or more prior felony convictions the prosecutor may, in his discretion, invoke the repeater statute. Invocation of the statute and proof or admission that the defendant had one prior felony conviction doubles the statutory minimum and maximum sentences for the current felony conviction. If it is proved or admitted that the defendant had two or more prior felony convictions, the habitual offender act requires the trial judge to impose a sentence of not less than fifteen years.[20]

The statute is invoked more often in Kansas than in either Michigan or Wisconsin. However, even in Kansas it is used in only a small number of cases. It is most typically invoked to support the prosecutor's position in the plea bargaining process. Many prosecutors consider the statute invaluable in securing guilty pleas. It is common for the prosecutor to offer not to invoke the statute against a defendant with a felony record if the latter agrees to plead guilty in the pending case. This offer carries with it the threat, sometimes made express, that if the defendant refuses the deal, or accepts it but later changes his mind, the prosecutor will invoke the statute against him. If the defendant refuses to cooperate, as in the illustration case, many prosecutors feel that they must invoke the statute to maintain its credibility as a bargaining instrument.

While maintenance of the guilty plea system accounts for most cases in which the statute is invoked, in certain situations it may be used because of the characteristics of the defendant and without regard to his willingness to plead guilty. In these cases the prosecutor may even refuse to bargain with the defendant for a guilty plea. These instances are largely limited to defendants who have given enforcement officials unusual difficulty or who pose a particularly serious threat to the community.

b. *Michigan.*

Illustration No. 5: The defendant had been plaguing the prosecutor's office and courts with his frequent misconduct as a beggar. He had been arrested over thirty-five times and convicted twenty times, in each case on a charge of begging, punishable by ninety days in jail, or some related misdemeanor. On the occasion of his latest arrest, $199 in cash and two bank books showing deposits of $5700 were found on his person.

[20] Kan. Stat. Ann. §21-107(a) (1964).

It was felt by the prosecutor's office that it was time to teach the old man a lesson. He was charged with begging as a third offender, punishable by not less than six months nor more than two years' imprisonment.

Michigan's experience with its felony habitual offender statute raises the issue whether the statute should be mandatory or discretionary. At one time it was mandatory in Michigan for the prosecutor to file a supplemental information alleging prior convictions whenever a convicted felon came within the scope of the statute. If the prior convictions were proved or admitted, it was obligatory for the trial judge to impose the high minimum sentence provided by the act. Prosecutors in Detroit invoked the statute when the sentence on the current conviction was, in their opinion, inadequate. Trial judges resisted invocation of the statute, even to the point of dismissing some supplemental informations on extremely technical grounds. One result of this attitude was amendment of the statute to make its invocation discretionary with the prosecutor and to give the trial judge discretion to set the minimum and the maximum sentence.[21] The statute has remained substantially in this form.[22]

After adoption of the discretionary provision, prosecutors in Detroit filed supplemental informations without prior consultation with the trial judges in cases in which the judge's sentence on the current conviction seemed inadequate to them. The trial judges in Recorder's Court refused to increase either the minimum or the maximum sentence, preferring to take the defendant's criminal record into account in setting the minimum sentence within the statutory limits applicable to the current conviction only. As a result of this, the prosecuting attorney's office does not use the habitual criminal statute unless a judge of Recorder's Court, after studying the presentence report, decides that the statute should be invoked. The judge then contacts the prosecuting attorney and suggests that a supplemental information be filed.

There is no indication whether the mandatory provisions were used as a bargaining device in Michigan, as in Kansas, and the manner in which the discretionary provisions are invoked, when they are invoked, indicates they have no relation to the plea bargaining process in Detroit. One judge indicated the criteria for his decision to use the statute by stating that he will request the habitual criminal statute to be utilized only when the defendant, as evidenced by his record and current conduct, is really a "bad egg" and

21 A more detailed discussion of the operation of the statute in its mandatory form appears in Miller, Prosecution: The Decision to Charge a Suspect with a Crime (forthcoming).

22 Mich. Stat. Ann. §§28.1028–1085 (1954).

should be incarcerated for a longer period of time than would be permissible for the crime for which he stands currently convicted. A prosecutor indicated that, in most cases in which Recorder's Court judges have requested invocation of the statute, the defendant has demonstrated his "habitualness" by four or five prior felony convictions. Necessarily, then, this means that the statute is used in Detroit in only a small percentage of cases in which it could be employed. In Michigan, outside of Detroit, there has been virtually no use of the statute after it was amended to give the trial judge discretion. Thus generally the act is used rarely and then only at the initiative of the trial judge.

Many Michigan statutes defining misdemeanor conduct provide for increased sentences when the defendant has previously been convicted under the same statute.[23] Normally, these provisions are not used except when, as in the illustration case, the defendant by his extremely repetitive misdemeanor conduct has made himself a nuisance to law enforcement agencies and the community. The repeater provisions of the accosting and soliciting statute are an exception. Accosting and soliciting is punishable by ninety days in jail; second offenders are punishable by one year in jail and third offenders are punishable as felons by two years' imprisonment.[24] Police do charge prostitutes and homosexuals under the repeater provisions, and this practice is supported by the prosecutor and trial judges.[25] Of course, even when the habitual offender laws are not used, the defendant's criminal record is taken into account by the judge in setting the minimum sentence.[26]

c. *Wisconsin.*

> *Illustration No. 6:* Defendant was charged with indecent exposure, which carries a possible sentence of one year in the county jail, and which for repeaters increases the possible liability to three years' imprisonment. He pleaded not guilty with jury waiver to the indecent exposure charge but admitted the allegations of the prior convictions. He was found guilty of indecent exposure. His criminal record consisted of five convictions for indecent exposure, three of them within the last two years. He was given a sentence of two and a half years' imprisonment.

23 See, for example, Mich. Stat. Ann. §§28.364-28.365 (1962) (defining numerous common misdemeanors under the rubric "disorderly persons" and providing enhanced punishment for repeaters).

24 Ibid.

25 A discussion of this police charging program will be found in Miller, Prosecution (forthcoming).

26 See Chapter 3.

The Wisconsin habitual offender statute authorizes, but does not require, an increase in the maximum sentence for persons with one felony conviction or three misdemeanor convictions within the five years preceding conviction for the present offense. The statute applies when the current conviction is for a misdemeanor as well as a felony.[27] In recent years the statute has fallen into virtual disuse in felony cases. It has been used very selectively in misdemeanor cases to increase the sentence for repetitive misdemeanants with certain characteristics.

One class of misdemeanant is the exhibitionist. Indecent exposure is punishable by not more than one year in the county jail. When, as in the illustration case, a person habitually exposes himself and probation or jail sentences have had no effect on his conduct, he may be charged as an habitual offender in order to permit his isolation for a considerable period of time, thus relieving the community of a nuisance. In addition to the indecent exposure cases, the statute has on occasion been applied to the repetitive bad check passer and to the habitual drunk, the latter sometimes at the defendant's own request in the belief that a prison sentence will enable him to abstain from alcohol permanently. The reason for the failure to use the statute with felons is the ample authority provided by current statutory levels attached to most felonies. For the misdemeanant, however, the statutory levels are limited, inviting the use of the habitual offender act when a person commits only misdemeanors but commits them repeatedly.

2. *Multiple offenders.*

> *Illustration No. 7:* Defendant was convicted by jury verdict of the offenses of first degree murder and attempted first degree murder. He was accused of killing a police detective and wounding another officer when they were taking him to police headquarters for questioning about a fraud charge. A sentence of thirty years was imposed for the attempted murder, the longest permissible for that offense. A mandatory sentence of life imprisonment was imposed for the first degree murder. The trial judge then provided that the life sentence was to be consecutive to the thirty-year sentence.

Trial judges in most jurisdictions have authority to impose concurrent or consecutive sentences when a person is convicted of more than one offense. The authority to impose consecutive terms has wide theoretical applicability, since many persons sentenced to prison could have been charged and convicted as multiple offenders. Recent model legislation has attempted to limit the authority

[27] Wis. Stat. Ann. §939.62 (1958).

to use consecutive sentences on the ground that it is sometimes abused. Thus both the Model Penal Code[28] and the Model Sentencing Act [29] display a clear preference for concurrent over consecutive sentences, although neither would prohibit the latter entirely.

Laws in the three states differ on authority to impose consecutive sentences. Trial judges in Kansas[30] and Wisconsin[31] have authority to impose either concurrent or consecutive sentences, while in Michigan consecutive sentences have, in effect, been prohibited by the Michigan Supreme Court.[32] Despite this difference, the practice is roughly the same in all three states: Consecutive sentences are very rarely used. Most judges in Kansas and Wisconsin use concurrent sentences except in extraordinary cases. In most cases of multiple conviction, the judge simply imposes one fairly long sentence and makes the other sentences run concurrent to it. Thus, the multiplicity of offenses is taken into account without imposition of consecutive terms.

Consecutive sentences are so rarely imposed that it is difficult to generalize on the criteria used. A Kansas judge, after stating that he almost never used consecutive terms, indicated that those cases in which he did were probably explainable on grounds of (1) the defendant's reputation, (2) his prior criminal record, or (3) the seriousness of the offenses. A Wisconsin judge imposed long consecutive terms on two defendants he was convinced were professional criminals. In another Wisconsin case, abstracted in Illustration No. 7, long consecutive sentences were imposed because the victims were police officers, the judge commenting, "You had no justification for taking the life of either [police officer]. I think this case graphically shows that the service of a law enforcement officer . . . even on what would appear to be routine business is

28 Model Penal Code §7.06 (Proposed Official Draft, 1962).

29 Model Sentencing Act §22 (1963) provides: "Separate sentences of commitment imposed on a defendant for two or more crimes constituting a single criminal episode shall run concurrently. Sentences for two or more crimes not constituting a single criminal episode shall run concurrently unless the judge otherwise orders."

30 Kan. Gen. Stat. §62-1512 (1949) required the trial judge to impose consecutive sentences "when any person shall be convicted of two or more offenses before sentence shall have been pronounced upon him for either offense." However, this provision was interpreted to permit the trial judge to impose concurrent or consecutive sentences for all offenses charged in the same indictment or information. See McCarty v. Hudspeth, 166 Kan. 476, 201 P.2d 658 (1949). Amendment of this provision subsequent to the field survey gives the trial judge discretion to impose concurrent or consecutive sentences in all situations. See Kan. Stat. Ann. §62-1512 (1964).

31 Wis. Stat. Ann. §959.07 (1958).

32 Ex parte Allison, 322 Mich. 491, 33 N.W.2d 917 (1948), prohibits the use of consecutive sentences except when specifically authorized by statute. The effect is virtually to prohibit them altogether because they are apparently statutorily authorized only for escape from prison. See Mich. Stat. Ann. §28.390 (1962).

fraught with danger." The judge concluded by remarking that he wanted the parole board to know his feelings when it reviewed the case.

Probably the reason why consecutive sentences are so rarely used is that the permissible statutory penalties for most single offenses are sufficiently high to achieve the sentencing objectives of the trial judge and to allow the parole board to keep the offender until it believes release on parole is appropriate. When imposed, consecutive sentences may have very little effect on the time actually served in prison but, as in the illustration case, are imposed to demonstrate the judge's view of the seriousness of the offense or to accomplish purposes of deterrence. However, when a large number of short sentences are imposed consecutively, the effect will be to delay parole eligibility for a substantial period of time and thus result in a long prison term unless the minimum is reduced by executive commutation.[33]

The consequence of the practice of using concurrent sentences is that the multiple offender will usually be charged with one, or at the most two, of his offenses because police and prosecutors normally view charging additional offenses as useless paper work that will only result in concurrent sentences. Even when not charged, additional offenses committed by the offender will probably have an effect upon whether he is given probation and, if incarcerated, upon the length of his sentence. In Detroit the uncharged offenses are described in the presentence report to permit the trial judge to take them into consideration in setting the minimum sentence. One judge said that "the other [uncharged] offenses are very definitely called to his attention. The purpose, of course, is to influence the sentence to be imposed on the defendant. The presentence report is very explicit in terms of spelling out crimes for which the defendant is apparently guilty and not charged with. A good general rule would be that the severity of the minimum period of confinement varies directly with, and is proportionate to, the number and aggravation of the uncharged criminal activity."

In Milwaukee it is common practice to charge the multiple offender with the two offenses for which the evidence is most conclusive, thus permitting consecutive sentences in the unlikely event that the judge desires to impose them. Additional uncharged offenses are brought to the judge's attention prior to sentencing in the expectation that they will influence the length of the maximum sentence and will influence the decision to grant or deny probation. In cases in which a presentence report has been or-

[33] See Chapter 9 for a discussion of the practice of commuting consecutive sentences to concurrent ones to permit parole eligibility.

dered, descriptions of the offenses which were not charged are included in that report. When a postplea of guilty hearing is held, the uncharged offenses are brought to the attention of the court by stipulation of the parties.

The effect of the uncharged offenses on the judicially set minimum in Detroit and the judicially fixed maximum in Milwaukee depends upon the number and seriousness of the uncharged offenses. In a typical multiple offender situation, such as the forger who has stolen and passed a number of checks, it seems to make little difference whether he committed one or several offenses. In other cases, however, where the value of stolen property is large or where violence is used against the person, additional offenses of this seriousness may have the effect of lengthening the sentences imposed.

Since the Kansas trial judge has no discretion in setting the maximum or the minimum sentence, he is unable to take account of additional offenses, except in deciding whether to place the offender on probation. Prosecutors in Kansas stated that they rarely charge all offenses committed by the defendant, but that they do charge all offenses of similar seriousness committed within a reasonable period of time and that they do this primarily for plea bargaining purposes. Dismissal of added charges, or promises not to prosecute uncharged offenses, are given in exchange for a guilty plea.

3. *Sex offenders.* Statutes in Kansas and Michigan authorize an indeterminate civil commitment for certain sex offenders, a very common type of legislation. In Wisconsin specified sex offenders are subject to confinement under a criminal commitment for a maximum sentence, subject to an indefinite number of extensions of the sentence. It is important to know what criteria are used to invoke these special acts with their great increase in possible length of incarceration.

a. *Kansas.*

> *Illustration No. 8:* Defendant, charged with sodomy, punishable by 10 years' imprisonment, pleaded guilty to lewd and lascivious behavior, punishable by 6 months in the county jail. The victim was a 15-year-old boy. The trial judge ascertained that the 29-year-old defendant had been engaged in homosexual activity since the age of 13 or 14, involving 5 or 6 acts as an active participant and over 200 times as a passive participant. The trial judge informed the defendant that upon conviction he would be committed to the state mental hospital under the Kansas sex deviate act, but the defendant indicated that he still wished to plead guilty. The psychiatric

report from the mental hospital recommended probation. Defendant was placed on probation for 1 year subject to the special condition that he not associate with any person under the age of 21 years.

The Kansas Sex Deviate Statute provides that the trial judge may commit to a state mental hospital for observation and study any person convicted of "any offense against public morals and decency, as relating to crimes pertaining to sex, in which perversion or mental aberration, appears to be or is involved. . . ." [34] If the psychiatric report recommends institutional treatment outside the penal system, the trial judge has authority to make an indeterminate civil commitment to any state mental hospital, although he still retains the authority to impose a prison sentence or place the defendant on probation.[35] The act provides that "if after commitment to any state or county institution, it appears that the defendant has been restored mentally, he shall be returned to the court where convicted, and be sentenced or paroled [placed on probation] as the court deems best under the circumstances." [36]

The provision for commitment for observation and study is used extensively only in Sedgwick County, where the judge uses the provision frequently and always follows the recommendation contained in the report. Since in most cases probation is recommended, only a small number of offenders are actually given the indeterminate civil commitment authorized by the legislation.

b. *Michigan.*

Illustration No. 9: Defendant was charged with assault and battery, punishable by ninety days in jail. While sitting in a movie theater he had placed his hand on the thigh of a middle-aged woman. Defendant's criminal record consisted of five convictions for assault and battery, all committed under similar circumstances, and one arrest and release for the same offense. Until this time he had received either a ninety-day jail sentence or probation for each conviction. A petition was filed alleging defendant to be a criminal sexual psychopath and a commission of three psychiatrists was appointed to examine him. At the court hearing he was found to be a criminal sexual psychopath within the meaning of the Michigan statute and was given an indeterminate civil commitment to the state hospital commission.

The Michigan Criminal Sexual Psychopath Act provides an indeterminate civil commitment for "any person who is suffering

[34] Kan. Stat. Ann. §62-1534 (1964).
[35] Kan. Stat. Ann. §62-1536 (1964).
[36] Kan. Stat. Ann. §62-1537 (1964).

from a mental disorder and is not feeble-minded, which mental disorder is coupled with criminal propensities to the commission of sex offenses." [37] The act may be invoked against any person charged with, convicted of, or placed on probation for any felony or misdemeanor who has had the defined mental disorder for a period of not less than four months.[38] A commission of three psychiatrists must examine the defendant but the issue of deviancy must be determined by a judge or jury.[39] Once committed, the defendant may not be discharged until "there are reasonable grounds to believe that such person has recovered from such psychopathy to a degree that he will not be a menace to others" and must be discharged if he can prove to a judge or jury that he has recovered. There are provisions for annual review of his status by two psychiatrists.[40]

The act is used very little in areas of Michigan outside of Detroit; in Detroit about fifty commitments are made per year. In the Detroit prosecutor's office one assistant prosecutor has responsibility for reviewing cases to determine the applicability of the act to them. Other assistant prosecutors refer all likely cases to this assistant for a decision on whether a petition should be filed. The single most important criterion in this decision is the defendant's criminal record. The criminal sexual psychopath act does not require a prior conviction of a sex motivated offense, but it is the policy of the prosecutor's office not to bring a petition unless the defendant's record contains at least one such conviction. Usually, as in the illustration case, it contains several prior convictions. This self-imposed requirement arises out of the necessity of proving that the defendant has propensities toward the commission of sexually motivated offenses and that the mental disorder was in existence at least four months prior to the determination of deviancy.

The decision made in the prosecutor's office is the crucial one. Usually the decision to invoke the act is made at the same time as the charging decision. If a civil commitment follows, which it almost always does, the charges on the current offense are dropped. Because of the heavy emphasis on prior criminal convictions, the act, as it is administered in Detroit, becomes sort of a special habitual offender act.[41]

c. *Wisconsin.*

Illustration No. 10: Defendant was charged with lewd and lascivious behavior, punishable by one year in the county

[37] Mich. Stat. Ann. §28.967(1) (1954).
[38] Mich. Stat. Ann. §28.967(3) (1954).
[39] Mich. Stat. Ann. §§28.967(4), 28.967(5) (1954).
[40] Mich. Stat. Ann. §28.967(7) (1954).
[41] A more detailed discussion of the prosecutor's role in administering the statute appears in Miller, Prosecution (forthcoming).

jail, and with being an habitual offender, punishable by three years' imprisonment. Both the present and a number of past offenses involved indecent exposure. He pleaded not guilty with jury waiver to the substantive count and admitted the allegations of the prior convictions. After the finding of guilty, the question arose whether the defendant should be committed for a presentence sex deviate study. The defense attorney expressed approval of such a commitment, saying, "The defendant expressed a thought to me that he needs medical attention. I don't know where he will end if we don't do something like that." After study, defendant was found not deviate and was sentenced to three years' imprisonment under the criminal code.

The Wisconsin Sex Crimes Law requires commitment for presentence study to determine the need for specialized treatment of any person convicted of forcible rape, sexual intercourse without consent, and indecent behavior with a child.[42] Upon conviction of any other sex crime, defined as "any crime except homicide or attempted homicide if the court finds that the defendant was probably directly motivated by a desire for sexual excitement in the commission of the crime," [43] the court may commit the defendant for presentence study if the Department of Public Welfare certifies that facilities are available. If at the end of the sixty-day period of study the defendant is found not to be in need of specialized treatment, the court may place him on probation or sentence him to imprisonment under the ordinary provision of the criminal code. If the defendant is found to be in need of specialized treatment, the court may either place him on probation on condition that he receive psychiatric treatment or commit him to the State Department of Public Welfare for the full statutory maximum attached to the offense of which he was convicted.[44] The court has no discretion to select a shorter maximum.

Parole eligibility is immediate under the Wisconsin Sex Crimes Law — there is no minimum sentence.[45] The defendant must be released when he has served his maximum sentence less allowances for good time. However, the Department of Public Welfare has authority to petition the sentencing court for a five-year extension of the maximum sentence if the offender is found to be dangerous.

[42] Wis. Stat. Ann. §959.15(1) (1958).
[43] Wis. Stat. Ann. §959.15 (2) (1958).
[44] Wis. Stat. Ann. §§959.15(5), 959.16(6) (1958). Huebner v. State, 33 Wis.2d 505, 147 N.W.2d 646 (1967), requires a judicial hearing on the issue of sexual deviancy under the Wisconsin statute.
[45] Wis. Stat. Ann. §959.15(10) (1958).

The maximum sentence may be extended any number of times.[46] The commitment, then, is potentially completely indeterminate.

The Wisconsin Sex Crimes Law has been used more frequently than the civil commitment provisions in Michigan and Kansas. The most likely explanation for this is the attitudes of prosecutors, trial judges, and defense attorneys toward the act in Wisconsin in contrast to the attitude in the other two states. Defense attorneys in Kansas and Michigan apparently regard the civil commitments as life sentences and tend to resist their invocation on the ground they are unduly severe. Except for the trial judge in Sedgwick County, Kansas, and the trial judges and prosecutor's office in Detroit, the same attitude seems to prevail among trial judges and prosecutors. Probably because an additional court hearing is necessary to extend the maximum under the Wisconsin statute and because the Wisconsin program has a reputation of being treatment oriented, the act has received wider support from prosecutors, trial judges, and defense attorneys. This probably explains why the mandatory provisions of the statute have not been resisted by charge manipulations. There is also a noticeable willingness on the part of defense attorneys to have the terms of the statute invoked in situations where invocation is at the discretion of the trial court. In Illustration No. 10, the defense attorney apparently thought that a sex deviate commitment, provided his client were found deviate, would be in the client's best interest. Once it was determined that the treatment facilities of the sex deviate law were not available, however, the defense attorney then argued that his client should receive only a jail sentence because a three-year sentence was too severe under the circumstances. Defense counsel was apparently willing to have a three-year sex deviate sentence (with possibility of extensions) but not a three-year straight sentence of imprisonment.

[46] Wis. Stat. Ann. §959.15(13)–959.15(15) (1958).

C H A P T E R 8

Sentence Disparity

Disparity among decisions is a problem whenever discretion is exercised in the administration of criminal justice. Discretion in making arrests is not uniformly exercised in all cities or by all officers within a single police department.[1] Whether an offender is prosecuted sometimes depends as much upon which assistant prosecutor makes the decision as upon the facts of the case.[2] Whether probation is revoked often depends upon which combination of probation officer and trial judge has responsibility for supervising the probationer.[3]

Despite the presence of disparity throughout the criminal justice system, public discussion has focused primarily upon sentence disparity — unjustifiable differences in the use of probation and the lengths of prison sentences. This may reflect the fact that the existence of discretion in sentencing has long been recognized while the fact it exists at other stages in the criminal justice system has been either ignored or minimized.[4] Also, disparity at the sentencing stage is more visible than it is at other stages; it is easier to compile statistics on the use of probation by various trial judges than on the exercise of discretion not to arrest or prosecute.[5]

Sentence disparity presents serious problems. It manifests the

[1] See LaFave, Arrest: The Decision to Take a Suspect into Custody 61-164 (1965).

[2] See Miller, Prosecution: The Decision to Charge a Suspect with a Crime (forthcoming).

[3] See Chapter 5.

[4] With respect to the traditional failure to recognize the existence of police discretion, see LaFave, Arrest 61-82 (1965). Although the existence of prosecutor discretion has been recognized, there has been little concern with prosecutor charging disparity. Yet it is clear in the urban prosecutor's office, where several assistants make charging decisions, that disparity does exist. See Miller, Prosecution (forthcoming).

[5] Records are normally not kept on decisions not to arrest offenders. With respect both to arresting and charging, it is often difficult to determine whether the negative decision resulted from doubt as to the guilt or convictability of the suspect or because the decision-maker determined that action was undesirable. In sentencing, however, the fact of conviction eliminates any doubt that the decision-maker has authority to make the discretionary sentencing decision.

failure of the system to achieve the goal of equal justice under law. When it becomes notorious, it is likely to undermine public confidence in the administration of criminal justice. Sentence disparity is asserted to have severe demoralizing and anti-rehabilitative effects on prisoners who receive harsher sentences than others in comparable situations.[6] Perhaps most important, the existence of sentence disparity casts grave doubt upon the extent to which the goal of individualized correctional treatment can be achieved in practice because of inadequate knowledge about human behavior, a lack of consensus about the goals of the criminal justice process, a failure of the trial judiciary to develop a method of minimizing their differing views about sentencing, and a willingness often to give administrative convenience a higher priority than the proper disposition of the individual offender.

The data gathered during the field survey permit only a limited contribution to the sentence disparity discussion. Statistics were not gathered to demonstrate the extent of disparity; however, enough was learned to document the conclusion that unwarranted disparity exists in the three states. But more imporant, observation of current practice makes it possible to evaluate some of the proposals for dealing with sentence disparity and to suggest ways of minimizing the consequences of such disparity as occurs.

A. Approaches to Minimizing Disparity

There have been two general approaches to the problem of minimizing sentencing disparity. The first is to re-allocate responsibility for sentencing, eliminating or limiting trial court discretion. This is reflected in the provisions of the Model Penal Code for a legislatively fixed maximum sentence which would be imposed uniformly in all cases. It is also reflected in proposals for appellate review of sentencing. The second general approach is to retain broad discretion in the trial judge but to equip him better to impose sentences that are consistent with those imposed by his fellow trial judges. This approach is reflected in the federal sentencing

[6] James V. Bennett, former Director of the Federal Bureau of Prisons, stated that sentence disparity fails "to stimulate a respect for the law among the very persons whom the law is supposed to teach that respect. The prisoner who must serve his excessively long sentence with other prisoners who receive relatively mild sentences under the same circumstances cannot be expected to accept his situation with equanimity. And the more fortunate prisoners do not attribute their luck to a sense of fairness and justice on the part of the law but to its whimsies. The existence of such disparities is among the major causes of prison riots, and it is one of the reasons why prisons so often fail to bring about an improvement in the social attitudes of its charges." Bennett, Of Prisons and Justice, S. Doc. No. 70, 88th Cong., 2d Sess. 319 (1964).

institutes, in efforts to guide trial court sentencing through statutory sentencing criteria, and in the sentencing council used in the Eastern District of Michigan. To the extent that observation of current practice affords a basis for evaluating these proposals, it seems safe to conclude that no single proposal is, in itself, adequate to achieve sentencing consistency.

A difficulty with the legislatively fixed sentence is that it is not uniformly applied in practice. Prosecutors manipulate the legislative maximum in guilty plea bargaining[7] and in an effort to conform the legislative sentence to the perceived equities of individual cases.[8] Adequate implementation of this approach would require the development of means of insuring against prosecutor charging disparity, an objective that seems as difficult to achieve as the elimination of trial judge sentencing disparity.

Most systems of appellate review of sentencing serve the important, but limited, function of providing a check upon unduly severe trial court sentencing. Despite the hope of its advocates, appellate review has not resulted in the development of sentencing principles through appellate court opinions explaining sentence reductions.[9] It seems likely that the major impact of appellate review on criminal justice administration is to cause trial judges to be more cautious about imposing long sentences.[10]

The federal sentencing institutes made important gains in equipping trial judges to exercise sentence discretion in an informed and consistent manner.[11] Their limitations, however, lie in the fact that they can at most provide a forum for the exchange of views on the problems in sentencing: They serve a valuable education function for trial judges, but only indirectly assist them in deciding upon sentence in concrete cases.

Much the same limitations exist with regard to attempts to deal with disparity by providing statutory guidelines for sentencing. The Model Penal Code's criteria for choice of prison or probation, although helpful in directing judicial attention to the general considerations involved, provide little more than general guidelines.[12]

[7] See Chapter 6.

[8] See Chapter 7.

[9] See Comment, Appellate Review of Primary Sentencing Decisions: A Connecticut Case Study, 69 Yale L.J. 1453 (1960).

[10] See American Bar Association Project on Minimum Standards for Criminal Justice, Standards Relating to Appellate Review of Sentences 27-30 (Tent. Draft, 1967).

[11] For the purpose and format of the sentencing institutes, see 28 U.S.C.A. §334 (Supp. 1966); Pilot Institute on Sentencing, 26 F.R.D. 231 (1959).

[12] Model Penal Code §7.01 (Proposed Official Draft, 1962): "The Court shall deal with a person who has been convicted of a crime without imposing sentence of imprisonment unless, having regard to the nature and circumstances of the crime and the history, character and condition of the defendant, it is of the opinion that

In all probability they can do no more than perform the general education function provided by the sentencing institutes.

Unlike the statutory criteria and sentencing institutes, the sentence council, as it operates in the Eastern District of Michigan, is a device for dealing with sentence disparity on an individual case level. The trial judge with sentencing responsibility in an individual case consults with his colleagues on the bench, who have previously been provided with a presentence report on the case. The sentence thus normally reflects discussion focused on the facts of an individual case.[13] Important as the sentencing council is, it has inherent limitations. It requires a multijudge court and that effectively limits its use to urban areas.[14] Furthermore, its impact is limited to sentences imposed by that court.

Each proposal approaches the problem of sentence disparity from a different direction and each deals more or less successfully with a different aspect of the problem. No one proposal is itself capable of adequately dealing with the problem; and it may be doubted that all of them together, to the extent they are consistent with each other, are capable of dealing with it. As a consequence it continues to be important to know the capacity of the correctional process to minimize the effects of judicial disparity.

---

his imprisonment is necessary for the protection of the public because: (a) there is undue risk that during the period of a suspended sentence or probation the defendant will commit another crime; or (b) the defendant is in need of correctional treatment that can be provided most effectively by his commitment to an institution; or (c) a lesser sentence will depreciate the seriousness of the defendant's crime."

[13] Doyle, A Sentencing Council in Operation, 25 Fed. Prob. 27 (No. 3, 1961). See Levin, Toward a More Enlightened Sentencing Procedure, 45 Neb. L. Rev. 499 (1966); Smith, The Sentencing Council and the Problem of Disproportionate Sentences, 11 Prac. Law. 12 (No. 2, 1965). Other experiments have been tried. The following appeared in the St. Louis Post-Dispatch, Wed., Nov. 17, 1965, p. 3B, cols. 6 & 7.

"ORDER SEEKS UNIFORMITY IN SENTENCING GAMBLERS"

"Trenton, N.J., Nov. 17 (AP) — The state supreme court has ordered that one judge in each county will be responsible for sentencing gamblers.

"The court ordered the plan in an effort to get uniformity in treatment of gamblers. The directive requires the superior court assignment judge for each county to sentence gamblers or delegate one judge to do it for him, although other judges may have presided at the trial or accepted a plea from the defendant."

[14] The group sentencing approach of the sentencing council can only be approximated in a single-judge court. Some trial judges are careful to confer with the police, the prosecutor, the probation staff, and the defense attorney on the issue of sentencing. To some extent this may provide the same kind of checks on single-judge sentencing provided by the sentencing council. See Chapter 3.

B. Approaches to Minimizing the Effects of Disparity

Most discussion about sentence disparity has focused upon ways to prevent it. There has been less consideration given to ways of minimizing the harmful consequences of such disparity as occurs by taking disparity into account in making subsequent correctional decisions. It is clear that much of the harmful consequence of sentence disparity can be eliminated in the making of later correctional decisions. This fact is not, however, commonly acknowledged by correctional personnel who understandably are reluctant to claim for themselves the task of reviewing trial judge sentencing. The consequence is that the correctional process does not deal as effectively with disparity as it could were it to systematically try to achieve this as an important correctional objective.

One form of sentence disparity is the unduly long minimum sentence. Parole eligibility is normally determined by the minimum sentence; if it is not corrected a long minimum postpones release from prison. In many jurisdictions executive clemency, usually commutation of sentence, is used to avoid limitations on parole eligibility. While the Wisconsin parole eligibility laws are generally quite liberal,[15] eligibility can be greatly postponed by imposing a number of consecutive sentences thus accumulating the minimum terms. Most trial judges use few, if any, consecutive sentences,[16] but some use them with what correctional people regard as alarming frequency. If in the view of the parole board consecutive minimum sentences preclude the parole of an inmate who should be released, commutation of sentence can be used to eliminate this disability and make immediate release possible.[17] In Kansas where parole eligibility laws were more restrictive,[18] commutation of sentence was used more frequently than in Wisconsin. The pardon attorney, who exercises the clemency power in routine cases, takes many factors into account in making commutation decisions. He is likely to commute consecutive sentences that seem to him unduly severe. He also takes plea bargaining into account. He is much more likely to commute the sentence of an inmate when the information available to him indicates there was no reduction in charge; when he concludes that a charge reduction was given, he is likely to summarily deny commutation, remarking to

15 Wis. Stat. Ann. §57.06 (1957).

16 See Chapter 7.

17 See Chapter 9.

18 Kan. Gen. Stat. §62-1529 (1949), repealed by Kan. Laws 1957, Ch. 331, §37. See Kan. Stat. Ann. §62-2245 (1964).

the inmate, "You have already had your clemency." Therefore, one effect of his decision making is a tendency to correct for differences in sentences attributable to guilty plea bargaining.[19]

In Michigan, parole eligibility is determined by the judicially fixed minimum sentence.[20] Most minima are quite short and do not impose substantial restrictions on parole board discretion. When a long minimum sentence precludes parole, however, the parole board uses a statutory procedure that enables it to grant parole before the minimum with the consent of the sentencing judge. Most judges routinely consent when requested by the parole board.[21]

An unduly long minimum sentence undoubtedly is a matter for serious concern. It may demoralize the inmate and create doubts about the fairness of the sentencing process. However, its most serious consequence — postponing release from prison — is likely to be eliminated by subsequent decision-making in the correctional process.

Two other forms of sentence disparity, the unduly short minimum sentence and the unduly long maximum sentence, can be corrected by parole board action without the use of executive clemency. Since neither of these restricts parole board discretion, the release decision can be made without regard to them. At most, the short minimum requires the parole board to interview the inmate before it is willing to consider his parole seriously,[22] and the long maximum sentence creates the possibility of long incarceration if the inmate creates trouble in the institution.[23]

By contrast, the parole board cannot correct what it perceives to be an unduly short maximum sentence. Unless the inmate commits an offense in the institution, he must be released when he has served his maximum.[24] The most the parole board can do is keep him until his maximum or, perhaps, parole him just before his maximum to provide some supervision upon release.

Like the selection of maximum and minimum sentences, the trial judge's choice between probation and prison is subjected to a type of review in subsequent correctional decision making. Review of a decision placing a defendant on probation is uncertain and probably not very effective. If the supervising probation officer believes the defendant should have been sentenced to prison, he may supervise him more closely and seek revocation when otherwise he might continue supervision. The difficulty is that the same trial

19 See Chapter 9.
20 Mich. Stat. Ann. §28.2303 (1954).
21 See Chapter 9.
22 See Chapter 11.
23 See Chapter 11.
24 See Chapter 12.

judge who placed such a defendant on probation normally has responsibility for making the revocation decision. While it is arguable that a trial judge who uses probation freely will revoke probation freely, no data gathered supported that position. Occasionally, a trial judge places a defendant on probation with substantial doubt that he is making the correct decision and instructs the probation officer to provide close supervision and return the case to court for revocation for any misconduct. However, except for the fact that a probationer who should have been sentenced to prison may be likely to commit a new offense and have probation revoked for it, there is no very satisfactory mechanism in the correctional process for reviewing and correcting an inappropriate probation granting decision.

The trial judge's decision to impose a prison sentence is reviewed by the parole board. If the board concludes the inmate should have been placed on probation, it will grant parole at the earliest possible moment.[25] As a practical matter, however, the inmate will normally serve at least nine to eleven months before his case is reviewed by the parole board. Even in situations in which the inmate is theoretically eligible for parole as soon as he enters the institution, parole board review normally does not occur until nine months have been served.[26]

Because subsequent correctional "review" of judicial (and prosecutorial) sentencing decisions is not usually deliberately and consciously undertaken, it is of uncertain effectiveness as an approach to the disparity problem. If sentence review were to be regarded by correctional authorities as an important and proper function of their decisions the value of this kind of review would increase greatly. The correctional process presently has the capacity to make significant gains in solving the disparity problem. As a practical matter, however, legal authorization and approval of correctional review of sentencing may be needed before that capacity is fully utilized.

[25] See Chapter 11.
[26] See Chapter 9.

CHAPTER 9

Parole Eligibility

Legislatures in almost all jurisdictions have imposed some restrictions upon the parole board's authority to release an offender from prison. In many jurisdictions, specified categories of inmates are not eligible for parole at all.[1] In most jurisdictions, parole eligibility is postponed until a specified period of time has been served,usually a minimum sentence or a portion of the maximum sentence.[2] In a few jurisdictions there are no legislative restrictions on parole eligibility.[3]

Where there are legislative limitations upon eligibility for parole, there are usually also judicial,[4] administrative,[5] or executive

[1] Model Penal Code §305.10 Comment (Tent. Draft No. 5, 1956): "In spite of the common use of parole in some states it should be observed that only fourteen out of the fifty jurisdictions in the United States establish no statutory exclusions on parole eligibility. . . . The position taken in this draft is that there should be no categorical limitations on parole. On the contrary, all men who leave prison should be discharged under supervision."

[2] Model Penal Code §305.10 Comment (Tent. Draft No. 5, 1956): "In general . . . eligibility for parole depends upon the completion of a fraction of any definite sentence imposed by the court or upon service either of the minimum sentence or of the minimum less earned good time under indefinite sentences. . . . Special provisions are commonly made in relation to parole eligibility for prisoners sentenced to life terms, generally prescribing a minimum term that must be served before eligibility. . . . Parole eligibility is also commonly deferred for recidivists and for sex offenders."

[3] Model Sentencing Act 13 (1963): "The sentencing system should not impose restrictions — for example, a minimum term — on a parole board. A minimum term prevents a parole board from releasing a defendant who in its judgment is suitable for release before the expiration of the minimum term of eligibility. This Act does not authorize a minimum term."

[4] The Kansas and Wisconsin legislatures have authorized trial judges to sentence certain offenders to institutions where, by statute, there are no parole eligibility requirements. The Michigan judicially fixed minimum sentence can be viewed as legislative recognition of the need for flexibility in limiting parole eligibility; theoretically, however, the Michigan trial judge has as much authority to postpone parole by setting a high minimum as he does to permit flexibility by setting a low one.

[5] The Kansas legislature has authorized administrative officials to remove statutory requirements for certain offenders by transferring them to institutions where they will immediately be eligible for parole. The Michigan "lifer law" authorizes

procedures for avoiding the legislative limitation in an individual case in which early release is believed desirable. In the aggregate, these methods reintroduce flexibility in a legislative system which may lack flexibility. This seeming inconsistency apparently reflects a quest for certainty and consistency at the legislative level and an equally strong desire for individualization at the administrative level. The compromise often is a fixed legislative system which survives primarily because there are ways of amelioration where the facts of the individual case demonstrate this to be desirable.

The fixing of a mandatory, very low legislative minimum does not, of course, mandate early release by the parole board even though it does make early release possible. Certain inmates in Kansas and Wisconsin are by statute made immediately eligible for parole. However, by administrative rule they are normally not considered for parole until they have served a period of nine months to one year. This practice is justified on the ground that such a period is necessary to learn what must be known about the offender and to make any treatment progress at all. Therefore, to the extent legislative requirements do not postpone parole eligibility for more than one year, they almost never impose a significant limitation on parole board discretion.

A. The Kansas Requirements and Their Administration

Kansas statutes in force during the field survey[6] limited parole eligibility to inmates who had served the statutory minimum sentence less allowances for good conduct.[7] Some offenses are punishable by a life sentence or by either a life sentence or a definite sentence. Inmates convicted of these offenses are not eligible for parole since their commitment has no minimum term. Finally, statutes

---

administrative amelioration of the parole eligibility consequences of certain life sentences or sentences with very high minima. Also, the Michigan "special consideration" statute authorizes a case-by-case amelioration of parole eligibility requirements by joint administrative and judicial action.

[6] In 1957, Kansas made a substantial revision of the laws relating to sentencing, probation, and parole. Kan. Laws 1957, Ch. 331. See Kan. Stat. Ann. §§62-2216 to 62-2255 (1964).

[7] Kan. Gen. Stat. §§62-1525, 62-1529 (1949). The Kansas law was ambiguous about whether good time should reduce the minimum as well as the maximum, but the practice was to deduct it from both. See Kan. Gen. Stat. §§76-2421, 76-2451 (1949). It is not clear as a result of the research whether good time was awarded automatically or selectively, or whether it was awarded automatically and forfeited selectively. One hypothesis can be constructed to support the last possibility: The burden of figuring good time allowances and population pressures leads to a system of automatic deduction with only occasional forfeitures. The criteria for awarding and forfeiting good time should be subjected to careful study.

expressly declare that inmates who have served two previous terms in a penitentiary are ineligible for parole.[8]

Kansas legislation expressly provides for limited judicial and administrative amelioration of these requirements. Male offenders, twenty-five years of age or younger who have no prior felony convictions, may, in the discretion of the trial court, be sentenced to the reformatory instead of the penitentiary.[9] Reformatory inmates are always eligible for parole despite the general statutory limitations.[10] Penitentiary inmates who are transferred to the reformatory become eligible for parole as soon as they arrive at that institution.[11] Despite the statutory grant of immediate parole eligibility to reformatory inmates, by administrative rule parole consideration is postponed until they have served ten months without substantial disciplinary infractions. Furthermore, by administrative rule reformatory inmates serving sentences for "crimes of violence, robbery armed or with force, forcible rape, or crimes that are vicious or heinous in nature" are not considered for parole until they have served sixteen months without significant disciplinary infractions.[12]

Commutation of sentence, one of the governor's constitutional executive clemency powers,[13] is regularly used in Kansas to accommodate legislative restrictions on parole eligibility to the need for flexibility in determining the length of incarceration. During an 18-month period, 1424 applications were made for executive clemency. Commutation was granted on 225 of these applications.[14]

[8] Kan. Gen. Stat. §62-1529 (1949).

[9] Kan. Gen. Stat. §76-2306 (1949).

[10] Kan. Gen. Stat. §76-2315 (1949). Women inmates may also be paroled at any time, provided they are not over twenty-five years of age and are first offenders. Kan. Gen. Stat. §76-2505 (1949). The remainder of the female population is subject to the general statutory provisions postponing or excluding parole eligibility.

[11] Kan. Gen. Stat. §76-2311 (1949) authorizes the warden of the penitentiary to select from "among the youthful, well-behaved and most promising convicts of the state penitentiary convicted of felony, and transfer them to the reformatory, for education and treatment. . . ." The field research does not reveal whether transfers are ever made primarily to permit earlier parole consideration.

[12] Report and Recommendations of the Kansas Legislative Council, Part II Special, The Penal and Correctional Institutions of the State, Dec. 8, 1956, pp. 176-177.

[13] Kan. Const. Art. I, §7 provides: "The pardoning power shall be vested in the governor, under regulations and restrictions prescribed by law." The pardoning power has been held to include governor's parole, commutation of sentence, and conditional pardon, in addition to full and unconditional pardon. See Spiegel, Pardon, Probation and Parole in Kansas, 6 Kan. L. Rev. 421 (1958). Kan. Gen. Stat. §§62-2215 to 62-2222 (1949) prescribe procedures in applying for and granting clemency.

[14] Some of these 225 commutations were probably not directly related to manipulating the parole eligibility laws to attain flexibility in release. Commutation is used to permit early discharge from parole supervision. See Chapter 13. Commutation of sentence is also used to permit a person who has been paroled and who has committed a new offense for which he was sentenced to begin serving the new

During approximately the same period about 750 inmates were paroled from the state penitentiary.[15]

Although the power to commute sentences is formally vested in the governor, in practice it is exercised by his pardon attorney, whose recommendations for clemency are invariably accepted by the governor.[16] The pardon attorney has traditionally been a retired judge. An inmate who wishes commutation of his sentence must file an application for executive clemency and advertise the fact in the official newspaper of the county in which he was sentenced.[17] The trial judge and prosecuting attorney are notified of the application and the date of the clemency hearing.[18]

Prior to his hearing, each applicant is interviewed in the institution by the pardon attorney. The applicant is not permitted to be present at the clemency hearing, but his relatives and friends are often present at the hearing to argue his case. Applicants are frequently represented at the clemency hearing by a retained attorney or by a relative or close friend. Attorneys sometimes function earlier in the process by advising inmates of the possibility of clemency and assisting them through the formalities of applying. The pardon attorney conducts the clemency hearing much like a parole hearing. He is provided with a written brief, similar to the one used for parole hearings.[19] Sometimes there are letters from friends of the applicant urging clemency or from persons responding to the advertisement urging denial of clemency. In addition, the pardon attorney has a summary of the clemency interview with the applicant and the statements of persons who appear at the hearing speaking for or against clemency.

The factor of greatest weight in deciding whether to grant com-

---

sentence without the necessity of finishing the one on which parole was granted. Nevertheless, most of the commutations are for the purpose of circumventing the eligibility statutes and permitting release when the case seems to warrant it.

15 Report and Recommendations of the Kansas Legislative Council, Part II, Special, The Penal and Correctional Institutions of the State, Dec. 8, 1956, p. 19. An inmate of the penitentiary said that it was assumed by them that 10 to 15 per cent would have their sentences commuted. The inmate's reaction to the commutation process was that it is not entirely consistent, although the extent to which this attitude is held is not known.

16 Although this is clearly the case, the pardon attorney uses the governor's formal responsibility for clemency to take pressure off himself. On occasions when applicants' relatives were pleading for clemency in an emotional and somewhat intense manner, the pardon attorney would remark, "I do not believe the Governor would look upon this favorably."

17 This was required by Kan. Gen. Stat. §62-2216 (1949). The advertisement must be paid for by the inmate. The rates may run from as low as $3 in a rural county to as much as $12 in more populous counties. The state made no provision to aid indigent inmates in paying for their advertisement.

18 This was required by Kan. Gen. Stat. §62-2216 (1949).

19 For a description of that document see Chapter 10.

mutation is the attitude of the sentencing judge. The pardon attorney said that he considered the recommendation of the sentencing judge, or his successor, more than anything else in his granting of clemency. His long experience as a trial judge had convinced him that most judges were fairly accurate in their recommendations. He said that he almost never overrules a strong objection by the sentencing judge to the granting of clemency. An unfavorable attitude by the sentencing judge effectively precludes commutation unless the relatives or friends of the inmate can persuade him to change his recommendation. A favorable recommendation is given great weight and virtually assures commutation. A consequence of this policy is to give the trial judge limited control over parole in many cases since he can effectively prevent early parole consideration by opposing commutation and can encourage early parole consideration by favoring or at least not opposing commutation. The general practice of trial judges is to respond to the notice of a clemency hearing if they oppose commutation and to make no response if they are not opposed.

Another significant factor is whether the applicant was convicted on a reduced charge. From the commutation brief and other sources of information, the pardon attorney attempts to determine whether the applicant's conduct would have justified a more serious charge than that upon which he was convicted. If he concludes there was a charge reduction, he assumes it was made to induce a guilty plea, taking "judicial notice" of the negotiated plea practice in Kansas. A charge reduction is weighed against commutation, because the pardon attorney views it as a grant of "clemency" at the adjudication stage in the process. It seems clear, then, that one of the objectives the pardon attorney attempts to attain by executive clemency is to equalize what might be called prosecutor charge reduction disparity.

Other factors also influence the decision. The pardon attorney stated that he took into consideration the inmate's prior record, his institutional adjustment, his attitude during the interview, and the outlook for successful adjustment on parole.[20] Cases in which commutation is sought fall into four categories, corresponding to four major types of legislative restrictions on parole eligibility.

1. *The high legislative minimum.*

Illustration No. 1: The applicant had been convicted of first degree manslaughter for which he had received a sen-

[20] The pardon attorney normally will not grant commutation if the applicant has a detainer lodged against him. Typically, the pardon attorney will instruct the relatives and friends of the applicant that his sentence cannot be commuted until the detainer is dropped and that they should attempt to persuade the authorities who filed the detainer to quash it.

tence of five to twenty-one years. He had already served thirteen months but had another two years to serve before the expiration of the minimum sentence less good time. Commutation had been denied once before. The prosecuting attorney and sheriff spoke against commutation because the applicant had caused them considerable difficulty in the past due to his excessive drinking. The pardon attorney noted that he had received several letters from residents of the sentencing county protesting commutation. The pardon attorney said that he would deny commutation because (1) it appeared to him that the applicant was really guilty of first or second degree murder, and (2) he had not served enough time to receive commutation consideration even for manslaughter.

Although many offenses carry legislative minima that are sufficiently low as not to seem unduly harsh in most cases,[21] many other offenses carry legislative minima as high as five[22] or ten years.[23] Persons sentenced for these offenses are eventually eligible for parole, but in many cases parole eligibility appears unnecessarily postponed due to the high minimum. Commutation of sentence plays an important role in reducing these high minima, thus permitting parole consideration to be given to the case earlier. Commutation does not, of course, assure parole upon expiration of the new minimum less good time, but it is an expression by the pardon attorney that parole consideration at that time would not be unreasonable.

2. *The "flat" or definite sentence.*

Illustration No. 2: The applicant had been convicted of second degree murder, for which he received a thirty-year sentence. He had already served three years and three months but he had another fourteen years and five months before the expiration of his sentence less good time. The applicant's father, wife, and two sons were present to argue in favor of commutation on the ground that the applicant was needed at home. The pardon attorney had received a number of letters from the sentencing county in favor of commutation, but the sentencing judge and the prosecuting attorney had written expressing opposition. The pardon attorney indicated

[21] Forgery, Kan. Gen. Stat. §21-631 (1949), and grand larceny, Kan. Gen. Stat. §21-534 (1949), have no minimum sentences specified in the offense-defining statutes. A general statutory minimum of one year applies to all offenses of this type. Kan. Gen. Stat. §21-109 (1949).

[22] Kan. Gen. Stat. §21-534 (1949) provides such a minimum sentence for grand larceny of an automobile.

[23] Kan. Gen. Stat. §21-530 (1949) provides such a minimum sentence for first degree robbery.

that he would not commute the sentence because (1) the applicant had already received clemency in the form of a charge reduction from first to second degree murder, and (2) he had not yet served sufficient time to warrant having his sentence commuted.

Persons convicted of second degree murder may be given a life sentence or a sentence of any term of years exceeding ten years.[24] Persons convicted as third offenders under the habitual criminal statute may be given a life sentence or a sentence of any term of years exceeding fifteen years.[25] If a term of years (also called a "flat" or "definite" sentence) is imposed under these statutes, the inmate is not eligible for parole because the parole laws apply only to persons given a minimum and maximum sentence under the indeterminate sentence act.

Definite sentences present two problems to officials responsible for individualizing the length of incarceration: first, while the inmate is entitled to release from incarceration at the expiration of his definite sentence less allowances for good time, this period is frequently unduly long in relation to the circumstances of the case; second, even if the definite sentence were commuted to a shorter definite sentence, the inmate would receive an unconditional release,[26] while officials feel that many of them would benefit from a period of parole supervision. These twin difficulties are overcome in some cases by commuting the definite sentence to an indeterminate sentence. The old definite sentence becomes the new maximum sentence and a lower minimum sentence is set to permit the applicant to present himself before the parole board at such a time that parole, in the opinion of the pardon attorney, would not be unreasonable.

3. *The life sentence.* A life sentence may be imposed on persons convicted of first degree murder,[27] second degree murder,[28] or as third offenders under the habitual criminal act.[29] Since a life sentence is not an indeterminate sentence as that term is used in the Kansas parole statutes, persons serving a life sentence are not eligible for parole at any time. Unlike those sentenced for a definite term, lifers are not entitled to unconditional release at any time. Frequently, then, life sentences are commuted to indeterminate sentences, which permits release on parole after service of the mini-

24 Kan. Gen. Stat. §21-403 (1949).

25 Kan. Gen. Stat. §21-107a (1949).

26 At the time the survey was conducted, Kansas had no conditional release law. One was adopted in 1957 as a part of the general revision of probation and parole laws. See Kan. Laws 1957, Ch. 331; Kan. Stat. Ann. §62-2246 (1964).

27 Kan. Gen. Stat. §21-403 (1949).

28 Ibid.

29 Kan. Gen. Stat. §21-107a (1949).

mum less good time and unconditional release after service of the maximum less good time.

4. *The "three-time loser."*

Illustration No. 3: The applicant was convicted of forgery and sentenced to a term of one to ten years. Since he had served two prior terms in the penitentiary, he was ineligible for parole. He would be unconditionally released at the expiration of ten years less good time, or about six years. He had already served two years. The applicant's father was present to plead for commutation. The pardon attorney had received letters from the sentencing judge and the prosecuting attorney expressing opposition to commutation at this time. The pardon attorney told the applicant's father that he could not commute his son's sentence since he had not yet served sufficient time to warrant it.

Kansas statutes make persons who have twice served sentences in any penitentiary ineligible for parole.[30] Though these persons must be sentenced to an indeterminate term, their only chance for release is unconditional release at the expiration of the maximum sentence less good time, unless commutation intervenes. Even commutation, however, cannot grant this kind of applicant parole eligibility.[31] However, the maximum sentence is frequently commuted to a lower maximum sentence in cases in which it seems that release should not be postponed as long as the original maximum sentence would require. There is apparently no later parole board decision in these cases; the inmates are unconditionally released automatically at the expiration of the new maximum sentence less good time allowances.[32]

B. The Michigan Requirements and Their Administration

Michigan statutes limit parole eligibility to inmates who have served the judicially set minimum sentence less allowances for

[30] Kan. Gen. Stat. §65-1529 (1949).

[31] The data are not clear on whether persons with two prior penitentiary sentences are paroled after their sentence is commuted. This parole restriction is unlike the other three because it involves a legislative declaration that the inmate is not eligible for parole, while parole eligibility is postponed or excluded in the other categories because of the length of or the nature of the sentence. Commutation changes the sentence, but it is doubtful if it can grant parole eligibility to one who is expressly declared by statute not to possess it. The uncertainty exists because the difference between the declaration of ineligibility for three-time losers in Kan. Gen. Stat. §62-1529 (1949) is often confused with the ineligibility resulting from a "flat" sentence imposed on a third felony offender under the habitual criminal act, Kan. Gen. Stat. §21-107a (1949).

[32] Governor's parole is occasionally used for persons in this category.

good conduct.[33] Inmates sentenced to life imprisonment are not eligible for parole without the use of special statutory procedures or commutation of sentence.[34] The Michigan legislature has provided two statutory procedures to ameliorate its parole eligibility requirements: special consideration and the lifer law. In addition, commutation of sentence is sometimes used for that purpose.

1. *Special consideration.* "Special consideration" is a statutory procedure designed to solve the problem of the excessively high, judicially set minimum sentence. The statute authorizing special consideration provides:

> [P]risoners shall be eligible for parole prior to the expiration of their minimum terms of imprisonment whenever the sentencing judge or his successor in office shall give his written approval of the parole of such prisoners prior to the expiration of such minimum terms of imprisonment. . . .[35]

The details of the special consideration procedure are not prescribed by statute.

An inmate normally receives his first parole hearing about a month before he reaches parole eligibility, which, in the case of a high, judicially set minimum, may be after several years in prison. Institutional personnel usually initiate the special consideration process by recommending to the parole board that a particular inmate be given early parole consideration. The recommendation is considered by the parole board in executive session and a decision is made whether to conduct a parole hearing. If the board decides that the case warrants a hearing, one of the members visits the sentencing judge to discuss it with him.

> *Illustration No. 4:* The sentencing judge said he was reluctant to approve early parole board action in this case but said he would not disapprove. The inmate had been recommended by the institution on the basis of a good institutional record and an outstanding work record. He had also completed a correspondence course and it was felt that he had matured in the more than four years he had served. The judge said he believed all armed robbers should serve a long term regardless of the circumstances. He also said that long sentences are a deterrent to crime. He made it known that, if the inmate received special consideration, the co-defendant should also be investigated with the possibility of early parole. The board member informed the judge that the parole board

33 Mich. Stat. Ann. §§28.2303, 28.2304 (1954). Good conduct allowances are determined by statutory formulae. See Mich. Stat. Ann. §§28.1403, 28.1514 (1954).

34 Mich. Stat. Ann. §28.2304 (1954).

35 Mich. Stat. Ann. §28.2303 (1954).

always investigates a co-defendant when special consideration is being considered for an offender. He also told the judge that the victim's attitude and the feeling in the community would be investigated by the local parole officer.

Once the approval of the sentencing judge is secured, the inmate is interviewed by two members of the parole board. The parole hearing obtained by special consideration is conducted the same as those regularly scheduled, and the parole decision criteria are the same.[36] After the parole hearing is conducted, the case returns to executive session and the decision to grant or deny parole is made, subject to final written approval by the sentencing judge.

Illustration No. 5: This special consideration case was recommended by the institution. The sentencing judge also approved early parole. The inmate had only two prior arrests, one in 1941 and one in 1953, both drunkenness. The institution recommended him highly for parole, stating that although he was alcoholic, he had gained much insight into his problem. In discussing the case, the board members concluded that the judge should have placed the man on probation instead of sending him to the institution. When the inmate had been interviewed by the two members of the parole board, he had made a favorable impression on them. The decision was to grant parole if the sentencing judge gave final approval.

In practice, special consideration is used with relative infrequency. Institutional personnel have complained that, while they often recommend special consideration, the parole board frequently refuses to follow their recommendations. Research of case files indicated that the parole board refused to grant favorable parole consideration to almost 80 percent of the inmates recommended for special consideration by institutional personnel.[37]

One of the primary reasons for the infrequent use of special consideration is that most of the parole board members feel the excessively long minimum sentence does not present a serious problem — that only rarely is the minimum sentence set by the trial judge so high that it prevents the board from paroling an inmate whom it would like to parole. On the contrary the board expressed concern for the unduly short minimum sentence, one that forces it to

[36] The parole criteria are discussed in Chapter 11.

[37] The research was conducted on an informal basis by a member of the Michigan Corrections Commission in response to complaints he had received from institutional personnel. The Commissioner was rather annoyed at what he perceived to be the parole board attitude toward special consideration, commenting, "Does the parole board mean to say that they know more about the inmates than the warden, the counselors, the work foreman, and the chaplain?"

hear a case with no chance for parole. Sentencing statistics available to the board illuminate its attitude toward minimum sentences: two-thirds of all minimum sentences were two years or shorter; only 7 percent were five years or longer; the balance, over 25 percent, were between two and five years. From these data the board concluded that a special consideration program is needed only for the group sentenced to five years or longer, which constitutes only 7 percent of the cases. A second reason for the relative nonuse of special consideration is the availability of the "lifer law." Persons sentenced with very high minima are eligible for parole under that procedure after they have served ten years in the institution. It seems clear that special consideration would otherwise be used for many of these cases.

Special consideration is theoretically as much the responsibility of the sentencing judge as the parole board, because the approval of the sentencing judge is required by statute.[38] In practice, however, many trial judges routinely approve requests for special consideration. In Detroit Recorder's Court judges asserted that "times and people change," and in their opinion the parole board is in a better position to ascertain an inmate's qualifications for release after several years of incarceration. All the judges said they routinely approve parole board requests for special consideration.

2. *Lifer law procedure and commutation of sentence.* The "lifer law" is a statutory provision that permits the parole of persons, other than those sentenced for first degree murder, who have served ten years in the institution.[39] It is used to parole inmates who are ineligible for routine parole consideration either because they have not yet served a high minimum sentence or because they are serving a life sentence. Administration of the lifer law is primarily the responsibility of the parole board, although action under it can be blocked by the sentencing judge or his successor in office.[40] A public hearing, similar to the one required for clemency matters, is necessary.[41]

Commutation of sentence is one of the governor's constitutional clemency powers.[42] The parole board is required to review in a public hearing the cases of inmates who have applied for commutation and forward its recommendations to the governor.[43] In prac-

[38] See note 35 *supra* and accompanying text.

[39] Mich. Stat. Ann. §28.2304 (1954).

[40] Mich. Stat. Ann. §28.2304 (1954). In this respect, the lifer law resembles the statutory special consideration procedure.

[41] Mich. Stat. Ann. §28.2304 (1954). The statutory provisions governing clemency public hearings are Mich. Stat. Ann. §§28.2313 to 28.2315 (1954).

[42] Mich. Const. art. VI, §9 (1908). The 1963 Constitution made no changes in the governor's clemency powers relevant to this discussion. Mich. Const. art. V., §14.

[43] Mich. Stat. Ann. §28.2314 (1954).

tice, the commutation power is exercised by the parole board because the governor routinely accepts whatever recommendations it makes.[44] While there are no formal limits on the use of the commutation power, other than the constitutional limitation that it may not be used in cases of treason or impeachment,[45] in recent years it has been used almost exclusively to complement the lifer law by enabling the parole of inmates convicted of first degree murder.[46] Although the lifer law and commutation of sentence are different in legal conception, they have become merged into a single procedure in their administration. They serve the same purpose and together permit the parole of all inmates who have served long terms but who still are ineligible for parole under the general statutory provisions.

The parole board has established the position of "parole eligibility examiner" and has staffed that position with a person whose duties are full time and who is not a member of the parole board. The examiner conducts a continuing survey of the long-term population and prepares their cases for parole board consideration. Inmates eligible for release under the lifer law receive their first interview with the parole eligibility examiner during their ninth year. Subsequent interviews are conducted at least annually. Persons serving sentences for first degree murder are not given their first interview with the eligibility examiner until they have served fifteen years. They, too, are subsequently interviewed at least annually.

> *Illustration No. 6:* The inmate, forty-six years old, appeared before the examiner for his annual interview. He had received a life sentence in 1935 for first degree murder. He had no criminal record prior to that. The offense occurred one evening when he met on the street a girl whom he knew slightly. The inmate drove the girl to a secluded spot where they had sexual intercourse, and then he strangled her. The examiner questioned the inmate on the events in his life since their last interview. After the interview was concluded, the examiner remarked that, although in terms of institutional adjustment the inmate might seem ready for parole, because he is still a comparatively young man and is apparently capable of repeating his crime, the parole board is likely to regard him as a poor parole risk for some time to come.

[44] An experienced member of the parole board said that in twenty years the governor has not rejected a parole board recommendation for commutation of sentence.

[45] Mich. Const. art. VI, §9 (1908). See note 42 *supra*.

[46] Before the enactment of the lifer law in 1941, commutation was used for all long termers, much like its use in Kansas during the field survey.

Illustration No. 7: The inmate, age forty-nine, had been sentenced to life for armed robbery. He was received at the institution in 1930. The robbery was regarded as very serious, partly because a bank guard had been wounded. The examiner spent most of his time assuring the inmate that the public hearing was forthcoming and that he would be released shortly. At one point, he said, "What else can I tell you? I'm telling you you're going to be released but it's just a question of when the public hearing date is set. You know how little can go wrong in a public hearing and you're just as good as out."

The interview with the eligibility examiner serves several different functions. When there is no chance for parole within the foreseeable future, the interview simply serves to demonstrate to the inmate that somebody is watching his progress in the institution and that his case is being considered. As in Illustration No. 6, the examiner is careful not to arouse hopes of early release. During an interview, the examiner said to the inmate:

> You fellows have a different meaning for the word "consideration" than we have. Every lifer case is given consideration every year, but you men take the word to mean favorable consideration and I'm afraid some of you build up your hopes without a sufficient basis.

In other cases, however, the interview simply serves to facilitate the release of a person who has already received a favorable parole board decision. The sole function of the interview in the second illustration was to give the prisoner assurance he would be released soon. When the release procedure is commutation, the inmate must make a formal application for clemency.[47] This is normally not done until a favorable decision has been made by the parole board. Often in such cases the examiner interviews the inmate to give him the application forms and to instruct him on how application must be made.

Once a year the eligibility examiner reports to the parole board on all the cases he interviewed during the year. In content the reports are very much like presentence reports, containing information under the following headings: previous parole board action; prior record; sentencing judge's statement; inmate's statement; accomplices; institutional record; biography; release plans; community attitude; opinion and summary; prospects for adjustment; conclusions; and recommendations.

The parole board meets in executive session annually to con-

[47] Mich. Stat. Ann. §28.2313 (1954).

sider the reports of the eligibility examiner. It is at this point that the parole decision is made. If the decision is negative, the inmate will be interviewed by the examiner during the next year and his case will again be reviewed by the parole board. If the decision is affirmative, the parole board orders a public hearing on the case. It is clear that the decision made by the parole board in executive session is the important one. All that remains after that, including the public hearing, is largely formality.

The statutes require that the attorney general, the sentencing judge, and the prosecuting attorney be notified of the public hearing.[48] Although it is not required to do so by statute, the parole board also notifies the press of its public hearings. If the inmate is serving time for first degree murder, the formalities of an application for commutation must be completed before the public hearing.

In form, the public hearing is adversary. The people are represented by the attorney general's office. The inmate is present and may be represented by a privately retained attorney. The hearing is conducted by two members of the parole board, who are required by statute to give the rules of evidence a liberal construction.[49] A standard procedure is followed. The attorney general's representative makes an opening statement summarizing the offense and institutional adjustment of the inmate, using the parole eligibility examiner's report as his source of information. The examiner himself is then sworn in and questioned about the contents of his report and any other information he may be qualified to give. The inmate and any witnesses who appear on his behalf are examined by the two parole board members. The warden's report, the recommendation of the parole eligibility examiner, the institution classification report, and any psychiatric reports are summarized and reviewed. Finally, it is determined whether anyone at the public hearing has objection to parole.

Several formalities remain after the hearing is concluded, but these do not represent significant decision points in the process. The results of the hearing are discussed by the parole board in executive session and parole is formally granted. In the case of commutation, the parole board formally recommends that the governor commute sentence and, after this recommendation is accepted, it formally paroles the inmate.

[48] Mich. Stat. Ann. §§28.2304, 28.2314 (1954).
[49] Mich. Stat. Ann. §28.2314 (1954).

C. The Wisconsin Requirements and Their Administration

A statutory formula determines parole eligibility for the majority of Wisconsin inmates. Eligibility is limited to inmates who have served the minimum sentence, one-half of the maximum sentence, or two years, whichever is shortest.[50] Inmates serving life sentences are eligible for parole when they have served twenty years less allowances for good conduct.[51] Male offenders thirty years of age or younger, except those convicted of murder or who have previously been convicted of a felony, may in the discretion of the trial court be sentenced to the reformatory instead of the penitentiary.[52] Reformatory inmates are immediately eligible for parole.[53] Certain inmates may administratively be transferred from the penitentiary to the reformatory.[54] By administrative policy, inmates of the reformatory are normally not considered for parole until they have served nine months or one-half of the maximum sentence, whichever is shorter.[55] Offenders sentenced to the penitentiary under the Sex Crimes Law are immediately eligible for parole[56] but, by

[50] Wis. Stat. Ann. §57.06(1) (1957).

[51] Ibid. Good time is determined by a statutory formula. See Wis. Stat. Ann. §53.11(1) (1957). An inmate serving a life sentence who remains free of disciplinary infractions becomes eligible for parole after serving eleven years and three months.

[52] Wis. Stat. Ann. §§959.045 (1), 959.09 (1958). The murder and prior felony restrictions were later eliminated. See Wis. Stat. Ann. §§959.045(1), 959.09 (Supp. 1967).

[53] Wis. Stat. Ann. §57.07 (1957). Women prisoners, except those serving life sentences, are also immediately eligible for parole. Ibid.

[54] Wis. Stat. Ann. §3.18(2) (1957). When a prisoner is transferred, the statute does not specify whether his parole eligibility is affected. Wis. Stat. Ann. §53.18(5) (1957) provides: "Any person who is legally transferred by the department to a penal institution shall be subject to the same statutes, regulations and discipline as if he had been originally sentenced to that institution, but the transfer shall not change the term of sentence." The administrative interpretation of this section was that "Persons transferred from the Reformatory to the Prison or from the Prison to the Reformatory are subject to the eligibility laws and policies with respect to the institution in which they are actually serving." Wisconsin State Department of Public Welfare Division of Corrections, Parole Board Procedures and Practices 7 (1959). This interpretation has since been changed: "The term of sentence includes parole eligibility. For example, a man committed to the Wisconsin State Prison at Waupun with a parole eligibility of two years and transferred to the Wisconsin State Reformatory will still have to serve two years including time served at the Prison prior to transfer before he is eligible for parole at the Reformatory." Wisconsin State Department of Public Welfare Division of Corrections, Parole Board Procedures and Practices 11 (1963).

[55] However, the Social Service Department may deviate from this policy and request a parole hearing for an inmate at any time. Wisconsin State Department of Public Welfare Division of Corrections, Parole Board Procedures and Practices 7 (1959).

[56] Wis. Stat. Ann. §959.15(10) (1958).

administrative policy, they are normally not considered until they have served one year.

The governor of Wisconsin, like his counterparts in Kansas and Michigan, has the power to commute sentences as one of his constitutional powers of executive clemency.[57] Because there are few legislative limitations on parole eligibility in Wisconsin, there is little need for executive intervention. From 1952 through 1957 only twenty-three commutations were granted for the purpose of creating parole eligibility for inmates who had not satisfied the statutory requirements. Nine of these involved life sentences with the mandatory minimum of twenty years; seven involved consecutive sentences with accumulation of the minima; and seven involved advancement of the relatively low two-year statutory parole eligibility requirement.[58]

The commutation procedure is in many respects similar to the one in Kansas. The statutory procedure expressly applicable to pardons is in practice applied to commutations as well.[59] An application must be made, the fact of application must be advertised in a newspaper published in the county of conviction, and the sentencing judge and prosecuting attorney must be notified of the application.[60] The Department of Public Welfare is required by statute to make recommendations on pending commutation cases when requested to do so by the governor.[61] The case is heard by the governor's counsel, who makes a recommendation to the governor.[62] The applicant is not present at the clemency hearing, but he may be represented by a privately retained attorney.

Some indication of the considerations that support a reduction of a minimum in order to accelerate parole eligibility can be seen in two excerpts from the governor's biennial report to the legislature.[63]

> *Illustration No. 8:* The applicant was convicted on June 20, 1949, of the crime of first degree murder and sentenced

[57] Wis. Const. art. V, §6, vests clemency powers for all cases except treason and impeachment in the governor.

[58] These statistics are taken from the reports of the governor to the legislature, found in Wisconsin Assembly Journal 24 (1953); Wisconsin Assembly Journal 1985 (1955); Wisconsin Assembly Journal 54 (1957).

[59] See Wis. Stat. Ann. §§57.08 to 57.10 (1957).

[60] Wis. Stat. Ann. §57.09 (1957).

[61] Wis. Stat. Ann. §46.03(6)(d) (1957).

[62] Although field data were not obtained on this particular point, it seems likely that the governor's counsel's recommendation is routinely followed by the governor.

[63] Wis. Const. art. V, §6, requires the governor to "annually communicate to the legislature each case of reprieve, commutation or pardon granted, stating the name of the convict, the crime of which he was convicted, the sentence and its date, and the date of the commutation, pardon or reprieve, with his reasons for granting the same."

to life imprisonment. This man killed his fiancée's sister, who threatened to tell the family that his fiancée was pregnant. It appeared that the applicant merely intended to frighten his fiancée's sister, but he had a loaded revolver with which he threatened her and which was discharged and killed her. He subsequently married his fiancée, who remained faithful to him throughout his seven years or more of imprisonment. He had an excellent adjustment at the prison, where he took full advantage of his educational opportunities. Because of the widespread and sensational publicity that overwhelmed the authorities at the time of the trial and conviction it seems clear that the extenuating circumstances surrounding the shooting were not fully considered. Because of these extenuating circumstances, because of the applicant's exceptionally satisfactory development at the prison and unusually good prospects of an excellent adjustment under parole supervision, he merited a reduction in his life sentence.

On January 4, 1957, the life sentence was commuted to a term of not less than fourteen or more than twenty-five years, the term of the commuted sentence to commence as of the date of the sentence imposed by the court.[64]

Illustration No. 9: The applicant was convicted on June 18, 1951, and sentenced for a term of five to six years for the crime of larceny as bailee, twenty counts, obtaining money by false pretenses, two counts, and forgery, three counts, and sentenced to a term of one to two years on each of the counts, all consecutive and also consecutive to the term of five to six years. This man was convicted of numerous criminal offenses arising out of his defalcations and frauds during the period after his return from military service and before his conviction in June of 1951. The sentences as imposed were much too severe and would have resulted in his conditional release on expiration of all sentences before ever becoming eligible for parole. The sentencing judge advised that he had been misinformed as to the effect of the sentences imposed upon parole eligibility. On June 1, 1954, all of the consecutive sentences of one to two years were commuted to consecutive sentences of three months to two years each, thereby making the applicant eligible for parole consideration in 1959.[65]

64 Abstracted from Wisconsin Assembly Journal 70 (1957).
65 Abstracted from Wisconsin Assembly Journal 1988 (1955).

C H A P T E R 1 0

Parole Information

The quality of parole decision making depends a great deal upon the adequacy and reliability of information available to the parole board, and there are significant differences in the amount of information available. For example, one of the major criteria used by parole boards in Michigan and Wisconsin is whether the inmate had undergone changes in attitude since the offense was committed.[1] Substantial information is available for the parole board to make that judgment. By contrast, in Kansas, at the time of the field survey, parole decisions were not based to any substantial degree upon that criterion. It was not that the Kansas parole board considered inmate personality change unimportant; rather, information bearing upon that issue was simply not available. But even when parole information is adequate, in the sense that data are available on all factors considered important in parole decision-making, there still remains the problem of the reliability of the information. This involves many of the issues typically discussed in the context of presentence information,[2] including the question whether some information should be disclosed to the inmate or his counsel.

Legislatures have left the responsibility for developing adequate and reliable parole information to correctional officials. There are very few statutory mandates or restrictions. In practice, most of the information upon which parole decisions are based is contained in the parole board's case file. These documents are normally not disclosed to the inmate, although the basis for the parole board's decision, once it is made, may be explained briefly to him. This information in the file may, to a limited extent, be verified and supplemented at the parole hearing by asking the inmate questions designed to either verify existing information or add information not otherwise available.

There are occasions when the parole board would like to know

1 See Chapter 11.
2 See Chapter 2.

why the trial judge selected the sentence he did. If the sentence seems to the board to be unusually long or short, it may be because the trial judge had information about the offender which is not available to the board. Reasons for trial judges' sentences are usually not reflected in the file, with the result that judicial sentencing may sometimes appear capricious. Trial judges do often indicate their reasons at the time of sentencing. The difficulty is that transcripts of sentencing proceedings, which reflect trial judges' stated reasons for selection of sentence, are not usually readily available to parole boards. The consequence is that the length of incarceration in an individual case, which is a product of the combined decisions of trial judge and parole board, may be made without any effective communication between the two agencies that share responsibility for the decision.

A. Legislative Provisions

Existing legislation in Kansas, Michigan, and Wisconsin does not systematically regulate parole information.[3] Instead, with few exceptions, the legislatures have preferred to leave the development of adequate and reliable parole information to administrative policy or informal parole board practice. Furthermore, the legislative provisions that exist are worded to imply that an inmate cannot require compliance with them and that noncompliance should not affect the validity of the parole decision; they are suggestions, not requirements.

Kansas statutes require the judge and prosecuting attorney to furnish to the parole board, at the time of the inmate's commitment, a statement based on such information as they possess concerning the character of the inmate and his prospects of rehabilitation.[4] The parole board is given power to require similar information from any person and is directed that "where practicable [it]

[3] By contrast, Model Penal Code §305.10 (Proposed Official Draft, 1962) contains a detailed provision on parole information: "Before making a determination regarding a prisoner's release on parole, the Board of Parole shall cause to be brought before it all of the following records and information regarding the prisoner: (1) a report prepared by the institutional parole staff, relating to his personality, social history and adjustment to authority, and including any recommendations which the institutional staff may make; (2) all official reports of his prior criminal record, including reports and records of earlier probation and parole experiences; (3) the presentence investigation report of the sentencing Court; (4) recommendations regarding his parole made at the time of sentencing by the sentencing judge or the prosecutor; (5) the reports of any physical, mental and psychiatric examinations of the prisoner; (6) any relevant information which may be submitted by the prisoner, his attorney, the victim of his crime, or by other persons; (7) the prisoner's parole plan; (8) such other relevant information concerning the prisoner as may be reasonably available."

[4] Kan. Gen. Stat. §62-1523 (1949).

shall procure such information from the people who have known the prisoner." [5] The Kansas statutes impliedly require a preparole report by providing that the parole board must have "satisfactory evidence that arrangements have been made, for [the inmate's] honorable and useful employment while upon parole in some suitable occupation, and also for a proper or suitable home, free from criminal influence." [6] The only remaining requirements are that an inmate must be given a physical examination, the report of which is presumably available to the parole board, and that the warden must make a record of any information coming to his attention "bearing upon the question of the parole or final release of the prisoner." [7]

Michigan legislation requires the parole board to have brought before it "all pertinent information" concerning an inmate appearing for a parole hearing.[8] "All pertinent information" includes a record of disciplinary infractions in the institution, notations of changes in the inmate's social attitude, the inmate's industrial record, including a recommendation concerning the work he is best fitted to perform when released, and the results of any physical, mental, and psychiatric examinations that may have been conducted.[9] The statutes further require that all information assembled by institution classification committees shall be made available to the parole board,[10] and that "no prisoner shall be released on parole until the parole board shall have satisfactory evidence that arrangements have been made for such honorable and useful employment as he is capable of performing, or for his education, or for his care if he is mentally or physically ill or incapacitated." [11]

Wisconsin statutes provide that "no such prisoner shall be paroled until the department [of public welfare] is satisfied that suitable employment has been secured for him, unless otherwise provided for by the department." [12] The only remaining statutory provision is that "the district attorney and judge who tried the inmate shall be notified in writing at least 10 days before the first application for parole is acted upon and if they so request shall be given like notice of each subsequent application." [13]

[5] Ibid.

[6] Kan. Gen. Stat. §62-1525 (1949).

[7] Kan. Gen. Stat. §62-1524 (1949). The provisions in Kansas relating to parole information were repealed by Kan. Laws 1957, Ch. 331, §37 as part of a comprehensive revision of the parole laws and were replaced with new provisions appearing in Kan. Stat. Ann. §§62-2245, 62-2247 to 62-2249 (1964).

[8] Mich. Stat. Ann. §28.2305 (1954).

[9] Ibid.

[10] Mich. Stat. Ann. §28.2324 (1954).

[11] Mich. Stat. Ann. §28.2303(c) (1954).

[12] Wis. Stat. Ann. §57.06(2) (1957).

[13] Wis. Stat. Ann. §57.06(1) (1957). It has been held that a parole grant is invalid

Of the three states, only Michigan has a statutory requirement that an inmate must be given a parole hearing: "At least one month prior to the expiration of the minimum term of each prisoner eligible for parole, less good time or special good time allowances, it shall be the duty of the parole board to cause each prisoner to be brought before it, together with all pertinent information with regard to such prisoner." [14] There is no statutory requirement that a prisoner must be given further hearings if parole is denied at the initial hearing. As a matter of practice in all three states, an inmate is given his initial hearing shortly before he becomes eligible for parole and, if parole is denied, he is given subsequent hearings periodically thereafter.

B. The Case File

There are wide differences in the states studied with regard to the amount of documentary information made available to the parole board. The information available in Kansas at the time of the survey was very slight, amounting in most cases to no more than a two-page "brief." In Michigan and Wisconsin much more information was available, amounting in many cases to a large folder of documents. The Kansas parole board was not provided with enough information,[15] while in Michigan and Wisconsin there was, in a sense, too much information because there was more than the board had time to consult.

Information regularly available in case files falls into several categories: presentence reports; reports by institutional personnel, usually concerning the offender's conduct and progress in the institution; a preparole report on the adequacy of the job and residence plans of the inmate; and recommendations from police, prosecutor, and trial judge.

1. *Presentence report.* The nature of the presentence investigation and the contents of the presentence report have been described elsewhere.[16] Although presentence reports are designed primarily to aid the trial judge in making the probation decision, in those cases in which the defendant is sentenced to prison they are also a source of information for the parole decision. A presentence report, or a substitute if none is provided by the sentencing

---

unless the board complies with this provision. State ex rel. Zabel v. Hannan, 219 Wis. 257, 262 N.W. 625 (1935).

14 Mich. Stat. Ann. §28.2305 (1954).

15 A member of the Kansas parole board stated, "The parole board does as well as it can with the scanty information available to it. . . . Insufficient material is available to the parole board for deciding upon paroles."

16 See Chapter 1.

court, is available for parole board use in Wisconsin and Michigan.[17]

In Wisconsin it is within the discretion of the sentencing judge to order a presentence investigation.[18] When a presentence is conducted and the defendant is sentenced to prison, copies of the report are sent to the Division of Corrections' central office and are included in the parole board's file. In those cases in which a presentence was not conducted, an "admission investigation" is conducted shortly after the inmate arrives at the institution. A report of this investigation, similar in content to a presentence report, is included in the case file.

In Michigan a presentence investigation and report is required by law in all felony cases.[19] When a defendant is sentenced to imprisonment in a state institution, a copy of the presentence report must accompany him to the place of incarceration.[20] If it is determined at a parole board hearing that a presentence report is lacking,[21] the board continues the case and requests a "postsentence investigation," the report of which is similar in content to a presentence report.

It is not clear to what extent parole boards in Wisconsin and Michigan rely on the presentence report in their deliberations. The fact that most reports are fairly lengthy indicates that a careful reading of them is not possible in the time available for consideration of each case. On the other hand, the fact that the parole board in Michigan stops the parole hearing when a presentence report is lacking indicates that they are considered to be of value.[22] It is clear that the Michigan parole board considers the presentence report to be especially helpful in two particulars. First, it enables the board

17 At the time of the field survey, presentence investigations were not conducted in Kansas. As a part of its 1957 revision of the laws relating to probation, sentencing, and parole, provision is now made for a presentence investigation to be conducted in the sentencing judge's discretion. If a presentence investigation is conducted, a copy of the report must accompany the defendant to the institution in case he is sentenced to imprisonment, and the parole board must consider the presentence report in its parole deliberations. See Kan. Stat. Ann. §§62-2238, 62-2245 (1964).

18 For analysis of the factors considered in the decision to order a presentence investigation in Wisconsin, see Chapter 1.

19 Mich. Stat. Ann. §28.1144 (1954). It is within the discretion of the judge to order a presentence investigation in misdemeanor cases. Ibid.

20 Ibid. If the court referred the defendant for psychiatric examination and he was later sentenced to imprisonment, a copy of the psychiatric report must accompany the presentence report to the institution. Ibid.

21 At the time of the field survey at least two counties in the state did not send presentence reports to the institutions, contrary to the statutory requirement.

22 A study indicates that the Wisconsin parole board considers the presentence report to be the most important of its sources of information. Hendrickson and Schultz, A Study of the Criteria Influencing the Decision to Grant or Deny Parole to Adult Offenders in Wisconsin Correctional Institutions 49 (unpublished master's thesis, University of Wisconsin School of Social Work, 1964).

to ascertain the inmate's actual criminal conduct, thus securing more guidance than furnished by the label of the offense for which the inmate was convicted. This need arises in part from the practice of reducing charges in exchange for guilty pleas in Detroit. Second, the board uses the presentence report to determine whether an inmate convicted of a single offense actually committed additional offenses for which he was not charged, a situation that frequently arises because of the charging practices of the Detroit prosecutor.[23]

2. *Institution reports.* Studies and observations made of the inmate in the institution are principal sources of parole information. To some extent this information varies from institution to institution and is influenced by the staff-inmate ratio in each institution; institution reports from Wisconsin State Reformatory and Wisconsin Home for Women were more detailed than those from the state prison, largely because of the comparatively higher caseloads at the prison.

The institutional reports constitute the largest block of information not available to the sentencing judge. Whether the parole decision will be based on more adequate information than the sentencing decision, as has been asserted,[24] depends partly upon the adequacy of the institutional reports. In Kansas, for example, the institutional reports added little about the inmate that was not known to the sentencing judge without a presentence report. Indeed, in some cases the only extensive social history of the inmate available to the parole board was submitted by the sentencing judge.

In Kansas the institution prepares a "brief" on each inmate for parole board use. The brief, normally consisting of approximately one and a half pages of typed material, is the major source of parole information. It contains the charge upon which the inmate was convicted, the sentence imposed, the county of conviction, and the date of sentence. The description of the offense is normally quite brief, such as the following: "Charge here is Forgery 2/d and uttering and the crime was the writing of a check for $4.50 in Hutchinson, Kansas. Pleaded guilty. Victim: Pinkerton's Service Station." The inmate's F.B.I. record and any detainers on file against him are indicated. There is a brief description of each disciplinary infraction within the institution and the disciplinary measures taken. There is a brief report of the medical examination given upon ad-

23 See Chapter 1. A member of the Michigan parole board said that information is completely lacking on the victim of the offense, a matter sometimes considered to be very important to the parole decision.

24 See pages 169-172.

mission to the institution and reports of any hospitalization while in the institution.

Since there is no presentence report, all of the social history available to the parole board is contained in the brief, except in unusual cases when the sentencing judge includes social history in his recommendation for or against parole. The social history in the brief is normally a short summary of an interview with the inmate conducted by institutional staff and consists of the date and place of birth, marital status, education, vocational skills, race, and religion. There is also a description of the inmate's impression on the person conducting the interview; for example, "answers questions freely, makes a good impression at this time. Should be good reformatory material." Psychological data consist of intelligence test results. The institution makes no recommendation for or against parole.

In Michigan the institution provides considerably more information to the parole board. The principal documents are the reception diagnostic center report and the progress and classification report.[25] Upon entering an institution, the prisoner is processed at the reception diagnostic center. A copy of the report completed at the center, which includes information primarily of a sociological nature, is submitted to the parole board together with the results of all tests conducted there. The body of the progress and classification report contains the disciplinary record of the inmate, his financial account, a record of his work assignments, his religious participation, a psychological report, a report on educational activity in the institution, and a report on institutional vocational training. The cover sheet of the report contains a summary evaluation by the inmate's counselor and any comments the classification personnel wish to make. The report may be submitted to the board with or without a recommendation, at the election of the counselor.[26]

The parole board views the institutional counselor's recommendations as only marginally helpful. Because of heavy caseloads at

[25] In addition to these two reports, the file contains a record of the inmate's military experience and questionnaires which have been returned to the institution by the inmate's relatives. The questionnaires are sent to the inmate's relatives in order to obtain some indication of the role the parole board and institutional counselors can expect they will assume when the inmate is paroled.

[26] A board member said that one of the major problems relating to institutional reports results from transfers. A prisoner may be in one institution for a long period of time and then be transferred to another institution shortly before becoming eligible for parole. It then becomes necessary for the counselor at the new institution to prepare the progress and classification report without the benefit of observing the individual in the institution where he served most of his time. The parole board member indicated that this presents the board with a gap they must fill by questioning the inmate at the parole hearing.

most of the institutions, the parole board feels that many recommendations are based on the social history reports of the inmate and, at best, on only one or two interviews with him.The board also feels that the pressures of inmate population lead the counselors to make unjustifiably favorable recommendations in many cases. But when an inmate has been under intensive treatment by a counselor, and the parole board is aware of this, his recommendation is given more weight in the parole decision.

In Wisconsin the institutions furnish the parole board with much of the information in its case files. A form summarizes the offense, sentence, parole eligibility date, and mandatory release date. The inmate's institutional adjustment and work record are indicated, as are his financial status at the time of the hearing and his F.B.I. and State of Wisconsin criminal records. Reports of psychiatric, psychological, and medical examinations are included. There is a chronological history of all contacts with the inmate by the institution's social service department. If the inmate has previously appeared before the parole board, the decision and the board's comments are indicated.

In each institution there is a screening committee, composed of representatives of the various departments within the institution,[27] that reviews each case scheduled for parole hearing. The screening committee prepares a summary of the case and makes a recommendation for or against parole. At the prison the screening committee's recommendation is normally accompanied by a brief statement of its reasoning: "Repetition of assault behavior. Little could be accomplished on parole that could not be accomplished on conditional release. Deny." At the reformatory, the screening committee makes a "preboard summary," stating the present status of the case, how many times it has been before the board for previous hearings, the inmate's present institutional assignment, his attitude and personality development, a diagnostic statement as to the major area of the inmate's problem, and some prognostic statement followed by a recommendation for or against parole.

In a large proportion of cases, the decision of the board is in agreement with the institutional recommendation. In contrast to the situation in Michigan, the parole board in Wisconsin grants parole slightly more frequently than the institutions recommend it.[28]

[27] At the prison and the reformatory, the screening committee consists of members of the custodial staff, vocational staff, and the educational, psychological, and social service departments. At the Home for Women, the committee is composed of the superintendent, six supervisors, and three social workers.

[28] The social service supervisor at the Reformatory said that institutional personnel sometimes become personally involved with inmates having difficulty in the

3. *Preparole report.* It is common for statutes to provide that arrangements must be made for suitable living accommodations and employment before parole may be granted.[29] In most systems, inmates are expected to develop parole plans — statements of where they intend to live and what they intend to do for support — by the time they appear before the parole board for a hearing. A preparole investigation may be conducted to verify the truthfulness of assertions of residence and employment arrangements made by an inmate in his parole plan and to assess the adequacy of the plan and community feelings toward the inmate. A report of this investigation, usually conducted by the parole agent who will supervise the inmate if he is granted parole, is often available to the parole board in time for consideration in its decision to grant or deny parole.

Kansas statutes require the parole board to have "satisfactory evidence that arrangements have been made, for [the inmate's] honorable and useful employment while upon parole in some suitable occupation, and also for a proper or suitable home, free from criminal influence." [30] In practice, parole is sometimes granted when the board feels that, although arrangements for employment have not been completed, they will be made within a reasonable time and the inmate should be released as soon as possible. In most cases, however, arrangements must be made for residence and employment before parole will be granted.[31] The inmate states his parole plan in his application for parole. The primary purpose of the preparole investigation in Kansas is to verify the employment and living arrangements alleged in the parole application. Typically, the parole officer visits the home of the parents or wife of the inmate and inquires whether the family has made arrangements for a job for the inmate. During the course of the conversation, the parole officer determines whether it is feasible for the inmate to return home or whether other living arrangements will have to be made. Often a parole officer has a large number of preparole in-

---

institution, such as breaking regulations. He said that the parole board in many cases is more objective on such matters and grants more paroles than are recommended.

[29] See Model Penal Code §305.11, Comment (Tent. Draft No. 5, 1956); Dawson, The Decision to Grant or Deny Parole: A Study of Parole Criteria in Law and Practice, 1966 Wash. U.L.Q. 243, 293-295.

[30] Kan. Gen. Stat. §62-1525 (1949).

[31] One Kansas parole officer stated that a rule requiring a parolee to have a job before he can be released from the institution is too rigid, because it is sometimes difficult to find employment when an employer has never seen the inmate applicant. This is especially true, according to the parole officer, if the prisoner is being paroled to a community where he is not known.

vestigations to make each month.[32] As a consequence, he may be able to do little more than verify employment and residence arrangements and to enlist the support of the family in an effort to create an environment conducive to successful parole adjustment.

Wisconsin statutes impose no requirements about residence and employment arrangements. A statute provides that "no such prisoner shall be paroled until the department [of public welfare] is satisfied that suitable employment has been secured for him, unless otherwise provided for by the department." [33] This has been administratively interpreted to permit parole without prior employment arrangements in any case the parole board thinks appropriate. Nevertheless, efforts are made to provide employment arrangements before parole is granted. The preparole investigation is used in Wisconsin as a supplement to other sources of information on employment, residence, and community sentiment. Parole officers, in addition to their active cases, have a number of institution cases — inmates still serving time but who are expected to reside in the officer's territory when they are paroled. The parole officer visits those inmates while they are still in the institution. On such occasions, discussions often center on the inmate's parole plan and what would be the best parole placement for him. Notations are made of these conversations and they are available to the parole board. They often serve as a substitute for a preparole report.

Preparole investigations are not routinely conducted; the institution must specifically request them.[34] An institution committee[35] determines whether a preparole investigation is necessary, taking into account (1) the extent and nature of the discussions between the inmate and his parole officer at the institution, (2) the extent of change in the family or community situation since the inmate's admission to the institution, and (3) the likelihood that the inmate will be paroled at the impending hearing.

When a preparole investigation is made, the report is available for parole board use. In his preparole report, the investigating officer verifies the inmate's parole plan, comments on its adequacy, and often attempts to assess community feeling toward the inmate. If upon investigation the parole officer decides that the inmate's plan is inadequate, he may visit the inmate in prison and attempt

[32] A parole agent in Kansas City, Kansas, stated that in some months he has had thirty to forty preparole investigations to complete.

[33] Wis. Stat. Ann. §57.06(2) (1957).

[34] Occasionally a parole officer submits a preparole report when none has been requested. This is interpreted by the parole board as a recommendation for parole.

[35] At each institution a special committee, composed of the social service department supervisor and a representative of the Division of Corrections, reviews cases scheduled for parole hearing for the sole purpose of determining whether a preparole investigation is needed.

to work out an acceptable plan. Sometimes, the parole board paroles an inmate when no residence and employment arrangements have been made. In such cases he is held in the institution until a plan can be devised.

Michigan statutes provide that "no prisoner shall be released on parole until the parole board shall have satisfactory evidence that arrangements have been made for such honorable and useful employment as he is capable of performing, or for his education, or for his care if he is mentally or physically ill or incapacitated." [36] In Michigan the field investigation of residence and employment arrangements is made after the parole board has granted parole. The board grants parole "subject to home and job placement," which is an authorization for the institution to release the inmate when it becomes satisfied that adequate arrangements have been made. If the field investigation discloses problems in residence or employment arrangements, the institution reschedules a parole hearing to permit the board to reconsider its decision in light of the new information. Because the parole board does not ordinarily have a verified plan before the parole hearing, it uses the hearing extensively to obtain information about the inmate's parole plan.[37]

4. *Recommendations from police, prosecutor, and trial judge.* In Kansas a preparole form is sent to the sheriff, police, prosecuting attorney's office, and the judge in the sentencing county, notifying them that the prisoner is being considered for parole and inquiring as to their attitude toward his release. Normally, these agencies briefly note their approval or disapproval on the form and return it to the institution. The police and sheriff agencies voice disapproval in practically all instances; the prosecuting attorneys and the judges disapprove in a minority of the cases. Failure to respond is considered by parole board to indicate approval.

In a few instances a more detailed summary concerning the social and criminal history of the inmate is submitted by the sentencing judge or the prosecuting attorney. However, the typical recommendation is given in a line or two with only slight explanation for the reasoning involved:

> This individual was given a bench parole [probation] which he violated; his conduct evidenced intentional disregard of his responsibilities toward society, contempt for the moral code, and lack of self-discipline. Consequently, I disapprove of a parole at this time.

In Wisconsin the department of public welfare is required by law to give ten days written notice to the prosecuting attorney and

[36] Mich. Stat. Ann. §28.2303(c) (1954).
[37] See pages 256-257.

the judge who tried the inmate before he can be paroled.[38] Many officials do not reply and, when they do, the response frequently is in the form of a list of those for whom they oppose parole. The prosecuting attorney of Milwaukee County, for example, uses this method. Infrequently a judge or a prosecuting attorney submits a letter setting forth his reasons for supporting or opposing parole. These communications become a part of the inmate's parole board file.

The Michigan parole board may solicit recommendations from other agency personnel, but it is not required to do so except in "special consideration" cases, paroles under the "lifer law," and commutation and pardon cases. In all of these cases, the statutes require that the sentencing judge or his successor be notified and asked for a recommendation. In both "special consideration" and "lifer" cases, the sentencing judge is not only consulted but can veto parole.[39]

It was at one time the practice of the Michigan parole board to notify the police, the prosecuting attorney, and the sentencing judge prior to considering a case for parole. These notifications were sent out automatically when an inmate became eligible for hearing. In addition to serving as notification, the forms solicited recommendations from the agencies. The procedure has been abandoned. One board member indicated that the procedure was first established by the board as a protective device to avoid being accused of "sneaking" an inmate out of the institution. It served primarily to notify the agencies responsible for having committed the inmate that he was being considered for parole. Comments of these agencies were solicited and eventually the procedure became formalized so that each of the agencies was asked for a recommendation. The prosecutor and the judge would usually indicate that they they preferred to reserve comment, leaving the matter to the discretion of the parole board. The police would consistently report that they did not concur in the release and would recommend that the man be required to serve the maximum period of his sentence.[40] The types of response became so predictable that the in-

38 Wis. Stat. Ann. §57.06(1) (1957). See State ex rel. Zabel v. Hannan, 219 Wis. 257, 262 N.W. 625 (1935).

39 See Chapter 9.

40 A detective lieutenant in the Detroit Police Department stated that it is always the policy of the police department to recommend that the prisoner serve the maximum sentence. He feels that the department of corrections would like the police department to approve a recommendation of parole so that they might have somebody to pin the responsibility on in the event that the individual again violates: "We have such a hell of a time getting a man into Jackson Prison, we're not going to be the ones to do anything to get him out early."

quiry lost all value as a source of parole information and merely served to notify the agencies of impending parole hearings.

5. *Information not regularly available.* In most parole systems the board attempts to secure every piece of relevant information reasonably available. There are, then, in many systems types of information not regularly available, but which, when present, are considered by the parole board. In Kansas an inmate's relatives, friends, and attorney[41] are permitted to attend the parole hearing. In approximately one-fourth of the cases heard on one particular day, from one to three members of the inmate's family were present at the parole hearing. A board member would first ask the inmate to identify the persons. The board would then ask the family if a job were available. On some occasions it would ask if they could help keep the inmate out of further trouble. In most cases, the parents or relatives indicated that they were willing to provide a home and aid the inmate in securing employment.[42]

In Wisconsin relatives, friends, and attorneys are not permitted to attend parole hearings. They may, however, present their views to members of the parole board in person at the parole board office in the state capitol. A memorandum regarding the conversation is prepared for the board's case file by the member contacted. Letters favoring or opposing parole also become part of the case file.

Similarly, in Michigan, while friends, relatives, and attorneys are not permitted to attend the hearing, they may contact members of the board at its central office. One day per week a member of the board is at the office in Detroit to hear persons interested in inmates scheduled for parole hearings. The board member records the general content of the discussion for inclusion in the case file. Correspondence relating to an inmate is also made part of the case file.

Institutional personnel are often present at the parole hearing. On occasion they provide information not contained in the case file, such as clearing up uncertainties in the file or providing the board with developments in the inmate's case that have occurred

41 See Chapter 16 for a discussion of the function of the attorney at the parole hearing.

42 In one case, the appearance of an older brother actually caused the inmate to be deferred for six months. The inmate had a very poor institutional record, having been cited fifteen times for breaking institutional rules. When the board chairman turned to the brother to ask how he could parole a boy who consistently broke the rules, the brother indicated that he felt some people were "nervous" and could not be bound by rules as easily as other persons. Before he had finished, the brother had managed to talk the inmate into an additional six months in the institution and, in addition, cast doubt on his capability of ever being able to provide a proper home for the younger brother. The parole board members agreed that the older brother would be a bad influence on the inmate.

since the file was completed. Inmates who have served long terms and have come before the board for numerous hearings become known to both the parole board and the institutional personnel. Often this personal knowledge enables a parole board member to arrive at his decision with only slight reference to the latest developments in the case. In Michigan, inmates serving life sentences or sentences with long minima may be released under the lifer procedure. In such cases, the lifer examiner interviews the prisoner and a copy of this interview is made part of the parole board case file.[43]

In Wisconsin trial court transcripts are sent to the institution in about half the cases. These transcripts are available to the parole board upon request. Occasionally, when there is a question as to the facts of the offense, the transcript may be requested and, if it is at the institution, will be used to aid in clarifying the uncertainty.[44] In Michigan the parole board has the services of a special investigator who regularly carries out assignments made by the director of the department of corrections. The parole board uses this investigator when there is some doubt about the facts in a case or, sometimes, when the board believes unethical pressure is being used to secure a parole grant.[45]

C. The Parole Hearing

Parole hearings are conducted as a part of the parole decision process in virtually all American jurisdictions.[46] Although a prisoner is given a statutory right to a hearing in some jurisdictions,[47] the predominant pattern is for the parole hearing to be conducted as a matter of administrative rule or informal parole board practice. The use of a parole hearing in the overwhelming majority of jurisdictions probably attests to its values, but it is far from certain what functions it performs.

[43] See Chapter 9 for a description of the lifer procedure and the role of the lifer eligibility examiner.

[44] For use of the trial court transcript in Wisconsin to secure the views of the sentencing judge on the case, see pages 258-260.

[45] The investigator has a police education and is trained in detective work. He occasionally carries out investigations of department of corrections personnel against whom complaints have been registered. The National Probation and Parole Association surveyed the parole system in 1953 and 1954 and objected to the use of a special investigator for checking on parole personnel on the grounds that the honesty and efficiency of personnel should be a responsibility of the immediate supervisor of these employees. Accordingly, they recommended the abolishment of the investigator's position. See National Probation and Parole Association, Adult Probation and Parole in Michigan 87, 89, 90 (1954).

[46] Model Penal Code §305.10, Comment (Tent. Draft No. 5, 1956).

[47] See, for example, Mich. Stat. Ann. §28.2305 (1954).

In the states studied the parole hearing can perform three functions relating to parole information: (1) it serves as a focal point for gathering parole information and making the parole decision; (2) it provides an opportunity for the parole board to verify information contained in its case file and for the inmate to dispute the reliability of such information; and (3) it provides an opportunity for the parole board to secure information not contained in the case file and for the inmate to furnish new information to the parole board.

The parole hearing performs functions other than the securing of parole information. It can be viewed as a part of the institutional treatment program. Thus, the authority of the parole board can be used to encourage participation in institutional programs. The parole hearing may be a necessary part of the decision process, not as an information source, but as a device for giving that decision an appearance of deliberation and fairness to the prisoner. The parole hearing may simply be an opportunity for the parole board to view the prisoner and thus satisfy the psychological need to see a person about whom it is in the process of making an important decision. These functions of the parole hearing are discussed here because they are inseparable from its parole information functions.

1. *The parole hearing as the focal point in the decision-making process.* In most cases it can be said that the parole decision is made at the parole hearing. The date set for a parole hearing serves as a deadline for the completion of the case file. Sometimes there is a review of the case file by one or more members of a parole board before the hearing is conducted. In some cases, although the decision is made at the parole hearing, there may be an administrative review of this decision, either by the full parole board in executive session or by an administrator in the department of corrections, or even theoretically by the governor. The parole hearing, then, is the point to which all sources of information are channeled and the place where the parole decision, sometimes subject to earlier screening and later review, is made.

In Kansas the parole decision is made at the conclusion of the hearing. Decisions to parole inmates of the penitentiary in theory are recommendations to the governor because by statute his assent is necessary to make a parole grant valid.[48] The governor's consent is not necessary for paroles from the reformatory and women's prison.[49] In practice, however, his consent is automatic and there is no actual gubernatorial review. By the time an inmate makes his

[48] Kan. Gen. Stat. §62-1529 (1949).
[49] Kan. Gen. Stat. §§76-2315, 76-2505 (1949).

appearance before the parole board, it has a completed case file. There is no review of the case file by the parole board prior to the hearing; the small file can be studied by the board members during the short hearing. Often as many as 135 hearings are held during a single day. The chairman of the board said there was really no need to conduct longer hearings because presentence reports, social histories, and substantial reports of the inmate's experiences in the institution are not available. After an inmate is excused from the hearing, the parole board makes its decision, which is later communicated to the inmate by a member of the institutional staff.

In Wisconsin the parole board receives a complete file on each inmate a few days before his hearing. The parole board members examine the file for five to ten minutes immediately before the appearance of the inmate for interview. Occasionally there is some discussion at this point; more commonly the members individually review the file until the chairman believes, on signal from the others, that they are ready for the interview. The files of women inmates are reviewed more leisurely than those at either of the men's institutions. The records provided and the time available to the parole board members for considering a case are both more extensive.

Hearings at the prison and the reformatory take from five to fifteen or, at the most, twenty minutes each. The board members try to make the hearings seem unhurried, and the length of an interview is not arbitrary. Occasionally, when an inmate wishes to discuss a serious problem with the board, it is more extensive. An interview terminates when the discussion appears to indicate that neither the inmate nor any board member wishes to say anything more.[50]

The parole board is an advisory group to the director of the department of public welfare, who alone has legal authority to grant parole.[51] Its decision is technically a recommendation to the director. The board does not vote on its recommendation until the inmate has left the room and does not tell him its decision at the hearing.[52] Parole board recommendations are forwarded to the director of the department of public welfare only when the decision

[50] In only one case observed, when an inmate continued to ramble on about subjects unrelated to the purpose of the hearing, was an interview cut short. In all other cases the board allowed the hearing to continue even when the inmate merely wished to use it as a visit, knowing that he had no chance of parole at that time.

[51] Wis. Stat. Ann. §§46.014(1), 46.03(6) (c), 57.06(1) (1957).

[52] The inmate is informed of the decision in writing later. Subsequent to the field survey, the Wisconsin parole board adopted the policy of informing the inmate of its decision at the parole hearing. Under this more recent procedure, the inmate is heard, leaves the room while the board makes its decision, and then returns at which time the board informs him of its decision and attempts to give him some of their reasons for it.

is for parole to be granted. If the majority decision is for parole to be denied, deferred, or continued, the decision is not referred because no action by the director is required. A unanimous recommendation for parole is sent to the director of public welfare who, in almost all cases, accepts the board recommendation. When the three-member hearing panel is not unanimous for granting parole, the case goes to the director of the division of corrections who, in his capacity as *ex officio* chairman of the parole board, examines the material and makes a personal recommendation. The file is then sent to the office of the director of public welfare for final action. Normally the majority recommendation of the board is finally adopted.

In the Michigan system the parole board consists of five persons. By statute, a majority of the board must approve before a prisoner can be released on parole.[53] Two members of the board conduct each hearing. The parole board members hearing the case do not ordinarily read the case files before their visit to the institution. One parole board member stated that the members hear so many cases they find it difficult to retain information about particular cases even when they do review the record. He added that there is enough time for all of the material to be reviewed during the hearing and the board members do not consider time of prime importance but take as much as is needed for each case. The board member said that in any event it would be necessary to review the case at the time of the hearing in order to refresh one's memory on the details of any particular case.

The board has developed a screening procedure in which a member who will not interview the inmate at the institution reviews the parole board file and makes a recommendation. If the screening member votes to deny parole, a second screening member reviews the file and adds his recommendation. If after the hearing, three members have agreed on a disposition, the decision is communicated to the inmate immediately. If a majority of the five-man board has been unable to agree upon a disposition, the case is referred to executive session of the parole board for further discussion and consideration by the entire board.

2. *Use of the parole hearing to verify information.* The question of disclosure of presentence information to the defendant or his counsel and of providing them opportunity to rebut assertions contained in the presentence report is one of current discussion.[54] A similar question arises at the parole stage with regard to information contained in the case file.

[53] Mich. Stat. Ann. §28.2305 (1954).
[54] See Chapter 2.

In practice, little attempt is made to verify information contained in the case file by questioning the inmate at his parole hearing. In Kansas, when the file discloses that an inmate committed a disciplinary infraction at the institution, a parole board member normally asks whether the report is true. It is difficult to describe this as verification because if the inmate denies the report or tries to absolve himself from responsibility, the board automatically assumes that the report is correct and the inmate is lying or attempting to rationalize his behavior. In Michigan the material in the case file is often used as a starting point for a discussion designed to determine the inmate's attitude toward himself, his family, and the offense. Only rarely does the board seek to determine the factual accuracy of the file by questioning the inmate.

Generally, the questioning by the board reveals only selected items of information in the file. The board makes no systematic effort to disclose to the inmate the important information on which the decision depends. In Michigan and Wisconsin the inmate has the opportunity to rebut any information contained in the case file about which he has knowledge. Generally, the hearings are held in a leisurely fashion, the inmate is given opportunity to ask questions, and the parole board makes it a practice to ask him if there are any questions he would like to ask or statements he would like to make. In Kansas, however, the hearings are quite brief — two or three minutes — and the board asks the inmate a few questions, after which he is dismissed with little opportunity to say anything other than answer the questions put to him.

3. *Use of the parole hearing to gather additional information.* In Michigan and Wisconsin, the parole hearings are designed to enable the board to supplement the information contained in the case file. Hearings are conducted in such a manner as to get the inmate to talk about himself, his institutional experiences, and his plans for parole, on the theory that this reveals his insights and attitudes. In Wisconsin one of the first questions usually is "Why do you think you're ready for parole?" The last may be "Do you have anything more you wish to say?" Generally, an inmate will be given the opportunity to make any statement he may wish and is encouraged to do so. It is not clear to what extent the inmate's attitudes are revealed at the parole hearing. It is also not clear what importance his attitudes are in relation to all the other factors that bear on the decision to grant or deny parole. The boards in Michigan and Wisconsin clearly regard one of the primary purposes of the parole hearing as ascertaining the inmate's attitudes and consider his attitudes relevant to their decision.

The hearings in Kansas are so brief there is little opportunity to inquire into the inmate's attitudes and to permit him to make statements.

In Michigan one of the uses of the parole hearing is to obtain some idea of the inmate's parole plans, and questions frequently center on the inmate's job and residence arrangements if he is granted parole. The board explained that this was necessary because they are not provided with a preparole report prior to the hearing. Although they make all paroles subject to job and home placement, the board nevertheless feels that the type of placement is an important factor in its decision. In both Michigan and Wisconsin discussion of the inmate's parole plan may be used to elicit responses from the inmate that enable the board to learn something of his attitudes and motivations.

4. *Other functions of the parole hearing.* In Wisconsin the parole board encourages inmates to participate in institutional programs. The parole hearing is used to alert the inmate to the resources of his institution and to the fact that the parole board expects him to utilize them. This is accomplished in several ways, for example by questions as to whether the inmate has joined Alcoholics Anonymous or has sought psychotherapy. This is emphasized particularly at the reformatory. More time is taken there than at the other institutions to explain to the inmate what he can do to hasten his release. The board feels that at the prison such explanations are less necessary, although they do occur, because inmates there are more experienced and remain in the institution a longer period of time. Many reformatory inmates are experiencing their first incarceration, are young, and are expected to be released within a relatively short period of time.

In Michigan the parole board members sometimes use the hearing to lecture offenders about their attitudes, their prospects for the future, or various conceptions they have of themselves and others. Board members also stress the importance of increased participation in prison programs to inmates who have shown no inclination to take advantage of them. The parole board's concern with the nature of the offender's prison adjustment also has the effect of directing his attention to improving his prison adjustment as a way of securing parole.

In both Michigan and Wisconsin an inmate is permitted to appear before the parole board at any time it is sitting at his institution, even though he is not yet eligible for parole. Often the purpose of these hearings is to explain to the inmate the board's position on what he needs to do in order to be paroled and to interpret the meaning of the eligibility rules to him.

In Michigan and Wisconsin parole board members are careful not to hurry the parole hearing. The fact that the inmate appears before the parole board and is given opportunity to present his case to it probably increases his sense of the fairness of the parole release procedure. In some observed cases it was apparent that the inmate would not be paroled but he was permitted to continue talking to the board simply as an outlet for him.

In Michigan the parole decision is communicated to the inmate at the parole hearing. When the decision is a denial, the parole board may go to some length to explain to the inmate its reasons for the decision and what he must do in order to increase his chances of parole. In some cases when the board decided to give the inmate a "three-year flop," [55] it was careful to explain to the inmate that if he showed great improvement before the end of three years he could get a special hearing prior to that time.

D. Interpreting the Judicial Sentence

In sentencing structures that divide discretion to determine the length of incarceration between the sentencing judge and the parole board, there is obvious need for coordinating these two decisions. The sentencing decision is sometimes influenced by the trial judge's expectations of the probable parole decision[56] and the parole decision is influenced by the sentence selected.[57] But this influence is the product chiefly of reciprocal conjecturing by judge and board. In the states studied attempts at communication on a case-by-case basis between the sentencing judge and the parole board have not been successful. This lack of communication manifests itself in the difficulties the parole board has in interpreting the sentence imposed by the trial judge, whether it is the maximum sentence in Wisconsin or the minimum sentence in Michigan. In many cases the sentence without accompanying explanation is ambiguous. A parole board member in Michigan stated:

> The parole board does not know what a judge's intentions are when he sets either a very low or very high minimum sentence. They do not know whether, in the case of a low minimum, the judge is leaving the matter of release up to the board or if he really intends for the individual to be released at the earliest

[55] When the Michigan parole board denies parole it immediately determines when the next parole hearing will be granted. Normally, the hearing is scheduled for one year after the present hearing. Occasionally, when an inmate with a long sentence is denied parole, the board schedules the next hearing in three years, referred to by board members as a "three-year flop."

[56] See Chapter 7.

[57] See Chapter 11.

> possible date. On the other hand, when a high minimum sentence is set, they are not certain whether the judge intended the individual to serve at least the minimum, or whether, if the circumstances warrant it, the judge can be approached for release prior to the minimum by special consideration.[58]

Another member of the Michigan parole board said:

> There is no way in which the board learns of the feelings of the sentencing judge at the time the individual is committed to the jurisdiction of the Department of Corrections. There is no form by which the judge informs the department or the board of his feelings at the time the individual is sentenced. The board most commonly must grope about in the dark in order to determine what a judge had in mind at the time he sentenced.

There are several interpretative aids available for parole board use in understanding the judge's reasons for the sentence he selected. For one reason or another, however, these devices have not been helpful.

In Wisconsin the sentencing judge is requested to submit a recommendation for or against parole at the time of the inmate's initial parole hearing. Through this recommendation with accompanying explanation, the judge could make the basis of his sentence known to the parole board. The value of this device has been limited. Most judges do not respond to the request for a recommendation, perhaps because the request normally comes at least one year after the time of sentencing. Unless the judge is able to recall the facts of the case from the description in the request, responding will require him to go over his records in order to refresh his memory. It seems likely that in the routine case the judge would not regard this worth the effort.

At one time in Michigan there was a statutory requirement that, upon sentencing, the judge had to make a recommendation on when the defendant should be paroled;[59] this is no longer the law.[60] One judge in Michigan still makes such recommendations, which accompany the commitment papers to the institution. Typically, however, he recommends that the defendant be paroled at the minimum, and it seems clear that this is what most of the Michigan judges mean when they select a minimum — that they approve of parole at that time.

A statute in Wisconsin requires the trial judge to submit a transcript of the proceedings in his court to the prison if he sentences

[58] For an explanation of the special consideration statutory procedure see Chapter 9.

[59] Mich. Comp. Laws §15859 (1915).

[60] See Mich. Stat. Ann. §28.1080 (1954).

the defendant to incarceration.[61] This would present the opportunity for the trial judge, at the time of sentencing, to put his reasons for the sentence selected on the record for parole board use. It is clear that the judge in Milwaukee uses the transcript for this purpose. In Wisconsin, however, only about half of the cases sentenced to prison are accompanied by transcripts. The parole board has access to the transcripts only by special request to the institution records office. Since the information is not readily available in its case file, the parole board rarely refers to the transcript. When it does so, it is usually for the purpose of ascertaining the details of the offense committed and not to determine the reasons the judge had for his sentence selection.

[61] Wis. Stat. Ann. §252.20 (1957).

CHAPTER 11

The Decision to Grant or Deny Parole

The parole decision is almost entirely a matter of administrative discretion. The paroling authority's discretion is slightly limited by statutory parole eligibility restrictions[1] and by occasional procedural requirements,[2] but once these are met the parole board is free to make whatever decision it wishes without that decision being subject to further legal limitations.

Statutes normally provide the parole board with little or no guidance on the criteria to be used in making its decision.[3] When statutory criteria exist, they typically admonish the parole board to act in the public interest and not to release an inmate who will commit another crime.[4] Parole boards do not regard existing statutory criteria as authoritative limitations on decision making; in most states the legislature has made it clear that the final decision rests with the parole board [5] and in some states it has specifically

1 For a discussion of these restrictions and their manipulation in practice, see Chapter 9.

2 See Chapter 10.

3 For a survey of statutory parole criteria, see Dawson, The Decision to Grant or Deny Parole: A Study of Parole Criteria in Law and Practice, 1966 Wash. U.L.Q. 243, 289-295.

4 Mich. Stat. Ann. §28.2303(a) (1954) provides that "no prisoner shall be given his liberty on parole until the board has reasonable assurance after consideration of all of the facts and circumstances, including the prisoner's mental and social attitude, that he will not become a menace to society or to the public safety." Wis. Stat. Ann. §57.07(1) (1957) authorizes parole of Reformatory and Home for Women inmates when "their conduct for a reasonable time has satisfied the department that they will be law-abiding, temperate, honest and industrious." Wis. Stat. Ann. §959.15(10) (1958) authorizes parole of inmates committed under the Sex Crimes Law when they are "capable of making an acceptable adjustment in society."

5 Many statutes are careful to indicate that the parole board alone determines whether the statutory criteria have been met. For example, the Standard Probation and Parole Act, which has had a substantial influence on state correctional legislation, authorizes the board to grant parole "when in its opinion there is reasonable probability that the prisoner can be released without detriment to the community or to himself" and when the board "believes that he is able and willing to fulfill

precluded judicial review of parole board decisions.[6] Even when judicial review is not specifically prohibited by statute, courts invariably refuse to review parole board decisions.[7]

Although in some states parole boards are theoretically subject to administrative review by a director of corrections or similar officer, in practice meaningful systems of administrative control have not developed.[8] To the extent there are identifiable administrative criteria on the basis of which the parole decision is made they exist as a matter of informal parole board practice. Boards make little attempt to formalize their criteria or systematically to assess their policy implications. The American Law Institute's assessment of criteria for parole decision making emphasizes their informality:

> Under present parole practice, the release of eligible prisoners is purely discretionary and no formal criteria have been established in the statutes, aside from general principles relating to public safety. Nor has there been any standardized administrative policy in this matter: parole decisions rest on the intuition of the paroling authority, largely unguided by the laws that establish this broad grant of power or even by specific board standards. . . .[9]

Although the field survey data tend to support that conclusion, they also reveal consistent patterns of parole decision making; these suggest that the intuition of parole board members about particular cases is less important than their habitual responses to recurring situations.

Of those factors considered by parole boards, the likelihood that the inmate will commit a criminal offense if released on parole is most significant. This may be expressed in terms of a desire to achieve rehabilitation of the offender or as a desire to minimize the risk to society that release would entail. Despite its importance, parole decisions are not made solely on the basis of the probability of recidivism. In many cases, inmates are paroled

---

the obligations of a law-abiding citizen." National Council on Crime and Delinquency, Standard Probation and Parole Act §18 (1955 rev., reprinted 1964).

6 For example, Mich. Stat. Ann. §28.2304 (1954) provides: "The time of his release on parole shall be discretionary with the parole board. The action of the parole board in releasing prisoners shall not be reviewable if in compliance with law." Model Penal Code §305.19 (Proposed Official Draft, 1962) provides: "No court shall have jurisdiction to review or set aside, except for the denial of a hearing when a right to be heard is conferred by law: . . . (2) the orders or decisions of the Board of Parole regarding . . . the release or deferment of release on parole of a prisoner whose maximum prison term has not expired. . . ."

7 See, for example, Garvey v. Brown, 99 Kan. 122, 160 Pac. 1027 (1916); Tyler v. State Dept. of Pub. Welfare, 19 Wis. 2d 166, 119 N.W.2d 460 (1963).

8 See Chapter 10.

9 Model Penal Code §305.14, Comment (Tent. Draft No. 5, 1956).

despite the board's belief they are likely to commit a new offense. Conversely, in some cases parole is denied despite the board's belief that the inmate is extremely unlikely to repeat this offense.

A. The Probability of Recidivism as a Consideration in the Parole Decision

The principal consideration in the decision to grant or deny parole is the probability that the inmate will violate the criminal law if he is released.[10] If for no other reason, parole boards are concerned with that because of the criticism they receive when a parolee commits a serious criminal offense. But they also regard the parole decision as an integral part of the rehabilitation process and consider the probability of recidivism to be an index of the extent to which the inmate is rehabilitated.

Parole boards do not use a fixed or uniform standard of recidivism probability to determine whether an inmate should be paroled. A parole board may demand a low probability of recidivism in some cases while it may be willing to grant parole despite a very high probability in other cases. It is clear from the field study that in no case does a parole board require anything approaching a certainty of nonrecidivism. It is also clear that in all cases the parole board requires at least some evidence the inmate would be law abiding if released. The standard varies from great doubt about parole success to great confidence. It varies according to the seriousness of the offense the parole board anticipates the inmate might commit if he violates parole. If a parole board believes an inmate has assaultive tendencies and that if he violates parole he may do so by committing a physical assault, perhaps homicide, it demands a great deal of proof he will not repeat before releasing him. If, on the other hand, an inmate has limited his offenses to forgery and it seems unlikely he will do anything more serious than violate parole by becoming drunk and forging a check, the board may be less concerned about the risk of repetition. There are a number of other factors, discussed later, which affect the emphasis which a parole board will place upon the likelihood of recidivism.

While the standard varies from case to case, the factors to which the board looks to determine the likelihood of recidivism remain relatively constant. Obviously not all of them are present in every

[10] A parole board is likely to think of the probability of recidivism in terms of the probability of parole success. A parolee who completes his parole period without revocation of his parole is a success; one who has his parole revoked — in most cases for criminal conduct — is a failure.

case. A number recur with sufficient frequency to permit them to be identified and discussed.

1. *Psychological change.*

Illustration No. 1: The inmate, age twenty-three, had originally received a two- to five-year sentence for auto theft. He was paroled and was returned to the institution within four months for parole violation. About three months after his return, he and two other inmates escaped. He was apprehended quickly and was given a three- to six-year sentence for the escape. Two and one-half years after the escape he was given a parole hearing. Despite his escape record, he was recommended for parole by the institution screening committee, and the psychologist's report showed that he received, and apparently benefited from, frequent counseling. A parole board member asked him the usual questions about any altered viewpoint on his part or any change that had taken place within himself. The inmate was able to explain that he had begun to understand himself better after many talks with the psychologist and felt that his past behavior would not be repeated since he now understood how senseless it had been. The psychologist's report indicated that the inmate had actually gained much insight into his motivation. The board unanimously decided to grant parole.

The indication of parole success most frequently searched for at parole hearings in Michigan and Wisconsin is evidence of a change in the inmate's attitudes toward himself and his offense. This is commonly referred to as an inmate gaining "insight" into the problem that caused his incarceration. The criterion is based on the assumption the offense was the result of a personal problem, and unless gains are made in solving that problem the likelihood of recidivism is high. Rehabilitation, then, becomes a matter of changing the problem aspects of the inmate's personality.[11] There are some cases in which the parole board feels that the offense was truly situational — that is, the result of a peculiar combination of circumstances external to the inmate that are unlikely to recur.[12] These are rare, however, and it is an unusual case in which a parole board becomes confident of success without evidence of basic personality change. Paroles are often granted with-

[11] Probably the most dramatic examples of psychological change occur in the plastic surgery cases. In one case in Michigan, the parole board gave as the major reason for the parole of a long-time recidivist the fact that plastic surgery on his disfigured nose gave him an entirely different attitude toward life. For a description of the plastic surgery program at the Connecticut State Prison at Somers, see National Council on Crime & Delinquency News, Jan.–Feb. 1965, p. 3.

[12] See pages 277-278.

out evidence of psychological change,[13] but the parole board considers it the best indication of successful adjustment on parole.[14]

In Kansas at the time of the field survey evidence of psychological change was not usually a factor in the parole decision. This was not because the parole board considered it irrelevant; rather, it was because the parole board had very little social and psychological data on parole applicants. There were no programs in the institutions for aiding in changing attitudes, and the time spent in parole hearings was inadequate to permit questioning beyond cursory inquiry into disciplinary infractions and the parole plan.

The factor of psychological change is frequently expressed in terms of when the inmate has reached his peak in psychological development. The problem of parole selection becomes one of retaining the inmate until he has reached his peak and then releasing him; incarceration after this point is regarded as detrimental to adjustment on parole.[15] Often the institutional summary and recommendation indicate that further incarceration will not help the inmate — that the institution has done as much for him as it can. Conversely, when an inmate is receiving counseling or therapy and it is reported that he has made some gains in insight but more can be done, the parole board is likely to take the position that the inmate has not reached his peak and will deny parole to permit further treatment. This notion may not be applied to alcoholics and narcotic addicts; some parole boards take the position that the longer their incarceration the better the chances of rehabilitation. These inmates are sometimes denied parole at the initial hearing for this reason despite other favorable factors.

Parole board members recognize it is often very difficult to apply the criterion of psychological change. A member of the Michigan parole board stated: "A parole board's most difficult task is to determine if any worthwhile change has taken place in an individual in order that he might take his place in society." In Michigan the parole board frequently questions the inmate about his offense in order to determine whether he freely admits his guilt and has feelings of remorse for his conduct. These are regarded as favorable signs that an inmate has taken full responsibility for his offense and has begun the process of rehabilitation. Denial of guilt or lack of remorse does not preclude parole, because criteria

13 See pages 278-289.

14 The emphasis placed by parole boards on psychological change creates problems when dealing with mentally defective inmates because of the extreme difficulty of effecting change with present prison resources.

15 When a parole board releases an inmate who has served a long term, it sometimes refers to the psychological change in the inmate in terms of maturation. Some parole board members have remarked that for certain types of offenders the only hope of rehabilitation lies in the slow processes of maturation.

other than probable success are considered, but it is an extremely unfavorable factor.

The difficulty parole board members experience in attempting to determine whether there has been a change in the inmate's attitudes finds expression in a universal fear of being "conned." [16] The parole board shows considerable concern about the inmate who is too glib, who seems to have everything down pat and is so smooth that every detail of his story fits neatly into place. Board members resent inmates who seem to be trying to "con" them or to "take them in." One parole board member in Michigan showed considerable concern over the difficulty "psychopaths" cause a parole board that looks for signs of psychological change in inmates:

> I believe the psychopath is especially adept at simulating rehabilitation and reformation and gives parole boards as much trouble as he does psychiatrists. I believe that they can be characterized only through a careful case history of their actions and that any standard description of them lacks a sharp focus unless it relates to their past behavior extended over many years.

Board members suspect simulation in the claims of inmates who report remarkable insight and gains from therapy. For this reason, they frequently question such an inmate on whether he found it difficult at first to talk about his problems in therapy. They are much more favorably disposed toward the inmate who found insight hard to gain at first, rather than one who claims he found it easy to understand himself and to profit from counseling or psychotherapy.

> *Illustration No. 2:* The screening committee of the institution recommended granting parole in this case. The inmate had received intensive psychotherapy, four months in group therapy and ten months individual therapy. The committee felt it should concur with the psychiatrist, who recommended parole because of the progress made in therapy. The parole board granted parole.

Difficulty discovering whether an inmate has made progress in understanding himself accounts in large part for the great reliance parole board members place on the recommendations of counselors and psychiatrists who treat inmates. The Michigan parole board pays close attention to psychological and psychiatric reports when available. Because of personnel shortages, many

[16] This fear prevailed even among members of the Kansas parole board, which puts little emphasis upon psychological change in making its decisions. In one case, the inmate seemed to the parole board to be too glib, so it quickly dismissed him and denied parole on the ground he was a "con man."

inmates are not diagnosed or treated by psychologists, psychiatrists, or social workers. However, examinations are made on repeated offenders, those with case histories involving assaultive criminal acts and those who exhibit some apparent psychological disturbance. The parole board very often follows the recommendations of psychiatrists treating the inmate. In Wisconsin both the institutional committees and the parole board place considerable emphasis upon the recommendations of psychiatrists who have observed or treated particular inmates.

If an inmate receives therapy and the prognosis is hopeful, it weighs heavily in favor of parole, although this fact alone may not be sufficient to persuade the board to grant it. However, if an inmate makes no effort to obtain therapy, or worse, refuses it, he is almost sure to be denied parole unless other very important positive factors are present. A negative recommendation from a psychiatrist treating an inmate almost invariably results in denial of parole.[17]

2. *Participation in institutional programs.*

> *Illustration No. 3:* The inmate, sentenced for forgery, was an experienced electrician. The institutional recommendation was for parole denial, characterizing him as a "chronic offender." The social services supervisor noted that no one had observed any change in him and he had not requested psychotherapy. When he was called into the parole hearing room, the first question was whether he had a job plan if released. The prisoner indicated that he wanted to look for work as a refrigeration mechanic. A parole board member then noted the inmate's drinking problem and its probable effect in the future. The prisoner indicated that he felt he could make it. The parole board member then asked the inmate if he had done anything about his alcohol problem while confined. The inmate indicated he could not do anything about it because he was working seven days a week in the institution. The parole board member asked which was more important, working in the institution or seeking psychiatric help concerning the very problem that would bring him back to the institution. He told him if he really wanted psychotherapy he could have received it despite the seven-day work schedule at the institution. The inmate was asked what in his present situation had changed that would make him a good

[17] In one Wisconsin case the screening committee's recommendation was as follows: "Paranoid psychosis. Thinks wife maneuvered him into murdering her. Psychiatrist reports too dangerous for release. Deny." The parole board quickly denied parole on the basis of the psychiatric recommendation.

parole risk. To this the prisoner replied that he would have to make it or give up. He claimed that if he works steadily he has no problems, and that as long as he has work on the outside he feels he can adjust on parole. A parole board member then noted to him that working was not the problem because he always had a good work record and was considered a very skilled person. He was told that this type of case was the most difficult to decide, principally because of the alcohol problem involved. After the hearing, the board unanimously denied parole.

In many institutions there are numerous programs and activities designed to assist the inmate in changing his attitudes and eliminating the problems thought to be causative of his criminal conduct. Examples of these are group and individual therapy, Alcoholics Anonymous, self-improvement (Dale Carnegie) courses, academic education and vocational training, and opportunity for religious training and worship. One of the indications of parole success used by the board is the extent to which the inmate has availed himself of these programs. This is viewed as indicating that the inmate is making a serious attempt to rehabilitate himself. The inmate who participates in these programs is regarded as a better risk even if no noticeable change is effected than is the inmate who is just "serving his time" with no genuine effort at change. Failure to participate is an extremely negative factor in the parole decision.

If an inmate appears before the parole board with a problem that might be alleviated by participation in any of these programs, he may be urged to participate if parole is denied. He may in fact be told that in his case participation is the surest way to be paroled.[18]

One of the difficult problems in applying this criterion is the availability of institutional programs,[19] particularly psychotherapy. This is a problem of particular concern to the Michigan parole board because at the state prison the average caseload per counselor is 325. One parole board member stated:

> What good does it do to select a good risk for a parole camp,[20] thinking that fresh air and sunshine will automatically rehabilitate him, and not provide him with anyone to discuss his personal problems with over a period of three or four years? I have asked

[18] See Chapter 10.

[19] A Michigan parole board member criticized the institutions for not awakening religious interests in inmates who have shown a desire for religious counseling and instruction. He said this is partially due to the "determinist" philosophy of those on the institutional staffs with training in the social sciences.

[20] See Chapter 13 for a discussion of the Michigan parole camp program.

dozens of inmates if they have ever had an opportunity to discuss personal problems with anyone during a period of many years' imprisonment and most of them have said that they have not. I believe that psychological treatment, counseling, and guidance must begin with the inmate's entrance into an institution and should be a continuing process leading up to parole. I do not believe that custodial care alone ever led to any spontaneous rehabilitation of an inmate.

Concern over lack of personnel for bringing about change in imprisoned offenders is illustrated by the statement of another board member. "It would almost be better not to have any counseling or psychotherapy available than to have a negligible amount and claim we have sufficient to cause any change for the better in an inmate."

The availability of programs is an important factor in the weight given to participation or failure to participate in programs. In Wisconsin's medium security institution many programs are available, and the parole board gives even more attention to participation in programs there than it does at other Wisconsin institutions.

There is evidence that in some cases in which parole is denied the parole board may be concerned about the effects on the other inmates of a parole grant to one who has not availed himself of any of the institutional programs. One parole board member in Wisconsin said that if an inmate appeared for parole and all prognosticating factors were in his favor for adjustment under supervision, and even if he, the parole board member, thought the individual would successfully complete parole, he still would vote to deny parole if the inmate had made no effort at all to change himself by participation in institutional programs. Thus conceived, the parole decision becomes a means of encouraging participation in the institution programs, much as it is used to encourage compliance with the institution's rules of discipline.[21]

3. *Institutional adjustment.*

Illustration No. 4: The inmate had received concurrent sentences totaling three to fifteen years for assault with intent to rob, assault and armed robbery, and larceny. He had served four years at the time of the hearing. Parole had been denied at two previous hearings. The inmate had continually maintained his innocence. Institutional reports said he was a guardhouse lawyer, was always critical of other inmates, had a quick temper, and was difficult to get along with. His adjustment in his work assignment in the laundry was satisfactory, although he was always finding fault with the institution. The institu-

21 See pages 291-293.

tional committee recommended denial of parole because of the inmate's hostility to authority. At the hearing, the inmate still asserted his innocence. In denying parole, the board listed the following reasons: "resents institutional authority, jailhouse lawyer, denies offense, has a bad temper, has a generally poor institutional adjustment."

One factor in the parole decision is the way in which the inmate has adjusted to the daily life of the institution. In Michigan and Wisconsin records of conformity to institutional disciplinary rules, work progress, and other contacts by institutional personnel bearing on adjustment are contained in the case file. In Kansas information on the inmate's institutional adjustment is limited to a record of disciplinary infractions. The parole board in each of the states regards the inmate's ability to conform to the institution's rules and to get along with other inmates, custodial personnel, and supervisors as some indication of his probable adjustment under parole supervision. Most inmates appearing for parole have a record of fairly good institutional adjustment. The fact that for many of them parole is denied indicates that good adjustment itself is not sufficient to achieve parole. It is likely that good adjustment is a minimum requirement for parole, one which must be met in order to qualify an inmate for favorable parole consideration but which is itself not sufficient for a favorable decision. In Kansas, where parole information is scanty, the fact that the board has a record of disciplinary infractions probably gives the factor of institutional adjustment greater weight than in the other two states. Also, both members of the Kansas parole board were former wardens, persons who would be expected to give more weight to institutional adjustment.

In all three states poor adjustment can be a negative factor in the parole decision, sufficient in itself for a parole denial. For example, if an inmate with a record of assaultive behavior continues this pattern within the institution, this is regarded as evidence that there has been no personality change. It is often difficult to determine whether the board is interested in the inmate's disciplinary record as an indication of his probable adjustment on parole or whether it is concerned about the effect which parole of an inmate with a bad institutional record would have on the efforts of the institutional administrator to maintain discipline. In many cases it seems likely the board is interested in both.[22]

4. *Criminal record.*

Illustration No. 5: The inmate was a fifty-three-year-old

[22] For a discussion of the maintenance of prison discipline as a factor in the parole decision, see pages 291-293.

man serving two concurrent terms of three to five years for forgery. He was an eleventh offender. He had served almost two years of the present sentence and was appearing for his first parole hearing. He had made a good institutional adjustment, but the screening committee of the institution recommended a denial of parole because of his criminal record. His record began in 1927 and involved convictions and prison sentences for abduction, rape, larceny, and forgery. The interview did not last longer than two or three minutes, only long enough for the inmate to smoke a cigarette. He was asked if he had a final comment to make and after he left the hearing room, the board briefly discussed his prospects if released. No parole plan had been developed. The board members unanimously denied parole without further discussion.

Most inmates appearing for parole hearing have had at least one criminal conviction prior to the one for which they are presently incarcerated. The extent and nature of the criminal record is a factor of considerable importance in the parole decision.[23] The inmate's criminal record is regarded as evidence of his potentiality for "going straight" if released on parole. Other factors being equal, it will take more evidence of change in attitude to convince the parole board that an inmate with a long record has reformed than would be needed for an inmate without such a record.

Statutes in some states exclude the possibility of parole or postpone parole eligibility of inmates with prior convictions.[24] A Kansas statute provided that inmates who had served two prior terms in a penitentiary are ineligible for parole.[25] Even in a jurisdiction with liberal parole eligibility laws, an extensive prior criminal record may result in a routine denial of parole at the first hearing.[26] In the illustration case, the inmate received his first parole hearing under Wisconsin law[27] after two years. Although there would normally be a strong expectation that a forger would be released at the

[23] In a study of parole criteria used by the Wisconsin parole board, the inmate's prior criminal and juvenile record was the factor mentioned by the board most frequently as a strong reason for denial of parole. Hendrickson and Schultz, A Study of the Criteria Influencing the Decision to Grant or Deny Parole to Adult Offenders in Wisconsin Correctional Institutions 36-37 (unpublished Master's thesis, University of Wisconsin School of Social Work, 1964).

[24] For a collection of these statutes see Model Penal Code §305.10, Comment (Tent. Draft No. 5, 1956).

[25] Kan. Gen. Stat. §62-1529 (1949), repealed by Kan. Laws 1957, Ch. 331, §37.

[26] The supervisor of the Social Service Department at Wisconsin State Reformatory and a member of the Wisconsin parole board agreed that although all inmates are given their initial parole hearings after serving nine months at the Reformatory, offenders with long criminal records will not be released at the initial hearing unless there is a remarkable improvement in attitude.

[27] Wis. Stat. Ann. §57.06 (1957).

end of two years in Wisconsin,[28] parole was routinely denied because of the long criminal record. It could theoretically be asserted that routine denials due to prior record would be less likely to occur in a jurisdiction like Michigan where parole eligibility depends upon a judicially set minimum sentence, because the trial judge could be expected to increase the minimum as a result of the prior criminal conduct.[29] The Michigan parole board has frequently complained, however, that inmates sentenced from Detroit with long records are often given minimum sentences that are so short they compel routine parole denial at the first hearing. This can be explained largely by the necessity of keeping minimum sentences low in Detroit in order not to interfere with guilty plea bargaining.[30]

Although routine denials at the initial hearing because of prior record are common in Michigan, the parole board has consciously refrained from using a rule of thumb excluding parole consideration for serious recidivists. One member of the board said that he does not believe in any rule of thumb, such as four-time losers cannot be rehabilitated, but believes that in many cases the process of maturation comes late with persons and that rehabilitation can take place within the personality of a multiple offender as well as a first offender.

In many cases the board may be more concerned with whether the inmate has had prior penitentiary experience than with the criminal record itself. Indeed, an inmate with a juvenile record, an adult arrest record, or adult convictions resulting only in probation may, in a limited sense, be regarded as a "first" offender by the institution and the parole board. Parole may be granted rather early despite prior failure under community supervision[31] on the theory that the inmate's first adult institutional experience may have had a shock value.

The parole board is concerned with prior offenses whether or not there was a conviction. In both Michigan and Wisconsin an offender who has confessed to a number of offenses is normally charged with only the one or two most serious ones. The uncharged offenses are described in the presentence report for consideration by the trial judge in sentencing.[32] The presentence report describing the uncharged offenses is normally included in the parole board case file and will influence the board in its decision.

[28] See pages 278-280.

[29] The defendant's prior criminal conduct is a factor tending to increase the judicial minimum. See Chapter 7.

[30] See Chapter 6.

[31] See pages 273-274.

[32] See Chapter 1.

Members of the Michigan parole board stated they consider the presentence report to be particularly valuable in determining the extent and nature of the uncharged offenses. A member of the Wisconsin parole board said that uncharged offenses were not per se an important factor in the board's estimation of probable parole success. As an example, he cited a case of a young man who for the first time in his life went on a drinking spree and committed ten burglaries. The mere fact that he committed ten burglaries probably would not influence the parole board in its decision to grant parole. The parole board member added, however, that he did not intend to say that, if the numerous offenses committed by an inmate, whether charged or not, indicated a pattern of serious behavior and a seriously disturbed personality, they would not be taken into consideration. He concluded that what the offenses represent in terms of the inmate's entire personality and the risk to the community is considered, rather than the isolated fact that he committed a certain number of offenses.

5. *Prior community supervision.*

> *Illustration No. 6:* The inmate was serving a sentence of one to four years for larceny. He was sentenced in December 1953, paroled in July 1955, and violated his parole in November 1955. The violation consisted of drinking and absconding. This was his first parole hearing since his return as a violator nine months ago. Prior to the sentence for this offense he had been on probation for a different offense and had violated probation. The Board unanimously denied parole. One member, in dictating his comments on the case, said the inmate had been back in the institution only nine months and, while his institutional adjustment was good, he was a previous probation and parole violator, had an alcohol problem, and was not interested in treatment.

The inmate's experience under community supervision is an important consideration in the parole decision. Many of the inmates appearing for parole hearings have had probation, which they may or may not have violated, and some of them are serving a sentence imposed because they violated probation.[33] Many inmates with long criminal records have had experience on parole as well as

[33] There is indication that inmates committed to Wisconsin State Reformatory for probation violation are frequently denied parole at their initial hearing held after nine months in the institution. But the nature of the probation violation may be more important than the fact of violation. In one case at the reformatory, an inmate who was appearing for his initial hearing on a probation violation commitment was denied parole. He had been placed on probation on a conviction for armed robbery and had violated probation by carrying a gun and the probation was revoked. He admitted to the parole board he had intended to use the gun in a hold-up to get money to abscond from the state.

probation. This is regarded as an especially important indication of what behavior can be expected of them if they are paroled.[34]

The extent the parole board should rely on the inmate's parole experience is a problem that inevitably arises when, as in Illustration No. 6, an inmate who has been returned to the institution as a parole violator appears before the board in a hearing for reparole. More evidence of a change in outlook is required to convince the board to parole him than when he originally was given parole. The parole boards in the states studied do not have a flat rule with regard to reparoles. Many inmates are given second paroles and some even third paroles, although the board may warn them that this is their "last chance," and that a violation of this parole will result in service of the maximum sentence.[35]

> *Illustration No. 7:* The inmate was sentenced to two and one-half to five years for larceny by conversion. He had already served twenty months. He had a long criminal record and had previously been in three other prisons in various states on charges of breaking and entering. All of his prior commitments were "flat" sentences and he had never been on parole. The inmate demonstrated some signs of beginning to understand his problem. His case was continued for ten months, an indication he probably would be paroled at his next hearing.

The absence of experience on parole may be a favorable factor. In Illustration No. 7, one of the parole board members said they were in effect promising a grant of parole at the next hearing because, although the inmate had a long prior record, he had never had a parole from any institution and it was not actually known what he could do under supervision. The board is understandably unwilling to assume that recidivism without parole is a clear indication of a high probability of recidivism with parole.

6. *Parole plan.*

> *Illustration No. 8:* The inmate, a youth, had no family to

[34] Again, it is clear the nature of the violation is as important as the fact of violation, particularly whether the violation and the original offense form a pattern that seems to indicate a personality trait and whether there is any evidence of a change in the problem aspects of the inmate's personality.

[35] Probably many of the reparoles are granted because the mandatory release date is approaching and the board prefers to give the inmate some community supervision even though in the past he has shown a tendency not to profit from it. See pages 280-281.

In Michigan, the parole board, with the consent of the sentencing judge, can parole an inmate prior to his legal eligibility under a statutory procedure called "special consideration." See Chapter 9. There is an indication that a violation of such a "special parole" weighs particularly heavily against reparole because the board has, in a measure, vouched for the inmate by securing special parole in the first place.

whom he could return upon release. He indicated a desire to work as a machinist and live at the YMCA in a particular small city. The preparole report pointed out that it was probably impossible for a seventeen-year-old boy to secure employment as a machinist and, in any event, such positions in that particular small city were practically nonexistent. The parole officer conducting the preparole investigation reviewed the inmate's long juvenile record and concluded that placement in a YMCA was unrealistic because the youth needed considerably more supervision, was not a proper subject for a group home because he had leadership qualities that might lead other boys into trouble, and was too old for a foster home and probably would not adjust in that setting. Therefore, the officer felt the only alternative available was to place the inmate on a farm until he reached an age when he could support himself fully without control and discipline. The board paroled the inmate to a farm placement.

The inmate's parole plan — his employment and residence arrangements — is considered in some cases an important factor in determining the probability of parole success. It is considered a favorable sign if an inmate has made a serious attempt to develop a suitable parole plan because it indicates he is thinking about his future. Even when a parole plan has been developed and its feasibility verified by preparole investigation, it is still necessary to determine whether it will help or hinder the inmate's adjustment on parole.[36]

When an inmate's parole plan seems inadequate, the parole board may deny parole or defer it for a short time. If the original plan seems inadequate but an alternative has been developed by the parole officer conducting the preparole investigation, or is otherwise available, the parole board may immediately grant parole on condition that the inmate accept the new plan. Unlike other factors relating to probable parole success, then, the parole plan can be manipulated by the parole board to increase the probability of success. In Illustration No. 7, the job plan was not feasible and the residence plan was considered inadequate. A new job and residence plan was developed and parole was granted on the basis of it. In Wisconsin the Special Review Board, the release authority for persons incarcerated under the Sex Crimes Law,[37] makes extensive use of special parole plans for certain types of offenders.

[36] The preparole report in Kansas simply verifies home and job arrangements, if any. No attempt is made to evaluate community sentiment or the suitability of the placement plan. Parole board members frequently complained about the scanty information they received from the field.

[37] Wis. Stat. Ann. §955.15 (1958).

The Board's experience has been that the best solution in incest cases is to parole the inmate to a place other than that where the daughter-victim lives. Similarly, the Board has developed "protective placements" in rural areas of the state for higher risk indecent liberties cases. In this instance the term "protective" refers to protecting potential victims such as children, rather than the usual meaning of "protective placement," which protects the inmate from harm or temptation.

The unavailability of employment causes problems, particularly in states which require the inmate to have a job before he is released on parole.[38] Parole boards find it difficult to comply with these statutes and often must be satisfied with only a vague promise of a temporary job, or with an expectation that some job can be found shortly after release. If the board feels unemployment may seriously jeopardize adjustment on parole, it may deny parole until there is assurance of employment. With unskilled farm workers, this necessitates a denial of parole in the winter in the expectation that securing employment will be easier in the summer and the inmate can be paroled then.[39] Normally, the parole board will be satisfied if the inmate is employable, but in cases in which prior involvement with the law has repeatedly occurred during periods of unemployment, the board may refuse parole until there is a firm offer of substantial employment.[40]

Normally, the inmate's residence plan is investigated to verify that he will be accepted in the home or institution and to determine what the physical conditions are and who the inmate's associates will be. The parole board normally makes an attempt to persuade the inmate to return to his family if he has one and they are willing to take him back, especially if he is young, except in the cases where the criminal behavior is thought to be caused by overprotective or hostile parents.[41]

38 For example, Kan. Gen. Stat. §62-1525 (1949), repealed by Kan. Laws 1957, Ch. 331, §37.

39 Often employment is adverted to, almost as an afterthought, as one of several reasons for the parole decision. For example, one institutional recommendation for denial read: "Repeater. He has done nothing toward self-improvement. His type of work is available in fall as well as in spring." In another case, a reason given by a board member for denial of parole was that the inmate might be released in the summer because employment suitable to his defective mental ability would be easier to secure then.

40 In one case, the information before the parole board revealed that the inmate had a very unstable employment history and that all of his offenses, including the present burglary, were committed during periods of unemployment. One of the parole board members said he would not parole the inmate to another car washer, barber shop porter or other tenuous and unsubstantial job. It was agreed that parole should be granted on condition of no drinking and a substantial and firm job offer before release.

41 In one case, the inmate, upon being questioned concerning his parole plan,

The attitude of the community in which the inmate wishes to reside and work is sometimes considered an important factor in adjustment on parole. This is especially likely if the inmate plans to go to a small community, where the attitudes of a number of citizens may make a substantial difference. If the inmate plans to work and live in a large city, a negative attitude by some citizens may make less difference.[42]

7. *Circumstances of the offense.*

> *Illustration No. 9:* The inmate was convicted of armed robbery and was sentenced to two to fifteen years, of which he had served eighteen months at the time of the hearing. He had no previous convictions and only a few arrests for misdemeanors. The inmate's account of the offense was that he held up a bus and was arrested almost immediately. His file showed he was destitute at the time of the offense, was unemployed, and had been sleeping in parks. The file also showed a good work record when he was employed. He had a letter to show the parole board verifying the fact that if there were an opening he could get his old job back. He was granted parole subject to home and employment placement.

The basic indication of probable parole success used by the Michigan and Wisconsin parole boards is evidence of personality change during the period of institutionalization. There are cases, however, in which the parole board may regard the offense as situa-

---

responded that although he had a mother and two brothers living in another state he would like to be paroled in this state. One board member asked him if he didn't think it would be best for him to go back with his family. The inmate replied, "It makes me feel pretty bad to think of the way I've lived and I don't want to go back around them." The board member pointed out that the inmate would have a better chance if he had relatives to help him make his initial adjustment on parole. He explained that the parole board usually prefers to parole an individual where he has family ties because it finds the chances for success on parole are greater. The other board member intervened to say, "I'll go for parole but not if he stays in this state where he got into trouble due to drinking and bad associates." It was decided to parole the inmate to his family out of state, subject to approval of home conditions and employment plans.

In another case, the inmate, thirty-six years of age, had been convicted several times of check forgery. On most of these occasions, he had been placed on probation because his mother made restitution. The inmate's plan called for parole to the city where his mother lived. A parole board member asked the inmate if he felt he should return to the city in which his mother lived. The inmate replied that he could not let his mother interfere with his life this time. The other board member noted that perhaps such a long pattern of dependency on his mother would be hard to break and it would probably be best to consider placement elsewhere. It was decided to continue the case to investigate the possibility of placement with some of the inmate's other relatives.

[42] The concern of the parole board with the attitude of the community toward the inmate goes beyond its effect on parole adjustment and reflects, in part at least, the board's desire to remain free of public criticism of its decisions. See pages 296-298.

tional in nature and not necessarily the result of a personality defect. If the parole board has some assurance that the situational factors have changed during the period of incarceration, it may be willing to grant parole despite lack of evidence of personality change. In Illustration No. 9, the offense seemed to be the result of the inmate's prolonged unemployment, and the parole board became convinced that the probability of success on parole would be high if the inmate were employed.

The number of cases in which the boards seem to regard the situational factors as predominating is small. Certainly, in comparison with the number of cases in which inmates explain their criminal conduct in situational terms — bad associates, drinking, unemployment, family disputes — the number of cases is small. It is also difficult to determine whether the situational factors in the offense relate exclusively to the probability of parole success or also to a judgment of the moral blame the inmate should bear for his conduct. In Illustration No. 9, one member of the board concluded that although there was no excuse for the offense, the inmate's circumstances did appear to be desperate at the time he committed it, implying that the offense was "understandable."

B. The Decision to Grant Parole for Reasons Other Than the Probability of Recidivism

In practice, inmates are paroled who would not be released if the probability of recidivism were the sole criterion for the decision. Often, inmates are paroled despite the board's judgment that they are likely to commit new criminal offenses. That a parole board sometimes feels compelled to parole inmates who are not rehabilitated may in part reflect deficiencies in institutional treatment programs. It is clear, however, that even great advances in that area would not entirely eliminate the necessity for making decisions of this kind. Practices discussed in this and the following section demonstrate that parole decision making involves more than merely clinical determinations about individual inmates and does, in fact, require the paroling authority to make important policy decisions.

1. *Seriousness of the anticipated violation.*

   Illustration No. 10: The inmate, a fifty-year-old man, had served two years on concurrent sentences of one to five and one to seven years for forgery. No parole plan had been developed. He was a seventh felony offender whose record for forgery extended back to 1933. He had served two previous prison terms. The institution made the following parole recommendation: "Seventh offender. Chronic offender. Social adjustment in institution was good. Psychiatrist seemed to think superficial progress was being made, however, never accepted alcoholism as a problem. Deny." A parole board member began discussing with the inmate the necessity for accepting alcoholism as a problem and told him he knew he would be back as a parole violator if he did not stop drinking. He suggested the inmate join Alcoholics Anonymous after release. The board voted to grant parole.

Parole board interest in predicting behavior on parole does not end when the probability of the inmate's violation of the law becomes apparent. The board is also deeply concerned with the type of violation likely to occur if the inmate does in fact violate. The board is willing to parole on less evidence of probable success when it is apparent that a violation, if it occurs, is not likely to be serious. In Illustration No. 10, one of the parole board members said he was voting for parole because the inmate was the type of individual who just wrote small checks when drunk and who was not a serious threat to the community. Another board member said he was voting to grant parole and added that "all were granting with tongue in cheek." [43]

The potential benefit from further institutional treatment is also a factor in these decisions. Thus, although one inmate was clearly alcoholic and had a long record of arrests for public intoxication, he was paroled at his initial hearing. The parole board concluded he was a harmless person. It could see little point in keeping him in the institution any longer because he had shown little indication of having enough strength to stop using alcohol. The board concluded, therefore, not only had the institution been unable to do much for the inmate, but it was extremely unlikely he would ever be able to make significant gains in solving his problem.

Finally, the board is concerned in these cases about the effect of parole on the inmate's family. If the inmate is retained in the institution there is little opportunity for him to make significant contributions to the support of his dependents. If he is paroled, however, he at least has the opportunity to support his family. In Wisconsin nonsupport offenders normally are paroled as soon as

[43] In another case, the board paroled a twenty-four-year-old man convicted of check forgery. He had one prior conviction for the same offense on which he had been given probation. There had been other forgeries but he was not convicted of them because he had made restitution. When he was paroled one of the institutional personnel remarked that the inmate looked like a good parole risk. To this a member of the parole board replied, "Nonsense. Statistics show that 70 percent of all forgers are repeaters."

they are eligible. The parole board states there are three reasons for this policy: they are unlikely to commit a serious violation of the criminal law, the institutional program is of little aid in their rehabilitation beyond the first several months, and parole may provide temporary financial support for the family as well as the benefits that may accrue from having a father in the family again.[44]

2. *Mandatory release date near.*

> *Illustration No. 11:* The inmate was a nineteen-year-old girl serving a sentence of six months to one year for larceny. Her prior record consisted of one conviction for drunkenness, for which she successfully completed a one-year probation period. At the time of the hearing she had served eight months of the sentence. Her conditional release date would be reached in another three months. If parole were denied, she would be released then and, after one month under supervision, would receive an absolute discharge. The board decided to parole her.

Parole boards sometimes find themselves in the position of choosing between a need to retain the inmate in prison and a need for supervision and control over him after he is released. This occurs when at the time of the parole hearing the inmate has only a short period to serve until he must be released from the institution. These are all situations in which the maximum sentence, whether set by statute or by the trial judge, is, in the view of the parole board, too short under the circumstances. The parole board frequently paroles an inmate despite its estimate of a high probability of recidivism if, in its view, parole supervision is needed more than continued institutionalization.

In Kansas and Michigan the inmate must be released unconditionally when he has served his maximum sentence less allowances for good time.[45] No period of parole supervision follows release. When the inmate has only a short period to serve until his maximum less good time, the parole board frequently feels it is forced to parole him in order to provide some supervision and control over him when he is released.

In Wisconsin, the inmate must be released from the institution when he has served his maximum sentence less good time, but the

[44] In one case, the inmate asked for an unconditional discharge at his conditional release date, stating that he would be unable to complete one year on parole successfully. The parole board denied his request on the ground that he needed supervision and it might also help the inmate's minor children if he could be forced to contribute to their support. The board concluded that at least the family would benefit from the inmate's parole. In another case an inmate who had been convicted of larceny was paroled on condition that he provide regular payments for his minor child.

[45] See Chapter 12.

release is conditional and a mandatory period of parole supervision follows during which the releasee is subject to the same conditions and possibilities of revocation that apply to parolees released by act of the parole board. He must be discharged from supervision when he has served his maximum sentence without good time allowances.[46] When, as in Illustration No. 11, the maximum sentence is short, the period of mandatory parole supervision following release at the maximum less good time is, of necessity, quite short. In Illustration No. 11, the period of supervision would have been one month had the inmate been kept until her mandatory release date. Nevertheless, the parole board felt that further incarceration would be useful in her case. Thus, it was forced to choose between what it regarded as an inadequate period of institutionalization and an inadequate period of post-incarceration supervision. It chose to increase the period of supervision at the expense of the institutionalization.

The position might be taken that this is an important factor to consider in determining whether the maximum sentence should be fixed by the trial judge or set by statute. Thus, it could be argued that paroles based on the approach of the mandatory release date would be less frequent when the maximum is set by statute than when the trial judge sets it. One would expect to find, therefore, that this is more of a problem in Wisconsin than in the other two states. This does not seem to be the case. There may be a number of reasons for this, including, perhaps, the fact that the Wisconsin parole board may be more liberal in granting paroles than the boards in Michigan and Kansas. Another reason may be that in Wisconsin the mandatory release is followed by a mandatory period of supervision. Unlike the boards in the other two states, the parole board in Wisconsin must simply determine whether the period of supervision permitted under the good time awarded the prisoner is adequate.[47] It is only when the maximum sentence is quite short that there is any need for a parole to increase the length of the period of supervision. In Wisconsin one finds such paroles when the maximum is short, while in Kansas and Michigan one finds such paroles when the inmate has previously been denied parole or has been paroled and returned for a violation.[48]

[46] See Chapter 12.

[47] In Wisconsin juvenile boys transferred from the training school to the reformatory are subject to the release jurisdiction of the adult parole board. Because they are still juveniles, however, the conditional release law does not apply to them. When they reach the age of twenty-one, they must be released unconditionally. It is a common practice for the parole board to grant parole to juveniles who are approaching age twenty-one simply to give them a period of supervision in the community which would be denied them under release by operation of law.

[48] The problem was particularly acute in Michigan due to an administrative

3. *Length of time served.*

Illustration No. 12: The inmate had received a sentence of three to twenty years for armed robbery, auto theft, and forgery. He was paroled after three years but shortly thereafter violated his parole and received a new sentence for operating a con game. He had served three years since his last parole. His criminal career began twenty years previously and involved numerous convictions. The psychiatric report was that the inmate was "instinctively vicious. Any rehabilitative program will be futile." The institutional recommendation was that the inmate "has adjusted in excellent manner in institution. Has served lengthy sentence. Should be tried. Grant." The parole board decided to grant parole.

Every decision to grant parole reflects the opinion of the parole board that the inmate has served enough time, but there are some cases in which the length of time served is itself the most significant factor in the case. This typically occurs when an inmate has received a relatively long sentence, but fails to respond to the rehabilitative programs at the institution. In addition, he may have been tried on parole once or twice and had his parole revoked. The parole board then may be faced with the choice of denying parole when it is evident that further institutionalization will not increase the probability of success on parole or of granting parole to an inmate who presents some risk of violation.

In Illustration No. 12, one of the parole board members commented that "just maybe" the inmate will make parole after so long an institutionalization. He felt that in such cases institutionalization reaches a point when it serves no purpose in terms of rehabilitation, and the only question remaining is that of protection of the community. In this case, the board members all felt that they would have to try the inmate on parole sooner or later, but none expressed any confidence in his capacity for success.

A factor mentioned in many cases of this type is maturation. When a relatively young man receives a long sentence and serves a fairly long term before parole, the board may comment that despite the apparent absence of any effect of the institution's programs, he may have matured enough to enable him to live a lawful life in the community.

---

directive that prohibited the parole board from forfeiting good time earned in the institution when an inmate violated parole. This resulted in a number of returned violators having only a short time remaining until their mandatory, unconditional release date. In some of these situations the parole board felt it was forced to grant parole in order to provide the inmate with some community supervision.

4. *Parole to a detainer.*

Illustration No. 13: A twenty-seven-year-old man serving a one- to five-year sentence for larceny appeared before the parole board for a hearing. He had a long criminal and juvenile record. While on parole in Ohio, he came to Wisconsin and committed the offense for which he was serving time. An institutional psychologist said the inmate had admitted using narcotics and drugs; he stated that the prognosis was poor. The institutional committee recommended parole to a detainer, partly because only about seven months remained until conditional release would be required; he had served approximately three years of a one- to five-year sentence, and it was thought he might as well start on his Ohio sentence. The final decision of the board was to grant parole to the Ohio detainer. The chairman commented that he did not think that Ohio would come after the subject, in which event he would be detained at the prison until his conditional release date. None of the board members felt that this person could possibly adjust on parole. The board rationale in this case was recorded by the chairman: "Claims he owes Ohio five years. He has been locked up for the past sixteen years except for twenty-nine months. Gullible, ambitionless, and no insight. Has used heroin. Practically hopeless."

The parole decision may be influenced by the fact that a detainer has been filed against the inmate. The prisoner against whom a detainer is filed may be charged with a crime for which he has not yet been tried, may be a parole violator from another state, may be wanted for completion of a prison term interrupted by an escape, or may have been ordered deported. A detainer is merely a request for notice of the inmate's release and an opportunity to take him into custody upon release. Institutions invariably comply with such requests.

The effect of a detainer on the parole decision varies from state to state. In some states, a detainer automatically precludes the inmate from the possibility of parole.[49] Sometimes this position is based on the view that parole implies community supervision — that a "parole to a detainer" is not really a parole and, hence, not within the authority of the parole board. In the three states, the parole boards do parole to detainers, although this is specifically authorized by statute in only one of them.[50]

[49] Tappan, Crime, Justice and Correction 724 (1960): "In some states any prisoner who is wanted under a detainer for further court action or imprisonment is automatically rejected [for parole] unless or until the writ is lifted."

[50] Mich. Stat. Ann. §28.2303 (c) (1954).

The problem whether an inmate should be paroled to a detainer normally arises only when prior attempts to remove the detainer have failed. Sometimes the trial judge may be successful in removing a detainer at the sentencing stage. If a defendant whom the judge has sentenced to prison is wanted in other counties of the state, he may order that the defendant be taken to those counties and tried for the offenses before being transported to the correctional institution. If a defendant is wanted in another state or by federal authorities, the judge may arrange to increase the sentence in exchange for an agreement to drop the detainer, or he may grant the defendant probation or a suspended sentence and turn him over to the requesting authority.

In some correctional institutions, officials contact authorities that have lodged detainers against inmates in an attempt to discover their intentions. Effort is made to persuade the requesting authority to drop the detainer or at least to specify the circumstances, such as the number of years the inmate must serve, under which they would drop it.[51]

There are some circumstances under which an inmate of a correctional institution may demand disposition of a detainer against him as a matter of right. If the detainer represents an untried charge, the inmate may be able to require that he be taken from the institution and tried, or that the state be barred from ever trying him on that charge, on the ground that he is enforcing his right to a speedy trial.[52] In some states, statutes give an inmate this right.[53] Even in a state with full provision for mandatory removal of detainers, the problem of parole to a detainer remains with respect to detainers for revocation of probation or parole and deportation detainers. Unless institutional authorities are successful in negotiating their removal, the problem comes before the parole board.

In Kansas the parole board grants parole at the first opportunity to inmates with detainers. The board apparently does not distinguish among in-state, out-of-state, and deportation detainers, nor between detainers based on charges yet to be proved and detainers for revocation of probation or parole. During one day's hearings, seven inmates were paroled to detainers. In many of these cases, it was apparent that the inmate would not have been paroled had there not been a detainer lodged against him. In each instance, the board explained to the inmate that it could do nothing but parole

[51] See Tappan, *supra* note 49, at 724 n.32.

[52] E.g., State ex rel. Fredenberg v. Byrne, 20 Wis. 2d 504, 123 N.W.2d 305 (1963).

[53] E.g., Wis. Stat. Ann. §955.22 (Supp. 1967); Mich. Stat. Ann. §§28.969(1) to 28.969(3), 4.147(1) to 4.147(8) (Supp. 1968).

him to the detainer. Apparently, no effort is made during the inmate's confinement to determine whether the requesting authority is willing to drop its detainer. When an inmate has been paroled to a detainer and the requesting authority fails to take custody of him at the institution, the detainer is dropped and the inmate is scheduled for another parole hearing to determine whether he should be paroled to community supervision.[54]

The Wisconsin parole board's policy on paroles to detainers was detailed in a booklet published after the field survey was conducted but reflecting practices at the time of the survey:

> Persons eligible for parole under Wisconsin Statutes but against whom detainers have been filed by Federal, Immigration, Out-of-State or local authorities may be granted parole to the detainer. Normally, parole is not granted to a detainer unless the usual criteria for parole selection can be met.
>
> Institutions will be responsible for correspondence on parole planning with authorities who file detainers except when the detainer has been filed by a paroling authority.[55] In such cases the Parole Board will be responsible for the necessary correspondence. (Institutions should refer cases of this type to the Parole Board.)
>
> Detainers from other states placed against persons serving sentences in Wisconsin Correctional Institutions normally fall within three groups:
>
> 1. Those cases in which the individual was under field supervision at the time he was received.
>
> 2. Those in which the individual has been previously convicted in another state and it is expected that he will, upon release from a Wisconsin Institution, go to an institution in the other state to serve his unexpired term. As a matter of practice, parole is usually not granted to this type of detainer until such time as the

[54] The Kansas parole board's practice of paroling inmates with detainers at the first hearing has caused discipline problems at the institutions because inmates with detainers are certain they will be paroled to the detainer no matter what their behavior. Occasionally, the parole board has declined to parole a troublesome inmate to his detainer in order to enforce the institution's disciplinary code. See pages 291-293.

[55] An official in the Wisconsin Division of Corrections explained that the Social Service Departments of the various institutions have responsibility for requesting the other jurisdiction to remove detainers and do all the negotiating. The time when the Social Service Departments contact the requesting authorities is within their discretion. Usually, they prefer to let the inmate serve long enough on the Wisconsin sentence so that the other state will be willing to release the detainer, particularly in cases of detainers for prosecution. Negotiation occurs because usually no plan can be developed for release and no effective program can be formulated for a prisoner who is not sure where he is going to be. The same official indicated that with in-state detainers for prosecution, the Wisconsin institutions are successful in obtaining removal in about 75 percent of the cases. Frequently, these detainers involve bad check charges, in which removal is easily effected by making arrangement for the payment of restitution.

applicant has less time remaining to serve in Wisconsin than he will have to serve in the other state.

3. Those in which the individual has been charged with an offense in another state but has not yet been tried. In this situation, it is expected that the individual will be taken to court in the other state to face prosecution when paroled in Wisconsin.[56]

In Michigan paroles to detainers are specifically authorized. A statute provides: "Paroles-in-custody to answer warrants filed by local, out-of-state agencies or immigration officials are permissible, provided an accredited agent of the agency filing the warrant shall call for the prisoner so paroled in custody." [57] The effect of the detainer on the parole decision differs depending upon the type of detainer involved.

Detainers filed by agencies within Michigan are usually for the purpose of having the inmate answer an untried felony charge. If an inmate who has such a detainer filed against him is not regarded by the board as parolable at the time of his initial parole hearing, a "custody parole" is almost alway given to allow disposition of the untried charges. If the local requesting authority, upon notice of the parole, does not take custody of the inmate at the institution, then the detainer is considered dropped. If the requesting authority takes custody, the inmate is not permitted to make bond while waiting trial or disposition and, regardless of the outcome of the proceedings, he is returned to the institution after their completion. If a new prison term is imposed, he becomes eligible for parole again when he serves the new minimum sentence less good time. If no new prison sentence is imposed, he will be reconsidered for parole in the usual manner.

In acting on a detainer filed by another state to bring an inmate to trial in that state, the parole board decides whether the inmate should be paroled to the community. When an inmate is released on such a detainer it is with the intent that if he is found not guilty, or if the charges are dropped, he will be placed on parole supervision in the other state. Commenting on this type of parole to a detainer, one parole board member stated "We must handle such cases with the expectation that the inmate may be released entirely from custody, and we cannot afford to take the long risk if the person is deemed not a proper subject for return to society." The board apparently requires that the inmate be parolable under the usual criteria.

If the detainer issued by another state is for return of the inmate

[56] Wisconsin State Department of Public Welfare, Parole Board Procedures and Practices 11 (Feb. 1959).

[57] Mich. Stat. Ann. §28.2303(c) (1954).

as a probation or parole violator, or an escaped prisoner, the board has more indication of what treatment will be accorded the prisoner by the requesting jurisdiction. Because the risk of the inmate's being freed is considerably less than when the detainer is based on untried charges, the parole board is likely to be considerably more liberal in its attitude toward parole. The board learns the length of the sentence remaining for the prisoner to serve and the character of the parole supervision in the state. If, for example, the parole board considers the inmate a menace to society and learns that the period of time remaining to be served in the requesting state is quite limited, it would decide against paroling to the detainer. If the parole board believes the inmate is ready for community supervision, it may suggest to the requesting state that the inmate be released to that state for dual parole supervision.

The effect on the parole decision of a detainer filed for deportation of an inmate varies depending on the country to which the inmate is to be deported. In considering deportation to Canada or Mexico, the board, aware of the ease with which the parolee can return to Michigan, tends to be somewhat cautious in granting parole. Nevertheless, even in these cases, the board is sometimes willing to grant parole when otherwise it would not. One parole board member noted:

> In some quarters of this state, and particularly among some members of the judiciary, there is present a philosophy that we should not clutter up our institutions with persons who are deportable, and that we should, as a matter of fact, pursue a very liberal policy in such cases. I do not think that the board subscribes to this philosophy, nor does it operate under it to the extent that some would desire.

A greater degree of liberality is evident in considering paroles to detainers for deportation to countries overseas.

5. *Reward for informant services.*

Illustration No. 14: The inmate had been convicted of assault with intent to rob, for which he was placed on probation. After one year of supervision, he violated probation and received a prison sentence of one to ten years. This was his initial parole hearing. The sentencing judge and the prosecuting attorney both recommended a parole denial. He had a prior record of assault. His I.Q. was recorded as 63. Shortly before his hearing, the inmate had learned of an escape plot involving four inmates who were hiding in a tunnel. He tipped off a guard and the inmates were apprehended. The board decided to grant parole.

In current administration, the services of informants are sought and rewarded by enforcement officials. The most persuasive inducement and reward for information is lenient treatment of the informant. The leniency may take the form of failing to arrest for minor offenses,[58] refusing to charge an informant despite sufficient evidence, convicting him of a less serious offense, probation, or a lighter sentence.

Occasionally, the parole decision may be used as a reward for informant services, especially for information about the activities of inmates in the correctional institution. In Illustration No. 14, the inmate would not have been paroled on the basis of his rehabilitation. His informant services were not discussed during the parole hearing, but the board was told of them before the hearing and discussed them after the inmate left the hearing room.

In many states, statutes authorize the granting of special good time to inmates who perform extra work or other meritorious duties, including giving information to prison officials.[59] It is not certain how often these provisions are used to reward inmate informant services and, if they are used, whether they are effective in eliminating the need for using the parole decision for the same purpose.[60]

The chairman of the Michigan parole board indicated the difficulty the informant causes the board in reaching a decision:

> Parole was designed to serve society as a means of assisting the individual to make the transition from prison confinement to existence in the free community. There are times, however, when offenders render great assistance to law enforcement or perform some valorous or meritorious act. Testifying against dangerous criminal offenders and thereby placing their own lives in jeopardy, saving the life of an officer or helping him in a serious situation, giving information preventing a serious escape threat of dangerous persons are acts which seem to warrant special consideration. As valuable as these acts may be, they must be interpreted as to the intent of the individual in performing them. It is said that "virtue is its own reward," but sometimes people expect something more tangible — say, a parole! The motivation of the individual and the circumstances in which his valor was evidenced are as important here as they are in the crime for which he was sentenced. They may be sincere expressions of a better set of social values, or they may be selfish efforts to gain personal ad-

[58] See LaFave, Arrest: The Decision to Take a Suspect into Custody 132-137 (1965).

[59] The Kansas statute provided: "The board of administration is hereby empowered to adopt a rule whereby prisoners . . . may be granted additional good time for . . . giving valuable information to prison officials. . . ." Kan. Gen. Stat. §76-2451 (1949), repealed by Kan. Laws 1957, Ch. 331, §37.

[60] For example, it is probably true in Michigan that the great majority of prison inmates are routinely awarded the maximum possible good time and special good time.

> vantage even if it means taking a personal risk. Such acts can be a spectacular evidence of deep significance or only an exhibition of self-aggrandizement.[61]

In some situations there may be a need, which parole can meet, for removal of the informing inmate from the institution for his own safety. It is not clear how important a consideration this is in the decision to grant parole to the informant and, if so, whether a transfer of the informant to another institution would be a satisfactory alternative.

C. The Decision to Deny Parole for Reasons Other Than the Probability of Recidivism

Parole is often denied to inmates for reasons other than perceived probability of recidivism. Often this decision is made despite the board's own estimate that the inmate would very likely complete his parole period successfully if he were released. That this should occur is surprising in view of the chronic crowded conditions of most prisons. Ironically, however, in some situations prison overpopulation may be a factor contributing to a decision to deny parole despite a high probability of parole success. It might be argued, for example, that when a parole board denies parole to a good risk because it is enforcing prison discipline, a major reason it feels compelled to do so lies in the strain on prison discipline created by overcrowding.

It has been contended that parole boards tend to be too "conservative" in their release practices. In part this contention goes to the point that parole boards may require too high a probability of parole success before granting parole, but it also may go to policy considerations upon which parole denials are based in cases in which the board's own requirements of probable success have clearly been met. This may be the situation, for example, with regard to denials because the inmate has assaultive tendencies or because a parole grant would subject the correctional system to severe public criticism.

1. *Cases involving assaultive behavior.*

> *Illustration No. 15:* The inmate, thirty-one years of age, was convicted of carrying a concealed weapon and sentenced to one to five years. When he was arrested on the present offense, he was believed to be trying to draw a gun on the arresting officer. His prior record consisted of convictions for

[61] Address by R. H. Nelson, Chairman, Michigan Parole Board, at a meeting of Michigan prosecutors, July 1957.

> "shooting another" and for felonious assault. He had been denied parole at a previous hearing because of several misconduct reports from the institution, one of which consisted of possession of a knife. Since his last hearing, however, he had received no misconduct reports. When the questioning of one of the board members revealed he was thinking of a parole grant, the other member interrupted him, stating, "I want a discussion on this." The first member replied that the record showed the inmate had greatly improved his attitude since the last hearing. Nevertheless, the inmate was told his case would have to be discussed with the other members of the parole board and he would hear their decision in about a month.

Parole boards tend to be more conservative in their release practices when the inmate has demonstrated he is capable of assaultive behavior. Sometimes this consideration is regarded as sufficiently important to justify a denial of parole to an inmate who would otherwise be regarded as having a sufficiently high probability of parole success to justify release. The rationale is, of course, that the parole board has an obligation to protect the public from possible assaultive behavior which overrides its obligation to release inmates at the optimum point in their rehabilitative progress.[62]

The Michigan parole board has a practice of refusing to grant parole to an inmate with a demonstrated capacity for assaultive behavior until the case has been discussed by the full five-man membership of the board in executive session. In Illustration No. 15 one of the two parole board members said, after the inmate left the room, that he did not believe parole was appropriate because of the inmate's history of assaultive conduct. He said he believed a further psychiatric evaluation would be necessary since on at least three occasions the inmate has proved himself capable of serious assaultive behavior.

Shortly after the field survey was conducted, the Wisconsin parole board adopted the policy of requiring a discussion in executive session before an inmate with a history of assault may be paroled. In these cases, the two members of the board conducting the parole hearing tell the inmate a discussion with a third member is necessary before a decision can be made. The director of the social service department of one of the institutions noted that both institutional authorities and the parole board are more cautious in cases involving assault, particularly in cases of murder.

[62] The board is especially unlikely to release inmates who appear to be directing aggression against a particular person. In one case, for example, an inmate was continually denied parole because he persisted in sending threatening letters from prison to his wife.

Normally, the board determines whether the inmate is capable of assaultive behavior on the basis of his prior record and the offense for which he is serving time. The board may also have had the benefit of a psychiatric evaluation. In such cases, the latter is given great weight. An evaluation concluding that the inmate is still capable of assaultive behavior or is still too dangerous for release almost automatically results in a denial of parole.[63]

2. *Supporting institutional discipline.*

Illustration No. 16: The inmate, twenty-six years of age, was convicted of larceny in a building and was sentenced to one and one-half to four years. This was his first parole hearing. A parole board member first questioned the inmate about his institutional record, which showed he had three institutional reports, two for being "lazy" and refusing to work and one for having dice in his possession. He had several misdemeanor arrests and at one time had been arrested on a narcotics investigation charge. An immediate parole was not granted but the case was continued for office review in six months. It was explained to the inmate that his institutional report had been poor and that if he corrected this and tried to obtain some help from his counselor, he would be given consideration again in six months.

Maintaining discipline among inmates is a major concern of all prison administrators. Although there are wide variations among penal institutions as to the degree to which the details of daily living are regulated by the administration, even in relatively permissive institutions there are disciplinary rules and sanctions for their infraction. Infractions of prison discipline are often interpreted by the parole board as signs of what the offender is likely to do when he is released on parole. They suggest an inability of the offender to adjust to his position and to respect authority.[64] Quite a different consideration is primary, however, when the board denies parole because of the effect its decision may have on prison discipline. The major interest shifts from a concern with the future adjustment of the offender to a concern with order and control in the penal institution. Parole becomes an incentive for good behavior and a sanction against undisciplined conduct by inmates.

It is frequently not easy to distinguish between actions of the board that are designed to have an impact on the discipline of the institution and those that relate to the offender's future adjustment. It is likely that even the parole board members are unable to

[63] For example, an institutional recommendation such as that in note 17 *supra* is virtually certain to result in a parole denial.

[64] See pages 269-270.

articulate clearly their reasons for reacting as they do to inmates with disciplinary problems. In Kansas a parole board member may sometimes say, "How can you expect to be paroled when you can't even behave in the institution?" which might be interpreted by the inmate to indicate that the board feels he lacks sufficient control. On the other hand, the board member will sometimes say, "I can't parole anyone who has become involved in so serious a breach of prison discipline," which might more readily be interpreted as supportive of prison discipline. Treating misbehavior during confinement as an unfavorable sign for parole success leads in most cases to the same decision that would be made if the order of the institution were the sole consideration.

Parole is only one of many sanctions used to maintain discipline in penal institutions. Violation of prison rules may result in denial of certain privileges or in solitary confinement. Repeated violations may result in a transfer of the inmate to a less desirable institution. In most states good time laws permit reduction of the maximum or minimum sentences, or both, as a reward for infraction-free conduct and permit revocation of reductions already given for discipline violations. In some states parole eligibility is contingent on the existence of no recent disciplinary infractions.[65]

That parole is used to support institutional discipline may reflect the failure of these other devices to provide the necessary controls. This may be particularly true of the good time laws. In some institutions it seems clear that good time laws have degenerated into automatic reductions of sentence, possibly as a result of heavy pressures from prison overpopulation, and thus have little, if any, effect on the conduct of inmates. A member of the Michigan parole board indicated that in practice the good time system has broken down and that it is an exception for an inmate to appear before the parole board who has not earned all possible regular and special good time. The board member indicated that in order to be denied good time an inmate would have to "spit in the warden's eye."

It is difficult to determine whether it is possible, assuming for the moment that it is desirable, to strengthen the other control devices enough to enable the parole decision to remain free of the necessity for its use as a disciplinary device. It is probably true that, assuming administration of the good time laws has resulted in their uniform application without regard to conduct, the parole decision is currently a necessary device for control within the institution. Certainly the Model Penal Code regards it as a proper use of parole because it authorizes a denial of parole when the inmate's

[65] See Chapter 9.

"release would have a substantially adverse effect on institutional discipline." [66]

3. *Minimum amount of time.*

> *Illustration No. 17:* The inmate, age twenty-two, had been convicted of unlawfully driving away an auto, for which he received two years' probation. After he had served twenty-one months on probation, it was revoked for failure to report, failure to pay costs and restitution, and involvement in an auto accident. The judge imposed a prison term of six months to five years, stating to the inmate that he would probably be back home in about four and one-half months. He spent two months at the main prison and was then transferred to the prison camp where he had served almost a month by the time of his parole hearing. The camp recommended a short continuance of the case on the ground little was known about the inmate. Most of the hearing was consumed by the parole board attempting to explain to the inmate that he had been in the institution "too short a time for the offense" and, further, that the institution knew little about him. The board explained it could not conscientiously recommend parole for him in light of its lack of knowledge of his case. The case was continued for discussion in executive session.

A problem some parole boards must frequently face occurs when an inmate appears for his initial parole hearing after he has served only a short period of time, normally under six months. Whatever the reasons, the parole board is likely to be quite reluctant to give serious consideration to the case until the inmate has served more time. The normal disposition when such a case appears is to schedule a rehearing, or sometimes only a conference in executive session, in several months, at which time the decision to grant or deny parole will be given usual consideration.

Because of its sentencing structure, the problem is particularly noticeable in Michigan. There, the maximum sentence for most offenses is fixed by statute but the judge has discretion to set any minimum sentence he wishes.[67] Regular and special good time are deducted from the judicially set minimum to determine parole eligibility,[68] and the inmate normally receives his first parole hearing one or two months before he becomes eligible for parole. As a result, when the judge sets a minimum sentence of six months, the inmate is eligible for parole after he has served about four

[66] Model Penal Code §304.9(1)(c) (Proposed Official Draft, 1962).
[67] Mich. Stat. Ann. §28.1080 (1954).
[68] See Chapter 9.

months, and he appears for his first parole hearing after he has served only three months. The typical disposition of such cases is a continuance for six months or a year, at which time he will be given usual parole consideration.

It is possible, of course, to have a judicial minimum system that does not as readily lead to the difficulties experienced in Michigan. Under the judicial minimum system proposed in the Model Penal Code, the judge may not set the minimum sentence at less than one year.[69] With the necessary allowances for deducting good time and scheduling the hearing a month in advance of parole eligibility, this would normally result in an inmate's not receiving his first parole hearing before he has served nine months.

A potential problem of the same type was handled by parole board policy in Kansas and Wisconsin. There, inmates of the reformatories and women's prisons are by statute eligible for parole as soon as they arrive at the institution.[70] In each state, the inmate, although statutorily eligible for parole immediately, does not normally receive his first parole hearing until he has served nine or ten months of his sentence. This doubtless reflects a judgment that about that much time is necessary before it makes sense to consider the question of parole.

While there seems to be a consensus that a minimum amount of time, probably between nine months and one year, is necessary before serious consideration should be given to parole, there is lack of agreement as to why this is true. One reason given is that the institution is incapable of having any rehabilitative effect on the inmate in less time. The assumption is that all persons sentenced to prison are in need of rehabilitation, which takes time, or at least that it takes time to determine whether they are in need of rehabilitation.[71] A related reason sometimes given is that the parole system and institution are incapable of formulating sound post-release programs for inmates in less time. Further, parole boards sometimes contend that adequate parole information on the inmate cannot be obtained in less time and that, therefore, a short continuance is necessary in order to obtain information.[72] At other

69 Model Penal Code §6.06 (Proposed Official Draft, 1962).

70 See Chapter 9.

71 In one case the parole board denied parole to an inmate who had served only three months, commenting: "He has only been in the institution for three months and I believe this is too short a time to expect a change in him if it is possible for any change to occur in such an individual."

72 A similar basis exists for the provision that women misdemeanants may be committed to the Wisconsin Home for Women instead of local jails, but only if their sentence is six months or longer. Wis. Stat. Ann. §959.045(4) (Supp. 1967). An official in the Wisconsin Division of Corrections said that the six months require-

times, however, parole boards have indicated that a certain minimum time is necessary in order to justify the risk entailed by every decision to grant parole. The assumption in such cases is that the inmate has served such a short length of time that the parole board can afford to be more conservative in its release decision. Also implicit is the fear that if an inmate were granted parole after serving only four to six months and violated parole in a spectacular fashion, the parole board would be subject to more than the usual amount of criticism.[73]

4. *To benefit the inmate.*

Illustration No. 18: The inmate, a young man who appeared to be in his late teens, had come from what had been described as a "good home." He had two brothers, both of whom were ordained ministers, and his parents were respected members of the community. The inmate's father constantly demanded more of the inmate than the latter thought he had the ability to accomplish and continually compared him unfavorably with his older brothers. This comparison was also made by the inmate's school teachers because the inmate, although of high average intelligence, did rather poorly in school. Nevertheless, he had completed all but part of his senior year in high school by the time he had been sentenced to the reformatory. In its preparole summary, the classification committee of the institution recommended that the inmate be permitted to complete his high school education, on the grounds that it would aid him in the achievements of which he was capable. Some members of the parole board believed that if the inmate finished high school, he might go to college. The parole board decided to defer the case for five months to permit the inmate to complete his high school education prior to his release.

Cases sometimes arise in which it may appear to the parole board that a denial of parole would bring a benefit to the inmate that would be unobtainable if parole were granted. It is arguable, of course, that whenever the board denies parole because it believes the inmate has not reached the optimum time for release in terms of rehabilitation, this is, in reality, a benefit to the inmate. But there are other cases in which the benefit obtainable

---

ment exists because the board of parole and the institution could not develop enough information to formulate a program for them in less time.

[73] In denying parole to an inmate who had served only four months before the hearing, a parole board member commented: "There has not been a sufficient period of time to warrant the parole risk in this case."

only through a parole denial may be at least as real, but may have no direct connection with the inmate's rehabilitation. Perhaps the clearest examples are those in which the inmate is suffering from a physical illness that is correctable in the prison but which release to the community would aggravate, or those cases in which the inmate would benefit from devices, such as dental plates or a hearing aid, that could be provided at no cost to him if he remains an inmate but which may not be as readily obtainable on the outside. Illustration No. 18 is one in which the benefit accruing to the inmate by remaining in the institution is related both to his rehabilitation and to his more general welfare.

5. *To avoid criticism of the parole system.*

> *Illustration No. 19:* The inmate had been convicted of embezzling $25,000 from a veterans' service group. He had absolutely no prior criminal record. Before the offense he had been a prominent member of the community and was well liked. This was his initial parole hearing. When the parole board learned that, as a result of the offense, the attitude of the community was very much against the inmate, it voted to deny parole.

A feeling is shared among many parole board members that the success of the parole system depends in part upon whether it achieves public approval and confidence. In some states the parole board publishes literature on the parole system for the public, and members make speeches or give demonstrations of parole hearings to civic and social groups. The parole board may also invite community leaders to be present at parole hearings and observe how the board functions.

While a desire to remain free of adverse public criticism and to gain the confidence of the public is a characteristic common to all criminal justice agencies, the parole board seems to be particularly sensitive. Whatever the reasons for this concern, it is sometimes reflected in the parole decision. Parole boards are often reluctant to release assaultive offenders despite their own estimate of the high probability of parole success in individual cases.[74] One reason for this is the board's concern for the safety of the community; while the probability of recidivism may be low, the seriousness of the violation, if it occurs, is likely to be quite great. But another reason for the board's reluctance to release assaultive offenders is its concern over adverse public reaction if the offender violates parole in a spectacular manner.[75]

74 See pages 289-291.

75 One parole board member indicated that, although parole prediction studies

The concern about public criticism is even more clearly an important factor in trust violation cases. The parole board normally views public or private officials who have embezzled funds as good parole risks in terms of the likelihood of parole success. One parole board member even said he thought these persons should not be sent to prison since, because of the publicity usually surrounding their apprehension and conviction, they are very unlikely to repeat the same or similar offense. Nevertheless, the question whether they should be paroled raises the difficult problem of determining what weight the parole board should give to community attitudes. If the attitude of the community toward the inmate is good, he is likely to be paroled as soon as he is eligible. When the community attitude is negative, parole is likely to be denied. One reason may be that a negative community attitude is likely to seriously hamper the inmate's efforts to adjust in that community on parole.[76] Another reason, and probably the more important one, is that parole of such an inmate would expose the board and the parole system to adverse public criticism. One parole board member expressed his attitude toward the trust cases in terms of a dilemma, stating that to some extent a parole board must defer to certain community attitudes but that no parole board member can go beyond a certain point without violating his own conscience.

The board's concern with public criticism of the parole system also affects the parole decision in cases in which the inmate or a member of his family has attempted to put unusual pressure on the parole board for his release. This normally occurs in cases in which the inmate has received a long sentence, often a life sentence. The inmate may write letters to influential persons in state government or to anyone else whom he thinks might be able to influence the board. Sometimes, the inmate or his family hire attorneys whom they think have unusual influence with the board. The attitude of the parole board in such cases toward release of the inmate is likely to be extremely negative. In one case, a member of the board said that if a lifer who wrote great numbers of letters trying to get someone to influence the board would cease writing for six months, he would be released, but that so long as he persisted in his present behavior the board member is deter-

---

have shown that murderers, sex offenders, and men who have committed assaults are among the best parole risks, the fact remains that if one is paroled and repeats the same type of crime, the unfavorable publicity is many times that of a sixth forgery offender who is paroled and again forges checks.

[76] See page 277.

mined that he "does it all." [77] If the board were to grant parole to such an inmate on the merits of the case, it would expose itself to the accusation that the parole grant was the result of special influence. The board prefers to keep the inmate in prison rather than incur that risk.

[77] One parole board uses a special investigator to examine suspected attempts to secure parole through unethical pressure.

CHAPTER 12

Mandatory Release from Incarceration

The extent to which parole is used varies greatly from jurisdiction to jurisdiction.[1] Most inmates denied parole are released later when they attain the mandatory release date. Determining this date is important, especially in those states in which a relatively small percentage of inmates are paroled. Normally, the timing of mandatory release is regarded as a sentencing problem, because the mandatory release date is usually determined automatically once the maximum sentence has been selected. Also, whether mandatory release is conditional or unconditional is usually a legislative determination.

Although mandatory release decisions are normally made as part of the sentencing or legislative processes, in some instances they occur as part of the postsentencing correctional process. Three such decisions are of special importance: (1) the decision to advance the mandatory release date, and the implications of this practice for legislation prohibiting release on parole of certain inmates; (2) the decision to postpone the mandatory release date, and its implications for the problem of incarcerating the dangerous offender; and (3) the decision to grant an unconditional release when mandatory release is normally conditional, and its implications for the assumption that all inmates should be conditionally released. Each of these is discussed in this chapter.

A. Advancing the Mandatory Release Date

Illustration No. 1: The applicant was convicted of forgery and sentenced to a term of one to ten years. Since he had served two prior terms in a penitentiary, he was ineligible for parole. He would be unconditionally released at the expiration of ten years less good time, or about six years. He had al-

[1] Model Penal Code §6.09A, Comment (Tent. Draft No. 5, 1956), indicates that in 1954 the percentage of paroles of all releases from penal institutions varied from about 5 percent in South Carolina to 99 percent in Washington.

> ready served two years. The applicant's father was present to plead for commutation of the ten-year sentence. The pardon attorney told the applicant's father that he could not commute his son's sentence since he had not yet served sufficient time to warrant it. After the applicant's father left, the pardon attorney stated that the reason he denied commutation was that he had received letters from the sentencing judge and prosecuting attorney expressing opposition to it.

An inmate of a penal institution in Kansas, Michigan, or Wisconsin attains his mandatory release date when he has served his maximum sentence less allowances for good time. In all three states, the good time permitted by statute is routinely awarded and forfeitures of earned good time for misconduct in the institution are apparently rare. In most instances, determination of the mandatory release date follows automatically from selection of the maximum sentence. In Wisconsin, the trial judge has authority to select the maximum sentence within statutory limits. He normally does so, however, on the assumption that the offender will be paroled and, consequently, views the maximum as determining the length of time the offender will remain in prison and on parole. In certain types of cases, it seems clear to the trial judge, in Milwaukee at least, that the offender will not be paroled. In those cases he selects a maximum sentence that is considerably shorter than it otherwise would be on the assumption this is proper since the maximum in those cases determines release from incarceration rather than discharge from parole supervision.[2] The maximum sentence is set by the legislature for most offenses in Kansas and Michigan.[3] In practice, the legislative maximum appropriate to a particular defendant's provable criminal conduct is often not imposed because of an extensive system of granting charge reductions in exchange for guilty pleas. There is evidence defendants are motivated in substantial part to desire charge reductions out of fear of not receiving parole, perhaps because of misconduct within the institution,[4] and, hence, wish to attain an earlier mandatory release date.[5]

Although in most cases the mandatory release date follows automatically once the maximum sentence is selected and imposed, in an appreciable number of cases that date may be advanced at a later time. The mandatory release date may be advanced as an

[2] See Chapter 7.

[3] See Chapter 6.

[4] There is considerable evidence that if misconduct occurs within the institution the probability of a denial of parole is great. See Chapter 11.

[5] See Chapter 6 for a discussion of the effects of guilty pleas on sentences.

incidental consequence of advancement of the date of parole eligibility. Normally, the minimum sentence less good time determines the date of parole eligibility. In some cases the minimum, particularly if set by statute but even if set by trial judge, may seem to postpone parole eligibility unnecessarily. In such cases, it is not uncommon for commutation of sentence to be used to reduce the length of the minimum sentence in order to permit parole. It is normal under such circumstances to reduce the maximum sentences as well as the minimum sentence, thereby advancing the mandatory release date as well as the parole eligibility date.[6] If for some reason, such as subsequent misconduct in the institution, the inmate is not paroled when expected, he will be released when he attains his new mandatory release date.

Under other circumstances, advancement of the mandatory release date may be the primary motivation for commutation of sentence. Principal among these are cases in which a particular class of inmates is made ineligible for parole by statute.[7] One consequence of such a provision is the creation of added incentives to reduce the charge to one that carries the possibility of parole, in exchange, of course, for a plea of guilty.[8] But even if the defendant is imprisoned under such a statute, the mandatory release date may still be advanced through commutation of sentence. The Kansas practice under the so-called "three time loser" statute[9] prohibiting parole of any inmate who has served two prior terms in a penitentiary is illustrative. Even if the legislative maximum appropriate to the criminal conduct is reduced in exchange for a guilty plea, the sentence may seem unnecessarily long because of the impossibility of parole. As the illustration case indicates, it is regular practice in Kansas for such inmates to seek advancement of their mandatory release dates through commutation of sentence. The governor's pardon attorney, the official who actually makes the commutation decision, applies the same criteria used to advance parole eligibility — recommendations from the sentencing judge and prosecutor, whether or not the inmate se-

[6] See Chapter 9.

[7] The Model Penal Code indicates that in only fourteen states are there no statutory provisions excluding parole eligibility for certain inmates. Common provisions prohibit parole for inmates serving life sentences, for some habitual offenders, and for certain homicide offenders. See Model Penal Code §305.10, Comment (Tent. Draft No. 5, 1956).

[8] The effect of the twenty-year mandatory minimum sentence for sale of narcotics in Michigan on the charge reduction practices in Detroit supports the conclusion that one effect of a statutory exclusion of parole eligibility is greatly to increase the probability of a charge reduction to avoid the operation of the provision. See Chapter 6.

[9] Kan. Gen. Stat. §65-1529 (1949), repealed by Kan. Laws 1957, Ch. 331, §37.

cured a charge reduction in the disposition of his case, and a general judgment of the "risk" the inmate will pose when released.[10]

B. Postponing the Mandatory Release Date

Illustration No. 2: The inmate, a thirty-eight-year-old man, was originally sentenced to a term of five years under the Sex Crimes Act for sodomy and indecent behavior with a child. After serving one and one-half years he was paroled. He was under parole supervision for almost two years, but his parole was revoked because of a new offense of indecent behavior with a child. He was not prosecuted for the new offense. Since he would soon attain his mandatory release date, the Department of Public Welfare ordered extension of the maximum sentence as permitted by the Sex Crimes Act. In a hearing before the court that had originally sentenced him, the court concluded that the inmate posed a danger to society if released and confirmed a five-year extension of the maximum sentence.

The Wisconsin Sex Crimes Act[11] allows postponement of the mandatory release date if release of the offender at that time would pose a danger to society. Unlike most sex psychopath acts, which provide indefinite commitments, the Wisconsin Act permits the original commitment to be no longer than the maximum provided for the offense of which the defendant was convicted. The possibility of keeping the offender in prison is provided by permitting an unlimited number of five year extensions of the maximum sentence. The Department of Public Welfare may order an extension of the sentence, but this order must be reviewed by the court that originally sentenced the offender. The defendant has the right to a nonjury hearing, including the right to appointed counsel and the right to be examined by a doctor or psychiatrist of his own choosing.[12] If the court concludes that discharge of the offender "would be dangerous to the public because of the person's mental or physical deficiency, disorder or abnormality" it must confirm the Department's order.[13] This process may be repeated an unlimited number of times.[14]

[10] The Kansas pardon attorney also refuses to commute the maximum sentence of an inmate against whom there are detainers outstanding. For a more complete discussion of the criteria used to make the commutation decision, see Chapter 9.

[11] Wis. Stat. Ann. §959.15 (1958).

[12] Wis. Stat. Ann. §959.15(14)(a) (1958).

[13] Wis. Stat. Ann. §959.15(14)(b) (1958).

[14] Wis. Stat. Ann. §959.15(15)(a) (1958). Wis. Stat. Ann. §959.15 (15)(c) (1958) provides: "During any such period of extended control, but not oftener than semiannually, the person may apply to the court for a reexamination of his mental condition and the court shall fix a time for hearing the same." Wis. Stat. Ann.

In practice, extension of the maximum sentence has been used in only a small percentage of all sex deviate cases.[15] Much of its use involves inmates who have been paroled but whose parole has been revoked because of the commission of a new sex offense. In such cases, as in Illustration No. 2, the commission of the offense for which parole was revoked forms the basis for the judicial finding of dangerousness. Sometimes, extension of the maximum sentence may be used as an alternative to prosecution, conviction, and sentencing for the new offense. In other cases, the maximum may be extended for persons who have never been released on parole or it may be extended to increase the duration of the parole period for persons presently on parole.

The process of postponing the mandatory release date has significance for discussion concerning sentencing the dangerous offender. This problem has received attention in both the Model Penal Code[16] and the Model Sentencing Act.[17] The basic issue is whether dangerous offenders can be identified and, if so, what safeguards are necessary in the process of permitting longer periods of incarceration for such offenders. The problem has normally been regarded as one of sentencing. Therefore, it is thought necessary to identify the dangerous offender and set the long maximum sentence at the sentencing stage, at the very beginning of the correctional process. Current practice on the nonuse of such comparable devices as habitual offender statutes, consecutive sentencing provisions, and sex psychopath legislation[18] indicates that trial judges are often unwilling to make the decision necessary to permit long-term incarceration at such an early stage. This may stem from uncertainty as to whether knowledge of human behavior permits identification of dangerous offenders to be made with as much accuracy as needed for these purposes.

It seems clear that use of extended terms for dangerous offenders could be increased if the trial judge did not have to make the entire decision at the relatively early sentencing stage. If he could simply make a finding of dangerousness and sentence the offender to a term of normal length, but provide for later extensions of

---

§959.15(16) (1958) allows appellate review of trial court proceedings involving extension of the maximum sentence.

[15] A Wisconsin parole official reported that, while from June 30, 1951, through June 30, 1954, a total of 199 offenders were committed as sex deviates; in only 12 of those cases was the maximum sentence extended.

[16] Model Penal Code §§6.07, 7.03 (Proposed Official Draft, 1962).

[17] National Council on Crime and Delinquency, Model Sentencing Act §§5, 6 (1963).

[18] See Chapter 7 for a discussion of the sentencing practices under habitual criminal statutes, provisions for consecutive terms for multiple offenders, and sex psychopath legislation.

the maximum sentence, use of these provisions might increase. The finding of dangerousness at the sentencing stage would permit a limited number of extensions of the maximum sentence based on findings of dangerousness at the time each extension is sought. This would permit the mandatory release date to reflect the offender's conduct and attitude in prison and on parole, and remove the difficulties of making the decision at the sentencing stage.

C. The Decision to Grant an Unconditional Mandatory Release

Illustration No. 3: The inmate appeared before the parole board and asked for an "unconditional release discharge" instead of conditional release. His mandatory conditional release date was the following month and, if he were conditionally released at that time, he would have about eleven months of parole supervision. The inmate stated that he could not successfully complete the supervision period and objected to a parole officer prying into his personal affairs. The parole board denied his request for unconditional release, stating that parole supervision, even if it does nothing else, might be used to force the inmate to support his minor children, so at least they would benefit from it.

Under the Wisconsin conditional release law, an inmate who has served his maximum sentence less allowances for good time must be conditionally released from prison. When released he is placed under parole supervision and subject to reincarceration for violation of any of the parole conditions. He is required to remain on supervision following conditional release until he has served his maximum sentence without good time allowance, unless discharged earlier by the Department of Public Welfare.[19] The Department has authority to release an inmate unconditionally when he attains his conditional release date.[20] In practice, this decision is made by the parole board.[21]

[19] Wis. Stat. Ann. §53.11(7) (1957). The Wisconsin conditional release law does not apply to inmates incarcerated for crimes committed prior to the effective date of the act in 1951 nor to juvenile delinquents incarcerated in the Wisconsin reformatory.

[20] Wis. Stat. Ann. §53.11(7)(a) (1957).

[21] The parole board's recommendation for conditional release dicharge must be approved by the Director of the Department of Public Welfare but, in practice, approval is only very rarely withheld. Wisconsin State Department of Public Welfare, Parole Board Procedures and Practices 19 (1963), states: "If a parole applicant is within a year of his conditional release date and the Board elects to defer him to this date, it may also decide to recommend to the Director of the Department of Public Welfare that discharge of the case be effected on the conditional release

The so-called conditional release discharge is used by the parole board in one major type of case. In a number of instances, the parole board is faced with an inmate who is not a Wisconsin resident and who wishes to return to his home state when released from prison. The usual procedure in such cases is to seek the home state's agreement to accept supervision of him upon release, which sometimes involves considerable difficulty and delay.[22] If the inmate violates parole in the sister state, Wisconsin must go to considerable difficulty, often involving a sizeable expenditure of funds, to return him to a Wisconsin correctional institution. In some of these cases, the inmate is denied parole and, therefore, must be released upon reaching his mandatory conditional release date. If his original maximum sentence was fairly short, as is often the case under the Wisconsin judicially set maximum sentence system, the period of parole supervision following release will last only a matter of several months. In such cases, the parole board feels it is not worth the difficulty of securing out-of-state supervision and incurring the risks of parole violation in order to obtain for the inmate the benefits of a short period of parole supervision. In many of these cases, therefore, the parole board elects to release the inmate unconditionally when he reaches his mandatory release date. Members of the board indicated, however, that they never grant a conditional release discharge to an inmate who has had a history of assaultive behavior.

The assumption is often made that every inmate released from prison should be conditionally released and placed under supervision.[23] And, this is the premise upon which the Wisconsin conditional release law is based. As the practice indicates, however, there are a few instances in which the benefits of post-incarceration supervision may not be sufficient to justify the difficulties it entails. This is a practical limitation on attaining the stated ideal that all inmates should be released conditionally.

---

date. The Director of the Department of Public Welfare approves or disapproves orders for discharge just as he does orders for parole."

22 Out-of-state parole supervision is often effected through compacts entered into by the several states, e.g., Wis. Stat. Ann. §57.13 (1957).

23 Model Penal Code §6.09A, Comments (Tent. Draft No. 5, 1956), which provides for mandatory conditional release, states: "The draft thus proceeds on the view that conditional release on parole, with its accompanying supervision, is a normal and necessary phase in the transition from prison life to full freedom in the community; and that it should, therefore, be the invariable incident of any long-term prison sentence, not an exceptional act of grace bestowed on 'good risks' and withheld from the bad."

CHAPTER 13

Parole Conditions and Supervision

This chapter considers the decision-making processes involved in selecting and imposing parole conditions and the nature of parole supervision in current practice. Revocation of parole is considered separately in the following chapter.

A. Parole Conditions

Parole conditions are of such broad coverage that most parolees are unable to avoid violating at least one of them during the supervisory period. If the appropriate officials had knowledge of all the parole violations that occur, virtually every parole could be revoked at one time or another. Even when consideration is limited to violations of which parole officials have knowledge, revocation could occur in the great majority of cases.[1] Often vague and moralistic, parole conditions may seem oppressive and unfair to the parolee. Parole officers sometimes experience difficulty in convincing parolees they really must conform their behavior to the parole conditions when many violations are excused.[2] Although parole conditions impose numerous behavior requirements, their administration is characterized in large part by nonenforcement.

Some parole conditions are not intended to be enforced. They are statements of behavior ideals couched in vague terms, indicating an exhortation of good behavior rather than specific rules that

[1] A Michigan parole officer estimated that if the paroles of all known violators were revoked, the revocation rate would be 70 or 80 percent of all parolees. A Wisconsin parole official stated there was probably no parolee who could live up to all the conditions of parole and that minor transgressions might be expected during the parole period. Indeed, he stated that probably every parole would be revoked at one time or another if every single known violation was a matter for revocation.

[2] A Michigan parole officer stated that parole conditions prohibiting the drinking of intoxicants or associating with other parolees are not enforced because they are unrealistic. A Wisconsin parole officer stated that prohibiting the possession of hunting weapons by parolees in the hunting areas of the state is unrealistic.

are susceptible of being followed. Such conditions are regarded as helping the parolee to see what his ultimate personal goals should be, and it appears that they are not intended to provide a basis for revocation of parole.

A major purpose of parole conditions is maximization of control over the parolee by his parole officer. They are drawn to cover any contingency that might occur; the great fear is that a need may arise for a parole condition that has not been imposed. Parole conditions are both comprehensive in requirements and flexible in administration. This result is achieved by using, in addition to a general parole agreement, special parole conditions imposed by the parole board on a case-by-case basis, special conditions imposed by the parole officer, authority in the parole officer to waive certain parole conditions, and discretion in the parole officer not to seek revocation despite sufficient evidence of violation of a condition.[3]

1. *The parole agreement.* It is customary for an inmate who is paroled to sign a parole agreement, which is a document specifying the conditions of his release and including any special conditions that may have been imposed by the parole board.[4] The Wisconsin parole agreement is as follows:

PROBATION AND PAROLE AGREEMENT

In consideration of Probation or Parole being granted me, I agree to the following:

1. I will make a sincere attempt to avoid all acts which by law are contrary to public welfare or my own best interests.
2. I will, to the best of my ability, take advantage of the opportunities offered me by probation or parole; I will practice temperance, conduct myself honestly, and assume my obligations as a citizen and as a member of the community in which I will live.
3. I will keep the Probation and Parole Officer informed of my whereabouts and activities at all times and I will submit such reports as may be required.
4. I will secure advance approval from the Probation and Parole Officer in writing, if practicable, if at any time I wish to:

[3] Parole may be conditional in two senses. Often the parole board grants parole but conditions actual release upon certain contingencies, such as suitable job and home placement or willingness by the inmate to return to his state of origin. To the extent such conditions are significant in current administration, they are discussed in Chapter 11. The parole conditions discussed here do not determine whether, or when, an inmate will be released but instead determine the circumstances under which he can be reincarcerated.

[4] See pages 308-312.

a. Purchase or operate a motor vehicle.
b. Incur debts whether by borrowing money or installment buying.
c. Take on additional responsibilities, such as by marrying.
d. Change employment or place of residence.
e. Leave the state.
f. Own or carry firearms or other weapons.

5. I will be guided by such specific instructions as may be issued by the Probation and Parole Officer with regard to companions, hours, intoxicants, medical attention, family responsibilities and support of self, court obligations, or other special restrictions stated below.
6. If I prove myself unsuited to supervision, I will hold myself ready to be placed in the institution to which I was committed, returned to the court which placed me on probation, or to the institution from which I was paroled.

The Michigan parolee signs a similar parole agreement.[5] In addition to specifying the standard conditions of parole, the Michigan agreement designates the community to which the inmate has been paroled, the parole officer to whom he is assigned for supervision, and the length of the parole period. It also specifies the inmate's employer and place of residence.

2. *Special parole conditions.*

Illustration No. 1: The inmate, whose previous parole was revoked for breaking and entering in the nighttime, appeared before the board for reparole. Questioning by the board members revealed that the inmate had violated his parole during a period of unemployment and that his violation was partially due to drinking. The inmate admitted that his return to the institution was partly because of his drinking but stated he had gained some understanding of himself and had joined A.A. in an effort to control his drinking. The Board granted parole and imposed a special condition of no drinking, warning the inmate that any drinking at all would result in revocation.

Special parole conditions are formulated case by case and may be imposed either by the parole board before the inmate's release or by the supervising parole officer at any time during the parole period. There are few, if any, statutory limitations on the correctional agency's discretion in formulating and imposing special parole conditions. They permit individualization of parole conditions.

[5] The Michigan parole agreement is reproduced in 2 Gillespie, Michigan Criminal Law and Procedure §820 (1953).

Perhaps the special condition most frequently used by the Michigan parole board is, as in Illustration No. 1, the no-drinking condition. Although the Michigan parole agreement provides that the parolee shall not "use intoxicating beverages to excess," the parole board, when faced with an inmate who has a drinking problem, is likely to prohibit any use of intoxicants and to warn him that his parole will be revoked if any use is discovered. Similarly, although the parole agreement provides that the parolee shall not "use any narcotics or habit-forming drugs," the Michigan parole board invariably attaches the special condition that an offender previously involved with drugs in any way is not to associate with drugs users or peddlers. This is generally accompanied by an explanation such as "That means that if you are picked up in the company of anyone who is using, you are through — you understand that, don't you?"

The Michigan parole board uses special parole conditions for an inmate having family problems. In many cases, the offender has shown an inability or unwillingness to care for and support his wife or children. The parole board admonishes the offender to accept and discharge his obligation to his family during the parole period. When there are special problems, the board is quick to make the care and support of family a special condition of parole.[6] The use of a special parole condition under these circumstances is apparently viewed as a way of emphasizing the support obligation since a standard condition of parole provides: "I will provide for my family to the best of my ability." Similarly, if an inmate has a history of domestic disputes, the parole board may impose a condition of nonassociation, such as prohibiting the parolee from molesting his former wife [7] or living with his common law wife. [8]

[6] At a parole hearing an inmate was questioned about his marital status. He said that his wife would not let him see their child because he had not been providing regular support. He had heard that the court would arrange for him to see the child when he began making regular child support payments, and he indicated that he did not know the exact amount he was supposed to pay. A board member suggested that the parole officer be instructed to find out the amount the inmate was supposed to pay in support of his child. Parole was granted for eighteen months, with the special parole condition that the inmate support his child.

[7] In one case, for example, the inmate was paroled to the home of his father with the special condition that he was not to molest his former wife. Shortly after his release, he violated this special condition by visiting his former wife in the hope of a reconciliation. Although this was a direct violation of a special condition, the parolee was continued on parole, and, after the incident with his ex-wife, he requested a transfer to Detroit to live with his mother and stepfather.

[8] In one case the inmate was paroled with a special condition that he was not to live with his common law wife, by whom he had two children. He also had a wife and children living in the South, whom he had never divorced. Although he was forbidden from living with his common law wife, he contributed to the support of the children and was permitted to visit them.

Occasionally, the parole board uses special conditions to compel treatment of the parolee during his supervision period. This occurs only when the parole board views treatment as essential to parole success. Sometimes this involves continued medical treatment for a serious disability or deficiency, but more often it involves psychiatric counseling or special assistance with mental health problems.[9]

Although the Wisconsin parole board has authority to impose special parole conditions,[10] in practice it uses this authority infrequently because it believes that the standard conditions of parole are adequate to cover almost all situations.[11] The Special Review Board, the paroling authority under the Wisconsin Sex Crimes Act,[12] also has authority to impose special parole conditions. Even though resources are available for outpatient treatment or continued psychiatric care, the Special Review Board requires such treatment only in exceptional cases. Occasionally other conditions, such as no drinking, are imposed on certain parolees, particularly those who have a history of indecent liberties with children following a period of excessive drinking.

In both Michigan and Wisconsin when special parole conditions are imposed by the parole board, they affect the parole officer's discretion not to revoke parole. When a standard condition of parole is violated, the parole officer often handles the situation by measures short of seeking revocation.[13] If a special parole condition imposed by the parole board is violated, however, the parole

[9] A twenty-seven-year-old inmate was convicted of unlawfully driving an automobile and sentenced to serve one to five years. He had no previous adult convictions, but he had been in some trouble as a juvenile and had also been arrested for indecent liberties. At his parole hearing, one board member remarked, "The indecent liberties charge started as rape." The inmate's psychiatric report diagnosed him as a "passive-aggressive preschizophrenic." The inmate himself maintained that his weakness was gambling and that, if he could avoid gambling, he could stay out of trouble. A board member asked the inmate if he had ever talked with or visited his counselor or any of the psychologists. The inmate said he had not. The board member then asked him if he had ever talked to any of the custodial officers about his personal problems. The inmate said that he had not. The board member then said, "In the nearly two years you have been in here no one has talked to you about your problems, is that right?" The inmate said he had never discussed them with anyone. The board decided to parole him with a special condition that he have periodic interviews with a state psychiatrist.

[10] Wisconsin State Department of Public Welfare, Parole Board Procedures and Practices 19-20 (1963) provides: "The Parole Board upon recommending parole to the Director of the Department of Public Welfare may at the same time establish special conditions of parole. . . . The parole agent may, at any time, recommend to the Parole Board that such special conditions be modified or discontinued. Special conditions of parole determined by the Parole Board are typed on . . . the parole agreement . . . which is signed by the parolee prior to release."

[11] See pages 307-308.

[12] Wis. Stat. Ann. §959.15 (1958).

[13] See Chapter 14.

officer is much more likely to seek revocation.[14] The parole board may impose a special condition in order to limit the parole officer's discretion in particular problem areas of a case.[15]

At the sentencing stage, special probation conditions are frequently used to compel the payment of restitution to the victim of his crime.[16] A court may also require an expression of willingness to make restitution and evidence of financial ability to do so as a condition to granting probation in certain cases.[17] In neither Michigan nor Wisconsin parole practice, however, was there observed an instance of making restitution a special condition of parole, although it can be assumed that in many cases the victim has not been paid for his loss. The apparent reason is that, since the offender has served time in prison, rather than receiving probation, it would be unfair to impose restitution requirements upon him as a condition of parole. It is also likely that most inmates are unable to get the kind of employment which would enable them to support themselves and make restitution. However, there are cases where restitution could be made if required, and the fact that this condition is not imposed indicates that compensation to the victim is not a matter of concern to the parole board.

Parole officers in Michigan have authority to impose special conditions of parole. The administrative policy allowing the imposition of special conditions by the parole officer is as follows:

> At some time in dealing with an offender, it may be felt desirable to impose certain special restrictions or conditions relating to his activities. These are termed "Special Conditions." In some instances, the Parole Board may have entered them into the parole order at the time of granting the parole. In other cases, during the period of supervision, the parole officer may find certain of the parolee's activities that might well be curtailed or deterred by the addition of special conditions to the parole. In these cases, the parole officer may impose the conditions . . .
>
> Any conditions so imposed must be stated clearly and simply,

[14] Wisconsin State Department of Public Welfare, Parole Board Procedures and Practices 19-20 (1963) states: "In the event that these special conditions of parole are violated, parole *must* be revoked unless otherwise determined by the Parole Board." One parole official noted that, when the Wisconsin Special Review Board imposes a special condition, such as no drinking, the supervising parole officer takes this as "gospel" and is very likely to seek revocation if he discovers a violation of this condition.

[15] For example, it is apparent that the special support obligation imposed by the Michigan parole board does not enlarge upon the parolee's support obligations imposed by law or by the general parole conditions. The effect of restating the obligation as a special parole condition does, however, direct the attention of the parolee and the parole officer to the problem and makes it more likely that revocation will occur if the support obligation is not performed.

[16] See Chapter 4.

[17] See Chapter 3.

> and they must be acknowledged by the signature of the parolee. . . . Special conditions must be used sparingly, and only when a real need for them exists. They are not to be used as only a punitive weapon following a violation episode, or as only a threatening deterrent to future actions. They must be, rather, a definite part of the treatment plan, and imposed only when all parties concerned will understand their meaning and the reason for their implementation.[18]

In practice, a special condition is rarely imposed by a parole officer except as a response to a violation of a general parole condition. The most frequent basis for imposition of a special condition is excessive use of intoxicating liquors by the parolee, a violation of a general condition of parole. In such cases, the parole officer is likely to impose a "no-drinking" special parole condition.[19]

3. *Waiver of parole conditions.*

> *Illustration No. 2:* The parolee, a young man in his twenties, indicated to his parole officer that he wished to marry a sixteen-year-old girl. He and the girl had been dating for the entire six months since his release from the institution. The parole officer interviewed the girl, her mother, and the parolee in his office. The parole officer was informed that her parents were in favor of the marriage, and he concluded the young girl was a good influence on the parolee. The parole officer gave his consent to the marriage, but instructed the parolee he was not to marry until approval was secured from the central parole office.

Parole officers have authority to waive the applicability of certain general parole conditions. These conditions are specified in the Wisconsin [20] and Michigan [21] parole agreements. Requests for waivers are usually granted. Only a quick investigation by the parole officer and some delay are ordinarily required. As Illustration No. 2 suggests, permission to marry in Wisconsin normally

[18] Department of Corrections, Manual of Procedure for Michigan Parole Officers 45 (1954). The Michigan parole agreement provides: "I will live up to such special conditions of parole as are ordered by my parole officer."

[19] For example, in one case the supervising officer made the following parole violation report: "Despite the obvious violation of drinking to excess and moral laxity, further investigation has revealed that the subject was not the aggressor in the fight. Although his actions are not to be condoned, perhaps it would be too severe a penalty to return him to the institution at this time. A special condition will be imposed that the subject is to totally and absolutely refrain from the use of any alcoholic beverages . . . and the subject has been informed that any further violations of this nature will result in his return to the institution as a technical parole violator." Wisconsin parole officers also have authority to impose special parole conditions. See page 308.

[20] See pages 307-308.

[21] See 2 Gillespie, Michigan Criminal Law and Procedures §820 (1953).

involves interviewing the parties in the parole office, signing the appropriate forms, and securing approval from the district supervisor and the central office. In Michigan parole officers are directed to make the following inquiry when requested to grant permission to marry:

> 1. Are both the parolee and his prospective spouse legally free to marry?
> 2. Has the person been completely apprised of the parolee's criminal record?
> 3. Is he or she aware of the length of parole supervision and what same entails?
> 4. Some investigations should be made as to whether the prospective spouse has a criminal record; also if there are liable to be influences exerted by relatives which would have a tendency to disrupt marital harmony.
> 5. The reasons why the couple wish to marry should be determined as far as possible.
> 6. Lastly, it should be the parole officer's concern that there are sufficient finances so that disruption of marital harmony from this source will be minimized.[22]

In practice, the parole officer seldom refuses permission when informed by the parolee that he wishes to marry. The check made by the parole officer is usually limited to a determination that the future spouse is not already married or obviously engaged in criminal activity. Objection is not raised, for example, to marriage to a woman who is considerably younger than the parolee or who has a number of children.

In both Michigan and Wisconsin an adult parolee is usually given permission to purchase and operate an automobile if his doing so will not conflict with existing financial responsibilities. Such requests are routinely granted if the parolee has a valid driver's license and presents proof of adequate insurance coverage for property damage and personal liability. Youthful offenders are sometimes denied permission to purchase automobiles because of a belief that limitations on mobility result in fewer temptations to delinquency.

Both Michigan and Wisconsin prohibit a parolee from leaving the state without the permission of his parole officer. Wisconsin parole officers are authorized to grant permission for out-of-state visits for periods up to fifteen days; permission must be obtained from the central office for longer visits. Permission to leave the

[22] Michigan Department of Corrections, Manual of Procedure for Michigan Parole Officers 45 (1954).

state for such purposes as to attend a family funeral is freely given. The parolee must sign an "Agreement to Return from Other State," waiving his right to extradition.[23]

In the abstract, waiver of parole conditions and imposition of special parole conditions by the parole officer are clearly distinguishable. In the former case the conditions apply unless they are waived by the parole officer, while in the latter case no condition exists until it is imposed by the parole officer. In practice, however, the distinction is blurred. For example, Michigan prohibits association with other parolees without the parole officer's permission, while in Wisconsin "association" problems are handled by use of special parole conditions. In one Wisconsin case, however, the parolee wished to enter into business with another parolee and informed his parole officer of his desires. As applied to this situation, the Wisconsin parole agreement provided only that the parolee keep his parole officer informed of his activities and secure his permission before assuming additional responsibilities or changing employment. [24] The Wisconsin parole officer viewed this as an "association" problem, however, and presented the request to the central office in that light. Permission was granted for the parolees to enter into business together. In effect, this was a decision not to impose a special parole condition prohibiting such an association. Even when such practical problems are considered, however, there still remains an important distinction between waiver of conditions and imposition of special conditions by the parole officer: in the former instance, the range of possible conditions is specified in the parole agreement, while in the latter case there is no limit on the conditions that may be imposed.

Waiver of parole conditions and discretion not to enforce violations of parole conditions are closely related. As a general proposition, parole conditions that can be waived by the parole officer are considered of less importance than those that cannot be waived. This is reflected in the practice of readily granting waiver. But if waiver is not obtained, it is unlikely that revocation will result when a violation occurs, for the same reason. The view was commonly taken, for example, that the parole condition prohibiting firearms is impractical in Wisconsin where, at least in the northern areas, hunting is indigenous to the culture. As a result, permission is readily granted to obtain hunting weapons and, if permission is not sought, violations are usually excused.

23 Michigan also prohibits the parolee from leaving his county of residence without his parole officer's permission. In practice, permission is freely given to leave the county for such purposes as looking for work.

24 See pages 307-308.

4. *Discretion not to enforce parole conditions.*[25] An essential aspect of the operation of parole conditions in current practice is discretion not to revoke parole of known violators. Even with such individualizing features as special parole conditions and waiver of many general parole conditions, the range of behavior regulated by parole conditions is so broad that the entire system would be unworkable were it not for the exercise of discretion. Parole officials estimate that 70 to 100 percent of all parolees would be returned to correctional institutions if parole conditions were fully enforced. Officials respond to most violations with action short of revocation.

Ordinarily, parole officials do not view violations, other than the commission of crime, as significant in isolation, but only in relation to other violations and the entire "adjustment" of the parolee. They excuse numerous parole violations when revocation, for one reason or another, is not indicated, but use an accumulation of minor violations as a basis for revocation when that action seems indicated. Discretion not to revoke is used to accommodate the need for comprehensive coverage by parole conditions and their realistic administration.

5. *Communicating parole conditions to the offender.* In current practice parole officials expend considerable effort, before and after the offender's release from the institution, to communicate the conditions and requirements of parole to him. Most inmates paroled from Michigan correctional institutions are first transferred to the preparole camp where they live during the time between the parole decision and actual release to community supervision, normally less than thirty days. In the preparole camp they work in a conservation setting half-time and spend the remainder of the time in lecture and discussion sessions on such subjects as alcoholism, budgeting, family relationships, community resources, law enforcement, civil law problems, employment problems, and religion. Part of this lecture and discussion series is devoted to parole; a member of the parole staff meets with the men to discuss parole conditions, practices, and the attitudes of parole officers.[26]

[25] An extensive discussion of discretion not to enforce parole conditions appears in Chapter 14.

[26] The Michigan preparole camp is described in Kachelski, An Approach to Parole Preparation, 20 Fed. Prob. 29 (No. 2, 1956): "Although preparation for parole in the form of preparole schooling was being carried out in the state's penal institutions, no means existed to prepare the inmate for the abrupt environmental change he would encounter upon his release, nor could such preparation be made in a purely institutional setting. Furthermore, the usual preparole schooling primarily was directed toward acquainting the inmate with the purpose, conditions, and responsibilities of parole."

Before an inmate in Wisconsin is released on parole he has several sessions in a parole school. An official from the central parole office comes to the institution and conducts a session in which he explains the parole conditions. Each prospective parolee also has a private session with an institutional social worker in which the role of the parole officer and the parole conditions are explained in detail. Finally, the day before the inmate is released he is again counseled by an institutional social worker; the parole conditions are again discussed, and the inmate is told that if he needs help on any problem after release, he should seek it from his parole officer.

While the process of explaining and interpreting parole conditions to the offender continues throughout the period of supervision, it is especially important in the initial interview the parolee has with his supervising officer. The Michigan parole officers' manual gives the following advice with respect to the initial interview:

> This is one of the most important interviews of the entire parole. . . . The parole officer should make arrangements for interview to be conducted under conditions as ideal as possible and at the earliest possible moment after the parolee's release. Ideally, it should be unhurried, private, and in a comfortable place. In it, the misapprehensions and distortions the new parolee may have about parole and parole officers in general, or his parole officer in particular, may be dissipated or increased, depending upon the manner and attitude of the parole officer.
>
> The officer should remember that while such an interview is one of many similar ones for him, it may be the first such experience for the parolee. This meeting may determine the nature of the entire future relationship between the parole officer and the parolee. In it, it is advisable for the parole officer to go over all the conditions of parole, stressing those which seem most important to the individual situation. This is a good time, also, to review the parole program that has been arranged for the parolee. The parolee should be given a clear understanding of what he may expect and what is expected of him, and the interview should be terminated in such a manner that he will anticipate the next meeting with the parole officer.[27]

There is little indication that parole officers conduct their initial interviews for the purpose of developing a plan of supervision for the parolee. Instead, the initial interview serves most officers as a means of indoctrinating the parolee with the conditions of parole. One Michigan parole officer said that he "devotes as much as an hour to each new case in order to acquaint the parolee with

[27] Michigan Department of Correction, Manual of Procedure for Michigan Parole Officers 12-13 (1954).

the rules, regulations, and obligations of parole." He found it beneficial to have a thorough indoctrination period in the first interview to avoid disputes later as to what was expected of the parolee.

B. Parole Supervision

Parole conditions are the framework of the parole officer's authority over the parolee, but they do not tell him how to use that authority. Responsibility for administration is distributed among various officials. Important policy decisions are sometimes made from the central parole office; in the main, however, authority and responsibility rest with the parole officer individually or in concert with his immediate supervisor. By whomever made, supervision decisions are important to the parolee, the criminal justice system, and the entire community. At the same time, very little attention has been given to them, perhaps because they are less visible than other decisions in the correctional process, such as the decision to grant or deny parole or the decision to revoke parole.

Supervision objectives and techniques differ among the three states studied, and comparable differences no doubt exist in other states. There are also variations in practice in different areas of the same state. Primary attention is given here to supervision in the urban areas of the three states, principally in Detroit and Milwaukee. In the less populous areas parole supervision tends to be more personalized and the parole officer has fewer community resources at his disposal. These and other differences are noted as contrasts to the supervision process in metropolitan areas.

1. *The objectives of parole supervision.* In current practice, parole supervision is a control device to encourage behavior by the parolee that conforms to the requirements of law and of the parole conditions. It also serves a treatment purpose. The parole officer, acting as counselor himself or referring the parolee to psychiatric or other treatment resources, seeks to establish long-term lawful adjustment in the community through modification of attitudes or correction of mental problems. Parole supervision may also be used to perform services for the parolee or others, such as members of his family or his creditors.

Parole supervision objectives sometimes conflict with each other. This is particularly likely with respect to the control and treatment objectives:

> Parole supervision involves something other than surveillance. It is the final measure in a treatment process of an integrated cor-

> rectional system. It treats but does not immunize an individual against repeated criminal conduct. Through the utilization of social casework principles, it bridges the gap for the individual between the institution and the community. It can be the leavening ingredient in his efforts at personal reconstruction.
>
> The twin functions of . . . parole are the protection of society and rehabilitative service to the individual. The two are inextricably interwoven. Where a conflict of interests arises between the protection of society and the conduct of the individual, the former must, of course, prevail.[28]

The emphasis parole officers place on control or treatment is a measure of their attitudes about their jobs. This is expressed in the statement that a particular parole officer is "law enforcement" oriented or "social work" oriented. Michigan parole officers exhibit a wide range of attitudes, while parole officers in Wisconsin tend toward the social work orientation. A number of factors contribute to this difference. Recruitment policies in Wisconsin place great importance on graduate social work or behavioral science education, while those in Michigan do not. Also the caseloads are considerably smaller in Wisconsin, thus permitting greater implementation of treatment objectives.[29] Whatever accounts for differences such as these, the emphasis a parole system or individual officer places upon the various objectives of parole influences the techniques of parole supervision, its intensity, its policies and practices on parole revocation.

a. *Control.* One of the major objectives of parole supervision is the prevention of behavior that violates the criminal laws or conditions of parole.[30] The parole officer typically explains the parole conditions to his client, emphasizing those he considers particularly important and warning the parolee of the consequences of nonconforming behavior.[31] If a parole violation occurs, the parole officer may exercise his discretion not to revoke parole. In such an event, he is likely to take action to impress upon the parolee the seriousness of the violation and to deter him from further violations. Such actions range from reprimands and warnings through imposition of special parole conditions to periods of detention in the local jail.[32]

28 Wisconsin Division of Corrections, Bureau of Probation and Parole, Field Agents Manual, Ch. 1, §1.13 (Mar. 1, 1955).

29 See pages 332-333.

30 Generally, formal statements, whether appearing in professional journals or in parole officer manuals, tend to emphasize the treatment aspects of parole supervision, while observation indicates that in current practice the control aspects tend to receive emphasis.

31 See pages 315-317.

32 Discretion not to revoke parole, including actions of a disciplinary nature short of revocation, is discussed in Chapter 14.

The contacts between parole officer and parolee are significant instruments of control over the behavior of the parolee. Through written reports by the parolee, office interviews, and home and employment visits by the parole officer, the behavior of the parolee is subject to substantial surveillance. Contacts with the parolee's family and friends provide the parole officer with information on the parolee's personal and employment habits as well as whether he has reverted to criminal activity. In some instances, members of the parolee's family may volunteer information concerning the parolee's behavior.

Police agencies are important in the control of the parolee's behavior. Police consider a person previously convicted of crime a prime suspect for observation and investigation whenever a crime has been committed. Ex-convicts returning to the community in which they formerly lived, as many of them do, are subject to unusual scrutiny by the police, especially if that community is relatively small. If the former inmate is under parole supervision, moreover, police surveillance is likely to increase because the parole agency often notifies the local police of his presence, status, and background.

In all three states studied, the police are usually notified of the presence of parolees in their area. As part of the preparole investigation in Kansas, the parole officer obtains the local police or sheriff's comments about the inmate's parole plan. While the comments are uniformly in opposition to parole, and therefore of little use as parole information,[33] this procedure does provide notice that an inmate is being considered for parole and is expected to be in the area if he is released. The parole officer in Wichita provides the police with lists of local parolees about two or three times a year. The Kansas reformatory sometimes notifies the police of parolees released to their areas, but the penitentiary does not. It is the practice, however, for parole officers to notify the police of all out-of-state parolees who are coming into the area.[34]

The Detroit Police Department is notified of all inmates paroled to that city and it maintains a separate file of such parolees.[35] In one Michigan town, the local parole office and the police had an arrangement that out-of-state parolees would be photographed and

[33] See Chapter 10.

[34] Members of the Wichita Police Department complained that they receive no information on federal parolees in their area.

[35] The Michigan parole board may itself notify the Detroit Police Department in unusual circumstances. In one case, the parole board decided not to parole an inmate with a long record of sexual offenses. The inmate would, therefore, be released unconditionally at the expiration of his maximum sentence. The parole board arranged for notification to the Detroit Police Department at the time of release, since the inmate would probably return to Detroit.

fingerprinted at the police identification bureau. The police interpret this agreement to include all out-of-state parolees, while the local parole office contends that the arrangement is simply to provide them with basic indentifying material on out-of-state parolees from states that provide little or no information with the transfer of supervision. The local parole officer said that only about one-fourth of all out-of-state parolees are ordered to report to the police department.

The Milwaukee Police Department maintains a separate identification system for parolees. Each Wisconsin adult correctional institution sends the Milwaukee Police Department a photograph of every parolee released to supervision in the Milwaukee area. The Police Department maintains a separate gallery of these photographs.[36] The liaison parole officer in the Milwaukee office provides the police with a weekly list of all parolees coming into the Milwaukee area. The dates of release and expiration of sentence, the criminal record, and the address of each parolee are listed.[37] Parole officers in Wisconsin seem generally to favor notification to the police on the grounds it is necessary for community protection.[38]

Most parole officers felt that there was very little police harassment of parolees,[39] that the police did not often arrest parolees without adequate evidence, and that the supervising parole officer was usually notified quickly when one of his parolees was arrested. The parole officer in a rural Wisconsin district gives law enforcement officers in his area general authority to arrest any of his pa-

36 Each photograph has a color scheme marker on it, indicating the type of offense. A police official indicated that in the six months after the system was established four identifications were made.

37 Systems of notification have been developed in other Wisconsin cities on a local basis. In one city the parole officer requires all his parolees to report to the police department for fingerprinting and photographing. In another city the parole officer regularly sends lists of his parolees to the police and keeps these lists up to date. In still another city, the parole officer makes information on parolees available only to the detectives on the police force, because of prior experience with patrolmen using this information in casual conversation to demonstrate to friends knowledge of criminal activity.

38 The issue was discussed at a district meeting of parole officers in Wisconsin. While some parole officers feared that close cooperation with the police would make them policemen in the eyes of parolees, most of them favored a general system of notification, remarking that it is especially important in cases in which the parolee has never lived in the community before.

39 A Michigan parole officer reported that several years ago there was police harassment of parolees by certain young officers on the force, but that it has since ceased. It is uncertain what parole officers mean by the term "harassment." One parole officer said there was no police harassment, then told of a case in which a parolee was arrested on no evidence, held for in-custody interrogation, and finally confessed after he was threatened with revocation of his parole if he did not cooperate by taking a lie detector test. For discussion of use of the probation or parole hold for police investigative purposes, see LaFave, Arrest: The Decision to Take a Suspect into Custody 360-363 (1965).

rolees without specific evidence of parole violation. He stated that he would revoke the "authority" if it were ever abused and generally regarded this as a proper method for investigation and even prevention of crime.[40]

b. *Treatment.* While maximization of control over the parolee is one reason for legislative delegation of broad discretion in setting parole conditions and revoking parole, another reason, perhaps equally important, is the creation of opportunities for effective treatment of the parolee. Literature on parole supervision regards the parole officer more as a treatment worker than a control agent. The treatment ideal expressed in the literature may be realized in practice depending upon such factors as the size of the caseloads, the agency's personnel qualifications and recruitment policies, and the availability of ancillary treatment resources. In a particular parole system, "treatment" may involve some or all of the following: personal counseling by the parole officer, referral for psychiatric treatment, or use of specialized therapy resources for narcotic addicts or alcoholics. In some parole systems, treatment, as that term is used here, may simply not exist.[41]

Parole officers in Detroit do very little personal counseling.[42] Perhaps one reason for this is the availability of the psychiatric clinic. This clinic, which has been in existence for over eighteen years, is held twice a month in the Detroit district parole office. Three psychiatrists from a state mental hospital interview and examine parolees. On the day on which observations were made, twenty-one parolees were interviewed at the clinic. Most psychiatric examinations performed by the clinic are diagnostic, although some parolees appear regularly for "therapeutic interviews." After interviewing the parolee, the psychiatrist discusses

[40] As an example of the latter, the parole officer cited a case in which a parolee had a history of assault against his former wife. He worked on a boat on the Great Lakes. One weekened he returned to town intoxicated. A police officer, having knowledge of the man's background, arrested him for parole violation and held him until Monday morning when he was placed on a bus to return to work. The parole officer felt this probably prevented a recurrence of the assaults against the parolee's former wife.

[41] In Kansas, for example, parole officers did virtually no personal counseling and the only ancillary treatment resource known to be used was a chapter of Alcoholics Anonymous in Kansas City.

[42] In one of the few instances of counseling observed, the parole officer attempted to persuade his Negro client, who lived and worked in an all-white neighborhood, to attend a Negro church. He did this in the belief that meeting and associating with people of his own race would help the parolee control his alcohol problem. In another case, a parole officer stated that he was encouraging a young police detective in his efforts to persuade a parolee, in whom he had taken special interest, to avail himself of psychiatric resources. He said he did this because the police officer seemed to relate to the parolee better than he did.

the case with the supervising parole officer and makes recommendations to him. If extensive treatment seems warranted, the parolee may return to the clinic several more times or may be referred to the outpatient clinic at the hospital. In some of the more difficult cases, the psychiatrist may recommend a diagnostic commitment to the state hospital for a period of sixty days.[43] During this time a decision is made whether to commit the parolee indefinitely to a state mental hospital.

Criteria for referring cases to the clinic are not clearly established. A parole officer may notice behavior of a parolee that seems to him evidence of an emotional disturbance warranting commitment to an institution. In some cases the parole officer may spend considerable time persuading the parolee to attend the psychiatric clinic.[44] No case was observed in which attendance was ordered, but authority to do so is implicit in the parole officer's advice.

The narcotics clinic in Detroit serves primarily as a diagnostic facility for the courts, but it is occasionally used as a treatment resource by parole officers. If a parole officer discovers narcotics use by one of his parolees,[45] he may refer him to the narcotics clinic

43 In one case the psychiatrist made the following summary and recommendation: "The patient does considerable drinking, is physically abusive of his wife, and I feel he needs institutional care at the present time, which might either be hospital or prison. His wife does not want him returned to the prison because she feels that will be of little benefit and she is considering commitment to the state hospital. Certainly one of these two courses of action should be taken. If he is not committed to the hospital, then I feel he should be returned to prison as a parole violator."

44 In one case, although the parolee had a history of being extremely resentful of anyone in authority, the parole officer was able, after several months, to gain his confidence, and the parolee frequently and voluntarily visited the parole officer whenever problems arose. He lost several jobs because of arguments with his superiors and finally came to realize that his quick temper and hostility to those in authority were causing him a great deal of trouble. The parole officer was able to convince him that he should take advantage of the psychiatric treatment available in the outpatient clinic of the state hospital. Although he first resisted psychiatric treatment, he finally became a voluntary patient.

45 One of the problems is gaining the confidence of the parolee so that he will speak frankly about whether he is using narcotics. In one case, during a home visit the parole officer emphasized that, if the parolee was using narcotics, the only way he could help himself would be to confide in him and seek his help. The parolee denied he was using narcotics. The parole officer left but returned later in response to a telephone call from the parolee. He was told that, after his visit, the parolee and his wife had a serious discussion about his narcotics use and decided to confide in the parole officer while there was still relatively little narcotics use. The parole officer told them he would discuss the matter with the district supervisor and suggested that one way to help was for the parolee voluntarily to request treatment at the narcotics clinic. The parolee agreed to this, and the same day the parole officer went to the narcotics clinic and made an appointment for the parolee. Checking with the clinic by telephone later, the parole officer learned that the parolee had kept the appointment and was scheduled to return for another session.

for psychiatric diagnosis and treatment instead of revoking parole.

In Wisconsin treatment objectives are implemented more through personal counseling by the parole officer than in Michigan but less use is made of psychiatric resources. Initial contact by the parole officer begins prior to the parole decision. At the time an inmate is committed to an institution, he is assigned to a parole officer for "institutional supervision." The institutional visiting program is designed to give the officer who eventually will supervise the offender an opportunity to establish initial contact, develop rapport, and assist the inmate in planning for his eventual release. At the time he is assigned an inmate, the parole officer receives all information the Department of Public Welfare has about the case; the presentence or institutional investigation, institutional material, such as psychological or social service reports, and chronological histories. He receives additional reports as they become available.[46] Each parole officer is expected to visit his institutionalized cases periodically.[47]

In institutional visits observed, the parole officers counseled inmates concerning their use of time in the institution and special problems. Parole officers do not attempt to contact every case assigned to them at each visit. Usually, the inmates expected to be paroled in the near future are interviewed; others are interviewed periodically for continuity of contact. An inmate is transferred to the parole officer's active supervision caseload when he is released on parole. By this time the parole officer is expected to have established rapport and to have assisted him in developing an adequate plan for parole release.

The Field Agents Manual emphasizes the importance of the casework interview in the supervision of offenders:

> It is commonly accepted that skill in interviewing is a basic and essential tool of the agent in treatment of the offender. Development of this skill is dependent upon the basic knowledge of the theory of interviewing combined with the experience and personality makeup of the interviewer.
>
> In . . . parole, there are two general classes of interviews — the diagnostic interview and the treatment interview. The initial diagnostic interviews are primarily for the purpose of obtaining information regarding the client's background and developmental history. The objectives of the treatment interview are to help the client find a solution to his problems and to assist him to make an acceptable adjustment to society. In all interviewing

[46] A detailed description of the information available concerning an inmate appears in Chapter 10.

[47] Parole officers in Milwaukee County visit one institution a month for this purpose.

> the agent should be aware of establishing rapport and building a mutually satisfactory relationship with the client. All interviews should be planned by the agent and have predetermined objectives.
>
> Interviews shall be held in privacy and every effort should be made to avoid disturbance during this time. All information revealed by the client during the interview shall be confidential insofar as practical and consistent with the interests of society.[48]

The parole officers are intensely concerned with their relationships with parolees and attempt to carry out the casework objectives of the agency. The concern with treatment is strong enough that, when a parolee is in contact with another social agency, the parole officer may withdraw from counseling if a worker from the agency appears to have better opportunities for success.[49]

Psychiatric resources are used infrequently, although parolees committed under the Sex Crimes Law may occasionally receive psychiatric treatment from a state psychiatrist. In some instances, arrangements are made for sex deviate parolees to receive psychiatric treatment from a private psychiatrist at rates the parolee can afford.

c. *Services.* Parole supervision may include such services as helping the parolee find a job, referring him to a social service agency for help with domestic difficulties, providing medical or financial assistance, or helping him meet his obligations to creditors. Services of this kind are not part of the over-all control and treatment objectives of parole supervision but can be viewed as isolated efforts to help the parolee with specific problems and to diminish the likelihood of antisocial responses to those problems. This objective of parole supervision has an obvious relation to the other objectives.

In Michigan the most frequent type of service is helping the parolee obtain employment. Normally this is done by referring him to the Michigan State Employment Service, for only in rare instances is a parole officer able to find desirable employment for a parolee through direct contact with an employer. Another service commonly offered is helping the parolee obtain a loan from the prison prior to his release. There are inmates who have insufficient funds in their institutional account and lack other sources from which they may borrow money to sustain them-

[48] Wisconsin Division of Corrections, Bureau of Probation and Parole, Field Agents Manual, Ch. 3, §3.7 (Nov. 23, 1955).

[49] In one case, for example, a woman parole officer encouraged a private caseworker, employed by an agency to which the parolee's children were committed, to play an active role because the relationship between the parolee and this worker appeared to be a better one.

selves until they receive their first pay check. In such cases the parole officer arranges a loan, and it becomes his responsibility to be sure the parolee makes regular payments. Parolees are warned that, if the loan is unpaid at the time for termination of parole supervision, they will be kept under supervision until it is repaid.

In Wisconsin, as in Michigan, employment problems are normally dealt with by referring the parolee to the State Employment Service, since again it is only occasionally that a parole officer can obtain employment for parolees directly. Other services by Wisconsin parole officers are comparable to those provided in Michigan. For example, a parolee whose wages had been assigned to the Division of Corrections was loaned thirty dollars by his parole officer when the regular allowance check did not arrive as scheduled from central parole headquarters; a parole officer picked up the personal effects of a parolee held by a landlord in lieu of rent because he did not wish the parolee to return to his former place of residence, where he had experienced difficulties; a woman parole officer drove a young woman in her automobile to enroll for public assistance.

Wisconsin parole officers often use a wage assignment procedure for parolees in substantial debt who seem unable to budget their expenditures. Under this arrangement, the parolee agrees to have his wages paid by his employer to the Division of Corrections. His wages are then disbursed according to a budget to pay the debts, to meet new obligations, and to give the parolee a small allowance.[50] Parole officials emphasized that in no case is the wage assignment imposed as a parole condition. Although the wage assignment is in a strict sense voluntary, officials could remember only one parolee in recent years who had refused a wage assignment when it was suggested. They explained that parolees usually understood that the wage assignment was a method of getting creditors "off their backs" and normally viewed it as being advantageous.

When a woman parolee is pregnant with an illegitimate child, the normal procedure in Wisconsin is for the Division of Corrections to contract for hospital care in a private institution or in the state's general hospital. After birth, the child is normally placed in custody of the state or county welfare department for foster home care. The mother is then usually urged to relinquish

[50] In one case, while the parolee was incarcerated, his wife charged numerous items to his account and then divorced him. She since had remarried but the parolee was faced with responsibility for paying the bills. The parole officer stated that the parolee came to him and asked for help because he could not meet his obligations. The parolee agreed to a wage assignment.

the child for adoption. Male parolees who are fathers of illegitimate children sometimes face paternity actions, typically when the mother has sought public assistance. The father in such instances becomes subject to arrest and detention pending the hearing. The Division of Corrections obviates the arrest by guaranteeing the parolee's appearance at the hearing, thus preventing the loss of employment and other adverse effects of arrest.

2. *The techniques of parole supervision.* The objectives of parole supervision depend for their implementation largely upon personal contact between the parole officer and the parolee and other persons close to him. One important aspect of that personal contact is the frequency with which the parole officer sees his caseload;[51] another is the setting in which personal contact occurs. Here as in other aspects of parole supervision, there are major differences between formal statements and current practice.

a. *Home and employment visits.* In Michigan the Department of Corrections emphasizes the value of the home visit as a "treatment" technique in parole supervision:

> There is no substitute for a home call and no more revealing visit can be made during the parole. The observant parole officer may learn more about the parolee's general behavior and attitude during home calls than from any other type of visit. The physical condition of the home and appearance of its members, the manner with which the parole officer is received, feeling of the members toward one another and toward the parolee are valuable items to be noted. It is not sufficient, in recording these visits, for the parole officer to report simply what the parolee and the family or landlord say and do. More important, what the parole officer says and does to create or to perpetuate a helpful situation and attitude should be described also.
>
> It may be well for the parole officer to occasionally visit the parolee's room in the residence to observe its contents and general appearance.[52]

In practice, the home visit most frequently serves as a means of obtaining information on the parolee's compliance with the conditions of his parole. It implements the predominant parole supervision objective in Michigan — control of the parolee. The frequency of home visits is in practice left to the discretion of the parole officer. The Department of Corrections recommends that such visits be made on a monthly basis at the start of parole and, if all goes well, subsequently on a quarterly basis.[53] The district

51 See pages 332-333.

52 Michigan Department of Corrections, Manual of Procedure for Michigan Parole Officers 15 (1954).

53 Id. at 16.

supervisor of the parole office in Detroit stated that home visits are supposed to be made every two months but, with the large caseloads and the difficulty of finding anyone at home during daytime hours, this requirement is largely overlooked in practice. A Detroit parole officer stated that, although regular home visits are required as a matter of policy, parole officers can omit them without difficulty from superiors. Most officers, he continued, can justify omitting home visits because of the size of their caseloads and the pressure of other work, such as completing preparole investigations and dictating violation reports. This officer stated that these two duties, because they must be completed in a limited time, take precedence over routine home visits and, as a consequence, the home visits are often overlooked for long periods of time. Despite the lack of conformity to home visit policies in Detroit, however, routine home visits do occur and other visits are sometimes made for special purposes.

> *Illustration No. 3:* At about 10:00 A.M. the parole officer called at the home of a twenty-three-year-old-man released on parole two months previously after serving a term for breaking and entering in the nighttime. The parolee had a history of narcotics addiction. He answered the door and his appearance showed that he had hastily put on a pair of pants. The parole officer asked him what he was doing in bed at this hour since he should be looking for work. The parolee said he had worked the day before at a car wash rack but did not go to work today because it was raining. The officer said he should be out looking for a better job. When asked if any of his friends had called him, the parolee stated he is not having anything to do with them. The parole officer said, "If any of them calls on you, don't even answer the door. You know what will happen if you get with them and get hooked again." The parolee replied that he was "off the stuff" and did not want anything to do with his old companions. The parole officer told the parolee that he did not want to find him "in the sack" when he called again at a time when he should either be working or looking for work. After leaving the apartment, the parole officer said, "You can bet if he had known I was coming he would have been dressed and would have claimed he just came in from looking for a job."

When routine home visits are made in Detroit their usual purpose is simply to secure information about the behavior of the parolee, especially whether he is conforming to the parole conditions. This information may be secured from the parolee himself or his relatives or landlord. Typically, routine home visits occur when the parole officer must be in the neighborhood to conduct preparole investigations. In such instances parole officers find it convenient also to make a home visit.

The parole officer reviews the parolee's file immediately before visiting the home to familiarize himself with the important problems in the case. During the home visit he questions the persons there about the parolee's progress in handling these problems. The visit is normally concluded with a warning by the parole officer concerning the parolee's behavior. Cases were observed, for example, in which warnings were given about securing and keeping steady employment, moderation in use of alcohol, return to use of narcotics, association with former friends, frequenting places in which trouble occurred, and keeping reasonable hours. If no one is found at the parolee's place of residence, the parole officer leaves his card to indicate that a visit was made. If the parolee is not present and the parole officer talks to a relative or the landlord, he is likely to solicit the cooperation of that person in reporting any violations of parole conditions to the parole officer. In one case, for example, the parole officer asked the parolee's sister to keep him informed of her brother's behavior and assured her that he would not let the parolee know about any information she gave him. He explained that he needed to be aware of any tendency on the parolee's part to violate a condition before it was too late to do anything for him. The sister said she understood and would cooperate.[54]

> *Illustration No. 4:* As a result of inquiries by a police detective, the parole officer suspected that a parolee of his might have been involved in a recent drugstore burglary in the neighborhood. He decided to make a visit to the parolee's place of residence. There he talked to the parolee's sister, who stated that the parolee had returned home by 11:30 P.M. on the night of the burglary. This cleared suspicion from the parolee since the burglary occurred at about 2:00 A.M. the following morning. The parole officer requested the usual cooperation from the sister, reminded her of the parolee's report day, and left.

Parole officers in Detroit sometimes make home visits for special purposes. One occasion for such a visit may be suspicion that the parolee has engaged in criminal behavior or is in serious violation of the conditions of parole. Suspicion may be created by

[54] In each of the three states a preparole investigation of the inmate's job and residence plans is made. The parole officer making the investigation, often the same officer who will supervise the inmate upon his release, visits the inmate's proposed place of residence. As part of this visit he usually asks the cooperation of the relatives or landlord in reporting parole violations.

the police, as in Illustration No. 4, or even by relatives of the parolee.[55] A special home visit is also likely to be made if the parolee fails to report for the regular office interview.

The employment habits of a parolee are considered crucial indicators of his progress and adjustment. The Michigan Department of Corrections places great importance upon checking the employment status of the parolee:

> In most parole situations, employment is an aid to the reformation of the individual; and to the parole officer, the parolee's work habits will be an indication of the latter's entire attitude. Further, the economic security of the parolee and that of his dependents revolves about his work habits.
>
> Job checks are required at least every sixty days throughout the parole period. This means an actual verification by the parole officer that the parolee is employed at the place and in the manner he reports he is. The nature of the job check will depend upon the type of employment, but in no case will there be reason to forego it. . . . In checking employment, whether by actual visit to the job, contact with the employer or personnel office, review of pay stubs or however, the parole officer should note continuity of employment, progress on the job, and attitude of the parolee toward work.[56]

Parole officers in Detroit do not ordinarily make such an extensive check of the parolee's employment. Their interest in the parolee's employment is restricted to determining that he is working steadily, without reference to the nature of the job. Job visits are almost never made, but paycheck stubs are routinely used to verify employment. Parole officers indicate they regard it as futile to be concerned with the quality of parolees' employment because of the difficulty of obtaining any kind of employment for them.

In Wisconsin the Division of Corrections requires that each parole officer make at least one home visit to each of his parolees

[55] In one case the parole officer had received numerous phone calls from the parolee's parents. The first call was made by the mother who stated the parolee was not staying home evenings, was not working, and, in her estimation, was acting in a peculiar manner. The last statement was not elaborated upon except she did state she thought her son might be using narcotics. The parole officer made a home visit, found the parolee and his mother at home, and made inquiry about the fact that his typewriter was missing, a fact related by the parolee's mother. The parolee denied use of narcotics, stating that he pawned the typewriter to allow him to look for a job by bus rather than walking. Later a phone call was received from the father who requested the officer to incarcerate the parolee to "kind of shake him up" and to find out what happened to his clothing. Visiting the home again, the parole officer discovered the parolee had pawned his clothing, leading to the suspicion that he was in fact purchasing narcotics.

[56] Michigan Department of Corrections, Manual of Procedure for Michigan Parole Officers 17-18 (1954).

every two months.[57] Apparently this requirement is followed in the Milwaukee district.[58] As in Detroit, most home visits are unannounced. Parole officers stated that unscheduled home visits enable them to learn more about the parolee's activities, thus enhancing the control value of such visits, and also that appointments are inconvenient because parole officers often find they are unable to maintain a rigid schedule. Most home visits are routine; the parole officer simply talks to the parolee or others who may be at home about the parolee's activities, problems, progress.[59] Occasionally, additional home visits are made for special purposes. In one case, for example, the parole officer made an additional visit to two parolees who had been given permission to enter into business together because he promised to do so as an indication of interest in their venture and because he was fearful that they might be having difficulty controlling their alcohol problem.[60]

b. *Office interviews.* In all three states, parolees are expected to report to the parole office once a month for an interview and to submit a written report. The routine office visit is substantially the same in each state, but its relation to other supervisory techniques differs among the three states. In Kansas the office interview is the exclusive method of parole supervision. The size of the caseloads and the press of other duties, such as conducting preparole investigations, prohibit other types of supervision. In Wichita the parole officer interviews parolees and receives their monthly reports in an office provided by the Wichita Police Department in its headquarters building. The parole officer in Kansas City normally spends the first four or five days of each month receiving monthly reports in brief office interviews. Often as many as forty or fifty parolees are interviewed in a single day.

In Michigan the Department of Corrections gives the following advice with respect to office interviews:

> Office interviews are not to be relied upon as a major type of visit in any case; rather the best work will be done in visits outside the office, at the parolee's home, job or elsewhere, with office

[57] Wisconsin Division of Corrections, Bureau of Probation and Parole, Field Agents Manual, Ch. 3, §3.7 (Nov. 23, 1955).

[58] In exceptional cases, permission is obtained from the parole officer's supervisor to eliminate home visits to a particular parolee. The exceptions usually involve parolees who work days and who do not live with relatives or close friends. Home visits under such circumstances are believed to serve no useful purpose.

[59] A woman parole officer in Milwaukee stated she had no specific plans other than to visit with her parolees; she had not completed her May monthly home visits as prescribed by directives. She indicated that sometimes simply dropping in on parolees enabled her to find out more about their activities than an announced visit.

[60] The state parole officer in Wichita, Kansas, said it was possible for him to make very few home visits because his caseload approached 200 parolees.

> interviews held at a minimum. However, there may be times when the privacy or the business atmosphere of the office may lend itself best to handling a situation.[61]

In practice, the office interview constitutes the major supervisory technique in Detroit. Each parole officer in the Detroit office has two "report days" per month for routine office interviews. The caseloads, averaging nearly one hundred, make it necessary to see forty or fifty parolees in about ten hours.

Each Michigan parolee is expected to submit a written report once a month on the nature and place of employment, wages earned, steadiness of employment, debts incurred and to whom owed, names of friends and associates, and any arrests since his last report. Usually the parolee is required to visit the office on report day and submit his report then. If distance precludes travel for this purpose, he may be permitted to mail his report to the parole officer.

In addition to routine monthly interviews, special office interviews are used in Detroit. One purpose of these is to maintain unusually close supervision over the parolee. If the parolee has a history of unsteady work habits or a tendency to alcoholism, he may be required to report to the office more than once a month. Extra office interviews may be used as a disciplinary measure. If a parolee has failed to conform to the conditions of his parole, the parole officer may require him to make frequent office visits as a disciplinary measure. Delinquency in making regular monthly reports may result in that parole officer imposing a further restriction upon the parolee by requiring that he report more than once a month. If a parole officer suspects a parole violation, he may require an additional office interview in an attempt to ascertain the facts.

In Milwaukee, parole officers usually remain in the office after normal working hours at least once a week to permit parolees to make required monthly reports without interfering with their employment. During the course of a one- or two-hour period, as many as forty reports are submitted by parolees. The monthly report form in Wisconsin is similar to that in Michigan. In addition, parolees who are working are required to verify employment by pay check stubs, thus eliminating the necessity for a job visit to verify employment. Occasionally, there is time for a brief interview. One parole officer said that the most he attempts to do at the office interview is to point up major problems and that he does not attempt to undertake any counseling. If he discovers prob-

[61] Michigan Department of Corrections, Manual of Procedure for Michigan Parole Officers 19 (1954).

lems requiring further exploration, he will pursue them during the remainder of the month through home visits or additional office interviews.

3. *The intensity of parole supervision.* The objectives actually pursued in parole supervision depend in part upon the amount of time the parole officer has to supervise a parolee. Presumably, as available time increases, greater emphasis can be placed on treatment instead of control and more use can be made of supervision techniques other than the routine office interview. Correctional literature would suggest that the intensity of parole supervision, normally expressed in terms of the size of the caseload of each parole officer, is the major problem in current parole supervision.

Judged by current practice in the three states, there is no question about the relationship between size of caseloads and supervision objectives and techniques. That is, actual emphasis on treatment and use of supervisory techniques beyond the routine office interview depend upon reasonable caseloads. The relationship between caseload size and intensity of supervision is, however, not as direct as it might seem. It is possible, for example, for a parole officer with a relatively large caseload to provide intensive supervision for some cases by screening out other cases in which little or no supervision seems necessary. But if the caseload is quite large, the parole officer can do little more than give the absolute minimum of supervision to all of his cases.

The parole caseloads in Kansas are the largest of the three states. In addition to a caseload of 200, the Wichita parole officer is assigned to conduct preparole investigations on inmates whose parole hearings are scheduled each month. At times he has been assigned as many as thirty-six investigations to make in one month. He often must spend the first half of the month doing nothing but preparoles, since these reports have to be completed before the parole hearings. The parole officer in Kansas City, Kansas, has a similar caseload and also spends a great deal of time conducting preparole investigations. He stated that in many cases he does not see a parolee for five or six months but felt it could not be avoided since he is assigned a caseload which is impossible for one man to handle.

One parole official stated that, although Kansas needs to double the number of its parole officers, one major reason for large caseloads is the lack of an early discharge provision in the Kansas parole law. No parolee may be discharged from parole prior to the expiration of his maximum term, except by commutation of sentence, and many parolees are retained under supervision for an unnecessarily long period of time. This not only increases the size of the caseload "on paper" but the record keeping involved consumes a large amount of the parole officer's time.[62]

In Detroit the caseloads average about one hundred. Caseload information for the rest of Michigan was unavailable, but the Detroit figure is significant since 47 percent of all parolees under supervision in Michigan are supervised by the Detroit office. Routine parole supervision in Detroit involves approximately one contact by a parole officer with each of his parolees each month. Contact is increased in those months in which the parole officer makes a home visit to a parolee. Supervision is also intensified if the parolee experiences difficulty adjusting to the community, or if the parole officer has reason to suspect that he may have difficulty, and, in some cases, the parole board may direct that supervision be more intense than usual.

The caseloads are smaller in Wisconsin than in the other two states. Each male probation and parole officer in the Milwaukee District Office supervises an average of fifty-five adult male probationers and parolees. Each female officer supervises an average of thirty-two adult female probationers and parolees. In addition, each officer has an institutionalized caseload, made up of inmates of adult correctional institutions who will be supervised by the officer when they are released on parole. Supervision of institutionalized cases is, of course, much less intense than those on probation, parole, or conditional release. Each male officer in the Milwaukee District Office has an institutionalized caseload of approximately eighty-six adult male inmates, while each female officer has approximately thirty-five adult female inmates on her institutionalized caseload. As in the other two states, each officer is assigned preparole investigations to conduct. However, since the officers in Wisconsin are probation as well as parole officers, they must conduct presentence investigations. Even considering the added duty of conducting presentence investigations, parole supervision is more intense in Wisconsin than in the other two states.[63] The Division of Corrections provides:

> In general, the needs of each case should determine the frequency of contact with the client. The minimum requirement is one personal contact each month and a home visit at least once every two months unless written waiver is obtained from the district supervisor.[64]

62 See pages 337-338.

63 In Milwaukee County presentence investigations are made by the local probation department.

64 Wisconsin Division of Corrections, Bureau of Probation and Parole, Field Agents Manual, Ch. 3, §3.7 (Nov. 23, 1955).

4. *The duration of parole supervision.* The parole period defines the time during which the parole system must accomplish its objectives. If the parole period is too short, these objectives may be frustrated; if it is too long, risks of revocation for the parolee and burdens of supervision for the system continue after the benefits of parole have been exhausted. In practice, the duration of parole supervision is determined by three decisions. First, before the offender is released on parole, the initial parole period is determined either by statute or by the parole board. Second, in some instances this initial period may be extended after the inmate is placed under parole supervision. Finally, the initial period may be shortened, either through an exercise of discretion by a correctional agency or commutation of sentence.

a. *Setting the length of the parole period.* In Kansas and Wisconsin the length of the initial parole period is set by statute. When a Kansas inmate is paroled, his parole period extends from the date of release to the date of his maximum sentence, less good time earned while in the institution. Good time is not awarded to offenders for good behavior while on parole. When a parolee has reached his maximum sentence less good time he must be discharged from parole supervision.[65]

In Wisconsin good time is awarded to inmates of correctional institutions and to parolees.[66] When an inmate has served his maximum sentence less allowances for good time, he must be released from prison, but his release is conditional and he is placed under parole supervision until the expiration of his maximum sentence without allowances for good time.[67] When an inmate is released on parole, his parole period extends from the date of release to the expiration of his maximum sentence without good time allowances.[68] Good time earned in the correctional institution and on parole does not shorten the parole period, but it is of importance because it determines the time the parolee must spend

[65] Kan. Gen. Stat. §§76-2421, 76-2451 (penitentiary), 76-2313 (reformatory), 76-2512 (women's prison) (1949). Kansas enacted new parole laws in 1957. See Kan. Laws 1957, Ch. 331. Under this scheme, an inmate must be released conditionally when he has served his maximum sentence less good time. The initial parole period extends from the time of release on parole or conditional release until the maximum sentence without good time is served. Kan. Stat. Ann. §62-2246 (1964). The parole board may grant early discharge from supervision to a parolee or conditional releasee but not sooner than one year after release on supervision, unless the sentence expires sooner. Kan. Stat. Ann. §62-2252 (1964).

[66] Wis. Stat. Ann. §53.11(2a) (1957) provides: "A parolee earns good time at the rate prescribed in this section. The department may forfeit all or part of the good time previously earned under this chapter, for violation of the conditions of parole, whether or not the parole is revoked for such misconduct."

[67] Wis. Stat. Ann. §53.11(7)(a) (1967).

[68] Ibid.

under supervision before he is eligible for early discharge from parole.[69]

In both Kansas and Wisconsin while the parole board is unable to determine the length of the parole period directly, it is able indirectly to do so by its selection of the date for release on parole. Practice in Wisconsin indicates that achieving a parole period of desirable length is a substantial factor in the parole board's decision to grant or deny parole. When it is faced with an inmate who has a fairly short maximum sentence, or whose good time has been forfeited, such as for parole violation, it may parole him because, although release at the maximum less good time is conditional, the length of this period of supervision may seem inadequate. By paroling such an inmate instead of permitting his conditional release later, the parole board increases the length of the parole period to a term it considers to be more adequate.[70]

In Michigan good time is awarded for good behavior both while the inmate is in the institution and while he is on parole.[71] The inmate must be unconditionally released from the institution when he has served his maximum sentence less allowances for good time.[72] He must be discharged from parole supervision when he reaches his maximum sentence less good time earned in the institution and on parole. The Michigan parole board, unlike those in the other two states, has authority to set a parole period that is shorter than the sentence remaining to be served. At the time it makes the decision to grant parole, it normally announces the length of the initial parole period.

The Michigan parole board normally selects a two-year parole period. This means that if the parolee serves two years on parole he will be unconditionally discharged even though he has not yet served his maximum sentence less good time allowances.[73] The board may select a period other than two years for special reasons. In certain cases, a Michigan statute requires that the parole period be longer than two years: "No parole shall be granted for a period less than 4 years in all cases of murder, actual forcible rape, robbery armed, kidnapping, extortion, or breaking and entering an occupied dwelling in the night time." [74] The parole

69 See pages 336-337.

70 For a detailed discussion of the decision to grant parole in order to provide for supervision or to increase the length of supervision, see Chapter 11.

71 Mich. Stat. Ann. §28.2308 (1954).

72 See Chapter 12.

73 However, the initial parole period selected by the parole board is subject to extension at any time before it is served. See page 336.

74 Mich. Stat. Ann. §28.2312 (1954). In 1961 the legislature changed the four-year requirement to two years and added the following: "except where the maximum time remaining to be served on the sentence is less than 2 years." Mich. Stat. Ann. §28.2312 (Supp. 1965.)

board may select a parole period longer than two years if it regards the inmate as posing a higher than usual risk of parole violation. In one case, for example, the parole board imposed a three-year parole period on an inmate who had a history of drinking and unemployment and who had a prior parole violation. When the inmate has less than two years remaining until he reaches his maximum sentence less good time allowances, the board paroles the inmate for the balance of the maximum less good time.

b. *Extension of the parole period.* Since parole periods in Wisconsin and Kansas are based on the maximum sentence and the maximum less good time, respectively, they are not subject to extension once the inmate is released on parole. In Michigan, however, the parole period is in most cases set by the parole board for a length of time shorter than the balance remaining until the maximum less good time is served. Under Michigan practice[75] the parole board may extend its parole period at any time before it expires except, of course, it may not extend it beyond the maximum less good time.

Extension of the parole period occurs infrequently in Michigan. While theoretically the availability of this device permits reevaluation of the parolee's adjustment in the community and the individualization of the parole period on that ground, it is apparently almost never used for such purposes. The closest case observed involved extension of the parole period to make it administratively convenient to commit a parolee to a state hospital for treatment of mental illness. Extension is occasionally used to enforce the parolee's obligation to repay money borrowed from the Department of Corrections under its parolee loan program. The Department of Corrections requires an extension if the parolee has failed to repay his loan by the time his initial parole period expires.[76] In one case, because a parolee had failed to repay his loan of $12, his parole was extended for six months.

c. *Early discharge from parole supervision.* Under some circumstances a parolee may be discharged from parole supervision before he has served his entire parole period as initially determined. Authority for early discharge exists in Wisconsin but not in Kansas. In Michigan early discharge is largely unnecessary

[75] No specific statutory authority for the practice of extending the parole period was discovered. It is arguable that authority is implicit in the statutory authority in the parole board to set the parole period at less than the balance of the sentence. See Mich. Stat. Ann. §26.2312 (1954).

[76] Department of Corrections, Manual of Procedure for Michigan Parole Officers 46 (1954).

because the parole board has discretion to set the initial parole period.[77] The Wisconsin Division of Corrections has authority to discharge a parolee after he has served his maximum sentence less good time earned in the institution and on parole, but before he has served his entire maximum sentence.[78] Use of this authority was observed in two types of cases. When an offender with an extremely long sentence is paroled, he is likely to receive an early discharge from parole supervision when he has served his maximum less good time, if his adjustment is good. Even assuming early discharge, parole supervision in such cases lasts for several years. An offender with a relatively short sentence is likely to receive early discharge if he plans to leave the state to return to his state of residence. Under such circumstances, parole officials find it easier simply to terminate parole for purposes of permitting exit from the state rather than to go through the lengthy procedure of transfer of supervision for such a short period of time.[79]

Under Kansas law at the time of the field survey there was no authority for early discharge from parole.[80] This lack of authority plus the long sentences imposed by Kansas statutes resulted in extremely long periods of parole supervision for many Kansas parolees and it is likely that the intensity of supervision is decreased markedly during such times. The only possible way a Kansas parolee could obtain early discharge was through commutation of sentence. He had to comply with all the requirements applicable to commutation of the minimum sentence to advance parole eligibility, including advertising in a newspaper in the county in which he was sentenced. The governor's pardon attorney used essentially the same criteria as in commutation for prison inmates, including placing heavy reliance on the recommendations of local officials, especially the trial judge. In one case, for example, a parolee had a successful construction business after a long term on parole. His parole status interfered with securing bonds to pursue his business, but he was turned down on his commutation application because local officials had registered oppo-

[77] It would be entirely possible for the Michigan parole board to shorten a parole period selected by it just as it sometimes extends such a parole period. No such case was observed, however.

[78] Wis. Stat. Ann. §53.11(7)(a) (1957).

[79] The Wisconsin parole board has authority to grant an absolute discharge and release from prison to an inmate who has served his maximum sentence less good time in the institution. One routine basis for such a decision is that the inmate, if released conditionally, would have only a short time on supervision and he wishes to leave Wisconsin to return to his native state. See Chapter 12.

[80] Present Kansas law permits early discharge in the discretion of the parole board, after the parolee has served one year under supervision. Kan. Stat. Ann. §62-2252 (1964).

sition to further grants of clemency at the time they consented to commutation of the minimum sentence to permit release on parole.[81]

[81] See Chapter 9 for a detailed discussion of the commutation of sentence practice used in Kansas to advance parole eligibility of a substantial number of inmates.

CHAPTER 14

Parole Revocation

Parole revocation is a critical step in the correctional process. Discussion in this chapter will emphasize the grounds for revocation, the function served by revocation, and discretion not to revoke despite adequate grounds. In common with other administrative decisions, parole revocation raises issues of sufficiency of evidence, of basic policy objectives, and of procedures to assure accuracy and fairness.

One of the principal problems in parole revocation practice is the standard of sufficiency of evidence for the revocation decision. Must there be a violation of a condition of parole to justify revocation? If so, how certain must correctional officials be that a violation occurred? What are the principal sources of information of parole violations? Further, what measures are taken to assure that revocation does not occur unless the required evidence exists? Other problems revolve around the purpose of the revocation decision. What is the principal use of the revocation decision in current practice? Is parole ever revoked without at least a suspicion that the parolee has returned to criminal activity? In the majority of instances in which parole could be revoked, revocation does not occur, for a variety of reasons. What are the criteria used to determine when parole will not be revoked despite adequate legal grounds for doing so? What alternatives to revocation are available when discretion is exercised?

A. Sufficiency of the Evidence to Revoke Parole

Whether the contemplated official action is an arrest, prosecution, or conviction, laws require some evidence that the suspect is guilty of a crime before the step is taken. Although the probability of guilt required may properly vary depending upon the action contemplated, the central point of inquiry — whether criminal conduct occurred — remains the same. In parole revocation similar evidence sufficiency problems must be confronted.

In all jurisdictions persons released on parole are warned that failure to conform to their parole conditions may result in revocation.[1] As a matter of law it is often unclear whether parole can be revoked without proof of a violation of a parole condition. Statutes in some jurisdictions, including Kansas[2] and Michigan,[3] indicate that proof of a violation is necessary to justify revocation. In other jurisdictions, including Wisconsin,[4] the law implies that revocation may occur without regard to whether there was a parole violation. In still other jurisdictions the law quite explicitly states that parole may be revoked even when there has been no parole violation.[5]

In practice, parole officials proceed on the assumption that revocation is justifiable only when there has been a parole violation.[6] This is the practice even in Wisconsin where there is implicit legal authority to revoke without proof of violation. The reasons for the practice may involve the belief, correct or incorrect, that the law requires it; the reluctance to test a law which is unclear on this point; the consideration that fairness to the parolee requires that revocation occur only when he has failed to conform his conduct to a standard of which he had prior knowledge; or the belief that such a limitation minimizes bitterness over revocation and therefore increases the probability of rehabilitation of revoked parolees. Because the law in some jurisdictions requires proof of a violation of a parole condition to justify revocation and, more importantly, because parole officials behave as if there were such a requirement, it becomes important to ask what degree of certainty of a violation ought to exist before revocation; what sources of information are used to discover parole violations; and what measures exist to assure that revocations occur only upon sufficient evidence of a parole violation.

1. *Certainty of violation.* Should parole be revoked only upon

[1] See Chapter 13.

[2] Kan. Gen. Stat. §§62-1528, 76-2316, 76-2515 (1949). The present parole law is substantially the same. See Kan. Stat. Ann. §62-2250 (1964).

[3] Mich. Stat. Ann. §§28.2308 to 28.2310 (1954).

[4] See Wis. Stat. Ann. §57.06(3) (1957).

[5] See, e.g., Summers v. State, 31 Ala. App. 264, 15 S.2d 500 (1943).

[6] Michigan Department of Corrections, Manual of Procedure for Michigan Parole Officers 39 (1954) states: "A parolee is still serving his sentence while on parole, and thus is liable to be returned for sufficient cause; but that cause must be sufficient basis upon which to return him and permit the Parole Board to find him guilty of violation. First, there must be demonstrated proof of violation of one or more of the conditions of parole, or conviction for a felony or misdemeanor. Second, the parole officer must be convinced that the removal of the parolee from the community will be to the best interest of the community and/or the parolee. If the State Supervisor agrees that return to prison is the proper course of action, he will issue a warrant and request the prison warden to return the violator."

proof beyond a reasonable doubt that a violation occurred, upon proof by a preponderance of the evidence, or upon a standard similar to the "probable cause" arrest requirement? The law in the three states fails to distinguish between the evidence required for arrest for parole revocation and evidence required for revocation itself. The Kansas law contemplates that the revocation decision will precede the arrest of the parolee; it authorizes an arrest "when in the judgment of [the parole board] any such paroled prisoner has violated his parole. . . ." [7] No evidence requirements for revocation itself are indicated. Michigan law contemplates that revocation will occur after arrest of the parolee. It authorizes issuance of an arrest warrant for revocation "upon a showing of probable violation of parole" [8] and authorizes arrest without a warrant if the parole officer or peace officer "has reasonable grounds to believe that the prisoner has violated his parole." [9] The parole board then makes the revocation decision, but no evidence sufficiency standard for this decision is specified.[10] Wisconsin law provides no evidence sufficiency standards either for the arrest or the revocation.

The measures used in practice to assure that a violation of parole has occurred indicate parole officials feel it important that revocation should not occur without fairly clear evidence that a parole condition has been violated. But the standard used in practice is not verbalized and may vary from case to case. Where revocation follows conviction for a new offense, it is based upon proof beyond a reasonable doubt if there was a trial, and upon a lower standard if there was a plea of guilty.[11] In many cases, certainty of violation is very great because the grounds for the decision are minor violations of parole conditions that are easily provable or admitted by the parolee. In such instances, however, the motive for revocation is often belief the parolee has returned to criminality sometimes supported by considerable evidence but at other times by little more than suspicion.[12]

2. *Sources of information concerning parole violations.* Parole officers receive information concerning parole violations from a number of different sources. The parole officer himself discovers some violations, especially those of a minor nature. Often these are admitted by the parolee. A second major source of informa-

[7] Kan. Gen. Stat. §76-2316 (1949).

[8] Mich. Stat. Ann. §28.2308 (1954).

[9] Mich. Stat. Ann. §28.2309 (1954).

[10] See Mich. Stat. Ann. §28.2310 (1954).

[11] See Newman, Conviction: The Determination of Guilt or Innocence Without Trial 10-21 (1966).

[12] See pages 358-367.

tion is the police. If a parolee is arrested, the parole officer is usually informed of it and is given the opportunity to visit the parolee in jail and interrogate him about the arrest. Other persons coming in contact with the parolee provide information on parole violations. Members of the parolee's family are encouraged to do so by many parole officers. In other cases, employers or friends may provide information to the parole officer.

a. *Observation by the parole officer.*

> *Illustration No. 1:* In a routine check of his records, a parole officer discovered that a parolee had not reported for his monthly office interview for two months. Suspicious that the parolee may have absconded, the parole officer began investigation to determine his whereabouts.

Occasionally, at the monthly officer interview a parolee volunteers admissions of minor violations, for example, drinking to excess or changing residence or employment without prior permission. Absconding is usually discovered as a result of the parole officer checking his case records and noting an absence of monthly office interviews. Typically, the parole officer then calls the parolee's relatives, landlord, friends, or employer to determine his whereabouts. Some parole officers use the home visit to check on the behavior of the parolee. One parole officer stated that he could discover more about the conduct of a parolee by an unannounced home visit than by any other method.[13] Inspections are made if the parole officer for any reason suspects that the parolee has reverted to use of narcotics, but parole officers in the three states do not routinely inspect for needle marks on parolees who were narcotic addicts.

The instances in which initial suspicion of parole violations arises from direct observation by the parole officer are few in comparison to instances in which suspicion is aroused from a report by police or other persons. The principal role of the parole officer is to verify information received from other sources.[14]

b. *Police reports.* Despite a history of animosity between parole officers and police officers in many cities,[15] cooperation between these two agencies is quite good in the cities studied. Indeed, partly because of the encouragement of correctional agencies, police in the three states carry important responsibilities for the

13 See Chapter 13.

14 See pages 347-350.

15 In several of the cities studied, parole officers described a history of what seemed to them police harassment of parolees and general lack of cooperation with them by the police. In each instance, however, they were careful to note that in recent years the situation had changed greatly, frequently as a result of changes in personnel, and that there is presently a high degree of cooperation between the two agencies.

control aspects of parole supervision.[16] The police are the parole officer's major source of information concerning parole violations and virtually his exclusive source concerning serious new offenses committed by parolees. In each of the three states, and especially in Detroit and Milwaukee, local correctional authorities cultivate this source of information and rely heavily upon it.

(1) *Wisconsin.*

> *Illustration No. 2:* The liaison parole officer made his daily rounds of the Milwaukee Police Department and obtained the names of two parolees who had been arrested the previous night. He interviewed each of the arrestees to ascertain their identities, the names of their parole officers, the circumstances of the arrests, and whether they were employed. He obtained a detailed statement of the circumstances of the arrests from police files. He then decided to place a "hold" on both arrestees and arranged for their transportation to the county jail for detention pending disposition of the hold order.

One parole officer in the Milwaukee district office is assigned full time as the court and police liaison officer. Each morning he checks with the police department to determine whether any parolees have been arrested. The police department provides him with the names of arrested parolees, secured from their own files or from interviewing the arrestee,[17] and permits the liaison officer to interview the parolee. After interviewing the arrested parolees, the liaison officer decides whether to place a parole violation hold order on them. In making this decision he places emphasis on the likelihood that parole will be revoked, taking into account whether an offense was committed and its seriousness. If the nature of the offense indicates that revocation is unlikely, the liaison officer then considers the employment status of the parolee. If, after an interview with the parolee and verification with the employer, it appears that the parolee was employed at the time of arrest and that employment is still available upon his release, the liaison officer is very likely not to place a hold order, because to do so might result in loss of employment. If, on the other hand, the parolee's custody has no effect on his employment, the liaison officer is likely to place a hold order on him and turn the matter over to the parolee's supervising parole officer. In Illustration No. 2, one parolee had been arrested for drunkenness and the other had been arrested for investigation of robbery but interrogation failed to implicate him. Although revocation was

[16] See Chapter 13.

[17] See LaFave, Arrest: The Decision to Take a Suspect into Custody 360-363 (1965).

unlikely for either of them, the liaison officer placed holds on both because they were unemployed and retention of custody would make it convenient for the parole officer to interview them about the arrests and to work out employment arrangements.

The information concerning the circumstances of the arrest gathered by the liaison officer from police files and interviewing the parolee is transmitted to the parolee's supervising officer in an "Arrest Report." The supervising parole officer uses the arrest report to question the parolee about the circumstances of the arrest and then includes it in the parolee's case file to permit its use as a ground for revocation of parole at any later date. If a parolee is stopped and questioned on the street by police, but not arrested, the liaison parole officer may be given information concerning the circumstances of the stopping and questioning.[18] If so, he forwards this information to the supervising parole officer. In addition to information on arrests and stopping of parolees, the liaison officer provides supervising parole officers with a daily list of the progress of cases in the local courts involving parolees and a daily list of parolees held in custody in the county jail.

(2) *Michigan.*

> *Illustration No. 3:* The police liaison officer visited the Detroit Police Department headquarters where he obtained the names of six parolees arrested over the weekend. Some had been arrested only for minor traffic offenses and were already free on bond. Of those still in police custody, the liaison officer decided that only one, arrested for felonious assault, would be held for parole violation in order to give his supervising officer time to decide whether to revoke parole. One of the others had been arrested for suspicion of burglary, but police interrogation failed to implicate him. The liaison officer interviewed him. The parolee denied his guilt. When asked about his purpose in being so far from his own neighborhood at the time of arrest, he responded that he was "only riding around." The liaison officer ascertained that the parolee had obtained the permission of his parole officer to operate a motor vehicle. After the interview, the liaison officer authorized the immediate release of the parolee and made a report of the arrest to the supervising parole officer.

18 When a Milwaukee police officer stops and questions a suspect on the street, he sometimes submits a record of the event, called a "Field Interrogation Report," to the police department. See Tiffany, McIntyre, and Rotenberg, Detection of Crime: Stopping and Questioning; Search and Seizure; Encouragement and Entrapment 73-80 (1967).

The police liaison officer in Detroit functions much the same as his counterpart in Milwaukee. Each morning he visits police headquarters to obtain the names of parolees arrested since his last visit. From police records and from interviewing those parolees still in custody, the liaison officer writes a report of the circumstances of the arrest, which the supervising parole officer uses in interrogation of the parolee and as a basis for revocation later should the need arise. Except for minor traffic offenses, the police do not release arrested parolees without authorization from the liaison officer, even when, as in Illustration No. 3, they contemplate no further action. The liaison officer also keeps the supervising parole officers current on the status of criminal prosecutions pending against parolees.[19]

c. *Reports from other persons.*

Illustration No. 4: A parolee's wife called the Detroit parole office and told her husband's parole officer that the parolee had remained away from home the entire night and had not reported for work that morning.

Illustration No. 5: A parolee's grandmother called the Milwaukee parole office to tell her granddaughter's parole officer that the parolee had stayed out all night with a boyfriend, was unruly, would not work, and obtained money from prostitution. The grandmother also reported she suspected the girl was pregnant.

Friends and relatives of the parolee frequently provide information concerning parole violations. Some parole officers strongly encourage the parolee's relatives, or other persons who would be expected to be in frequent contact with the parolee, to report suspected instances of parole violations to the officer. If this is done, the parole officer sometimes explains to them, it is more likely that any problems can be corrected before they become so serious as to require revocation.[20]

Often parole violations reported in this manner are accompanied by general complaints about the behavior of the parolee and by requests that the parole officer do something to correct the situation. In Illustration No. 5, for example, the grandmother wanted the parole officer to remove the parolee from her home. Most such reports involve minor rules violations that do not lead to revoca-

[19] Parole staffs in Kansas were not large enough to require the development of a formal position of police liaison officer. Each supervising parole officer works closely with the police and attempts to keep informed on arrests of any of his parolees.

[20] See Chapter 13.

tion.[21] The parole officer assures the informant that he will do what he can to ease the trouble. He records the circumstances of the alleged violations for the case file. He then interviews the parolee about the report, seeking verification of the allegations, and, if he finds them to be true, takes corrective measures, normally a reprimand and warning that future incidents may result in revocation.

3. *Measures designed to assure that revocations occur only upon sufficient evidence.* An evidence sufficiency standard, whether imposed by law, directed by administrative policy, or evolved as a matter of practice, has much more significance if devices are used to assure compliance with that standard in individual cases. At the conviction stage, for example, the trial functions as such a device for some cases, while for many others, devices have been developed in the practice to assure that persons who plead guilty really are guilty.[22] Comparable devices exist at the parole revocation stage of the criminal justice process.

Kansas statutes authorize the parole board of the penitentiary to revoke the parole of any inmate paroled from that institution.[23] The parole board at the reformatory has authority to revoke parole of former inmates of that institution. The superintendent of the institution is authorized to return suspected parole violators to hold them for the parole board's decision, but there are no provisions for a hearing on the issue of whether there was a violation of parole conditions.[24] In Michigan the parole board is given authority to make the revocation decision. The parolee may be returned to the institution from which he was paroled, either with or without a warrant, upon a showing of probable violation of parole. After return, he must be given "a fair and impartial hearing of such charges within 30 days before 2 members of the parole board under such rules and regulations as the parole board may adopt." [25] Wisconsin statutes authorize the Director of the Department of Public Welfare to revoke parole. There are no provisions for a hearing.[26]

Despite variations in legal allocation of authority to revoke parole in the three states, the practices are quite similar. In each of the states the initial revocation decision is made by the supervising

21 Only one instance was observed in which such a report formed the principal reason for revocation of parole. In that case the parole officer was making a home visit when the mother of the parolee informed the officer that her daughter, a former narcotics addict, was at that very moment upstairs taking a shot of heroin. The parole officer immediately placed the parolee under arrest. Her parole was quickly revoked and she was returned to the correctional institution.

22 See note 11 *supra.*

23 Kan. Gen. Stat. §62-1525 (1949).

24 Kan. Gen. Stat. §§76-2315, 76-2316 (1949).

25 Mich. Stat. Ann. §28.2310 (1954).

26 Wis. Stat. Ann. §57.06 (1957).

parole officer. Normally, he takes steps to assure himself that there is an adequate basis for revocation and that revocation is desirable before he recommends it. In Michigan and Wisconsin the parole officer's recommendation for revocation is discussed with the supervisor of the district office in which he works. If the district supervisor concurs in the recommendation, which he usually does, it is forwarded to central parole headquarters. There an administrative official checks the revocation request for compliance with certain standards. In Wisconsin the revocation recommendation is then forwarded to the Director of the Department of Public Welfare, who has formal responsibility for revocation, where it is approved. The parolee is then returned to the institution to await his parole violation hearing. In Michigan the parole board hears the case and then makes the formal revocation decision, almost always concurring with the prior recommendations. In Wisconsin the parolee is given a hearing before the parole board despite the fact that the statutes do not require a hearing and even though the formal revocation decision has already been made. After hearing the parolee, the Wisconsin board decides how much good time should be forfeited because of the revocation and sets a date for a hearing to consider reparole.

a. *Verifying information on violations.*

Illustration No. 6: A parolee who worked as a busboy in a hotel was discovered by his employer to be in possession of a set of master keys without authorization. The employer suspected the parolee of stealing meat, hotel towels, and items from guests' rooms and reported his belief to the police. The police contacted the supervising parole officer. In the company of police officers and without a warrant, the supervising parole officer searched the parolee's room in a rooming house, securing the permission of the landlady. The only hotel property discovered was a few bottles of wine. The parolee was then informed of the search and was requested to take a lie detector test. The test results indicated that the parolee had stolen hotel property not in excess of $100 and was not planning to use the master keys to burglarize guest rooms. On the basis of this information, the supervising officer severely admonished the parolee but did not revoke his parole.

Illustration No. 7: Responding to calls received from the parolee's parents that the parolee was acting suspiciously and was probably using narcotics again, the parole officer had the parolee arrested and held in police custody. The parole officer and a detective from the narcotics squad visited the parolee in jail and, after questioning him at length, concluded there was a possibility he was "joy popping." Although there were no tracks visible, the detective said that was not unusual since the parolee had been in custody for four days and could have eliminated the tracks by a considerable amount of scratching. The parole officer ordered the parolee held in custody for further interrogation.

In some instances, such as the parolee's apprehension while committing an offense, violation of parole is so clear that no further investigation is necessary to enable the parole officer to make his revocation decision. In most instances, however, the initial suspicion of violation is not so well founded to permit the parole officer to make the revocation decision without gathering further information. Most often the parole officer simply interviews the parolee about the alleged violation. Interviews may occur even in those situations in which the violation is clear in order to establish the parolee's version of the incident. The parolee is also interviewed even though the parole officer is certain that the violation, if it occurred, is not serious enough to warrant revocation because this establishes a record that may be used, along with other violations, as a basis for revocation later.

Although the most frequent method of verification is interview of the parolee, other methods are also used. Two of these are the search and the lie detector test. When the question arises whether the parolee is in possession of stolen goods or contraband, the parole officer may undertake a search of the parolee's room or person. With respect to search of the parolee's room, warrants are normally not first obtained and the parolee's consent is not sought. If the parolee objects to a search of his person or his room (although in the latter case he is normally unaware of it until it is an accomplished fact), he may be warned that such objections may be taken as a failure to cooperate, may constitute a parole violation, and may result in revocation for failure to cooperate. One parole officer, when asked about his authority to search parolee's rooms, said he thought there were no problems and that parolees rarely, if ever, object to such searches.[27]

The lie detector is also used to verify information concerning parole violations. Parolees rarely refuse to consent to a lie detector test. One parole officer said that he always informs the parolee that he does not have to take the test but that refusal to consent may result in revocation of parole. On one occasion, after the parolee

[27] A recent California case held that the Fourth Amendment does not apply to searches of parolees by parole officers and, hence, that a search warrant, lawful arrest, or other justification for the search need not exist. See People v. Hernandez, 40 Cal. Rptr. 100 (1964).

"consented" to the lie detector test, the parole officer asked him what the test would show. The parolee responded, "Guilty"; it then became unnecessary to administer the test.

Some parole officers feel that the police are in a better position than they to interrogate parolees concerning suspected violations. They cooperate with police interrogation efforts by placing a parole violation hold order on the parolee to enable police to retain custody of him for purposes of interrogation. Sometimes they request the police interrogation themselves and may even participate in it.

In Michigan parole officers must file parole violation reports whenever a violation is discovered, whether or not revocation results. These reports are sent to central parole headquarters and are reviewed there. Before parole is revoked, the parole board insists on a clear demonstration of the existence of parole violation in the violation report. By administrative policy each parole violation report must contain: (1) a summary describing the salient features of the subject's behavior while on parole; (2) circumstances leading to and including the commission of the violation; (3) a concise listing of the violations incurred; (4) recommendations and comments by the officer evaluating the violator's behavior in general and recommending return to the institution or continuance on parole with or without further restrictions; (5) the date of the violations; (6) the date and place the violator can be found; and (7) if the subject is an absconder, his possible destination. A parole violation report may be completed by the parole officer subsequent to investigating an alleged violation even though the result of his investigation indicates that a violation did not occur.[28] The following is a typical listing of parole violations in such a report, complying with the second and third of the directives concerning violation reports:

1. Violation of Rule No. 2, changing residence without permission based on the fact that the subject admitted that he was not living at his parole residence but with various friends.
2. Violation of Rule No. 2, failure to keep steadily employed based on the fact that the subject has not sincerely tried to secure work.
3. Violation of Rule No. 4, excessive use of intoxicating liquors based on parole officer's examination of the subject and the police report indicating that the subject was arrested for being drunk.

[28] In one case a parole violation report was filed on the basis of a police in-custody interrogation of a parolee for suspicion of burglary, even though the interrogation did not result in prosecution and the police, convinced of his innocence, released the parolee. The parole officer concluded at the end of the violation report that he believed there had been no parole violation.

4. Violation of Rule No. 9, failure to keep parole officer informed as to his whereabouts, movements, and activities.

Writing the parole violation report forces the parole officer to indicate the grounds for his belief that the parolee violated his parole. A revocation request accompanied by an unsatisfactory violation report will be rejected by the district supervisor, the central administration, or the parole board.

b. *Administrative review of revocation recommendations.* In Michigan and Wisconsin there are systems of administrative review of parole revocation requests made by parole officers. Although these systems function as a check to assure that sufficient evidence exists to revoke parole in individual cases, they are primarily used as a check on whether revocation is desirable apart from evidence sufficiency problems and as a device for checking the quality of casework rendered by supervising parole officers. Judged simply in terms of the number of decisions overruled by this method, the review systems would have to be regarded as devices of marginal usefulness, since it is rare for a parole officer's revocation recommendation not to be followed. On the other hand, it is clear that the parole officer's revocation decision and the care with which he arrives at that decision are affected by the fact that a review system exists.

In Michigan a parole officer's decision to request revocation, made after the investigation methods discussed previously have been used, is subject to a two-stage review process before the parole board hears the case. The parole officer's decision must be approved by the supervisor of his district office. It is then sent to the assistant director of the Bureau of Pardons and Paroles who reviews the decision. If he approves, he issues a warrant for the apprehension of the parolee as a parole violator, although in most cases he is already in custody as a result of action taken without a warrant. When the warrant is issued, the parole violator is returned to the correctional institution to await his parole violation hearing before the parole board. The supervisor of a district office commented that it is sometimes necessary for him to overrule a revocation recommendation for technical violations made by an overenthusiastic parole officer. After he reviews the recommendation, it is very rare for the assistant director of the Bureau of Pardons and Paroles to turn it down. He said it would not happen more than 1 time out of 100.

In Wisconsin a parole officer's decision to revoke parole must be approved by the supervisor of his district office. The recommendation is then sent to one of two supervisors of field services of the

Division of Corrections for review. He reviews the request for its legality and quality of casework. The supervisor of field services for the western half of Wisconsin indicated that he rarely refuses to follow a recommendation that has the concurrence of the district supervisor. He indicated that perhaps the supervisor for the eastern half of the state turns down more requests because of the wide variety of parole officers operating out of the Milwaukee district office. If the supervisor approves the request, the parole violator is returned to the institution to await his parole violation hearing. In the meantime, the request is forwarded to the Director of the State Department of Public Welfare, who has formal responsibility for the revocation decision. A supervisor of field services said that the request is always concurred in by the Director and that, in the five years he has been a supervisor, he could not remember a single recommendation turned down by the Director.

c. *Parole violation hearings.*

Illustration No. 8: Revocation was requested on the ground the parolee had been convicted of larceny from a store. When asked to tell about the offense, he replied, "I didn't steal no radio and I didn't try to steal no radio." The parole violation report stated the parolee and three others took a radio from a store but were apprehended almost immediately. The parole board quickly declared his parole to be revoked and notified him he would receive a parole hearing in three years. At this the inmate became hostile and continued to deny the offense. The Michigan parole board reprimanded him for his attitude and advised him to seek assistance from an institutional counselor.

Illustration No. 9: Parole had been revoked prior to the violation hearing. The case history review submitted by the supervising parole officer had requested revocation because the parolee was not adjusting under parole supervision, had failed to work on his farm placement, had left his farm placement without permission, was continued on parole and permitted to take a factory job from which he was fired for unsatisfactory work performance, and was unable to handle his own funds. After the hearing, the Wisconsin parole board forfeited all good time previously earned and informed the inmate he would receive a parole hearing in nine months.

In all three states, parolees returned to correctional institutions for violation of parole receive violation hearings before the parole board. This is true despite the fact that in Wisconsin the power to revoke parole rests with the Director of the State Department of Public Welfare. This is also true despite the fact that a statutory right to a violation hearing is granted only in Michigan.

In Kansas parole violation hearings are held once every two months at the penitentiary and the reformatory. Typically, a parole board member begins the hearing with the question, "Did you violate your parole?" In most cases involving new offenses the answer is "Yes." The parolee is sometimes asked how the violation occurred and gives an answer such as, "I wrote two bad checks," or "I stole a car." Of nineteen parole violation cases heard in one day, the board revoked parole in seventeen. Of the seventeen cases, all but three involved the commission, although not necessarily conviction, of new offenses. Two others were absconders. In one instance, the board continued a person on parole because the revocation request had been based on his passing $35 in bad checks, and he had already paid back $25 and was willing and able to pay the remainder.[29] The parole board permits violators to appear with counsel at their own expense, but this occurs rarely.[30] When parole is revoked, a date for a new parole hearing is set at one year hence at the penitentiary and ten months at the reformatory.[31]

Michigan statutes grant all parole violators, except those convicted of a new criminal offense, the right to a parole violation hearing within thirty days of their return to the correctional institution.[32] In practice all parolees returned to prison, whether convicted of a new offense or revoked upon technical grounds, are given hearings before the parole board within the thirty day period.[33] The parole board has authority to make the revocation decision and may, but rarely does, order the violator continued on parole despite the revocation request.[34]

[29] No instances were observed or heard of in which the Kansas parole board refused to revoke parole because of doubt as to whether a parole violation occurred. Occasionally, as indicated in the text, revocation is refused because the board thinks that it should not occur despite its own belief that there was a parole violation.

[30] Whether significant or not, the instance reported in the text in which the parole board continued the alleged violator on parole because restitution was made occurred in a case in which the parolee was represented by counsel.

[31] These are approximately the same periods of time newly sentenced offenders must wait before receiving their first parole hearings. See Chapter 9.

[32] Mich. Stat. Ann. §28.2310 (1954).

[33] Parolees serving life or very long sentences, who are accused of violating parole and returned to the prison, sometimes do not receive a violation hearing within the statutory thirty-day period. This is because prison authorities feel that, if the parole board has too many cases to hear in a particular month, it is proper to schedule the lifers and long termers for hearing in the next month's session at the institution.

[34] It is not known what percentage of the parolees continued on parole by the board were handled in that manner because of lack of proof of parole violation,

Hearings conducted for parolees returned to prison for conviction of a new offense are brief and conducted in a routine manner.[35] Only two members of the parole board and the parolee are present. The violations with which the parolee is charged are read from the violation report submitted by the parole officer. Normally the parolee admits the conviction and his guilt. Even if he does not, he is pronounced a parole violator and his parole is formally revoked.[36] He is also told when he will receive a hearing for purposes of considering his reparole.

A parolee who is returned as a technical violator (has not been convicted of a new offense) is "arraigned" before two members of the parole board as soon as possible after his return to the institution. The allegations of the violation report are read to him, and he is asked whether he admits them. Normally he does. If the allegations are admitted, the parole board formally revokes parole and informs the inmate when he will receive his first parole hearing.[37]

If the parolee denies any of the allegations in the violation report, he is asked whether he wishes a public hearing. If he does, no further questions are asked. The parolee is entitled to be represented by counsel at his own expense.[38] A representative of the Bureau of Pardons and Paroles calls on the inmate to see if an attorney is to represent him and to obtain the names of the witnesses whom the inmate wishes to have subpoenaed in his behalf. He is

---

and how many were continued on parole because the board judged that the violation, although proved, was not sufficiently serious to warrant revocation.

[35] The statute does not require hearings for this class of violator. See note 32 *supra*. It is not clear why the parole board grants hearings to violators convicted of a new offense. Perhaps the board believes in the rehabilitative value of parole violation hearings. Hearings may also be given to prevent convicted violators from feeling they were unfairly treated because they did not receive a hearing; the great majority of parole violators have not been convicted of a new offense and, hence, receive hearings as a matter of right. It is clear that the parole board will not give a convicted parole violator the full public hearing they give other violators at their request.

[36] When a parolee is sentenced to prison for a new offense, revocation is automatic in the sense that refusal to revoke parole could not permit the parolee to remain outside the prison since he would be there in any case as a result of the new sentence. Therefore, parole is always revoked.

[37] By statute, parole board decisions must be made by a majority of the five-man board. See Mich. Stat. Ann. §28.2305 (1954). Since only two members of the board are present at the violation hearing, they are technically powerless to revoke parole without concurrence by at least one other member of the board. When the parolee admits his violation, the parole board hearing members are able to declare his parole revoked immediately since their decision is automatically ratified later by the full board in executive session.

[38] Mich. Stat. Ann §28.2310 (1954) provides in part: "Upon such hearing such paroled prisoner shall be allowed to be heard by counsel of his own choice, at his own expense. . . ." Some parole board members regarded the appearance of counsel at violation hearings as an unwarranted interference with an administrative matter.

entitled to have the government pay the expenses of having witnesses from within the state appear for his defense if he is unable to afford it.[39] Should the inmate not have counsel, the bill of particulars is mailed to him at the institution and the witnesses named by him are subpoenaed.

At the hearing the Bureau of Pardons and Paroles is represented by an assistant attorney general. The hearing is conducted before two members of the parole board. The supervising parole officer rarely appears at the hearing. According to a member of the parole board:

> What may be termed liberal rules of evidence apply at the public hearing. This does not mean hearsay evidence, however. At the outset of a public hearing, when counsel for the inmate appears, the rules and their interpretation are discussed and both counsel always stipulate the tentative admissibility of such secondary evidence as letters from doctors subject to later objection. In an atmosphere in which both counsel are anxious to determine the facts, serious objections scarcely occur. So far, no objections have ever been made at the time of hearing or later that the procedure was either too technical or too liberal.[40]

If the parolee is not represented by counsel, according to the same parole board member, "the rules of evidence become a shamble. However, before we get through we are certain the parolee's case has been adequately covered, even though he persists in asking leading questions without reserve, and eventually may, and usually does, testify in his own behalf, although he may be said to have done so with great latitude in the period prior to being sworn."

Only a very small proportion of the inmates who request a hearing have an attorney to represent them. One parole board member estimated that one out of every six such parole violators retains counsel. When the parolee at a public hearing cannot afford counsel, he is assured by the hearing members of the board that they will assist him and protect his rights. In conducting the hearing itself, the board is careful to avoid the prosecutor's role, which is left to the assistant attorney general. As one parole board member

[39] Mich. Stat. Ann. §28.2310 (1954) provides in part: "Upon such hearing such paroled prisoner . . . may defend himself, and he shall have the right to produce witnesses and proofs in his favor and to meet the witnesses who are produced against him. If such paroled prisoner shall make it appear to the satisfaction of the board that there is a material witness in his favor within this state without whose testimony he cannot safely proceed to a hearing, and that such paroled prisoner is without funds and cannot obtain the means to procure the attendance of such witness at the place of hearing, the assistant director, having obtained the place of residence of such witness, shall have the power to issue a subpoena to compel attendance of such witness, or any other witness."

[40] Mich. Stat. Ann. §28.2310 (1954) provides that the hearing shall be conducted "under such rules and regulations as the parole board may adopt."

commented: "Nor has it ever been said by a parolee after any hearing that he did not have a full and satisfactory hearing; nor at any time after his revocation, which is the usual outcome."

At the conclusion of a public hearing, final judgment is held in abeyance. Those present are informed that the matter is "to be taken under advisement." A majority of the board — three members — is necessary for a decision and only two members are present at the hearing. Final disposition is made at the next executive session of the board when the findings of the hearing members are presented to the others.[41]

The number of parolees returned to prison as technical violators who elect to have a public hearing has been small since the law providing for such hearings was passed in 1937.[42] Typically, five or six such hearings are held each year. The largest number of hearings held in a single year has been ten. The small number of public hearings is partially due to the care taken by parole officers in ascertaining the facts of a violation and their practice of refraining from initiating revocation procedures if the facts do not support the action. Most parolees brought before the board on charges of technical violations are quick to plead guilty to the counts cited against them. Occasionally a parolee will, when pleading guilty to the charges, present excuses for his misbehavior in an effort to win leniency from the board. Another reason for the small number of public hearings lies in the fact that a substantial number of parolees appearing before the board on charges of technical violations have, in fact, been arrested for the commission of a new offense. The police, prosecutor, or the court may have decided to dismiss the charges against the parolee provided that he is returned to prison as a parole violator. In such instances the parole officer will formally charge the parolee with the commission of technical violations, although the true nature of the situation will be noted in the violation report submitted to the parole board. When the parolee appears before the board, he usually is willing to plead guilty to the technical violations cited against him.[43]

In addition to making the formal revocation decision at the pa-

[41] Stenographic notes are made of the testimony at the public parole violation hearing, as they are of parole board hearings of all kinds. Only that portion of the hearing in which the parole board announces its decision and states its reasoning is transcribed immediately. If a question arises as to what occurred at a hearing, the stenographic notes are then transcribed. One member of the parole board stated that no attempt has ever been made to legally challenge a revocation decision made after a public hearing, and that a transcript of a public hearing has never been requested by a parolee or his attorney.

[42] Mich. Pub. Acts 1937, No. 255.

[43] Another reason may be that parole board members, because they dislike being subjected to public hearings, may subtly discourage parolees from requesting them.

role violation hearing, the Michigan parole board decides how much good time is forfeited because of the violation. Normally, the board forfeits all good time earned by the parolee on parole. An administrative directive prohibits them from forfeiting good time earned in the institution prior to release on parole.[44] At the violation hearing the board also decides when the inmate will appear before it for consideration of reparole. The board has discretion in this matter. In some cases, the board decides that the parole violator is to serve until his entire maximum sentence has expired and therefore sets no date for a parole hearing. Often a hearing is scheduled for one year, but it is not uncommon for the board to schedule a new hearing for three years.[45]

In Wisconsin authority to make the revocation decision rests with the Director of the State Department of Public Welfare.[46] The parole board does not normally participate in this decision. Although there is no statutory right to a parole violation hearing, as a matter of administrative policy hearings are granted to all parole violators except those who have been convicted of and sentenced to prison for a new offense. The parole board members have before them at the time of the hearing the information contained in their case file[47] and a "case history review" submitted by the parole officer at the time of the request for revocation, containing the grounds and reasons for the revocation request.[48]

The Department of Public Welfare has the authority to decide whether to forfeit good time previously earned by parolees who

[44] When the directive was announced, the parole board reacted in a manner to indicate that it resented what it regarded as an unjustifiable infringement upon its practices. It also regarded the directive as a violation of Mich. Stat. Ann. §28.2308 (1954) which provides: "The parole board, in its discretion, may cause the forfeiture of all good time to the date of the declared delinquency." The board members seemed in agreement that the reason for the directive stemmed from an attempt to alleviate the problem of overcrowding in Michigan correctional institutions. They noted that the directive presented great problems for the parole violator who had little time to serve unless good time earned prior to parole was forfeited. The board said that as a result of the directive, some parole violators served only a matter of months before they reached their new mandatory release date.

[45] A member of the Michigan Corrections Commission complained that the parole board was giving too many "three-year passes" and was in that way contributing unnecessarily to the crowded condition of Michigan correctional institutions. A Michigan parole officer noted that, when he is deciding whether to request revocation for a clear parole violation, he considers the fact that if parole is revoked, the parolee may have to serve as long as three years before he is considered for reparole. This, he stated, has lead him not to seek revocation in many cases in which he probably would otherwise have wished to revoke parole.

[46] Wis. Stat. Ann. §57.06(3) (1957).

[47] This is the same file the board uses to make the decision to grant or deny parole. See Chapter 10.

[48] The following is an example of a case history review: "W.S.P.—34027, John Doe, was sentenced to the Wisconsin State Prison on March 5, 1954, in the County Court of Chippewa County to two terms of five to seven years, concurrent, for

have been revoked. In practice, the parole board makes this decision at the violation hearing. It is the policy of the Department that parole and conditional release violators lose all good time previously earned in the institution and on parole.[49] In the violation hearings observed, the parole board forfeited all good time previously earned. At the conclusion of the violation hearing, the parole board informs the violator when he will receive his first hearing to consider reparole. The first hearing is granted at the end of nine months at the reformatory and at the end of one year at the penitentiary.[50]

While there are parole violation hearings in all three states, they do not serve the same purposes. In Michigan the parole board has authority to revoke parole and does not make this decision until after the violation hearing. Although few revocation recommendations are reversed by the Michigan parole board, the fact that it has formal authority to make the decision accounts for the care with which the parole board seeks to establish the existence of a parole violation at the hearing. Sometimes the parole board requests a more complete violation report when the one they have seems inadequate as a basis for making the decision. If the parolee denies any of the allegations in the violation report, the parole board seeks to determine whether he wants a full public hearing on the

---

forging and passing a check, sections 343.56, 343.57. Received at the institution on March 8, 1954. Released on parole April 30, 1956. Returned to the institution on May 17, 1956. Time out on parole: 7 days.

"1. The aforesaid has repeatedly given false information on his activities since being released on parole. He admits that on May 7, 1956, he spent the night at a hotel in Beloit in the company of a twenty-year-old female. Subject lied to supervising agent about the name of the hotel.

"2. The aforesaid has borrowed money from Lutheran ministers in Janesville area on various pretenses which could constitute fraud.

"3. The aforesaid has not worked when work was available and in general conducted himself in such a manner as to warrant revocation of parole."

On some occasions the parole board does not have the case history review at the time of the parole violation hearing. This is particularly likely when the parolee has been returned to the institution shortly before the board's scheduled monthly hearing sessions at the institution. In such cases, the board questions the parolee about the violation and proceeds without the information from the field.

[49] In addition to loss of good time earned in the institution prior to parole and while on parole, there is the problem of credit on the sentence for time served under community supervision. A parolee receives credit on his sentence for all time served while on parole until the time of the parole violation. He begins receiving credit for time served when he again enters the correctional institution. A conditional releasee, however, does not receive credit for any time served on conditional release status when that is revoked. Therefore, he enters prison as a violator with the same amount of time to serve as when he was given conditional release plus the time represented by forfeiture of good time previously earned.

[50] These are the same periods of time a newly sentenced offender must normally spend in a correctional institution before he receives his initial parole hearing. See Chapter 9.

issue of violation. Indeed, the entire statutory and administrative provision for the public hearing reflects the fact that it is the parole board that has authority to revoke parole.[51] In Kansas, by contrast, violation hearings are brief and routine despite the fact that there the parole board also has authority to revoke parole. The Kansas parole board clearly regards the violation hearing as a formality and denials of the fact of violation are met with the assumption that the parolee is lying. On rare occasions the board may continue a parolee on parole because in its judgment he should not have been returned despite a parole violation, but this is not inconsistent with its basic assumption that a parolee appearing before it is a parole violator.

In contrast to Michigan, the parole board in Wisconsin does not have authority to revoke parole. Indeed, parole has already been revoked by the Department of Public Welfare before the violator receives a parole violation hearing. The board exercises little discretion in forfeiting good time and the date for the first new parole hearing is set automatically. This raises the question of the function of the parole violation hearing in Wisconsin. Board members consider that it has a rehabilitative function. The hearing gives the parolee an opportunity to admit or deny the existence of a violation, although denials have no effect on the revocation decision. Further, parole board members feel that the violation hearing shows the parole board's continuing interest in the parolee and may serve to encourage him to work for reparole. Indeed, on some occasions the parole board may advise the violator as to what steps he can take to enhance the probability of reparole. It is clear that parole violation hearings in Michigan also perform these functions in addition to determining whether there has been a violation and setting the date for the first parole hearing.

B. The Decision to Revoke Parole Because of the Parolee's Criminal Conduct

Parole is most often revoked because the parole officer believes the parolee is engaging in serious criminal conduct. The other major reason for revocation is absconding. Occasionally, revocation is based on a belief that the parolee is "slipping" and will soon return to criminality if his parole is not revoked, although even in

[51] As one example of the board's attitude toward its function in determining whether there has been a violation of parole, a parole board member, asked whether violation hearings should be first or last on the monthly hearing schedule, said, "It should be made the first order of business. A parole violator is not actually a violator until we investigate the circumstances and declare him to be a violator."

these situations there may exist suspicion that the parolee is already engaging in serious criminal activity.

Occasionally, the grounds for revocation and the reasons for revoking parole are the same; a parolee who has been convicted of a serious criminal offense is usually revoked for that reason and on that ground. Many times, however, the grounds for revocation are violations of technical conditions of parole while the reason for revoking is suspicion of return to criminal activity. Parole officers are careful to determine whether there are sufficient grounds for revoking parole before they request revocation. Their requests are reviewed by various officials, in part to assure that adequate evidence of a parole violation exists. With respect to the reasons for revocation, however, the situation is much less clear. It is important to examine what assurances there are that parole is not revoked because of a belief (without evidence) that the parolee has engaged in criminal conduct.

1. *Parole revocation following conviction.* In all three states, conviction of a felony constitutes an "automatic violation" of parole; no independent inquiry is made whether parole has been violated. Conviction of a felony may also mean, as it does in Michigan, that the parolee is not entitled to a hearing on the question whether parole has been violated.[52] In addition, and more importantly, conviction of a felony constitutes an "automatic revocation" of parole.[53] This means that, following conviction of a felony, parole will be revoked except in very unusual circumstances. In the rare instances in which parole is not revoked following a felony conviction, the usual procedure is for the court to place the parolee on probation to be supervised by his parole officer. It is a decision which, in the formal sense at least, requires the concurrence of the trial judge with parole officials.[54] In some instances a parolee has committed a felony but officials feel that his parole should not be revoked; the new felony charge may not even be brought into

[52] The Michigan statute does not require a parole violation hearing when the basis for violation is conviction of a felony or misdemeanor. In Wisconsin all parole violators receive hearings except those convicted of new offenses and sentenced to prison on the basis of the new conviction.

[53] This is a matter of administrative policy in Michigan and Wisconsin.

[54] Some indication of the seriousness with which such action is regarded is obtained from statements from those responsible for continuing on parole a person convicted of a felony. A Michigan judge stated that normally he imposes a sentence on a parolee convicted of a felony but that, occasionally, when requested to do so by the supervising parole officer, he will consent to placing the parolee on probation to permit continuation on parole. A Wisconsin parole official stated that conviction of a felony is an automatic revocation of parole but that occasionally a judge will request that the parole officer recommend continuation on parole in meritorious cases. He stated that normally the parole officer complies with the judge's request.

court. In such cases, the new felony charge remains available for later use should the need arise.

In Wisconsin the sentence for the new felony conviction is usually made concurrent with the remainder of the parole term.[55] This is consistent with the general practice of imposing concurrent sentences when any offender has been convicted of more than one offense.[56] In the rare instances in which consecutive sentences are imposed, the reason is that there is little time remaining on the old sentence but the circumstances of the new felony offense (or more likely offenses) are such that a longer term seems warranted. Even in this situation the new sentence may be imposed concurrently because the longer of the two sentences governs the prison term and the other is completely disregarded. In some instances in Wisconsin, if the time remaining on the old sentence is long, the trial judge may suspend either the imposition or execution of the new sentence. This is done on the assumption and assurance that parole will be revoked immediately and because there seems to be no need to impose a new sentence in light of the time remaining to be served on the old. Some Wisconsin judges view this as a means of minimizing the criminal record of young parolees.

A Michigan statute requires that any parolee convicted of a new offense receive a consecutive sentence.[57] Service on the new sentence begins only after the old sentence has been completely served. The usual trial judge reaction to this statute is simply to impose the new sentence concurrently with the old. It seems clear that by virtue of the statute this is a consecutive sentence, although it is unclear how the correctional authorities regard such sentences.[58] In a substantial number of cases, however, the trial judge may suspend the imposition or execution of the new sentence upon receiving assurances that parole will be revoked in order to avoid the effects of the mandatory consecutive sentence law.[59] More felony sentences

[55] Wis. Stat. Ann. §959.051(5)(1958) specifically provides that consecutive sentences may be imposed under those circumstances: "and if the defendant is then serving a sentence, the present sentence may provide that it shall commence at the expiration of a previous sentence."

[56] See Chapter 7.

[57] Mich. Stat. Ann. §28.2308 (1954) provides in part: "Any prisoner committing a crime while at large upon parole and being convicted and sentenced therefore shall be treated as to the last incurred term, as provided under section 34 of this act." Section 34 (Mich. Stat. Ann. §28.2304 (1954)) states how the parole eligibility and mandatory release dates are to be computed when consecutive sentences are imposed.

[58] Possibly they take the position that they are bound by the determination of the trial judge that the sentences are to run concurrently and, therefore, treat the sentences as concurrent.

[59] One judge stated that he suspended sentence if the parole violator had a long enough period of time remaining on his original sentence because there is no need to impose an additional sentence. He feels that it is best to leave such

are suspended in Michigan than in Wisconsin under these circumstances and the Michigan statute seems responsible for the difference. It is also possible that the Michigan mandatory consecutive sentence law is a substantial factor in those instances in which new felony charges are not brought into court and parole is revoked.[60]

Conviction of a misdemeanor likewise constitutes an automatic violation of the conditions of parole but does not lead to an automatic revocation of parole. In many instances, new misdemeanor charges are not brought into court and the parolee is continued on parole with only a warning. Many parolees convicted of misdemeanors receive short sentences to local correctional institutions and are continued on parole during and after service of these sentences. They may, of course, also receive probation and be continued on parole.

Special problems arise when a parolee is convicted of a misdemeanor and it is contemplated that parole will be revoked. Misdemeanor sentences typically must be to local correctional institutions while revocation of parole results in return of the parolee to a state correctional institution.[61] The problem is aggravated because, in many instances, the sentencing decision must be made before the revocation request can be processed, which often occurs due to the relative speed of proceedings in misdemeanor courts. The usual solution to this problem is for the trial judge to sentence the parolee to a term in a local correctional institution to await the revocation decision. When that decision is made and communicated to the judge, the parolee is returned to court, his case reopened, and the misdemeanor sentence suspended, thereby permitting his immediate return to the state correctional institution to resume service of his original sentence. The misdemeanor sentence in these situations is only a device to permit continued custody of the parolee pending the formal revocation decision and return to the state correctional institution. This practice obtains in both Michigan and Wisconsin, although in the latter state a statute

---

questions up to the parole board if the violator can possibly be rehabilitated. The judge indicated that it is not always the normal procedure to suspend the sentence because much depends upon the man and the type of offense involved. If, according to the judge, the parolee before him has a serious character disorder, and there is little hope for rehabilitation, perhaps a consecutive sentence would be imposed. The "character disorder" would be shown by a long criminal career and a background replete with evidence of inability to adjust, failure to accept responsibility, a poor home condition, etc., all leading to the improbability of rehabilitation.

60 A judge might be unwilling to make the rather visible suspension of sentence decision and may, therefore, favor a disposition that would not involve taking the case into court. This would, of course, also have beneficial record consequences for the parolee.

61 See, for example, Wis. Stat. Ann. §57.072 (1957).

permits merger of a misdemeanor sentence into a felony sentence.[62] While this statute would theoretically' permit the parolee to be sentenced for a misdemeanor and to serve that and the remainder of the original felony sentence at the same time, it appears that the statute is never used. Perhaps one reason for this is that, frequently at the time the trial judge must impose the misdemeanor sentence, it is not known clearly that parole will be revoked.[63]

It is probably true that fewer parolees charged with new felony or misdemeanor offenses demand trial than do defendants generally. It seems clear that in those instances in which the parolee, although convicted of a felony or misdemeanor, is continued on parole the conviction is upon a plea of guilty, and the parolee is told of the probable disposition of his case before pleading, or pleads guilty in the hope of being continued on parole. Further, the guilty plea signifies "cooperation" and for that reason tends to make the parolee a fit subject for continuance of supervision. With respect to those parolees who are revoked after conviction, it is not clear the extent to which the conviction is based upon a negotiated plea of guilty. Charge reductions and sentence concessions, especially promises not to impose consecutive sentences, could be used in negotiations for pleas of guilty. On the other hand, guilty pleas might be entered on the basis of nothing more than a general expectation by parolees of a lenient sentence.

With respect to the sufficiency of the evidence to revoke parole, rarely is the test of trial used. There is no more assurance of guilt in these cases than in negotiated guilty plea cases generally. The state's position in bargaining for guilty pleas is enhanced because of the vulnerable position of the parolee. It is possible that this position is used to induce guilty pleas. If so, then parole revocation based on negotiated guilty pleas offers less assurance of underlying evidence sufficiency than do guilty plea convictions generally.[64]

2. *Parole revocation without conviction.* Many parole revocations that are based on a belief that the parolee is engaging in serious criminal activity occur without a conviction of the suspected crimes. Parole officials in Michigan and Wisconsin stated that most

[62] Wis. Stat. Ann. §959.051(5)(1958) provides in part: "If the defendant is sentenced to a state prison and to a jail on separate counts, both sentences shall be served concurrently at a state prison unless otherwise ordered by the court."

[63] Although normally sentence is suspended in misdemeanor cases, in one instance the court imposed a one-year sentence to a local correctional institution and provided that service of this sentence was to begin only after release from the state correctional institution where the defendant was being returned for parole violation. Although the parolee had at least six years to serve on his original sentence, the trial judge felt the consecutive sentence was warranted because of the intense publicity given to the case in the local newspapers.

[64] For a discussion of the practice of plea bargaining and of the problem of the sufficiency of the evidence upon a plea of guilty, see Newman, Conviction (1966).

revocations for technical violations of parole really involve a return to criminality by the parolee and that parole is revoked on technical grounds to avoid the necessity of a conviction. This may constitute a considerable percentage of the total revocations. During a two-month period in Michigan, for example, 30 percent of all revocations involved new sentences to state correctional institutions, 34 percent involved absconders, and 36 percent involved technical violators other than absconders.[65] It is likely that the great majority of the technical violators were returned because of a belief they were engaging in serious criminality.[66]

In most cases in which parole is revoked without conviction but because of the parolee's criminal conduct, it is clear the parolee is convictable of the offense suspected. Usually he has been arrested for the new offense and the prosecutor stands ready to prosecute him, confident of obtaining a conviction. If parole were not revoked, the parolee would be prosecuted and convicted. If convicted, it is quite likely that parole would be revoked more or less automatically.

The supervising parole officer, his supervisor in the district office, and the prosecuting attorney or one of his assistants, always participate in deciding whether to revoke parole in lieu of prosecution for the new offense.

Revoking parole instead of prosecuting conserves the limited resources available to prosecutors, police departments, and trial courts. If the parolee is prosecuted and convicted, the prosecutor, the police, and the trial court must spend additional time on the case even if there is a plea of guilty. If parole is revoked, the case is closed immediately as far as these agencies are concerned. If the parolee is convicted, his parole will be revoked. Often the sentence on the new conviction is suspended if the length of time remaining to be served, because of the revocation, is considered adequate under the circumstances of the case. Enforcement agencies see little advantage in prosecution and conviction while those steps require expenditure of additional resources. It should not be surprising, then, to find these agencies normally quite willing to turn the

[65] For the same 2-month period in Detroit alone, 27 percent of all revocations were for absconding, 36 percent were because the parolee had received a new sentence to a state correctional institution, and 37 percent were for technical violations other than absconding. During this 2-month period, 82 paroles were revoked in Detroit while 180 paroles were revoked in the entire state.

[66] A Michigan parole officer stated that there are very few revocations for minor technical violations. He said the revocations which do occur are the result of many technical violations and, usually, the parolee is strongly suspected of having engaged in illegal activity. The parole officer stated that he knows the number and seriousness of technical violations required by the central office for revocation. He stated that sometimes these are a pretext while the real reason may be that the parolee is viewed as a danger to the community.

defendant over to parole officials for revocation.[67] Of course, if little time remains to be served on the old sentence and if enforcement agencies view that time as inadequate because of the seriousness of the new offense or other reasons, then the parolee will be prosecuted, convicted, and sentenced for the new offense.[68]

For the parole system, one of the major advantages of revoking parole instead of prosecuting is the minimization of publicity adverse to the institution of parole. If the parolee is prosecuted, convicted, and sentenced, he is continually exposed to newspaper publicity which, at least in serious cases, may result in the formation of public opinion adverse to the parole system. Parole agencies are particularly sensitive to newspaper criticism[69] and may view revocation as a satisfactory means of avoiding it, at least in cases in which it promises to be severe. On the other hand, it is clear that police and prosecutors may be unwilling to permit revocation in lieu of prosecution in cases that have already received considerable notoriety. There is some evidence they fear being criticized for "going soft" on the recidivating parolee by not prosecuting. In at least one observed instance, the presence of unusual publicity caused the interested officials to abandon their discussion of revocation in favor of prosecution, conviction, and imposition of a consecutive sentence, despite the fact that the time remaining to be served because of revocation seemed adequate to them.[70]

Another advantage to the parole agency of revoking parole instead of prosecuting for the new offense is that such action puts it in a posture of cooperation with the enforcement agencies. In many cases, the benefits of the revocation alternative are greater for the enforcement agencies than for the parole system.[71] Nevertheless, the parole agency invariably complies with requests from these

[67] A Wisconsin parole official stated that the Milwaukee County prosecutor is always willing to permit revocation instead of prosecution and often initiates the procedure because it saves his office time and expenditure of limited manpower.

[68] Usually there is a great deal of time remaining to be served after revocation because all of the parolee's previously earned good time is automatically forfeited. It would be suspected that Wisconsin, because of the judicially imposed maximum sentence, would experience more need to prosecute parolees for new offenses than would Kansas or Michigan, where the longer legislatively set maxima obtain. There is no specific evidence to support or refute this expectation, however.

[69] See Chapter 11 for a discussion of the great impact of newspaper publicity on the decision to grant or deny parole.

[70] In that case the parolee had six to nine years remaining on the old sentence. The new offense was passing bad checks, normally not regarded as a particularly serious offense. However, because the parolee had feloniously assaulted a police officer a number of years before, the newspapers gave the case unusual publicity, emphasizing that aspect particularly.

[71] It saves the parole agency no resources to revoke before conviction rather than after conviction. In fact, it may result in the parolee receiving a parole violation hearing when he would not receive such a hearing if he were convicted of the new offense.

agencies to revoke the parole of a clearly convictable parolee. While the direct benefits of revocation in such cases may be minimal to the parole agency, its action aids efforts to secure the cooperation of police and prosecutor in their contacts with parolees.[72]

The advantages of revocation for the clearly convictable parolee are considerable. In some cases, minimization of publicity is as important to the parolee as it is to the parole system; the parolee may prefer revocation for this reason. If the parolee is prosecuted and convicted, his criminal record reflects another conviction for a serious offense, which is, of course, likely to have adverse effects upon him in later contacts with criminal justice agencies and in seeking employment. On the other hand, if his parole is revoked, his criminal record reflects his arrest and revocation but does not note a conviction. Normally the revoked parolee does not begin again the service of his old sentence until he is physically returned to the state correctional institution. The time from the violation to his return is "dead time" that does not count on his sentence even though he spends it incarcerated in a local institution. Revocation in lieu of prosecution reduces dead time and somewhat shortens the total time he may have to serve. This may be a considerable advantage to the parolee in urban areas with congested court dockets even when a plea of guilty is contemplated.[73] If the parolee is convicted, he faces the possibility of a consecutive sentence which considerably postpones his eligibility for reparole. Even if sentence is imposed concurrently, however, the minimum sentence may be longer than the time he would have to serve before his first parole hearing if there were no minimum sentence. This, for some parolees, may be a considerable advantage.

These advantages are premised on the assumption that the parolee is clearly convictable and would be prosecuted and convicted if parole were not revoked. This probably describes the great majority of cases; in other cases, however, the parolee's convictability may be subject to considerable doubt. Revocation in such situations presents quite different problems because there are no formal procedures to determine the parolee's guilt of the crimes suspected.

The extent to which such revocations occur is unknown. With respect to a similar aspect of revoking probation, a Kansas judge

72 Parole agencies cultivate police and prosecutor as a source of information concerning parole violations and need the cooperation of these offices in investigating and apprehending suspected parole violators. The parole agency's cooperation in revoking upon request may have considerable value in promoting cooperation from the enforcement agencies in areas in which the parole agency needs it.

73 In some instances, parolees have been known to request revocation in lieu of prosecution because of the effects on the "dead time" which would otherwise be served.

stated that one of the major problems he encounters is the constant requests by police officers, the prosecutor's office, and the F.B.I. to have probation revoked of a person suspected of a crime. He stated that he refuses to revoke probation merely because a law enforcement officer or a prosecutor suspects the probationer of having committed an offense. He concluded that when, however, there is "tangible proof" of the type which would bring about a verdict of guilty in a jury trial, then he would probably revoke. A parole official in Michigan stated that the police request revocation when they have a weak case as well as when the evidence is great. He did not indicate what the response of the parole agency was to such requests. On the other hand, a high-ranking police official in Detroit said, "Some people think that all policemen want to see everybody returned to prison at the slightest excuse. I don't think like this at all. I believe that a lot of men deserve parole, and I don't believe in returning a parolee when there is only suspicion of his activities to go on. I think we should have a clearcut case against a man before we can fairly expect his return as a violator."

No instances were observed in which a parolee was returned as a violator solely because of suspected criminal activities that could not be proved. There were cases observed in which this, along with other factors, resulted in revocation without conviction of the suspected offense. In one such case, a parolee, previously convicted of burglary, was strongly suspected of committing acts of indecent liberties with his twelve-year-old stepdaughter. Clear proof was lacking; the victim was reluctant to testify and there was a desire to save her from the ill effects of testifying to such acts in court. A psychiatrist diagnosed the parolee as a sexual deviate and pronounced him a danger to society. Certain other behavior of the parolee, though not constituting criminal offenses, strongly supported the psychiatrist's diagnosis. The parole officer decided to revoke parole. In this case, the police and prosecutor were not involved because the complaints concerning the parolee's behavior came directly to the parole officer from the parolee's wife.

One of the purposes of parole supervision is to prevent the recurrence of criminality by revoking parole when there are signs the parolee is "slipping" back into crime but before he actually commits criminal acts.[74] A clear example of such a revocation occurs when a sex deviate parolee who is alcoholic begins drinking again. If the parole officer discovers this, the parole is very likely to be revoked, despite a firm belief that the parolee has not recidivated, because of the assumed close relationship between drinking

[74] See Chapter 13.

and abnormal sexual acts. Revocations do not occur frequently under these circumstances and some parole officials believe they should not occur at all because of the difficulty of predicting that the parolee is about to return to criminal activity.[75]

C. The Decision Not to Revoke Parole Despite Evidence Sufficient for Revocation

Parole is often not revoked even when adequate grounds for revocation exist. Indeed, the exercise of discretion[76] in making the revocation decision is commonplace and revocations are unusual by comparison. Parole officers not only acknowledge the existence of discretion but emphasize its importance in the revocation decision. Typically, they assert that not every minor technical violation is a reason for revocation and that the "entire adjustment" of the parolee must be considered. On other occasions they may support a decision to continue a parolee under supervision despite a clear violation on grounds he lacked "criminal intent" or "malicious intent" in committing the parole violation; from the context it is clear such statements mean merely that the parolee should not be returned despite evidence of a violation.

One of the principal reasons for the frequent exercise of discretion in the revocation decision is that parole conditions are not intended to be fully enforced. The primary purpose of parole conditions is to maximize the parole officer's control over the parolee's behavior.[77] As a result, parole conditions tend to be numerous and to touch upon many aspects of the parolee's life, some of which are only remotely related to the causes of his criminality. The violation of many of these conditions usually does not indicate a failure of the parolee to adjust to community life or an imminent danger to society, but indicates instead a normal pattern of behavior well within that expected of usually law-abiding persons. The Michigan Department of Corrections, which is responsible for designing the Michigan parole conditions, states in its instructions to parole officers:

> Not every violation of parole need or should result in the return of the parolee to prison. Often the violation, if only of a

[75] A high-ranking parole official in Wisconsin questioned the validity of revoking parole to prevent criminality on the grounds of the difficulty of making such a determination. He said such revocations do not occur frequently.

[76] Here, as elsewhere in this series of volumes, "discretion" means a decision not to take action despite the presence of adequate legal justification for taking the step.

[77] For an elaboration on this theme, see Chapter 13.

> technical nature and not indicative of criminal or serious ill intent, may point up the area of poor habits or thinking in which the parolee needs help, warning, or simple advice. A majority of persons in trouble are there because they have not learned how to live in harmony with the community. It is a function of parole supervision to try to teach them how to get along without continuing further disruptions that their previous social disabilities have caused. Minor violations, then, may result in better understanding of the problem by the parole officer and improved handling of the case. Even conviction for a misdemeanor, if it fits the conditions above, may be treated by continuation on parole. The question is: Will the community or will the parolee be harmed if the parolee is continued under supervision?
>
> However, should the parolee repeat a pattern of violation, and do so in such a way as to indicate an inability or unwillingness to adjust to community life, stronger measures must be taken. This may be done with the parolee still given the opportunity to remain under parole.[78]

Administrative review of parole officer revocation recommendations is a standard-setting device for the exercise of discretion as well as a review of the evidence sufficiency aspects of parole revocation.[79] Michigan parole officers state they soon learn how serious parole violations must be in order to be approved for revocation by the central office and the parole board.

Even if parole conditions were intended to be enforced fully, such a policy would be unworkable. One parole official stated that, if parole were revoked for every known violation, every parolee would be reincarcerated at one time or other while under supervision. Another official estimated that full enforcement would result in a revocation rate of 70 to 80 percent of all parolees. The effects full enforcement would have upon overcrowded correctional institutions are obvious. If parole conditions were fully enforced, there would literally be no place for the returned parolees in the institutions. Some discretion, therefore, is necessary.

The fact that parole conditions are not intended to be enforced fully and that there is need for less than full enforcement created by prison population pressures explains the existence of discretion in the revocation decision. But it tells nothing of the criteria used in exercising discretion. It is, therefore, necessary to examine in detail the reasons for not revoking parole in a large number of individual cases. It is also important to understand what alternatives to revocation exist in practice, because the parole officer's

[78] Michigan Department of Corrections, Manual of Procedure for Michigan Parole Officers 37-38 (1954).

[79] See pages 350-351.

choice is not simply whether to revoke, rather it is a choice between revocation and a number of actions short of revocation that are designed to deter future violations.

1. *Criteria for the exercise of discretion not to revoke parole.*

Illustration No. 10: A parolee reported to his parole officer that he had left the state without permission and had become involved in an automobile accident while out of the state. The parole officer ascertained that law enforcement officials in the locale of the accident absolved the parolee of any fault. The parolee said, "Well, I guess you have plenty of grounds to revoke me if you want to." The parole officer replied that leaving the state without permission was a ground for revocation but that it appeared to him the parolee had suffered enough for his violation due to the injuries resulting from the accident. The parole officer lectured his client on the necessity for obeying the parole conditions and dismissed him. After the parolee left, the officer stated that since he had only a few weeks remaining on his parole period and had had no difficulty for the last year, it would take an extremely serious parole violation to justify revocation.

Illustration No. 11: The parolee posed a constant supervisory problem, losing many jobs and lying to the parole officer about her residence, among other activities constituting grounds for revocation. She had a number of prior experiences in correctional institutions. Prior to her latest parole, an institutional psychiatrist reported: "Her prognosis for adjustment is not good. However, it is questionable that she would profit by further incarceration, as is shown by her past record." The parole officer said that, although her client had not committed a serious offense while on parole, she had committed a number of technical violations. Nevertheless, she decided not to revoke parole because she believed that incarceration would not help the parolee. She stated she would consider the case a "success" if the parolee made it through the parole period without committing a serious offense.

Illustration No. 12: The parolee had been released from prison eight days prior after serving a term for armed robbery. He and a fellow inmate whom he had met in prison were arrested for petty larceny of a radio. The parolee's companion tried to absolve the parolee of responsibility, but the latter readily and fully admitted his guilt to the parole officer. Although associating with another parolee and petty larceny were both violations of parole conditions, the parole officer decided not to revoke parole because of the parolee's honesty and candor with respect to the offense. The parole officer felt this might be the turning point in the case and wished to continue the parolee under supervision.[80]

The factors affecting the exercise of discretion not to revoke parole are numberless. Most of them, however, can be grouped into three types of considerations: the seriousness of the parole violation, the adjustment of the parolee, and the consequences of revocation.

Conviction of a single felony committed while on parole almost always results in revocation of parole. Commission of a felony usually results in revocation, although occasionally the case may not be taken into court and the parolee continued on parole. Absconding also usually results in revocation, even when it does not involve a renewal of criminal activity.[81] Except for commission of a felony and absconding, however, no single parole violation is re-

[80] A few days later the parole officer learned that the parolee had turned down several good job offers, was borrowing money from several other parolees, had spent his institutional loan of $26 within four days after receiving it, and was suspected of burglary in addition to the petty larceny. The parole officer concluded that the parolee's apparent candor with respect to the petty larceny was only manipulative, and he decided to revoke the parole.

[81] A Kansas parole officer said there usually are four or five parolees on his caseload whom he cannot locate and who have moved from the last given address and have not notified him of any new address. He said that a parolee was usually safe if he reported within four months and gave his new address. If the parolee does not report in four to six months, the officer receives a typewritten statement from the central office stating that the parolee is an absconder. He said that when things go that far and the man is apprehended, his parole is automatically revoked. In Wisconsin absconding is the only technical violation which in itself is likely to result in parole revocation. The Wisconsin Division of Corrections has established rules to guide agents in reporting absconders and in recommending revocation: "Agents will notify the supervisor of field services and the district supervisor . . . as soon as they can determine that a client has absconded, noting the date of absconding, the known facts surrounding such act, and any suggestion as to the absconder's possible whereabouts or activities. . . . Recommendations to revoke are encouraged at the end of the fifteen days subsequent to absconding. Recommendations to revoke are *mandatory* thirty days after the whereabouts are undetermined unless the district supervisor or supervisor of field services approves a different course of action." Wisconsin Division of Corrections, Bureau of Probation and Parole, Field Agents Manual, Ch. 3, §3.12(3) (Nov. 23, 1955). The return of absconders is the responsibility of the institutions. If an absconder is located out of state, the Division of Corrections must approve his extradition or return. It is the policy of the Division to return all absconders with the exception of persons under conditional release with only one or two months of supervision remaining. The short period of possible incarceration is not believed to warrant the expense of return. However, the absconder who remains at liberty for a considerable period of time and who establishes a respectable mode of life has a chance of not being returned to the correctional institution. For example, a parolee who was located nine years after absconding was not returned because investigation revealed that he had established a very good business, was a respected member of the community, and was in no way suspected of having engaged in illegal activity.

garded as being sufficiently serious by itself to require revocation. Even conviction of a misdemeanor usually does not result in revocation. In most cases, then, revocation is not seriously considered unless there have been several parole violations. In these situations one factor which is carefully considered is the seriousness of the violations. In one case, for example, parole was not revoked despite the parolee's conviction for drunkenness that involved a barroom fight. After investigating the circumstances of the fight, the parole officer concluded the parolee was not the aggressor and decided not to revoke parole for that reason. In another case, the parolee was apprehended with a gun illegally in his possession, but his parole was not revoked because after investigation the parole officer concluded that the parolee, who had a fondness for hunting and target shooting, had no intent to use the gun in commission of a crime.[82] One parole officer stated that an important factor he considers when a parolee reverts to use of narcotics is whether there is evidence he is supporting his habit by criminal activity.

If the violation, although serious by most standards, is expected behavior in the parolee's subculture, the parole officer may decide not to revoke. In one case, a parolee was not returned to prison when he stole from his employer, a hotel, because the parole officer believed that hotel employees frequently engaged in such behavior due to low salaries. Several parole officers stated they do not attempt to enforce their moral code on parolees because they believe that for many parolees moral liberality, especially with respect to sexual conduct, is an important part of their subculture.[83]

The most frequently cited reason for not revoking parole is that the parolee is adjusting reasonably well. Violations that occur shortly after the parolee's release from prison are more readily excused because that period is regarded as the most difficult the parolee will face.[84] If a parole violation occurs after the parolee has spent considerable time on parole without violating, revocation is

[82] Although parole was not revoked, the parolee's gun was confiscated by the police and given to the parole officer.

[83] In one case, the parole officer indicated that although the parolee, a Negro woman, was undoubtedly receiving gifts from her "boyfriend" in exchange for sexual relations, she was not going to take steps to terminate the illicit relationship because she viewed it as a common situation in Negro culture and noted that one could not expect Negroes to live up to the parole officer's personal moral standards. In another case, the parole officer, when informed that one of his parolees was accused of accosting and soliciting a female under the age of sixteen, indicated he would not revoke parole, noting: "This is normal behavior in the parolee's environment and he would not be changed by ten years' imprisonment so there is no use doing anything to him."

[84] One parole officer noted that he expects parolees to become drunk several times immediately after release from prison and does not revoke parole or even severely reprimand them unless the drinking persists.

unlikely. This is also true if the parolee first violates parole but then improves his conduct before violating again. The parole officer's impression of the parolee's candor regarding his behavior is also an important consideration.

The consequences of revocation are also important. A parole officer may decide not to revoke the parole of a person who is adjusting poorly if he believes that reincarceration will not change the parolee's behavior. In such instances, the parolee may be continued on parole despite an unusual number of serious technical violations. Another consideration is the parole officer's estimate as to the length of time the parolee would have to serve before reparole. One Michigan parole officer stated that, because the Michigan parole board frequently does not consider reparole for three years, he is very reluctant to revoke parole for even a large number of technical violations. He stated that, if reparole were considered in six months or one year after return as a parole violator, his revocation practices would change sharply.[85] Some parole officers are reluctant to revoke parole when the parolee has only a short time remaining to serve until discharged from supervision. They feel that good behavior during the larger part of the parole period merits unusual consideration when violations occur just before supervision is to be terminated. In addition, the time remaining to be served if parole is revoked would often be too short to be of any benefit to the parolee or to the community. One parole officer stated that he is extremely reluctant to revoke the parole of young parolees because of a fear they will be sent to the penitentiary, which, he feels, may have an adverse effect upon them.

2. *Alternatives to parole revocation.*

Illustration No. 13: The police department informed the parole officer that one of his parolees was in the police ward of a hospital with a stab wound in his stomach. The wound was inflicted by another parolee during a fight. In his violation report the parole officer noted the parolee's conduct was a violation of the rule against associating with other parolees, but stated: "It appears that, after interrogation by precinct detectives, the subject has been cleared of any possible criminal activity. This meeting between the subject and the other parolee did not appear to be planned; from all indications it seems to have been an accidental meeting. The parole officer had a very lengthy talk with the subject regarding his parole

85 In many instances the Michigan parole board has been observed to warn inmates whom they release on parole that if they are returned as a parole violator, they will serve the remainder of the sentence without possibility of parole. It is not known whether this warning is ever communicated to the supervising parole officer.

rules and regulations and tried to point out the trouble that he can be involved in by disregarding these rules and regulations. Subject now seems to realize the close call he had and stated he would be more careful in the future. Thus, since the subject has only been on parole for a relatively short time, and the association with another parolee appeared to be only a chance meeting, it is the recommendation of the parole officer that the subject be continued on parole without further penalty."

Illustration No. 14: Over one year after his release from prison after serving a term for indecent exposure, the parolee was convicted of a misdemeanor sex offense. Parole was not revoked. Instead, the parolee received a six-month sentence to a local correctional institution and was continued on parole on condition that he receive outpatient psychiatric care at his own expense.

Although parole is often not revoked despite adequate evidence, it is unusual for no action at all to be taken when a parole violation comes to the attention of the officer. A number of disciplinary measures short of revocation of parole are used when parole is violated. The most frequent measure used instead of revocation is a reprimand or lecture by the parole officer. Most minor violations of parole conditions are handled by reprimand with a warning that further misconduct may result in revocation.[86] Sometimes the reprimand is accompanied by imposition of a special parole condition specifically prohibiting the troublesome conduct. For example, if a parolee frequently violates the parole condition prohibiting drinking alcoholic beverages to excess, his parole officer may impose a special parole condition prohibiting consumption of any alcohol and warn the parolee that violation of that condition will mean an automatic revocation of parole.[87]

If a parolee steals property, he may be permitted to make restitution of the goods taken and, if he is willing and able to make restitution, parole will not be revoked. In one case, a married pa-

[86] In one case, when the parolee reported for an office interview, the parole officer informed him that he was on the borderline and very close to being sent back to prison; the parolee had had a woman in his room and had not reported when he was ordered to do so. Furthermore, the parole officer pointed out that the parolee had changed his employment without notifying him. The parolee replied that he had quit his last job because he thought he was going to be laid off since the firm he was working for was laying off employees regularly. The parole officer again informed the parolee of the precariousness of his situation and indicated he was on the borderline of being sent back. He instructed the parolee to find another job. After the parolee left, the parole officer stated he hoped the "shock treatment" would have some effect on the parolee.

[87] See Chapter 13.

rolee stole $5000 from his paramour, who reported the theft to the police. A lie detector test verified her accusations. The parolee promised to repay the money to the complainant, which seemed to satisfy her. Parole was not revoked. Occasionally, a parole violation may result in the parolee receiving psychiatric or other treatment for his problem instead of revocation. The general lack of such treatment facilities prevents this being used as a regular alternative to revocation, and it is used most frequently when the parolee is financially able to obtain private treatment. In Detroit such an alternative is available without regard to financial status for parolees who are narcotics users. Parolees who are known or suspected to be using narcotics are quickly taken into custody by the parole officer for technical violations so that it can be determined whether there is narcotics use. The parole officer usually seeks to win the confidence of the parolee and get him to admit that he is "using." If the parolee admits the use of narcotics, the parole officer may continue him on parole on condition that he submit himself to outpatient treatment in the public narcotics clinic.

If the parole violations become too serious to permit handling by simple lecture and reprimand, the parole officer may resort to a short period of incarceration in a local correctional institution in an effort to deter future violations. Frequently, when parolees are arrested on drunkenness or disorderly conduct charges, the parole officer may encourage the judge to sentence him to a short period in the local jail. Most instances in which parole is not revoked following conviction of a misdemeanor involve parolees who have served short sentences in the local correctional institution as a result of the conviction. Sometimes the parole officer may on his own initiative order his client's apprehension and a short period of detention as a parole violator in an effort to alter his conduct. After the parolee has been detained for several days and the parole officer has talked with him several times, he is released and continued on supervision.

PART IV

The Correctional Process and the Legal System

> What is needed is to provide offenders under correctional authority certain protections against arbitrary action, not to create for all correctional decisionmaking a mirror image of trial procedures. What sorts of protections are proper will depend upon the importance of the decision. . . .
>
> It is too early to attempt to define absolute standards in this area but it is of utmost importance that a beginning be made in considering and experimenting with a variety of methods of safeguarding the rights of offenders.
>
> The President's Commission on Law Enforcement and Administration of Justice, Task Force Report: Corrections 84 (1967)

> Might every governmental function in any set of circumstances have an optimum position on the rules-to-discretion scale, so that discretionary power which is greater than the optimum may be expected to cause one set of harms and discretionary power which is less than the optimum may be expected to cause another set of harms?
>
> Davis, *Administrative Law* 82 (1965)

Traditionally, the correctional process has operated close to the discretionary end of the scale. This probably reflects the assumptions that offenders have only "privileges" not "rights," and that the objectives of rehabilitation and community protection can best be served if correctional personnel are free to make decisions on a case-by-case basis. One consequence of this is that there has been vested "in judges and parole and probation agencies the greatest degree of uncontrolled power over the liberty of human beings that one can find in the legal system." [1]

It is clear that correctional decisions are increasingly coming under close judicial scrutiny,[2] and there are proposals for closer legislative guidance of correctional programs.[3] The need is to find the optimum balance between discretion and rule. The history of governmental activity is that the pendulum swings from too great a reliance upon discretion to a preoccupation with formal rules.[4] It is obvious that this should be avoided if possible.

There are methods of external control of correctional decision-making in addition to legislation or court review. One is to insist that a judge make the decision rather than a correctional officer. This may be increasingly required for correctional decisions that are of great significance to the offender, such as the decision to invoke a sex crimes law with possible incarceration for life.[5] It is also possible to develop methods of "civilian" control as is done when the correctional agency is under the control of a board of public welfare. Finally, it is possible to create a system of checks and balances by dividing discretion between two independent decision makers.

Whatever the trend of external control over correctional decisions, it is apparent that there is a trend in the direction of increased attention to methods of reviewing important decisions within the correctional agency itself. There is greater willingness to view corrections as part of the administrative law process, to look upon correctional policy statements as administrative rules, and to subject correctional decisions to the requirements imposed upon other governmental, administrative decisions. This has caused many correctional administrators to give greater attention to the decision-making process within the correctional agency and to insure, for example, that decisions to revoke parole are subject to review either by a supervisory officer or by the parole board.

Chapter 15 deals with control over correctional decision-making. As correctional processes are increasingly subjected to requirements of formality and to judicial review and control, offender and

[1] Kadish, Legal Norm and Discretion in Police and Sentencing Processes, 75 Harv. L. Rev. 904, 916 (1962).

[2] See Kimball and Newman, Judicial Intervention in Correctional Decisions: Threat and Response, 14 Crime & Delinq. 1 (1968).

[3] The Model Penal Code proposals are all based on the assumption that closer legislative control of the correctional process is needed.

[4] M. Cohen, Law and the Social Order 259-267 (1933).

[5] See, e.g., Specht v. Patterson, 386 U.S. 605, 87 Sup. Ct. 1209, 18 L. Ed. 2d 326 (1967); Huebner v. State 33 Wis. 2d 505, 147 N.W.2d 646 (1967).

correctional official alike become more interested in and concerned about the legal system and find themselves more often confronted by lawyers or turning to them for help and advice. Chapter 16 deals with the lawyer and the correctional process.

CHAPTER 15

The Exercise and Control of Discretion in the Correctional Process

The law usually gives the correctional decision maker a wide range of choice, authorizing him to exercise discretion. But there are few legal standards to guide him in choosing from alternatives available. In the absence of legal norms, his decision is based upon such considerations as correctional agency policy, if any, the attitudes of his superiors, the manner in which the problem has been handled in the past, the values and theories of his profession, and his personal views. Even when discretion is apparently precluded by legislation as, for example, when a statute provides a mandatory sentence, precludes probation eligibility, or postpones parole eligibility, techniques used in practice may nullify these restrictions[1] and permit the exercise of discretion.

The existence of broad discretion in the correctional process seems to be the result of deliberate choice reflecting the assumption that effectiveness of the process depends upon the existence of maximum discretion. This is in contrast to earlier stages of the criminal justice system where discretion is either not generally recognized or thought to be a necessary evil.[2] Indeed, the existence and propriety of discretion in corrections is sometimes used to support arguments that it is desirable to minimize discretion in police, prosecutors, and trial judges.[3]

Broad discretion in corrections depends upon at least the acquiescence of courts and legislatures.[4] This avoids for them the difficult problems of setting standards and imposing controls that

1 See Chapters 3, 6, and 9 for discussion of devices used to avoid the impact of mandatory sentences and statutory restrictions on probation or parole eligibility.

2 See LaFave, Arrest: The Decision to Take a Suspect into Custody 61-82 (1965).

3 See, e.g., Hall, General Principles of Criminal Law 55 (1960).

4 For example, legislative parole criteria seem designed to insulate the parole board from judicial control rather than to guide parole decision-making. Also, legislatures sometimes expressly prohibit judicial review of parole decisions. See Dawson, The Decision to Grant or Deny Parole: A Study of Parole Criteria in Law and Practice, 1966 Wash. U.L.Q. 243, 285-303.

would otherwise exist. And for courts in particular, taking a "hands off" attitude toward the process avoids the increase in caseload they anticipate would soon follow more judicial intervention.

Broad discretion is exercised at all decision-making levels, from the most general policy decision down to individual judgments about particular offenders. Discretion is also exercised by all personnel in the correctional agency, from the administrator, through intermediate-level supervisors, to probation and parole officers, parole board members, and caseworkers in correctional institutions. Several examples demonstrate the wide variety of situations in which discretion is exercised.

Probation and parole officers exercise broad discretionary control over their clients. For example, a probation or parole officer often learns of violations committed by clients that technically justify revocation. However, officers seek revocation in only a small percentage of those cases. If the officer seeks revocation, the existence of violations and the desirability of revoking are reviewed by higher authority — the trial judge, the parole board, or a supervisor in the correctional agency. But a decision not to seek revocation despite the existence of provable violations is usually not reviewed. This is true even in the common situation in which the decision not to seek revocation is coupled with action by the officer designed to correct the violating conduct, action that may range from a reprimand or increase in reporting requirements through imposing new probation or parole conditions to detaining the client in a local jail for a period of days.

In most jurisdictions, the trial judge has broad discretion in sentencing the convicted offender. Most sentences are in fact a series of discretionary decisions made by the trial judge: choosing between incarceration and probation; selecting the maximum or minimum sentence, or both, when a prison commitment is imposed; selecting, in some instances, the institution to which the offender will be committed; imposing probation conditions such as restitution or a period of incarceration in a local jail; and setting the length of the probation period. In addition, the trial judge usually has broad discretion in revoking probation. Despite the increase in the number of jurisdictions that permit appellate court review of trial judge discretion in sentencing, in most jurisdictions the trial court decision is final. Sentencing decisions by a trial judge are arguably "judicial decisions" and thus not properly of concern in discussing the exercise of administrative discretion by criminal justice agencies. However, in fact the trial judge does, in sentencing, operate like an administrative agency in the sense that he does not surround his sentencing decision, as he does other decisions, with the attributes of judicial decision-making such as notice, disclosure, and right to formal hearing. As a consequence, it is both realistic and helpful to view the sentencing judge as a correctional decision maker.

Parole boards have broad discretion to release inmates eligible for parole. In some jurisdictions they also set parole conditions, determine the length of the parole period, and exercise discretion in revoking parole. By exercising discretion to approve applications for executive clemency, they sometimes even participate in creating parole eligibility for inmates who by statute are ineligible. When parole is denied, the board typically determines the date when it will next consider the possibility of release. When making any of these decisions, parole board discretion is virtually uncontrolled. Only decisions to grant parole typically receive administrative review and then it is often only minimal. Opportunity for judicial review is very limited.

The correctional agency administrator also possesses broad discretion, although it is not usually exercised with respect to individual cases. He may have freedom, for example, to decide whether inmates will receive parole hearings when their release is considered by the parole board, or whether parole violation hearings will be held as a regular part of the revocation process. He may also have discretion to determine whether inmates or parolees can be represented by retained counsel at parole hearings or parole violation hearings or whether documentary information upon which major correctional decisions are based will be disclosed in whole or part to the individual about whom the decision is made. He usually has broad discretion in deciding what conditions of probation or parole will be imposed, what effect institutional disciplinary infractions will have on parole eligibility or what effect the existence of a detainer will have on inmates' prison programs and opportunities for parole. He also has authority to provide guidelines for the exercise of discretion by front-line personnel and to require administrative review of their decisions.

The problems in controlling discretion in the correctional process are as complex as the variety of situations in which it is exercised. There is no simple answer; a number of approaches must be considered.

A. Greater Legislative Control

Legislatures have allocated discretion among various decision-making authorities but have prescribed few procedures for making decisions and have provided almost no criteria to guide the exercise of discretion. The Model Penal Code makes the assumption that an increase in legislative control is needed. Yet the suggestions of the Code have not been widely followed, and there remains doubt as to how much legislative control over correctional decision-making is possible or desirable.

1. *Precluding discretion.* In the past, most of the sporadic legislative efforts to control the correctional process have assumed the form of precluding the exercise of discretion in defined circumstances. Examples are statutes that preclude probation eligibility for certain offenders or offenses, and statutes that preclude or postpone parole eligibility for certain classes of inmates or provide mandatory sentences. Discussion elsewhere in this volume has indicated in detail how mandatory sentences and legislative declarations of probation ineligibility are circumvented through charge manipulations and why this is likely to occur whenever they are enacted.[5] The practice of manipulating strict parole eligibility requirements by commutation of sentence, thereby relieving overcrowded prisons and individualizing the timing of release on parole, has also been discussed in detail elsewhere.[6] Legislative attempts at control through enactments that preclude discretion are almost certain not to be fully implemented. The administrative pressures resulting from the necessity for handling large numbers of cases with inadequate manpower and the very strong need felt by judges and correctional professionals to reflect individual circumstances in their decisions lead, almost inevitably, to circumvention of such limitations upon discretion.

2. *Statutory criteria.* Legislatures have provided statutory criteria to guide discretion. However, these tend to be admonitions against releasing persons who are likely to violate the law or instructions to act in the best interest of the individual and of society. In practice, legislative criteria are commonly ignored. Most of them are too abstract to provide real control even if they were consulted with a desire to be guided by them. Others are not intended to provide control and are phrased in language intended to indicate that they are only suggestions. In any event, courts will not review decisions to determine whether statutory criteria were followed. Some of the criteria — an example is the common provision that the parole board cannot release an inmate unless there is a reasonable probability he will not violate the law — are often not followed in practice. For example, some parole boards perceive a strong need to release certain kinds of inmates whom they do not consider dangerous, despite their judgment they are likely to violate parole by committing a new criminal offense. When such a

[5] See Chapters 3 and 6.
[6] See Chapter 9.

case arises, parole is granted even though the board knows that a statute purports to preclude release.[7]

Because they set unrealistically high standards, are abstract, admonitory, and not judicially enforced, legislative efforts to control discretion through statutory criteria have completely failed. It is against this background that the recent Model Penal Code effort at statutory criteria must be evaluated. One of the distinctive characteristics of the Code's treatment of corrections is its attempt to provide statutory criteria for major decisions: the probation decision,[8] the parole decision,[9] and decisions to revoke probation[10] or parole.[11] They are carefully drafted and reflect many of the criteria used in practice. While they purport to exhaust the considerations that may properly go into decision-making, they are structured in such a way as to permit flexibility of application. First, they are not intended to operate as rules; rather, they are statements of policy in statutory form.[12] Second, the Code specifically precludes judicial review to determine whether the decision maker has complied with the criteria in individual cases.[13] The Code's criteria are intended to focus the attention of the decision maker upon what the draftsmen regard as the proper criteria. However, unless there is a change in the nature of correctional decision-making, it is doubtful whether the Model Penal Code criteria will have a great impact even if enacted by a state legislature. Correctional professionals are not accustomed to looking to legislation for guidance in making correctional decisions unless the legislative criteria are reflected in administrative policy within the correctional agency. For the Code's criteria to have a substantial impact on day-to-day decision-making they would have to be, in effect, ratified by the correctional administrator. If he instructs his personnel to be guided by the criteria, they are likely to follow his instructions; otherwise, the criteria are not likely to be stressed.

The correctional criteria provisions of the Model Penal Code

[7] See Chapter 11.

[8] Model Penal Code §7.01 (Proposed Official Draft, 1962).

[9] Model Penal Code §305.9 (Proposed Official Draft, 1962).

[10] Model Penal Code §301.3 (Proposed Official Draft, 1962).

[11] Model Penal Code §305.15 (Proposed Official Draft, 1962).

[12] This is stated most strongly in the section specifying criteria for the decision to grant or deny parole. Model Penal Code §305.9 (Proposed Official Draft, 1962) begins: "Whenever the Board of Parole considers the first release of a prisoner who is eligible for release on parole, it shall be the policy of the Board to order his release, unless the Board is of the opinion that his release should be deferred because. . . ." There follows a list of four criteria that justify parole denial.

[13] Model Penal Code §305.19 (Proposed Official Draft, 1962) precludes judicial review of parole release or revocation decisions. The Code contains no provision for appellate review of sentences.

have had only very limited impact upon state legislation.[14] It seems likely that the Code's suggestions may have a greater impact upon the development of administrative policy than upon the course of future legislation. Whether this is so depends upon whether the correctional field is, in the future, characterized by increased administrative responsibility for policy development and articulation. Absent an administrative willingness to do so, legislatures may become more actively involved and may well adopt criteria such as those proposed by the Model Penal Code.

3. *Decision-making procedures.* A major role the legislature could play in controlling correctional discretion is to impose procedural requirements upon the decision-making process. The legislature could impose a series of procedural requirements that, unlike statutory decision-making criteria, are likely to be enforced by the courts. Primary attention is usually given to three requirements: hearing, counsel, and disclosure of information used in decision-making.

Experience in the three states suggests that hearings will often be held as a part of correctional decision-making whether or not they are required by statute. While the Michigan legislature requires a hearing for probation revocation,[15] release on parole,[16] and parole revocation,[17] Wisconsin statutes are silent on those issues. Nevertheless, hearings are regularly held for those decisions in Wisconsin as a matter of trial judge or correctional agency policy.[18] It is likely that trial judges hold probation revocation hearings because they are accustomed to making decisions by having judicial hearings. It is probable that correctional administrators do not regard parole hearings or parole revocation hearings as safeguards against arbitrary decision-making but rather as useful to them in gathering information, as giving the individuals affected a sense of the fairness and deliberation of the decision-making process, and as therapeutic tools.[19] The impact of legislative hearing requirements

14 An exception is §65.00 of the recently revised New York Penal Law, which provides a modified version of the Model Penal Code criteria for making the probation decision.

15 Mich. Stat. Ann. §28.1134 (1954).

16 Mich. Stat. Ann. §28.2305 (1954).

17 Mich. Stat. Ann. §28.2310 (1954).

18 Parole hearings and probation revocation hearings are substantially the same in Wisconsin as in Michigan. However, the Wisconsin parole revocation hearing occurs after parole has been formally revoked by the Department of Public Welfare. The main purpose of the hearing is to determine how much good time to forfeit and to schedule a hearing for consideration of reparole, not to determine whether parole was properly revoked. See Chapter 14.

19 This seems to be true of the parole hearings held in Wisconsin as a matter of administrative discretion. See Chapter 10.

on the practice may be minimal, therefore, because correctional administrators see real advantage to themselves in using hearings quite independently of statutory requirements.[20]

Correctional attitudes toward the presence of counsel for the individual are quite different. Experience in Michigan and Wisconsin strongly suggests that, unless correctional agencies are required to permit counsel to appear at hearings, they will be excluded. By contrast, Michigan and Wisconsin trial judges permitted counsel to appear at probation revocation proceedings even though they were not then clearly required by law to do so. Trial judges seem to consider attorneys helpful to them in making decisions—although not helpful enough, at the time of the field survey, to appoint counsel for the indigent [21] — while correctional administrators do not regard them as helpful and, indeed, probably view them as obstructive to their therapeutic efforts. If counsel has a function to perform in correctional decision-making and his services are viewed as useful,[22] his presence at nonjudicial hearings is unlikely without a radical change in attitude by correctional administrators or intervention by legislatures or courts.

Correctional administrators have much the same attitude toward disclosure of information used in making decisions: they view disclosure as not helpful to them and as actually obstructive. By contrast, some trial judges, in Milwaukee for example, regularly disclose presentence information to counsel although not required by law to do so.[23] Again, it seems clear that disclosure is not likely to occur unless required by legislative or judicial mandate.

A legislature could require hearings for all major correctional decisions, establish the right to the presence of counsel, appointed and retained, and require the disclosure to counsel of all information used in making the decisions. These requirements could be enforced by the courts. The legislature could even establish a limited right to judicial review of correctional decisions, much like judicial review in administrative law contexts, to determine

[20] This is not to say that correctional administrators always provide the same kind of hearing that would be required by the legislature if it addressed itself to the question. Some statutory hearing provisions seem primarily concerned with protection of the individual, while others seem most concerned with administrative efficiency and flexibility. The Michigan statute dealing with parole revocation hearings, Mich. Stat. Ann. §28.2310 (1954), is an example of the former, while the provision on probation revocation, Mich. Stat. Ann. §28.1134 (1954), illustrates the latter.

[21] A federal constitutional right to appointment of counsel for the indigent now applies to probation revocation proceedings. Mempa v. Rhay, 389 U.S. 128, 88 Sup. Ct. 254, 19 L.Ed.2d 336 (1967).

[22] The roles of counsel in corrections are discussed in Chapter 16.

[23] See Chapter 2.

whether the administrator correctly interpreted the law and whether his findings of fact are based upon "substantial evidence" appearing in the record of the hearing. Whether this degree of formality is wise may be debated. Past experience would indicate a risk that elaborate hearing procedures will not necessarily have a major impact upon correctional practices, partly because counsel is often not requested, and even when requested is unlikely to be able successfully to challenge a discretionary decision made by a qualified correctional agent.

4. *Financial controls.* In the past, legislatures have used their power over appropriations to influence correctional decision-making, but only sporadically. One of the reasons correctional agency administrators are so sensitive to public criticism of decisions made by their personnel is its possible effect upon appropriations. An agency administrator may be criticized for an unwise decision — paroling an inmate who later committed a serious crime that attracted great publicity — when he testifies before appropriations committees. In a more indirect fashion, public criticism of any aspect of the correctional system may result in eroding legislative support.[24]

Though not common in the past, it is possible for major federal and state funding programs to influence correctional practices by the requirements which must be met to receive grants of funds. These requirements could, but have not in the past, stress the development of appropriate administrative procedures to insure against arbitrariness in the correctional process and to aid in making counsel available through programs of legal assistance.

B. Increased Judicial Control

Appellate courts have traditionally played a very limited role in controlling discretion in the correctional process. Observers of the process who perceive a need for greater control sometimes view the appellate judicial system as a suitable vehicle for attaining that goal. Greater control could be accomplished, it is argued, if only the appellate judiciary would forego its traditional reticence toward involvement in the correctional process and adopt an active role. The model is the role played by the United States Supreme Court in controlling preconviction criminal proceedings, particularly police activities. It is asserted that ample authority exists in constitutional provisions as well as in correctional legislation to

[24] The impact of public criticism on correctional decision-making is seen most clearly in the parole-granting decision. See Chapter 11.

justify greater intervention; all that is needed is the desire on the part of appellate courts to provide effective control over the process.

Appellate courts have always intervened in the correctional process to enforce specific statutory procedural rights, such as the right to a hearing or to the presence of retained counsel. They have also been willing to determine whether correctional agency interpretations of statutes, such as parole eligibility or good time laws, are correct ones. However, when appellate courts have determined that a challenged decision is within the statutory discretion of the decision maker, they have traditionally refused to review the propriety of the judgment made or procedures used. Since most correctional decisions are clearly discretionary and appellate courts have tended to find discretion quite readily in borderline situations, their impact on corrections has been quite limited. Despite the retention of traditional attitudes by most courts, there is clear evidence of a trend toward greater judicial intervention.[25]

1. *Reviewing decision criteria.* While appellate courts have always corrected trial court sentences that are in excess of limits permitted by statute, they have traditionally refused to review sentences that are within those limits. Although that is still the situation in over half the states, appellate review of trial court sentencing is available in an increasing number of jurisdictions.[26] In most states that have appellate review of sentences it was specifically authorized by statute; in a few states appellate courts themselves have assumed this role. In the three states under study, only the Wisconsin court has departed from the traditional position and has, since 1963, indicated a willingness to review sentencing under at least some circumstances.[27] The field data, therefore, shed no light on the important question of the effect of appellate review on the course of trial court sentencing. It would be expected, however, that appellate review would tend to decrease the incidence of extremely long sentences and, perhaps, eliminate the use of consecutive sentences altogether, because usually only the defendant can appeal the sentence and the appellate court normally has no authority to increase it. Where it exists, appellate review of sentencing includes not only review of trial court discretion in selecting the maximum or minimum sentences, but also discretion in making the choice between incarceration and probation.

[25] See Kimball and Newman, Judicial Intervention in Correctional Decisions: Threat and Response, 14 Crime & Delinq. 1 (1968).

[26] See American Bar Association Project on Minimum Standards for Criminal Justice, Standards Relating to Appellate Review of Sentences (Tent. Draft, 1967).

[27] State v. Tuttle, 21 Wis. 2d 147, 124 N.W.2d 9 (1963).

Although appellate courts will inquire into whether statutory authority exists for using the probation or parole conditions imposed, this is not a significant limitation because the statutory authorization is normally quite broad.[28] If the challenged condition is not prohibited by statute, it is usually upheld, and the appellate court is unlikely to inquire into whether the decision maker properly exercised his discretion. In extreme cases — a classic example is a condition that, in effect, banishes the offender from the jurisdiction — a condition may be held invalid even though it is not prohibited by statute.[29]

In most jurisdictions, trial courts have discretion whether to use presentence investigations and psychiatric examinations to obtain information for sentencing. Appellate courts have usually refused to upset a sentence because the trial court failed to use these resources. In *Leach v. United States,*[30] however, the United States Court of Appeals for the District of Columbia Circuit held that, on the facts of that particular case, the need for psychiatric information was so obviously critical that the trial judge abused his discretion in imposing sentence without referring the defendant for psychiatric examination.

While appellate courts have traditionally been willing to order the release of a prisoner whose sentence has expired — decisions that sometimes involve difficult problems of interpreting good time laws — they have uniformly refused to review discretion in denying or revoking parole. Intervention in the parole process has been limited almost exclusively to enforcing specific statutory procedural rights. Efforts to secure appellate court scrutiny of parole decision-making criteria from the broader perspective of their conformity to constitutional principles have usually failed.

2. *Reviewing decision procedures.* When reviewing probation revocation proceedings, appellate courts will enforce specific statutory requirements, such as notice of violations alleged, a hearing before the trial court, proof that a probation condition has been violated, or limitations upon the kind of evidence that can be used to prove a violation. In addition, some appellate courts have shown recent willingness to examine the procedures used in revoking probation without regard to specific statutory requirements. In *State v. Strickland,*[31] for example, the Wisconsin Supreme Court held that the federal constitution requires the appointment of

[28] See Chapters 4 and 13.

[29] E.g., Loving v. Commonwealth, 206 Va. 924, 147 S.E.2d 78 (1966), *rev'd on other grounds,* 388 U.S. 1.

[30] 334 F.2d 945 (D.C. Cir. 1964).

[31] 27 Wis.2d 623, 135 N.W.2d 295 (1965).

counsel for the indigent in trial court proceedings for sentencing or revocation of probation. And in *Mempa v. Rhay*[32] the United States Supreme Court extended the federal constitutional right to counsel to revocation of probation. Intervention in the parole granting and revocation process has been limited to enforcing specific statutory rights. Unlike probation revocation, there is no perceptible trend toward scrutiny of procedures from the perspective of broad constitutional principles. However, in *Hyser v. Reed,*[33] the United States Court of Appeals for the District of Columbia Circuit liberally interpreted the federal parole revocation statutes to require procedural rights in the parole revocation process, including the right to an administrative hearing on the alleged violations at the place the parolee was apprehended. While the court expressly refused to apply constitutional principles to the revocation process, its interpretation of the federal statutes led to a set of procedural requirements that the court thought were better suited to the problems posed by the revocation process than would result from a wholesale application of constitutional safeguards.

Several conclusions about appellate court intervention in the correctional process are apparent. First, appellate court intervention is greatly influenced by action taken by the legislature. If statutes prescribe specific procedural requirements, appellate courts will scrutinize the decision-making process to determine whether they are followed. Second, appellate courts are more likely to apply constitutional principles to those correctional decisions that present issues most closely analogous to the issues in the criminal trial and to those stages that are chronologically closest to adjudication. They view the problem of procedural due process in corrections as an extension of due process at the criminal trial. This was clearly the notion in *Mempa v. Rhay,*[34] in which the United States Supreme Court extended the right to counsel to probation revocation proceedings. Third, even if the full range of procedural due process were applied to the correctional process, it would provide a form for decision-making but not necessarily substantive control, so long as the criteria for correctional decisions remained broad and unarticulated. Fourth, there is very little indication that appellate courts are anxious to assume greater responsibility for reviewing correctional decisions. In most jurisdictions with appellate review of sentencing, it was specifically authorized by the legislature. Even where appellate review exists, it has not resulted in the development of a body of principles,[35] which serves to articulate

[32] See note 21 *supra.*
[33] 318 F.2d 225 (D.C. Cir.), *cert. denied,* 375 U.S. 957 (1963).
[34] See note 21 *supra.*
[35] See Chapter 8.

criteria for important correctional decisions. In decisions reducing sentences, no principle emerges that can be used as a guide for future action; the appellate court often simply notes that the sentence seems severe in relation to the total circumstances of the case. In brief, judicial review of correctional decisions is likely to have a limited impact upon the daily operation of the correctional process.

3. *Shifting authority to the trial court.* The approach of increasing judicial control over discretion in corrections is usually thought of as judicial review of administrative action. There is another conception of judicial control over the correctional process. Some correctional decisions can be made by trial judges on the basis of information obtained in a judicial hearing. In this system the trial judge does not function as the first level of judicial review upon petition; rather he makes the correctional decision himself as a regular part of the decision-making process. The trial court might or might not have discretion in making the decision, but it would have exclusive authority to make it.

The question whether some correctional decisions can best be made by the trial judge rather than correctional personnel is important particularly in light of recent indications that the federal constitution requires a judicial hearing and a trial court decision for at least some determinations in the correctional process. In *Specht v. Patterson*,[36] the United States Supreme Court held that federal due process of law requires trial-type hearing and judicial determination of the issue whether a convicted offender comes within the scope of a sex offender act that increases the possible length of incarceration. Mr. Justice Douglas, writing for the Court, indicated that criminal trial-type constitutional protections are required because the sex offenders act increases the possible length of incarceration on the basis of issues not determined in the adjudication of guilt:

> Under Colorado's criminal procedure, here challenged, the invocation of the Sex Offenders Act means the making of a new charge leading to criminal punishment. The case is not unlike those under recidivist statutes where an habitual criminal issue is "a distinct issue" . . . on which a defendant "must receive reasonable notice and an opportunity to be heard." . . . Due process, in other words, requires that he be present with counsel, have an opportunity to be heard, be confronted with witnesses against him, have the right to cross-examine, and to offer evidence of his own. And there must be findings adequate to make meaningful any appeal that is allowed.[37]

[36] 386 U.S. 605, 87 Sup. Ct. 1209, 18 L. Ed. 2d 326 (1967).
[37] Id. at 610, 87 Sup. Ct. 1212, 18 L. Ed. 2d 330.

Although the full implications of the case are not known, it could be interpreted to mean that, whenever the law authorizes correctional action only if certain facts are found to exist, the federal constitution requires giving the individual affected the constitutional procedural protections available in the trial of criminal cases. Such an interpretation would have important implications for proceedings to revoke probation or parole, where not infrequently statutes authorize revocation only if the individual has violated a condition of his probation or parole.[38]

While it is not possible to compare correctional decisions made by the trial judiciary and those made by correctional professionals with any degree of certainty, some tentative conclusions can be advanced on the basis of the field survey data. The closest analogy in practice is the role of the trial judiciary in revocation of probation. Statutes typically grant the trial court power to revoke probation. Whether it is required by statute or not, trial judges insist upon proof of violation of a probation condition before they exercise their discretion to decide whether to revoke. In form, the trial judge has exclusive power to revoke probation, but in practice he functions more as a reviewing authority than as the initial decision maker. The supervising probation officer typically receives information on probation violations from the police, the probationer himself, or his friends or relatives. In most instances, he handles the violation without consulting the sentencing judge. He may reprimand the probationer or take other action to correct the problem. He returns the probationer to the trial court only if he wishes action that requires court participation, such as revocation or a judicial reprimand. The trial judge conducts a probation violation hearing; the probationer is informed orally or in writing of the alleged violations, and the trial judges in the states studied require fairly close adherence to the rules of evidence in receiving proof of the violations alleged. The probationer is permitted representation by retained counsel; the right to confrontation and the privilege against self-incrimination are granted. The probation officer presents any witnesses needed to prove the violations and makes a recommendation whether probation should be revoked. A stenographic record of the proceedings is made. In Detroit the probationer is required to plead guilty or not guilty to the violations alleged; most plead guilty and the formal hearing discussed above occurs only when a not guilty plea is entered.

While probation revocation proceedings approximate a criminal trial without a jury and embody many of the protections required by the United States Supreme Court in the *Specht* case, there is

[38] See Chapters 5 and 14.

one major difference: Probationers were represented by counsel only in a very small percentage of cases, since this was before *Mempa v. Rhay* and the trial judges did not advise them they could be represented by counsel. This is a significant difference that is difficult to take into account; certain conclusions can, nevertheless, be drawn from the experience in the three states. First, when the trial judge is given authority to make a correctional decision he is likely to exercise it seriously; this is in marked contrast to trial judge performance in routinely approving police and prosecutor requests for arrest warrants. There, he relies very heavily upon prior administrative screening.[39] While it is clear most trial judges rely upon the views and recommendations of probation officers in deciding whether to revoke, they do exercise independent judgment and sometimes refuse to revoke despite proof of violations and a request for revocation by the supervising officer. The reasons for this difference in attitude are not entirely clear; perhaps judges feel that adequate means exist at later stages in the process for reviewing the propriety of arrest and search warrant decisions while they know there is no effective review of a judicial decision to revoke probation.

Second, trial judges know probation officers do not return all violators to court and they approve, indeed, insist upon screening by the probation staff. Violations are too numerous and usually too inconsequential to justify judicial scrutiny of each one. The trial judge has other functions to perform, such as the trial of civil or criminal cases, that cannot be delegated. This indicates that when a trial judge is given discretion to make a correctional decision, he is likely to delegate major responsibility to the correctional staff, reserving for himself only those cases the staff feels are in need of action which the law gives the trial judge exclusive authority to take. Although it is clear that much administrative screening is a reflection of known or believed judicial attitude toward whether a court hearing should be requested, it is also clear that correctional personnel exercise considerable independent judgment in deciding what action to take.

Third, very few disputes over facts occurred at the probation violation hearings in the three states. There are several explanations for this. Probation officers do not return a probationer to court without first investigating the case and deciding they can prove the relevant facts to the satisfaction of the trial judge. Normally when a probation officer is considering requesting revocation, the probationer has committed several violations and the officer is able to omit doubtful ones while still presenting a strong case

39 See LaFave, Arrest 15-52 (1965).

for revocation. Finally, the probationer usually admits the violations alleged against him; the admissions may be made to the probation officer in prehearing interviews, to the court at the hearing, or to both. In Detroit a formal plea to the allegations is required, and the great majority of probationers plead guilty. The staff screening was such, in Milwaukee and Detroit at least, that it is doubtful whether even the presence of counsel on a regular basis would result in uncovering many allegations that cannot be supported. Even when there is a denial of allegations of violations, there is almost always at least one provable violation that has occurred. Many violations that occur quite frequently can be proved easily. Examples are failure to report according to schedule and failure to make required payments for family support, restitution, or court costs. The trial judge's real decision, therefore, is usually whether he should revoke probation, not whether it can legally be revoked.

Fourth, trial judges tend to defer to the judgment of the probation staff on those questions they consider to lie within the staff's special competence. One example is the judgment of the likelihood of recidivism if an offender is granted probation or continued on probation after proof of violation. The necessity for making this judgment is one reason trial judges tend to rely upon the probation officer's recommendation in violation hearings. It would be expected, therefore, that the trial judge would rely heavily upon psychiatric evaluation to make the finding required by the statute in the *Specht* case that the defendant "if at large, constitutes a threat of bodily harm to members of the public, or is an habitual offender and mentally ill." [40] However, the requirement of a judicial hearing is one way of permitting the defendant the significant opportunity to present an independent psychiatric evaluation.

If the analogy is correct — if the trial judge would perform in other situations as he does in the revocation of probation — then the gains from extending trial judge decision making to other determinations in the correctional process may seem limited. The likelihood of extensive prehearing staff screening, the probability of heavy judicial reliance on staff recommendations, especially for critical social-medical determinations, and the infrequency with which factual disputes are likely to arise all indicate that shifting responsibility to the trial judiciary may not significantly increase the fairness of decision making. On the other hand, some of the characteristics of the judicial hearing, especially the opportunity to learn of the information utilized by the person responsible for making the decision and the opportunity to present different informa-

[40] Col. Rev. Stat. Ann. §39-19-1 (1963).

tion and views, may seem appropriate safeguards to employ for some correctional decisions whether they are made by trial judges or correctional personnel.

C. Controls Imposed by Dividing Discretion between Decision-Makers: the Checks and Balances Approach

One method of controlling discretion is to divide it between two decision-makers. In that way each may provide some control over the power of the other. Dividing discretion between the trial judge and the parole board has been used in the correctional process to determine length of incarceration. The critical inquiry is how this system of divided responsibility works in practice. In the states under study, the Michigan trial judge has discretion to select the minimum sentence (while the maximum is set by statute for most offenses), and in Wisconsin the judge has discretion to select the maximum sentence (with the minimum set by statute).[41]

The experience in Michigan, particularly in Detroit, is that judicial authority to set the minimum sentence does not control parole board discretion to any significant degree. This is true despite the fact there are no statutory upper limits on the minimum sentence, thus granting the trial judge theoretical power to preclude parole board discretion by selecting a minimum sentence very close to the statutory maximum. In fact most minima are set at one or two years. A major reason for this is the need felt by the trial judiciary in Detroit not to interfere with guilty plea bargaining by setting high minima. The guilty plea bargaining system and its advantages to the trial court pose substantial limits on the ability of trial judges to control parole board discretion by selecting the minimum sentence.[42]

The field survey data in Wisconsin indicate that judicial authority to select the maximum sentence constitutes a substantial control over parole board discretion. While it would be possible for trial judges routinely to set high maximum sentences to grant broad discretion to the parole board, that did not occur in fact. Like their Michigan counterparts, Wisconsin trial judges use sentencing discretion to encourage the disposition of cases by guilty pleas.[43] This requires the selection of maximum sentences that are substantially shorter than statutory upper limits in the great ma-

[41] The Kansas trial judge was required to impose both sentences as provided by statute. See Chapter 6.

[42] See Chapter 6 for a detailed discussion of judicial selection of the minimum sentence in Michigan.

[43] See Chapter 6.

jority of cases involving guilty pleas. Whereas plea bargaining in Michigan tended to decrease judicial control over parole board discretion because it resulted in short minima, in Wisconsin it tended to increase judicial control because it resulted in short maxima.

The real impact of the Wisconsin judicial maximum sentence upon parole board discretion can be measured by the substantial number of instances in which the maximum prevents the parole board from postponing release. Wisconsin's mandatory conditional release law, requiring parole supervision of inmates released upon service of the maximum less good time, means that practically no inmates are unconditionally released from incarceration.[44] Despite the fact that release at the maximum is conditional and under supervision, in a substantial number of cases the Wisconsin board paroled inmates solely because their mandatory release date was approaching and the board felt they needed a longer period of supervision than that provided by law.[45] The judicial maximum sentence system could have an even greater impact on parole board discretion in a jurisdiction without a mandatory release supervision program.

Although it is clear Wisconsin's judicial maximum system has a substantial controlling effect on parole board discretion, it is necessary to examine the operation of that system in more detail. The system assumes there is communication between the two decision-makers. It assumes the trial judge is familiar with parole board practices and can, on the basis of that knowledge, select a maximum sentence that reflects his values and gives sufficient allowance to the legitimate needs of the parole system. It also assumes that the parole board understands the reasons the trial judge had for selecting the sentence imposed, and that it will consider those reasons in exercising its discretion. The length of incarceration would reflect, therefore, the values and needs of both the sentencing judge and the parole board. Without such communication and understanding, there is a risk that the system of divided responsibility, while controlling discretion, would also impose needless obstacles to realizing the needs and values of the decision-makers.

In practice, the communication assumed by the system does not exist. It seems clear that sentencing judges sometimes select maxima on the basis of supposed parole board practices that do not in fact exist and that parole boards lack an adequate understanding of the basis for judicial sentencing. Trial judges sometimes impose

[44] See Chapter 12.
[45] See Chapter 11.

maxima that deny the parole board flexibility in timing release and prevent a period of parole supervision that is long enough to be effective. Whether the initiative should be taken by parole boards or trial judges, it does seem clear that trial judges need more information about paroling practices to effectively exercise discretion in selecting the maximum sentence. Despite several efforts to provide parole boards with the reasons trial judges have for selecting the maximum imposed in particular cases,[46] in practice parole boards usually do not know why the sentence was selected. They do not know, for example, whether a long maximum reflects the trial judge's opinion that the inmate should be detained for a long period of time, whether it reflects his opinion that the parole board should have flexibility in timing release, or whether it reflects his opinion that a long period of post-incarceration supervision is needed. Yet, knowledge of the factual basis for the trial judge's opinion would be of great assistance to the parole board in exercising discretion. To the extent trial judges select maxima on the basis of erroneous impressions of parole board practices, communication of the basis for selecting the sentence would give the board an opportunity to explain its release criteria to the sentencing judge.

To achieve its purpose, a system of divided responsibility must be based upon adequate communication between the decision makers. Without it, a workable system of checks and balances will not develop.

D. Controls Imposed by Community Involvement in the Correctional Process

Officials and agencies in the correctional process, like other governmental authorities in a democratic society, are responsible ultimately to the public. This tradition of accountability to the public and public scrutiny of governmental action places limits on the exercise of discretion in the correctional process. Trial judges and correctional agencies are quite sensitive to public comment on their decisions and their desire to avoid public criticism is sometimes an important factor in making discretionary judgments. In addition, correctional agencies perceive a need for public understanding and support of their programs and conduct active campaigns to secure it, a process that requires describing correctional programs in a way understandable and acceptable to the public.

[46] See Chapter 10.

Finally, community involvement in corrections is sometimes formalized into policy-making boards composed of persons representative of the community.

Much community involvement in corrections is at an informal level and occurs mainly through news media. Numerous examples of the fact that concern over public criticism influences correctional decisions made by trial judges, parole boards, probation or parole officers, and correctional administrators have already been given. The problem of the effect of newspaper and broadcast publicity upon official decision making is not limited to the criminal trial. It is a fact of life in correctional decision making with which officials must deal more often than they would wish. When correctional administrators handle a case that has engendered considerable newspaper publicity, they are likely to carefully explain their decisions to the news media in an effort to obtain public support. In the states studied, administrative steps have sometimes been taken in an effort to provide assurance against adverse public reaction to correctional decisions; for example, the Michigan practice of notifying prosecutors and trial judges of parole hearings, now abandoned, was instituted to avoid public comment that the parole board was "sneaking" inmates out of prison, and the Wisconsin requirement of administrative review of parole grants exists largely to keep the correctional administrator informed of decisions likely to receive publicity and to permit him to veto any that might harm the correctional program by engendering public criticism. Correctional administrators believe public criticism of correctional decisions limits the effectiveness of their personnel, who must sometmes enlist the support of local employers and community leaders, and has possible adverse effects on future legislative appropriations.

Many correctional agencies seek to enlist public support for their programs through community information efforts. They publish literature for public distribution, describing correctional programs in a way that can be understood by people in the community.[47] They invite civic, social, and school groups to tour correctional institutions and sometimes ask small groups of community leaders to observe parole board hearings. Probation and parole officers give speeches to community groups explaining the correctional program. While these efforts hardly provide community control over the correctional process, they do demonstrate the concern of correctional administrators for public understanding of and support for their programs.

[47] E.g., Mich. Dep't of Corrections, Parole in Michigan (undated); Wis. Dep't of Public Welfare, Parole Board Procedures and Practices (June, 1963).

There have been attempts to formalize the responsibility of the correctional agency to the public. These have usually taken the form of a policy-making board composed of representatives of the community, similar to policy-making boards that govern voluntary social agencies.[48]

In Wisconsin, the statutes create a State Board of Public Welfare, composed of nine members who serve without compensation. The governor is required to appoint the members of the Board "on the basis of recognized and demonstrated interest in and knowledge of the problems of public welfare." [49] The Board appoints the Director of the State Department of Public Welfare.[50] The Board's functions are "regulatory, advisory and policy-forming and not administrative or executive" [51] while the Director has the "administrative and executive powers" of the Department to be exercised by him "subject to the policies and in accordance with the principles established by the board." [52] Michigan statutes establish a similar pattern of citizen control over the Department of Corrections.[53]

Although the apparent legislative purpose in creating both the Wisconsin State Board of Public Welfare and the Michigan Corrections Commission was to provide substantial citizen control over the professional agencies, there was no indication they have in fact provided that control. By the very nature of its structure, a citizen board is limited in the policy-making role it can play. To expect laymen serving part time to obtain detailed knowledge of the daily functioning of a complex administrative system is unrealistic. The citizen board makes decisions on questions chosen for it by the professionals, usually on the basis of background information prepared by the professionals. In the case of the Wisconsin State Board of Public Welfare, the professionals even recommended the position to be taken by the Board, which is followed in an overwhelming majority of the cases.

The ultimate question is how much responsibility for the exercise of discretion should lie with the professionals who make the decisions and how much should lie with external groups with a different and sometimes broader perspective. As professionalism

[48] These boards, however, are quite different from the police civilian review board because the correctional policy-making board does not normally pass upon the propriety of individual decisions of agency personnel. It seems clear correctional agencies would resist the civilian review board in much the same fashion as the police.

[49] Wis. Stat. Ann. §46.012(1) (1957).

[50] Wis. Stat. Ann. §46.013(2) (1957).

[51] Wis. Stat. Ann. §46.013(1) (1957).

[52] Wis. Stat. Ann. §46.014(1) (1957).

[53] Mich. Stat. Ann. §§28.2271–28.2273 (1954).

increases in administering the correctional process, there is increasing need for assurance that the correctional program is responsive to public needs, while at the same time it becomes increasingly difficult for nonprofessionals to provide informed and intelligent control.

E. INTERNAL CONTROLS: THE PROCESS OF SELF-REGULATION

Normally, control over discretion in corrections is viewed in terms of legislative or judicial controls. It is unusual to find recognition of using administrative discretion to control administrative discretion although such a recommendation was made by the President's Crime Commission.[54] To assert that this approach should be explored is not to say that formal legal controls are unnecessary because existing internal controls are adequate. Quite the contrary, it seems clear that internal controls are presently not sufficiently developed to justify placing primary reliance upon them. Rather than assuming an either-or approach to controlling discretion through external or internal controls, it is important to ask what combination of methods will provide the necessary control without producing harmful rigidity. Internal controls may be needed to assure maximum use of professional knowledge and experience, while external controls may be viewed as necessary to assure compliance with broader decision-making norms.

Although it seems likely discretion in the correctional process will be subjected to greater control in the future, the form that control will assume depends upon a number of variables. For example, whether appellate courts and legislatures directly intervene in the correctional process to a greater extent depends in part upon whether internal controls are developed that provide assurance of fair decision-making. If correctional administrators and trial judges assume greater responsibility for controlling discretion, the necessity for direct external intervention will lessen; however, if these officials do not exercise their power to control discretion, legislatures and appellate courts may feel they have little alternative to increased direct intervention. Conversely, appellate courts and legislatures could encourage the development of internal controls by recognizing a duty on the part of officials and agencies to control discretion and by directly intervening in the correctional process only when that duty has been inadequately performed.

[54] The President's Commission on Law Enforcement and Administration of Justice, The Challenge of Crime in a Free Society 181 183 (1967): "Correctional agencies should develop explicit standards and administrative procedures to enable those under correctional control to test the fairness of key decisions affecting them."

There are several kinds of internal controls. One is policy making by the official or agency with ultimate responsibility for making the correctional decision. This may involve prescribing decision-making procedures, precluding discretion in certain situations, or providing guidelines for the exercise of discretion. Another is casework supervision. This may involve guidance at the time of decision making, as when a probation or parole officer confers with his supervisor about a decision he is in the process of making, or it can be a method of gathering information for future control, as when a supervisor audits the records of his caseworkers. A third method of internal control is administrative review of initial correctional decisions. This may involve reversing improper decisions, gathering information for future policy-making, and setting standards for future decision-making.

1. *Controls imposed by policy-making.* Some correctional policies are expressed in formal administrative regulations that may be filed with a state official or even published in a code of administrative regulations. In other instances, the policy may be contained in an agency personnel manual or in various training materials. In still other instances, the policy may be expressed in the form of a directive to agency personnel. The policy need not be in writing; it may be communicated orally to personnel individually or in staff meetings. Sometimes practices developed over a long period of time become routine and receive at least the implicit approval of the agency administrator who expects them to be followed in the future; as a practical matter, firmly established practices of this kind are the equivalent of agency policy. Whatever form it assumes, correctional policy is a generalized decision applicable to a class of cases that is expected to determine or guide the outcome of those cases in the future.

It is important to distinguish between two situations: in the first, the person ultimately responsible for a correctional decision does not make the decision initially. He may not even review it. However, he has administrative control over persons who make and review the decision. Probation officers, parole officers, and institutional personnel usually have initial responsibility for making correctional decisions but are subject to the administrative control of superiors in their agency. In the second situation, the person ultimately responsible for making the decision is the same person who makes it initially. He is subject to little or no administrative control over the way he makes decisions. Trial judge decisions with respect to granting or denying probation or selecting the length of a prison sentence are made initially by the same person who has ultimate responsibility for the decision. There is also some recognition that the parole board, because of the quasi-judicial nature of its functions, should be isolated from administrative control over its decisions.

The potentiality of control through policy making is clear in the first situation. In addition, however, it can and does exist in the second. Parole boards that sit in panels sometimes adopt formal policies in executive session to govern the decisions of panel members. Trial judges in multiple-division courts sometimes adopt policies to control or guide decision making by individual trial judges. In addition, individual trial judges may adopt positions that become known and that they commit themselves to follow.

Correctional agency administrators exercise some control over the discretion of their personnel through policy making. However, much agency level policy making concerns personnel matters that have little or nothing to do with discretionary decisions but that are necessary for the efficient management of a large organization. Policies that affect the exercise of discretion in individual cases are less frequent.

Typically, the correctional agency has established firm policies with respect to major decision-making procedures. For example, parole agencies usually specify in considerable detail the procedural steps that must be followed for parole revocation, such as verifying violations by the parole officer, writing a violation report, conferring with a supervisor, conducting parole violation hearings, and administrative review of the revocation decision. Probation departments typically specify procedures for probation revocation up to the point of judicial hearing.

In some instances, correctional agency policy assumes the form of precluding the exercise of discretion. For example, a correctional agency may specify that no inmate can be considered for parole who has committed institutional disciplinary violations within a specified period of time. Some correctional agencies have taken the position that an inmate with a detainer lodged against him is ineligible for parole. Some agencies have established categories of automatic revocation of parole; for example, the agency may require a revocation request when a parolee has absconded and has not been located within a specified period of time.

It is rare for correctional agencies to attempt to provide guidelines for exercising discretion. Although it would be possible to provide guidance for making correctional decisions by discussing appropriate and inappropriate criteria and by analyzing recurring situations, there are several reasons why this has not occurred. First, providing guidelines for exercising discretion is much more difficult than specifying procedures — there are many more variables. To the extent guidelines are attempted in practice, they usually involve little more than a general specification of the goals of the agency expressed in broad terms of the protection of society and the rehabilitation of the offender. Obviously, such statements provide very little control over the exercise of discretion.

Second, correctional agencies rely upon the educational background and training of their personnel to provide guidelines for making decisions. The assumption is that decisions should be made in accordance with professional norms and that those are provided by professional education. One of the difficulties with that position is that correctional personnel come from a wide variety of professional backgrounds — some have graduate study in social work, psychology, or sociology but most have at best an undergraduate degree in practically any field.[55] With that diversity of background, it is difficult to take the position that professional education provides guidelines for making decisions. In-service training and correctional literature provide some guidelines, but the fact remains that much correctional decision-making is based upon personal norms modified by experience and informal communication among correctional personnel. Current personnel recruitment and training programs, then, provide little assurance of uniformity of approach to correctional problems or that well considered, intelligent criteria are being used.

Third, there is a notion that it is unprofessional to control correctional personnel closely. The argument runs that, if correctional personnel are professionals, they must be treated as professionals and must be given latitude to exercise professional judgment. This is closely related to the notion that discretion in the correctional process is beneficial, that it ought to be maximized at all levels of service, and that attempts to control discretion should be resisted. The feeling seems to be that providing guidelines for decision-making would destroy discretion; there is little recognition that guidelines can provide assurance that appropriate criteria are being used and at the same time permit the flexibility necessary for making individual decisions.

2. *Casework supervision.* Probation officers, parole officers, and institutional caseworkers are normally under the control of a casework supervisor. His job is to assist the new caseworker in handling cases and to provide some control over the quality of services the officer renders. The officer is expected to confer with his supervisor when he encounters problems and the supervisor is expected to audit the casework files of his officers.

[55] The President's Commission on Law Enforcement and Administration of Justice, Task Force Report: Corrections 197 (1967).

Obviously, casework supervision is potentially important as a means of controlling discretion. The supervisor could assure the implementation of agency policy, serve as an important source of information for reexamining existing policies and developing new ones, and provide some assurance of uniformity of approach by workers under his supervision. In its present form, however, casework supervision does not provide this control. One reason for this is that the purpose of casework supervision is usually directed to the effectiveness of casework, rather than to the fairness of decision making. This may be a carryover from casework in voluntary social agencies where fairness does not present the problems involved in correctional decision making. In order to provide control over discretion, it would be necessary to broaden the supervisor's task to include concern about the fairness and consistency of worker decisions as well as the effectiveness of casework services rendered. Another important limitation upon the ability of casework supervision to perform administrative control functions is the little time most supervisors can devote to actually assisting caseworkers. The supervisor himself may have a caseload or may be charged with responsibility for conducting social investigations. He is likely to have responsibility for a large number of caseworkers. In addition, the caseworker has little time to compile a supervision file that does more than tersely indicate the contacts that have occurred between officer and client. Auditing supervision records, therefore, provides very little insight into the criteria used by the officer to make decisions.

For casework supervision to play an important role in administrative control of discretion, it would be necessary to broaden the goals of supervision and to increase the manpower allocated to the supervision function. Supervisors would have to be given more time to supervise, and means would have to be found to make casework records more accurate reflections of decisions actually made.

3. *Administrative review.* Some correctional decisions are subjected to administrative review, a process that holds obvious potential for controlling discretion. Whether administrative review is provided and, if so, the form it takes is determined by the official or agency that has ultimate responsibility for making the decision. In practice, there are major differences in the availability and form of administrative review.

Although administrative review of parole grants is available in Kansas and in Wisconsin, but not in Michigan, in fact there is very little review of parole board decisions in any of the three states. Under Kansas statutes in force during the field survey, parole board decisions granting parole had to be approved by the governor. In practice, such approval was given routinely, and no gubernatorial review actually occurred. Wisconsin statutes vest parole-granting power in the Director of the State Department of Public Welfare. Parole board decisions denying parole are not reviewed, but an elaborate two-stage system of administrative review of parole grants has been established by the Director. In practice, virtually all parole-granting decisions are approved routinely without real review. Michigan statutes vest parole-granting authority in the parole board and specify that its decisions shall be final. Although administrative review of parole board decisions does not occur in practice, the parole boards in Michigan and Wisconsin have established systems of review within the boards themselves. Michigan statutes require that a parole grant be approved by three of the five-member parole board. Since only two members are present at the parole hearing, a third member reviews the case file before the hearing and votes to grant parole, deny parole, or defer to the judgment of the hearing members. If the screening member and hearing members do not agree on a disposition, the case is reviewed by the full board in executive session and a decision is reached there. The Wisconsin parole board, which hears cases in panels of two members, has established the procedure of requiring full board consideration of all cases that involve assaultive conduct. In such cases, the hearing members report their judgments to the full board in executive session and the decision is made there.[56]

Administrative review of the conclusions and recommendations in presentence reports is common. In Detroit the supervisor of each Division of Recorder's Court Probation Department discusses the report, especially its conclusions and recommendations, with the investigating officer. He indicates his approval or disapproval of the recommendation before the report is submitted to the court. In Milwaukee a similar process of administrative review occurs. In each department the view is that the recommendation contained in the presentence report is the official departmental position and that approval at an administrative level is necessary.[57]

By contrast, there is no administrative review of a probation officer's decision whether to seek revocation of probation. If he has difficulty deciding whether to seek revocation, he may confer with his supervisor, but there is no requirement of approval at that level. Perhaps the reason for this is that revocation requests must be approved by the trial judge, who bears ultimate responsibility for revocation; this may be viewed as eliminating the need for ad-

[56] Administrative review of parole board decisions is discussed in detail in Chapter 10.

[57] See Chapters 1 and 2.

ministrative review. The trial judge who reviews the case, however, is the judge who happened to place the defendant on probation, and there is little assurance of uniformity of approach at the judicial stage of the revocation process. If the probation officer decides not to seek revocation despite the presence of violations, his judgment is normally not reviewed.[58]

The most elaborate systems of administrative review have been established for revocation of parole. In Wisconsin a revocation request must be approved by the supervisor of the district office in which the officer works. The actual revocation decision, formally vested in the Director of the State Department of Public Welfare, is made by an official in the state central office. A decision to revoke results in returning the parolee to a correctional institution, where he receives a hearing before the parole board to determine such matters as forfeitures of good time and scheduling a hearing for reparole. In Michigan approval at the district and state level precedes a parole violation hearing before the Michigan parole board, which has ultimate responsibility for revocation. A revocation decision made at the conclusion of that hearing is not reviewed. A decision not to seek revocation made by the individual parole officer or at the district office level is not reviewed by the parole board.[59]

There are serious limitations upon the usefulness of present systems of administrative review as controls over discretion. First, many important correctional decisions are not subjected to administrative review. Examples are the wide variety of supervision decisions made by probation or parole officers and decisions not to seek revocation despite the presence of provable violations. The only effective review in the parole-granting process occurs internally within the parole board, despite the presence of other forms of administrative review in two of the three states. Second, the purposes of administrative review when it exists are often not so much to determine whether discretion has been exercised fairly and sensibly, but to protect the agency or department from the possibility of public criticism of an unwise decision. Administrative review of parole granting in Wisconsin is the best example of this limitation, but it exists elsewhere as well. To be effective as control devices, existing systems of administrative review must undergo changes in their objectives. Third, with the exception of the parole violation hearing in Michigan, existing systems of administrative review do not involve participation by the individual about whom the decison is made. He does not request administrative review; indeed,

[58] See Chapter 5.
[59] See Chapter 14.

he may not know it occurs. He has no opportunity to present before the reviewing authority any reasons he may have for criticizing the decision. This is in marked contrast to administrative review as that concept is understood in traditional administrative law contexts. There it usually means at least an administrative hearing requested by the individual affected by the initial decision at which he has an opportunity to challenge the initial decision. An example is the "fair hearing" required for administrative review of determinations in federally-financed public assistance programs, such as Aid to Families with Dependent Children.[60] It is this kind of administrative review with which courts usually deal when they impose a requirement of exhaustion of administrative remedies before permitting judicial review. Of the systems of administrative review existing in the three states, only the statutorily imposed parole violation hearing in Michigan meets those standards. Existing systems of administrative review would have to be changed to provide assurance that they subject discretion to control. Simply because they are presently inadequate for control purposes, however, does not eliminate the possibility they can be strengthened to provide adequate control.

[60] 42 U.S.C.A. §602(a) (1964).

CHAPTER 16

Lawyers and Controlling Discretion in the Correctional Process

There is a trend toward greater involvement by attorneys in the correctional process. However, many of the functions they perform are not directly related to controlling discretion and are only of peripheral concern here. This is true of the increasing lawyer involvement in representing clients to challenge the validity of their convictions by appeal or collateral attack. It is also true of increasing lawyer representation of the legal aid type to deal with civil legal problems of persons who are in the correctional process. And it is true of legal representation of clients to challenge nondiscretionary correctional action, such as the interpretation of good time laws.

Major concern in this chapter is with legal representation of individuals in the correctional process to influence the outcome of discretionary decisions. This involves (1) representing clients in correctional hearings — sentence hearings, parole hearings, commutation of sentence hearings, and hearings for the revocation of probation or parole — and (2) representing clients to seek administrative or judicial relief from discretionary decisions that may or may not have involved a correctional hearing as part of the original decision-making process.

A. The Extent of Legal Representation in the Correctional Processes of Kansas, Michigan, and Wisconsin

Lawyers appear frequently at the sentencing stage. Generally, if the defendant was represented by counsel at the adjudication of his case, that representation continues until the sentencing decision is made. The frequent appearance of attorneys at sentencing is largely a by-product of the appointment of counsel for the indigent at adjudication. By contrast, although retained counsel was permitted to represent clients in judicial proceedings for revocation of probation, it was the practice in all three states not to notify a probationer of this right or to appoint counsel for the indigent. Consequently, counsel appeared only very rarely in these proceedings. Presumably, legal representation at probation revocation proceedings will increase as a result of the recent Supreme Court decision recognizing a constitutional right to appointment of counsel for the indigent at that stage.[1]

Public hearings are held in all three states as part of the commutation of sentence decision-making process.[2] Although the statutes are silent on the right to representation by counsel at the hearings, as a matter of practice retained counsel is permitted to be present and represent the interests of the applicant for clemency. Since counsel is not provided for the indigent, attorneys are present in only a minority of commutation hearings.

The Kansas parole board permitted retained attorneys to appear for inmates at parole hearings and for parolees at parole violation hearings, but in practice legal representation was very rare.[3] Counsel is not permitted to appear at parole hearings in either Michigan or Wisconsin, but attorneys are permitted to communicate with the parole board prior to the hearing.[4] The same policy prohibits the appearance of counsel at parole violation hearings in Wisconsin, but in Michigan there is a statutory right to retained counsel at parole violation hearings.[5] In practice, counsel appears very rarely.

Under the Wisconsin Sex Offenders Law, the length of incarceration can be extended for five-year periods by the Department of Public Welfare, subject to approval of the sentencing court. The statutes require appointment of counsel for the indigent in judicial proceedings in which approval of a five-year extension is sought.[6]

The failure to appoint counsel for the indigent and to permit the appearance of retained counsel at some hearings resulted in almost no legal representation in correctional hearings other than judicial proceedings to determine initial disposition. Moreover,

1 Mempa v. Rhay, 389 U.S. 128, 88 Sup. Ct. 254, 19 L. Ed. 2d 336 (1967).

2 See Chapter 9 for a discussion of commutation of sentence.

3 Kan. Laws 1957, Ch. 331, §23 authorized the parole board to exclude attorneys from parole hearings. See Kan. Stat. Ann. §62-2248 (1964).

4 Wis. Dept. of Public Welfare, Parole Board Procedures and Practices 10 (Feb. 1959): "Attorneys, members of inmates' families, or others are not permitted to make appearances either for or against parole at parole hearings. Such persons may, if they wish, make their views known to the Parole Board by letter or can arrange to see the Board at its offices in Madison."

5 Mich. Stat. Ann. §28.2310 (1954).

6 Wis. Stat. Ann. §959.15(14)(a) (1958).

the field data revealed no instances of legal representation outside the context of a correctional hearing.

B. The Role of Counsel as a Control Over Discretion

Because legal representation increases the ability of the individual to influence discretionary decisions affecting him, it has considerable potential as a control over discretion. Commenting on this function of legal representation, Professor Kadish has noted:

> There is no apparent reason why there should be abandoned in the area of sentencing or paroling offenders the traditional value, associated closely with the root idea of a democratic community, that a person should be given an opportunity to participate effectively in determinations which affect his liberty. Indeed, the cultivation of a sense of fair dealing in the offender would appear to be helpful, if not essential, in attaining one of the principal goals of these correctional processes, the rehabilitation of the offender.[7]

The control significance of legal representation at correctional hearings is obvious: Counsel has access to the decision maker and an opportunity to present facts and arguments favorable to his client. However, many correctional decisions are made without opportunity for a hearing. This is true of many probation or parole supervision decisions and of some institutional decisions not involving release. While the opportunity for significant legal representation is less, important functions can be served by seeking administrative relief from these decisions or, when necessary, judicial relief.

1. *Functions of counsel in a correctional hearing.* Discussion of the functions of counsel in correctional hearings is made difficult because counsel appears regularly only at the sentence hearing. The field survey revealed such few instances of counsel appearing at other correctional hearings that generalization based upon direct observation is impossible. Nevertheless, if the assumption can be made that counsel would function in other correctional hearings as he does at sentencing, it is possible on the basis of observed instances of legal representation at sentencing to arrive at tentative conclusions about representation at correctional hearings generally.

The regular appearance of counsel at the sentence hearing probably more reflects the fact that sentencing is regarded as an incident of adjudication than it reflects a feeling that counsel has significant, independent functions to perform in sentencing. Since

[7] Kadish, The Advocate and the Expert — Counsel in the Peno-Correctional Process, 45 Minn. L. Rev. 803, 830 (1961).

the criminal prosecution is not concluded until the defendant is committed to prison or placed on probation, counsel is expected to represent his client until that occurs. The same reasons probably explain the appearance of the prosecuting attorney at sentencing. This is not to say that either the prosecutor or the defense attorney regards sentencing as unimportant. It does seem clear, however, that they regard their role in sentencing as unimportant, or more precisely, that they regard their role at the sentencing stage as unimportant. Counsel is likely to think of his function with respect to sentencing as securing a charge reduction or sentence promise (or expectation) in exchange for a guilty plea or of maneuvering his client's case before a judge who has a reputation for sentence leniency. In comparison to these sentence-related attorney functions, he probably regards the services actually performed at the sentencing stage as being comparatively unimportant.

a. *Guarding against the use of prejudicially incomplete or inaccurate correctional information.* One of counsel's major goals at the sentencing stage, and presumably at correctional hearings generally, is to prevent damage to his client's opportunity for leniency as a result of the use of incomplete or inaccurate correctional information. One of the major determinants of counsel's ability to achieve this goal is whether he has access to the information upon which the decision will be based.

At the sentencing stage in jurisdictions that employ the postplea of guilty hearing[8] as the major source of presentence information, assuring accuracy of information is relatively simple and involves the kinds of services attorneys are accustomed to performing. Because presentence information is obtained through judicial proceedings involving examination and cross-examination of witnesses, it is relatively easy for counsel to guard against incomplete or inaccurate information prejudicing his client. He can cross-examine witnesses to question the accuracy of their testimony or to elicit information not disclosed on direct examination. He can also introduce evidence of his own to present his client's case in its best light. If counsel understands the criteria used in sentencing and, hence, what items of presentence information are critical and what of little importance, he can function with ease in the postplea of guilty hearing.

When a presentence investigation is used, however, counsel's opportunity to guard against prejudicially incomplete or inaccurate information is more limited. Counsel's ability to eliminate inaccurate information depends in part upon whether he is permitted to see the presentence report when the investigation is complete. In

[8] See Chapter 1 for a discussion of the postplea of guilty hearing.

Detroit counsel was not permitted to view the report, but he was able to glean some of its contents from comments made to him by the judge in conference prior to sentencing, to the defendant upon the imposition of sentence, or from statements made by the judge for the record justifying the sentence selected. Usually, however, information gained in that manner comes too late to be helpful.

In Milwaukee it was routine practice for the trial judge to provide the defendant's attorney (but not the defendant himself, even if he was unrepresented) with a copy of the presentence report prior to sentencing. Counsel was permitted to examine it and to question the investigating probation officer about it. Normally, counsel had very few comments to make about the report. No instance was observed in which he questioned its completeness or accuracy either in open court or in the judge's chambers prior to sentencing. It was not usual for counsel to confer at length with the defendant after reading the report but prior to sentencing, and there may have been an expectation that counsel would not reveal to the defendant any of the contents of the report. Furthermore, counsel would be unlikely to make an issue of a factual inaccuracy unless he thought it to be of critical importance to his client's chances for leniency, and it is possible that, because investigating probation officers know of the disclosure practice, such inaccuracies do not often occur.

Counsel's access to correctional information varies at other correctional hearings. Access is likely to be fullest at proceedings for revocation of probation because at least some trial judges insist that all information they receive be introduced at the hearing in the presence of the probationer. In such proceedings counsel could provide as much assurance of accuracy as he does in a jurisdiction that uses the postplea of guilty hearing as the major source of presentence information. Furthermore, the issues at probation revocation are usually clearly defined in terms of allegations of specific violations of probation conditions, thereby focusing counsel's attention upon some of the critically important facts.

In other correctional hearings, however, the important information is likely to be in documentary form, much like the presentence report. This is true at the parole hearing and is usually true at parole revocation hearings. Confidentiality of such information is sometimes even more guarded than the presentence report. The ability of counsel to test the accuracy of data considered by the decision maker is, therefore, quite limited as those hearings are presently conducted.

b. *Seeking maximum leniency for his client.* Observation of sentence hearings in the three states indicates that counsel is likely to regard his main function at correctional hearings as seeking maximum leniency for his client. He will usually define leniency as the disposition that involves the least deprivation of his client's liberty. At sentencing, the usual practice is for counsel to emphasize to the judge those facts about his client's case that argue for lenient treatment. In a jurisdiction using the postplea hearing, he usually attempts to bring out such facts by examining the defendant or cross-examining the investigating police officer. At the time of sentencing, however, it is rare for counsel to reveal facts not already known to the judge. His contribution is to emphasize their importance to the disposition of the case. Although counsel normally argues for probation, it is unusual for him to present to the judge any plan for his client, such as a change in residence or a new job. Counsel seems to assume that the investigating probation officer has explored these areas. Typically, the defendant says almost nothing at the sentence hearing, whether or not he is represented by counsel.

Counsel's arguments for leniency typically involve the obvious sentencing criteria — prior record, seriousness of the offense, effect of a prison sentence upon the defendant's family. It is unusual for counsel to appreciate the importance of other factors in sentencing, such as the timing and pattern of prior offenses or the availability of alternatives to prison other than "straight probation." It can be hypothesized that at the parole hearing, for example, most attorneys would be at a loss to know what factors are important in making the decision and would, perhaps, miss opportunities to emphasize significant factors in their clients' favor. Nevertheless, an individual's "case" for lenient treatment is more forcefully presented by counsel, even though he may be unfamiliar with all the factors affecting the disposition, than by the individual himself.

c. *Maintaining a posture of cooperation with the decision-making authority.* One of counsel's objectives at the sentence hearing is to place himself and his client in a posture of cooperating with the court. It would probably be an important objective at other correctional hearings as well. This limits counsel's ability to present or cross-examine witnesses at the postplea of guilty hearing, to question the accuracy of statements of fact contained in the presentence report, or to take any other action that would prolong the proceedings or create other difficulties for the decision maker. Counsel may appreciate that a trial judge at sentencing has great discretion that cannot be overturned except under extraordinary circumstances. He is, therefore, in a position to insist upon very little as a matter of right. If he should conduct himself in such a way as to incur the disfavor of the judge, he runs the risk that his client will suffer for it. And, if counsel conducts himself in such a way as to prolong the sentencing proceedings except for the most important reasons, he runs the risk of losing whatever benefits he may have achieved by his client's plea of guilty. When a defendant pleads guilty, he has committed himself to a course of cooperation with the court and there is a general expectation that it will continue at sentencing as well. Whatever the reasons, the uniform practice of seeking to appear cooperative places limitations upon the controls that counsel's presence might otherwise provide.

2. *Function of counsel in a nonhearing context.* Although the major correctional decisions are usually made in a hearing context, other decisions are made without a hearing. Examples are numerous decisions made during probation or parole supervision, such as imposing new conditions, changing the frequency of reporting, approving residence and employment arrangements, and waiving compliance with certain conditions. During incarceration decisions involving transfer from one institution to another, the forfeiture of good time for disciplinary violations, or the imposition of other discipline sanctions, such as deprivation of privileges or confinement in a discipline cell or ward, are made without hearing or with a summary hearing soon after the alleged misconduct. In addition, administrative and judicial review of these decisions are normally not available, at least on a regular basis. The question is raised, therefore, whether counsel has a function outside of a hearing context.

Although counsel is unlikely to be able to represent the interests of his client when these decisions are made originally, he may be able to obtain relief from decisions that seem inappropriate. Typically, well-defined channels of administrative relief do not exist and counsel must, therefore, proceed upon an informal basis. This involves discussing the case with various administrators in an attempt to obtain reconsideration of the decision. Although empirical data are lacking concerning counsel's functioning in this manner, the point is that simply because a discretionary decision is made without a hearing and without well-defined steps of administrative review, counsel is not precluded from representing the interests of his client and, to some extent, influencing the way in which discretion is exercised.

Although appellate courts limit the availability of review of correctional decisions, judicial relief is a possible course of action in at least some instances. Perhaps as important as the function of counsel in assuring that meritorious claims are presented to the court is his function in discouraging the filing of frivolous claims that would otherwise be pressed by unrepresented persons. This might have the effect of encouraging courts to give more serious and careful consideration to the claims that are advanced and of making the judicial system a more effective means of control. Again, empirical data on the function of counsel in presenting such claims and in screening out those without merit are largely lacking.[9]

3. *Function of counsel in strengthening internal controls.* From the viewpoint of the attorney representing a correctional client, his function in increasing the visibility of the correctional process is simply a by-product. However, from a broader perspective, it may be his most significant function. Since counsel for the individual views the process from the perspective of the client, he may be able to uncover and present problems to correctional administrators that are unknown to them. He also may be able to give an outside group — the legal profession — information about a process that is generally unknown to them. The President's Crime Commission Task Force Report on Corrections notes that programs providing legal representation for individuals in the correctional process

> can serve a number of important functions in addition to guaranteeing access to the courts. They can provide increased visibility for a system that has generally been too isolated, helping to mobilize public opinion and bring political pressure to bear where needed for reform. The mere presence of outsiders would serve to discourage illegal, unfair or inhumane practices. . . . Such programs can, moreover, help indigent inmates with meritorious claims present those claims to correctional authorities as well as to courts, and could be instrumental in helping develop better protective procedures within corrections.[10]

As discussion in Chapter 15 indicates, there may be a variety of ways of assuring sound exercise of discretion. Whether or not counsel is needed for control purposes, then, depends in part upon how adequate these other methods are or can be made. It is perfectly possible to have a correctional process that functions fairly without the presence of counsel in any significant number of cases. A correctional administration committed to a goal of fairness of decision making and willing to take steps needed to assure achieving that goal would seem necessary at a minimum.[11] It is, however,

[9] See 1967 Wis. L. Rev. 514 for discussion of the value of legal representation of prison inmates in screening out frivolous court petitions.

[10] The President's Commission on Law Enforcement and Administration of Justice, Task Force Report: Corrections 85 (1967).

[11] There is a possible role for lawyers in controlling discretion in corrections that has been omitted for lack of empirical data, namely, the potential use of correctional agency lawyers to assist correctional administrators in designing decision-making procedures, creating adequate systems of administrative review, and guiding discretion through policy-making.

uncertain whether a workable system of administrative self-control is likely to develop without the presence of counsel to stimulate the necessary concern on the part of correctional officials and administrators.

CONCLUSION

Corrections in the Future

The major purpose of this book has been to describe current correctional practices carefully and objectively, giving emphasis to aspects that raise sharply conflicting value choices. Doing this leads one to conclude that the correctional process, like the criminal justice process generally, will have to make major changes if it is to respond adequately to rapidly changing social and behavioral problems.

There is need for greater recognition of the fact that corrections is an integral part of the criminal justice system and it is, therefore, essential that correctional practices be understood as they exist in, are affected by, and, in turn, affect the over-all criminal justice system. Failure to recognize this has, for example, led legislatures to enact high, mandatory penalties which have put irresistible pressure upon police, prosecutors, and trial judges to restore necessary flexibility to the process. This failure has also meant that too little attention has been given to the impact of correctional programs upon the effectiveness and fairness of enforcement and prosecution practices. For example, an inability to develop effective correctional programs for the prostitute, the homosexual, and the drunk has resulted in a process of improvisation by enforcement agencies sometimes involving unfortunate techniques such as harassment of prostitutes. Finally, the failure to recognize corrections as an integral part of the total criminal process has caused us to think of corrections as a stage that comes after conviction, with the consequence that too little attention has been given to the development of correctional programs that can serve, in appropriate cases, as alternatives to prosecution and conviction.

Corrections is also an obviously important aspect of community life and of the community's effort to minimize social deviancy, and is therefore bound to be influenced by social change, particularly the very rapid social changes that are occurring today. Corrections can have a significant role to play in the urban crisis, either in dealing with the causal factors or in adapting correctional programs to meet the particular problems raised by ghetto living. But, to date, correctional involvement in the community has been limited even in the most advanced correctional systems. Apart from the immense problems of the ghetto, there is need to treat the sex offender's family as well as the offender himself; the family of the alcoholic as well as the alcoholic himself. The trend seems away from the large institutions and in the direction of greater emphasis upon treating the offender in the community, a trend that will have profound implications for corrections and the criminal justice system as a whole.

Corrections is a major setting in which governmental power is exercised. Correctional agencies have more in common with economic regulatory agencies than with voluntary social agencies. Like regulatory agencies, they have been delegated broad powers to make governmental policy, adjudicate individual cases, and exercise discretion without hearing safeguards or opportunity for judicial review. Because of this, it is as important in corrections as in other governmental endeavors to be concerned with whether practices conform to appropriate standards of administrative "due process." It is not enough to be concerned with effectiveness — whether corrections rehabilitates offenders and protects society from them — nor to assert that the "best interests of the inmate" underlies the program, or that offenders have only "privileges" and not "rights." In the exercise of broad governmental power there must be assurances of fairness and consistency. Pursuit of these goals has important implications for the qualifications correctional leaders should have, for the education, training, and professional standards of correctional personnel, and for correctional manpower needs. How these questions are dealt with in correctional administration will surely have great influence over the amount of legal involvement there will be in the determination of appropriate future correctional programs.

A. Corrections and Criminal Justice Administration

Corrections has traditionally been viewed as something separate from criminal justice administration, as a distinct process affixed to the end of the criminal justice system, rather than an integral part of that system. This traditional conception obscures the substantial interrelationship and mutual dependence that characterize the actual operation of the total system.

There is an important relationship between guilty plea bargaining and the correctional process of the particular jurisdiction. When the trial judge has discretion in choosing between probation and prison or selecting the length of the prison term, he is likely to exercise that discretion in a way that encourages guilty pleas. When his discretion is eliminated, other means of encouraging guilty pleas are used. The result may be a system of charge reductions that may complicate and frustrate the correctional process.[1]

There is increasing recognition that corrections has a considerable stake in the way criminal cases are handled prior to conviction. If the defendant has been dealt with unfairly, he may enter the correctional process with a bitterness and hostility toward authority that impedes correctional efforts at control and treatment. It is thus of considerable importance to corrections whether the defendant has received adequate legal representation and has been dealt with fairly by the police, the prosecutor, and the courts. There are obvious limitations upon the ability of corrections to contribute to the fairness of precorrectional criminal justice administration. In many instances corrections can do little more than support efforts by others to improve the fairness of the process. In others, however, a more direct contribution may be possible. For example, probation departments have been active in instigating and operating programs for the pretrial release of indigent offenders without bond. In part, this merely reflects the fact that the decision-making technique in recognizance programs is based on the correctional social investigation model. However, it also reflects recognition by correctional leaders that needless pretrial detention often has adverse effects upon later correctional efforts.

Concern for effective correctional treatment of offenders extends beyond the fair treatment of persons who are later convicted and enter the formal correctional process. Effective correctional treatment of the adult, as the child, may be enhanced if treatment is available as an alternative to prosecution and conviction rather than being limited to those who have been convicted. While the juvenile justice system may be adopting some of the procedures of the adult system,[2] there is a trend in the adult system to adopt some of the informal treatment dispositions found effective in dealing with juveniles. Many criminal cases terminate without conviction. In some instances they are not pursued for lack of evidence to support an arrest, prosecution, or conviction. But in many other instances they are terminated because, although full invoca-

1 The relationship between sentencing discretion and the mode of adjudication is examined in more detail in Chapter 6.

2 Application of Gault, 387 U.S. 1, 87 Sup. Ct. 1428, 18 L. Ed. 2d 527 (1967).

tion of the criminal process is possible on the evidence, advantage is perceived in not pursuing the case through to conviction. In many of these latter instances, cases are dismissed with simply a lecture or warning to the offender. Others, however, involve the use of sanctions and techniques similar to those used in the formal correctional process. They raise difficult problems about intervening in the lives of persons without a formal determination of guilt.

There seems a clear trend toward viewing correctional treatment as an alternative to conviction. Administrative and other advantages are perceived in diverting persons from the criminal process as early as possible if effective alternative means are available for handling the case. In part, this trend is related to the trend toward greater use of community-based corrections. As correctional programs become increasingly community-based instead of institution-based, there appears to be less and less need to pursue cases through to conviction because equivalent methods of control and treatment can be used without conviction. Moreover, important correctional objectives are often furthered by avoiding prosecution and conviction. The offender's formal criminal record is minimized, thus perhaps avoiding some obstacles to obtaining employment. Pretrial detention is usually shortened and sometimes eliminated, and corrective measures are instituted sooner.

Whether preconviction correctional programs are operated by correctional agencies or other criminal justice agencies appears to be largely a matter of chance. The great majority of nonsupport offenders are handled by negotiation of support agreements without conviction. In many states the agreements are negotiated and their performance supervised by the prosecuting attorney's office. In Detroit, however, the adjustment division of the probation department does it. If the offender fails in his performance of the agreement, he may be convicted of criminal nonsupport and placed on probation to be supervised by the probation department. The principal purpose of supervising nonsupport offenders before or after conviction is to obtain support for dependents, and obtaining support payments dominates the supervision process whether conducted by a correctional agency or another agency; nevertheless, because these programs are merely another form of probation, correctional leaders should be concerned with the way they operate even when they are the responsibility of a noncorrectional agency. The same considerations support correctional concern with other programs of preconviction disposition. For example, it seems clear that correctional agencies have a contribution to make to the way domestic disputes are commonly disposed of without prosecution, sometimes by individual police officers and sometimes in formal programs operating out of police departments or prosecuting attorneys' offices.[3]

While it may be neither feasible nor desirable for correctional agencies to assume operational responsibility of even those programs of preconviction disposition that involve probation-like supervision or complex psychological problems, their assistance at the level of program planning and training of personnel seems potentially valuable. It seems likely that use of these programs will continue to increase with or without the advice and assistance of corrections professionals. Recognition by correctional leaders and other leaders in criminal justice that corrections has a contribution to make with respect to preconviction disposition practices seems necessary before constructive action can begin. Perhaps the most basic problem is recognition by all persons concerned that many of these practices should be regarded as essentially correctional programs even though they occur outside the formal correctional process that follows conviction.

The stake of police, prosecutors, and trial judges in the correctional process seems as great as the importance of preconviction criminal justice administration to correctional agencies. The criminal justice system through conviction can be viewed as an elaborate intake process for corrections — as a method of selecting the persons who should be subjected to correctional control and treatment. Thus conceived, the goals of the criminal law are largely realized in the correctional process, and an ineffective correctional process can nullify the efforts of police, prosecutors, and trial courts.

Moreover, the effectiveness of the correctional process has an impact on how these officials make their decisions: An important consideration in arrest, prosecution, and conviction decisions is whether meaningful correctional programs are available for offenders. It is not overstating the argument to say that a meaningful correctional process is essential to make the criminal justice system work the way it is intended to work. The system is premised on the belief that meaningful corrective treatment is available and that criminal justice officials will for that reason desire to pursue cases through to conviction so that offenders can receive correctional treatment.

The important question is whether the correctional process has a meaningful program for offenders viewed from the perspective of police, prosecutors, and trial judges. Thus, if the police, correctly or not, perceive sentencing and correctional action as ineffective in controlling crime, they are not likely to make the effort necessary

[3] These and many other practices of preconviction disposition are discussed in Miller, Prosecution: The Decision to Charge a Suspect with a Crime (forthcoming).

to invoke the correctional process. Instead, they may impose summary sanctions of their own. For example, the fact that much petty vice activity is sanctioned by only a small monetary fine leads police to adopt programs of harassment arrests of such offenders without gathering the evidence necessary to support a conviction. There are obviously other reasons for harassment programs, but the perceived ineffectiveness of the correctional sanction is a major factor.[4]

Furthermore, whether the police view the correctional sanction as meaningful has an important impact on the effectiveness of the exclusionary rule as a control over police conduct. The exclusionary rule is premised on the belief that the police wish to obtain convictions; illegal methods of obtaining evidence are deterred by excluding evidence so obtained from the criminal trial, thus making conviction difficult or impossible. Whether police in fact desire a conviction depends to a large extent upon how they view the correctional sanction. If the police view the sanction as meaningless in controlling crime, they will not be deterred by the exclusionary rule, and harassment practices are likely to result.[5] This is not an argument for more severe sentencing in these areas because of the impact it might have on law enforcement. Rather, the point is that police and prosecutors, as well as courts and corrections professionals, have a large stake in correctional decision-making and that an important objective of correctional planning should be to give maximum support to the criminal justice system in dealing with offenders through arrest, prosecution, and conviction or, where that is not feasible, to encourage the development of alternatives such as diversion to other community agencies to deal with the conduct.

B. Corrections and a Changing Society

One of the major trends in corrections is a movement away from institution-based control and treatment of the offender toward community-based correctional programs. Probation and parole are more effective rehabilitative tools than correctional institutions, it is argued, because they avoid the negative effects of institutionalization and permit resocialization by giving the offender a supervised experience while living in a law-abiding community. Put differently, one cannot expect an offender to learn to live a law-abiding life in the free community by confining him in an institu-

[4] See LaFave, Arrest: The Decision to Take a Suspect into Custody 437-489 (1965).

[5] The United States Supreme Court recognized these limitations upon the exclusionary rule in Terry v. Ohio, 392 U.S. 1, 88 Sup. Ct. 1868, 20 L. Ed. 2d 889 (1968).

tion with other offenders. The increased use of halfway houses and work-release programs, instead of total confinement, is based on the same arguments made for increased use of probation and parole.

Many persons under correctional control come from areas of cities that have long had high crime rates and that have recently experienced great social unrest and often widespread violence, and will return to these areas when released from the process. This alone should mean that corrections has a stake in improving conditions in the urban ghetto. The environment in which the correctional client lives and works has a substantial influence on whether he will return to crime, and the urban ghetto will increasingly become the setting in which corrections makes its rehabilitative efforts, if the trend toward community-based corrections continues.

How should corrections respond to the urban ghetto and its implications for community-based correctional programs? One approach might be to increase efforts to find residences for correctional clients outside of ghetto areas. Another might be for corrections to conclude that such a course of action is not possible for many offenders and instead attempt to provide closer supervision for probationers and parolees living in ghetto areas, reallocating resources to make such supervision possible. A third approach might be for corrections to take positive steps to improve the environment in which many of its clients live. While there are obvious limitations on the ability of corrections to improve conditions in the urban ghettos, correctional personnel may have understanding of local conditions that would be helpful to others in attacking ghetto problems. Despite the emphasis upon keeping offenders in the community, there is little evidence that correctional leaders view such courses of action as part of their responsibility for developing effective correctional programs.

The effectiveness of community-based correctional programs may depend upon efforts to work with the offender's family as well as efforts to improve community conditions. There are difficult questions about the authority of correctional agencies to undertake treatment of the families of offenders; yet in some cases it may be necessary for the offender's rehabilitation. As correctional programs move from institutions to the community, new problems are encountered and new responsibilities must be assumed. It is not sufficient to proceed on blind faith that treatment in the community is, under all circumstances, preferable to treatment in an institution. Is it entirely clear that an offender's prospects for rehabilitation are better if he lives in an urban ghetto than if he is in prison, even if he later must return to the ghetto? As corrections moves into the community, the community's problems become increasingly important to corrections. The relationship between correctional treatment and community life requires careful study and thought.

C. Corrections as an Exercise of Governmental Power

There is growing recognition that correctional agencies exercise a very significant form of governmental power, even more important to the lives of individuals than most governmental agencies. Concurrently, there is a changing view of the nature of the correctional process. Although there is great need for the effective application of behavioral science knowledge to the treatment of the socially deviant, there is also need to do so in ways that are just and that inspire in the offender, as far as possible, and in the community a confidence in the justice of the correctional process. The objective, to be achieved, requires correctional leadership to be knowledgeable about the exercise of governmental power in a democratic society and the relationship of legislatures and courts to the administrative process in general and to corrections in particular as a very important part of the governmental administrative process.

The corrections profession has tended to regard its major contribution to criminal justice administration as providing casework services for convicted offenders within a framework of concern for the immediate protection of society. Correctional leaders, like leaders in the police field, have focused their attention almost exclusively upon the effectiveness of programs, the effectiveness being often measured in terms of achieving a low recidivism rate. This is similar to the police concern with crime rates and offenses cleared by arrest. But corrections, like the police, is now faced with the necessity of reexamining its methods because of the imposition of new legal standards for correctional procedures.[6] The new standards raise important questions for corrections about the relationship of corrections to the legislative and judicial processes and about its responsibilities as an administrative agency with broad governmental powers over the liberty of individuals.

Corrections could adopt a hard line and criticize the imposition of greater legal control over its process as an unnecessary and harmful interference with its discretion. It could argue that the

[6] These standards are discussed in Chapter 15.

imposition of legal standards runs against the public interest because it interferes with correctional action designed to protect the public by rehabilitating the convicted criminal offender. This would be similar to the position adopted by many police leaders who criticize Supreme Court decisions on the ground that they impede effective police work. One difficulty with this position is that it is counter-persuasive: If it has any effect, it is to convince legal authorities that even more control is needed because high-level administrators will not readily take steps to require their personnel to comply with existing legal standards.

Alternatively, corrections could silently accept the new legal standards as and when they are imposed, taking the position that the fairness of its processes is exclusively within the province of legal authorities. This position assumes that the corrections profession has no contribution to make to the development of legal standards for its own administrative processes. Correctional concern with the fairness of its processes would be limited to reacting to legal standards by conforming to them as they are imposed.

However, correctional leaders could take the position that greater legal control is desirable, or at least inevitable, and seek to influence the form those controls will assume by taking steps to insure that legitimate correctional interests are considered in the formulation of new legal standards. This position asserts that corrections has an active and creative role in the lawmaking process and that its experience and knowledge are badly needed to make the new legal standards intelligent ones, appropriate to the decisions they regulate rather than blindly doctrinaire and unnecessarily sweeping in their reach. To play this creative role in lawmaking, corrections would have to implement systematic programs of empirical research into the procedures and criteria involved in its decisions and make a sustained effort to accommodate correctional needs with the concerns reflected in legal standards. Presenting this information and thought to legislatures and courts may require legal counsel as knowledgeable in corrections as in legal doctrine.

But the most important question is whether corrections should actively be concerned with the fairness of its processes beyond conforming to legal standards and participating in the creation of new ones. Legislative and judicial standards for the conduct of administrative agencies are necessarily minimum standards. Neither legal authority can effectively supervise an administrative process to the extent necessary to assure that day-to-day decision-making is as fair as possible to the individuals affected. Reliance must be placed upon the administrative agency itself to achieve that goal. Recognition of this leads to the conclusion that an administrative agency has an important responsibility to insure the fairness of its processes beyond merely complying with minimum legal standards.

Acceptance of this notion would have significant implications. It would mean that correctional agencies have the responsibility to insure that the broad discretion given them is exercised fairly and consistently. Correctional decision-making procedures may have to be examined and, where necessary, changed. Greater control over criteria used by front-line personnel in exercising discretion may be needed. This may mean agency research to determine the criteria actually used, more guidance of decision criteria through agency policy-making, and a reexamination of processes for administrative review of initial correctional decisions.

There are also implications for the education, training, and professional standards of correctional personnel. Agency concern may have to extend beyond the effectiveness of casework services and include the ability of correctional personnel at all levels to exercise the agency's governmental power in a fair and consistent manner. The correctional agency may also need the services of staff legal counsel to assist it in achieving these goals.

Perhaps the most important implication lies with correctional leadership. Correctional leaders will determine how the profession discharges the responsibilities placed upon correctional agencies by virtue of the fact that they exercise important governmental powers. It would not be sufficient for correctional administrators to have a humane concern for the welfare of convicted offenders, a knowledge of effective casework in a correctional setting, and an ability to operate a large organization. In addition, correctional leaders would need an appreciation of the relationship of administrative agencies to the legislative and judicial processes and an understanding of how governmental administrative power should be exercised in a democratic society.

INDEX